Those Magnificent First Flying Machines

Aeroplanes and Engines Before 1912, and
How to Build a Biplane and Monoplane

Edited by C.B. Hayward

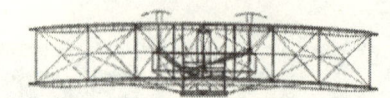

American Aeronautical Archives

Foreword and back cover copyright © 2015
by Michael A. Markowski
All rights reserved under Pan American and
International Copyright Conventions

Published by Markowski International Publishers

American Aeronautical Archives is an imprint of
Markowski International Publishers
www.AeronauticalPublishers.com

This Markowski edition is an unabridged facsimile of the original work, compiled and edited by C.B. Hayward, and first published in 1909, 1910, and 1912 as the aeroplane volume of the Cyclopedia of Automotive Engineering. It includes all the original aeronautical photographs and illustrations. The introduction was specially prepared for this edition.

Publisher's Cataloging-in-Publication

C.B. Hayward, Editor
   Those Magnificent First Flying Machines: Foreword by Michael A. Markowski, p.cm.
   Originally published in Chicago, Illinois by American School of Correspondence
   Copyright © 1909, 1910, 1912
   ISBN: 978-0-938716-98-3

1. Flying Machine-History.   2. Aeronautics-History
I. Title

Manufactured in the United States of America

Authorities Consulted

THE editors have freely consulted the standard technical literature of America and Europe in the preparation of these volumes. They desire to express their indebtedness, particularly, to the following eminent authorities, whose well-known treatises should be in the library of everyone interested in the Automobile and allied subjects.

Grateful acknowledgment is here made also for the invaluable co-operation of the foremost Automobile Firms and Manufacturers in making these volumes thoroughly representative of the very latest and best practice in the design, construction, and operation of Automobiles, Motorcycles, etc.; also for the valuable drawings, data, illustrations, suggestions, criticisms, and other courtesies.

CHARLES E. DURYEA
Consulting Engineer
First Vice-President, American Motor League
Member, American Motor-Car Manufacturers Association
Author of "Roadside Troubles"

OCTAVE CHANUTE
Consulting Engineer
Past President of the American Society of Civil Engineers
Author of "Artificial Flight," etc.

E. W. ROBERTS, M. E.
Member, American Society of Mechanical Engineers
Author of "Gas-Engine Handbook," "Gas Engines and Their Troubles," "The Automobile Pocket-Book," etc.

BENJAMIN R. TILLSON
Director of H. J. Willard Company Automobile School
Author of "The Complete Automobile Instructor"

SANFORD A. MOSS, M. S., Ph. D.
Member, American Society of Mechanical Engineers
Engineer, General Electric Co.
Author of "Elements of Gas Engine Design"

GARDNER D. HISCOX, M. E.
Author of "Horseless Vehicles, Automobiles, and Motorcycles," "Gas, Gasoline, and Oil Engines," "Mechanical Movements, Powers, and Devices," etc.

AUGUSTUS TREADWELL, JR., E. E.
Associate Member, American Institute of Electrical Engineers
Author of "The Storage Battery: A Practical Treatise on the Construction, Theory, and Use of Secondary Batteries"

Authorities Consulted—Continued

THOMAS H. RUSSELL, M. E., LL. B.
Editor, *The American Cyclopedia of the Automobile*
Author of "Motor Boats," "History of the Automobile," "Automobile Driving, Self-Taught," "Automobile Motors and Mechanism," "Ignition Timing and Valve Setting," etc.

CHARLES EDWARD LUCKE, Ph. D.
Mechanical Engineering Department, Columbia University
Author of "Gas Engine Design"

VICTOR LOUGHEED
Founder Member, Society of Automobile Engineers
Member, The Aeronautical Society
Formerly Editor, *Motor*
Author of "Some Trends of Automobile Design," "How to Drive an Automobile," and "Vehicles of the Air"

R. P. HEARNE
Author of "Air Ships in Peace and War," and "Motoring"

H. DIEDERICHS, M. E.
Professor of Experimental Engineering, Sibley College, Cornell University
Author of "Internal Combustion Engines"

JOHN HENRY KNIGHT
Author of "Light Motor Cars and Voiturettes," "Motor Repairing for Amateurs," etc.

WM. ROBINSON, M. E.
Professor of Mechanical and Electrical Engineering in University College, Nottingham
Author of "Gas and Petroleum Engines"

W. POYNTER ADAMS
Member, Institution of Automobile Engineers
Author of "Motor-Car Mechanisms and Management"

ROLLA C. CARPENTER, M. M. E., LL. D.
Professor of Experimental Engineering, Sibley College, Cornell University
Author of "Internal Combustion Engines"

ROGER B. WHITMAN
Technical Director, The New York School of Automobile Engineers
Author of "Motor-Car Principles"

Authorities Consulted—Continued

CHARLES P. ROOT
  Formerly Editor, *Motor Age*
  Author of "Automobile Troubles, and How to Remedy Them"

W. HILBERT
  Associate Member, Institute of Electrical Engineers
  Author of "Electric Ignition for Motor Vehicles"

SIR HIRAM MAXIM
  Member, American Society of Civil Engineers
  British Association for the Advancement of Science
  Chevalier Légion d' Honneur
  Author of "Artificial and Natural Flight," etc.

SIGMUND KRAUSZ
  Author of "Complete Automobile Record," "A B C of Motoring"

JOHN GEDDES McINTOSH
  Lecturer on Manufacture and Application of Industrial Alcohol at the Polytechnic Institute, London
  Author of "Industrial Alcohol," etc.

FREDERICK GROVER, A. M., Inst. C. E., M. I. Mech. E.
  Consulting Engineer
  Author of "Modern Gas and Oil Engines"

FRANCIS B. CROCKER, M. E., Ph. D.
  Head of Department of Electrical Engineering, Columbia University
  Past-President, American Institute of Electrical Engineers
  Author of "Electric Lighting;" Joint Author of "Management of Electrical Machinery"

A. HILDEBRANDT
  Captain and Instructor in the Prussian Aeronautic Corps
  Author of "Airships Past and Present"

T. HYLER WHITE
  Associate Member, Institute of Mechanical Engineers
  Author of "Petrol Motors and Motor Cars"

Authorities Consulted—Continued

ROBERT H. THURSTON, C. E. Ph. B., A. M., LL. D.
  Director of Sibley College, Cornell University
  Author of "Manual of the Steam Engine," "Manual of Steam Boilers," etc.

MAX PEMBERTON
  Motoring Editor, *The London Sphere*
  Author of "The Amateur Motorist"

HERMAN W. L. MOEDEBECK
  Major and Battalions Kommandeur in Badischen Fussartillerie
  Author of "Pocket-book of Aeronautics"

EDWARD F. MILLER
  Professor of Steam Engineering, Massachusetts Institute of Technology
  Author of "Steam Boilers"

ALBERT L. CLOUGH
  Author of "Operation, Care, and Repair of Automobiles"

W. F. DURAND
  Author of "Motor Boats," etc.

PAUL N. HASLUCK
  Editor, *Work*, and *Building World*
  Author of "Motorcycle Building"

JAMES E. HOMANS, A. M.
  Author of "Self-Propelled Vehicles"

R. R. MECREDY
  Editor, *The Encyclopedia of Motoring, Motor News*, etc.

L. ELLIOTT BROOKES
  Author of "The Automobile Handbook"

S. R. BOTTONE
  Author of "Ignition Devices," "Magnetos for Automobiles," etc.

LAMAR LYNDON, B. E., M. E.
  Consulting Electrical Engineer
  Associate Member, American Institute of Electrical Engineers
  Author of "Storage Battery Engineering"

Foreword

What Were Those Magnificent First Flying Machines Really Like?

Wow! I first became aware of this great, extremely rare book back in 2000, when my good friend Leo Opdycke, founder of *WWI Aero—The Journal of the Early Aeroplane*, called it to my attention. It's the most amazing book I have ever read on early flight—a real trip back in time—and it's my pleasure to make it available to you.

This book was compiled, written, and edited by the eminent authorities of the day in the fields of transportation, engines, aeronautics, engineering, and flying. With contributions from men like Charles Duryea, Octave Chanute, Victor Laughead (Lockheed), Sir Hiram Maxim, and many others, this book, like none since, presents the true picture of how aviation was in its infancy. It is a true classic in aeronautical literature.

You'll learn, in great detail, exactly how those early aeroplanes were built and how they flew. Reading it will give you a real sense of what was going on in aviation back then, and you'll feel like you're at the controls of the various aircraft! You'll learn about their performance, stability, and handling, and the truth about their engines. The aeroplanes of Antionette, Farman, Voisin, the Wright brothers, Bleriot, Curtiss, Santos-Dumont, Roe, Cody and many others come alive on these pages.

You'll also learn about the first aeronautical engines. The discussions of the various types, four-cylinder vertical, V-types of 2 to 16 cylinders, horizontally opposed, 3- and 5-cylinder fan types, rotaries and radials, air cooled and water cooled are amazing. How well were they built and how reliable were they? Names like

Wright, Curtiss, Indian, Hamilton, Deuthil-Chalmers, Darracq, Anionette, Renault, Wolseley, Anzani, Gnome, and R.E.P. are enough to stir the soul of any early aviation enthusiast.

It's truly amazing what those early pioneers had accomplished by 1912, when every flight was an adventure. It was a time when flying was considered the miracle of the ages and its intrepid birdmen were the heroes and idols of the day. By understanding these early flying machines and engines, you'll gain a deeper appreciation of just how far we've come since flight's humble beginnings.

Those Magnificent First Flying Machines also features a couple of chapters devoted to the actual building and flying of a Bleriot monoplane and a Curtiss biplane. There's also a section that discusses gliders, and how to build and fly model airplanes, both rubber and gas powered.

It's curious to see how the early aeroplanes compare to modem ultralights, which fly at nearly the same speeds. And it's refreshing to read about a simpler, slower, gentler age when, as with ultralights, aeroplanes were flown mostly for sport and to experience the exhilaration and joy of flight.

During the first decade of the 20th Century, mankind had finally broken the surly bonds of Mother Earth and was discovering that the sky was not the limit; it was the gateway! Those brave early flyers saw what others didn't, leading the way to the development of the fastest, most exciting and comfortable form of transportation there is.

Enjoy reading the book.

Blue skies and tailwinds,

Mike Markowski

Publisher

PS. While four volumes of *The Cyclopedia of Automobile Engineering* were published, only one dealt with aviation. We have taken the liberty to give it the descriptive title it deserves.

Table of Contents

VOLUME IV

TYPES OF AEROPLANES . . *By C. B. Hayward* † Page *11

Standard Types: Wright, Curtiss, Voisin, Farman, Sommer, Cody, Antoinette, Santos-Dumont, Bleriot, Grade, Pelterie, Pfitzner—Comparison of Standard Types—Special Types: Paulhan, Nieuport, Bleriot, Tatin-Paulhan, Antoinette, Short Two-Motor, Dunne, De Marcay-Mooney, Variable-Speed Aeroplanes, Etrich Bird-Wing, Queen-Martin, Albatross, Breguet, Tubavion, Morane, Deperdussin, Valkyrie, Hanriot, Curtiss Racer, Fairchild, H. Farman, Herring, Baldwin, Waldon-Dyett, Multiplanes — Hydroaeroplanes: Advantages, Early Attempts, Fabre, Curtiss, Burgess, Brown, Detroit Flying Fish, Transatlantic

AERONAUTICAL MOTOR . . . *By C. B. Hayward* Page 159

Early Types—General Motor Requirements: Automobile vs. Aeronautical Motor, Fundamental Features of Design, Standard Forms—American Motor Types: Wright, Curtiss, Four-Cylinder, Water-Cooled, Horizontal-Opposed, Eight-Cylinder, V-Type, Two-Cycle Motors, Rotary Type — Foreign Motor Types: Horizontal-Opposed, Four-Cylinder, V-Type, Water Cooled Types, Fan-and-Star Types, Gobron-Brille X-Form, Gnome Revolving-Cylinder

BUILDING AND FLYING AN AEROPLANE . *By C. B. Hayward* Page 225

Building Aeroplane Models: Rubber-Band Motor, Gasoline Motor—Building a Glider: Simple Type, Glider with Rudder and Elevator, Learning to Glide—Building a Curtiss Biplane: Cost, General Specifications, Details of Construction: Main Planes and Struts, Making Turnbuckles for the Truss Wires, Running Gear, Outriggers, Ailerons for Lateral Stability, Covering the Planes, Making the Propeller, Mounting the Engine, Controls, Tests, Assembling the Biplane—Building a Bleriot Monoplane: Motor, Fuselage, Truss Frame, Built on Fuselage, Running Gear, Wings, Control System, Covering the Planes, Installation of Motor—Art of Flying: Use of Elevating Plane, Aeroplane in Flight, Center of Gravity, Center of Pressure, Ground Practice, First Flight, Warping the Wings, Making a Turn, Starting and Landing, Planning a Flight, Training the Aviator—Accidents and Their Lessons—Amateur Aviators

---

* For page numbers, see foot of pages.

† For professional standing of authors, see list of Authors and Collaborators at front of volume.

A FRENCH ARMY CAPTAIN READY FOR A START WITH A MILITARY TYPE BLERIOT MONOPLANE
This Photograph Protected by International Copyright

TYPES OF AEROPLANES
PART I

STANDARD TYPES

General Survey. In view of the fact that aeroplane design can hardly be said to have progressed beyond its inception, it may appear to be somewhat of a misnomer to refer to standard types. There are, however, a certain number of designs in biplanes and monoplanes, constructed according to well-defined models, and after which the majority of others are patterned. While these are more or less similar in their fundamental characteristics, they vary from one another in important details of size, arrangement, and efficiency of their parts. For the purpose of comparison, a discussion of their distinguishing features, as well as their merits and demerits, is appended. A study of this will be found of the greatest value as a means of obtaining a knowledge of the chief characteristics of the best-known aeroplanes.

The fifteen most prominent and distinctive types are described in detail, the order in which they are taken up not being based on any quality of the machines themselves. The biplanes are eight in number, as follows: Wright, Wright Racer (Baby), Curtiss, Voisin, New Model Voisin, Farman, Sommer, and Cody.

The monoplanes are seven in number, as follows: Antoinette, Santos-Dumont, Bleriot XI, Bleriot XII, Grade, Pelterie, and Pfitzner.

With few exceptions the machines in question as described in the following paragraphs have been flown thousands of miles and used over extended periods by a great number of aviators and amateurs, and they have likewise been copied in hundreds of other machines, but as the result of the experience thus gained, their builders have inaugurated various changes, not merely of dimensions, but of construction in some cases and of principle in others. Most of these changes have been brought about during 1911. In not a

Copyright, 1912, by American School of Correspondence.

few instances, the changes have been of sufficient importance to warrant giving the new machine a new title. Wherever the changes have altered the machine materially, the details are given just after the description of the standard type.

In addition to the foregoing, there are some special types the distinguishing features of which merit reference. Many other types of successful biplanes and monoplanes are in use, but they differ so slightly from one or another of those described here that any detailed mention of them would only lead to confusion. The great number of machines now being built in this country by individual experimenters or by manufacturers are either replicas of those detailed or are modifications of them.

Nomenclature. Despite the phenomenally rapid development of aviation, its terminology has kept pace so that there are a number of expressions the meaning of which must be explained before attempting a description of the machines themselves.

SUPPORTING PLANE. By supporting plane is meant the main lifting surface as distinguished from all auxiliary or stabilizing surfaces.

DIRECTION AND ELEVATION RUDDERS. Direction rudder refers to the movable, vertical surface used for steering to the right or left, while the elevation rudder is a horizontal surface the function of which will be obvious.

TRANSVERSE CONTROL. Transverse control is the device employed for the preservation of lateral balance when flying straightaway and for maintaining an artificial inclination of the machine when rounding turns.

KEELS. Keels are fixed surfaces intended to aid in the preservation of stability; they exert neither lifting effect nor rudder action.

SPREAD. Spread is the maximum horizontal dimension perpendicular to the line of flight.

DEPTH. Depth is the dimension of the plane parallel to the line of flight.

ASPECT RATIO. By "aspect ratio" is meant the proportion of spread to depth and it constitutes a factor for defining the shape of the supporting plane.

For the purpose of more clearly showing the variation in size of the different types, detailed and dimensioned plans and elevations of each machine are given. Most of these are drawn to the same scale, thus enabling a direct, graphic comparison of the types. But it must be borne in mind, inasmuch as aviators are constantly changing and rechanging the dimensions of their machines, without recording such alterations, many of the dimensions given here are necessarily approximate. In all cases, however, the most recent

TYPES OF AEROPLANES

and accurate data, as furnished by the large number of references consulted as well as by close personal inspection, has been employed.

BIPLANES

Wright. This Wright machine, Fig. 1, is the original Wright type of which many are made and used in England, France, and Germany, there being Wright companies in those countries devoted to their manufacture and exploitation. The more recent Wright machines do not require a rail or weight for starting and the front elevation rudder has been discarded. Among the biplanes the Wright is almost twice as efficient as any other type, this being ascribed by French writers, particularly Berget, to the fact that a great deal of weight is saved by the starting device. This is what the latter was originally adopted for, but as no increase in power was found necessary when it was discarded for the four-wheeled chassis now employed, the contention does not hold good. In view of its much rougher construction as compared with the finely finished French machines, its efficiency is extremely high, owing in large measure, doubtless, to the employment of two propellers revolving at a comparatively slow speed.

Frame. Clear spruce and ash are used throughout in the construction of the frame, which is very simply but solidly built. The bracing wires are steel and are made to fit exactly, while the struts or separators are of elliptical form with the small edge facing the direction of motion. These struts are equipped with hooks at each end fitting in rings in the frames of the two planes. All exposed parts of the machine are painted with an aluminum mixture.

Supporting Planes. Two identical and superposed surfaces of canvas (fine, closely woven duck) stretched over and under wood ribs of light but strong built-up construction support the machine in the air. These surfaces, or planes, are 3 inches thick near the center and have a somewhat flatter and more regular curve than that commonly employed. The planes, which are spaced 6 feet apart, have a spread of 41 feet, a depth of 6.56 feet, and a total area of 538 square feet.

Elevation Rudder. In the Wright biplane the rudder is so constructed that when elevated it is automatically warped concavely on the under side, and when depressed it is curved in the

TYPES OF AEROPLANES

opposite way. This materially adds to the force exerted. It is double surfaced, constituting a small biplane itself and has 70 square

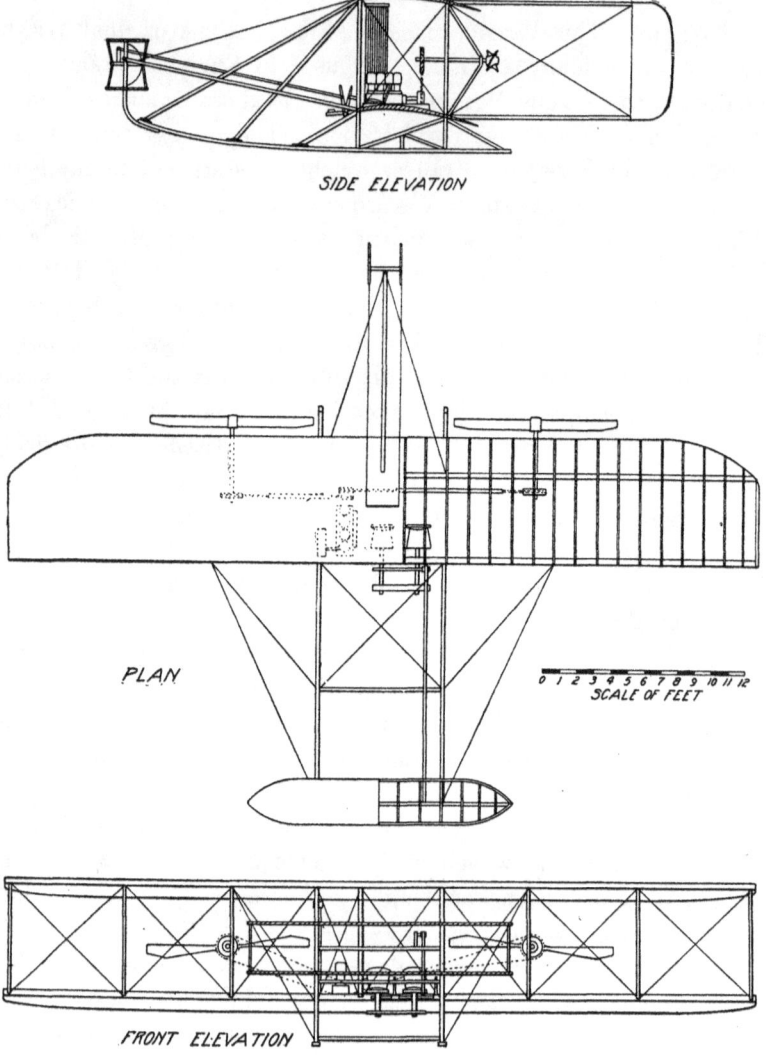

Fig. 1. Original Type of Wright Biplane

feet of area; it is placed well forward of the main planes, being supported on an extension of the landing skids. This rudder is controlled by a lever worked by the operator's left hand. To rise, the aviator pulls the lever toward him. This motion, transmitted to the rudder mechanism by a long, wood connecting rod, causes the rudder to turn upward relative to the line of flight and consequently the machine rises. Reversing the movement causes it to descend.

Direction Rudder. The direction rudder is placed in the rear on the center line, and consists of two identical and parallel vertical surfaces with a total area of 23 square feet. It is governed by the right-hand lever, turning to the left being accomplished by pushing out and to the right by pulling in on it. The control is not employed exactly in this manner, however, as a sidewise movement of the same lever also serves to warp the planes—a feature indispensable to lateral equilibrium in rounding turns. The two motions of the lever are very intimately connected in their effect upon the control.

Transverse Control. Transverse control is the famous warping device invented by the Wrights for the preservation of lateral balance and for artificial inclination in making turns, and is employed in a similar or modified form in almost every aeroplane thus far constructed, the Pfitzner monoplane constituting the most radical departure from it. To permit of this warping, the rear vertical panel of the main cell, or double plane, is divided into three sections. The central panel is solidly braced and extends on either side of the center to the second strut from each end. From these struts, the rear horizontal crosspieces are merely hinged instead of being continued portions of the crosspiece at the center, and the two vertical panels on either end are not cross braced. These two rear end sections of the cell are, therefore, movable vertically. The entire front of the machine, as well as the ribs inside the supporting planes, however, are perfectly rigid, there being no helical torsion of the ribs themselves, as commonly supposed. Cables connect these two sections of the planes together and lead to the right-hand lever. The operation is as follows: If the machine suddenly tilts or dips down, at the right end, for example, the lever is moved to the left. This action pulls down the rear right ends of the surfaces and at the same time pulls the left ends upward. An increase in the incident angle of the outer end of the plane on the depressed side and a decrease of the incident angle on the opposite side, are thus brought about, righting the machine at once. During this operation, the entire front face of the cell as well as the rear central section remain perfectly rigid in every sense.

The warping apparatus is also interconnected with the direction rudder and the simultaneous action of both is depended upon. This is one of the chief claims of the original Wright patent, and in actual practice the direction rudder and transverse control of the machine are rarely, if ever, worked separately. To make a turn to the left, for example, it is evident that if this same lever is moved in an arc, outward and to the left, somewhat similar to

Fig. 2. Tail of Short Wright Biplane Showing Addition of Horizontal Keel at Rear

the contour of the desired turn, not only will the surfaces be warped so as to raise the right end, but the direction rudder is also set to give the desired change of travel, and the combined action of the two is prompt and very effective.

There are no keels on the original Wright biplane, but since the elimination of the forward elevating rudder, these have been introduced in the later type, Fig. 2. In the older machine, a small, pivoted, vertical surface is placed in front to indicate any change in direction of the relative air current.

TYPES OF AEROPLANES 7

Power Plant. The power plant consists of a four-cylinder, vertical, four-cycle, water-cooled motor built by the Wrights themselves and rated at 25 to 28 horse-power, which drives two double-bladed propellers in opposite directions by chains and sprockets. The propellers are of laminated wood construction, made of clear spruce, measuring 8.5 feet in diameter and having a 9-foot pitch. They rotate at 400 r.p.m., or only about one third the speed at which the usual single propeller is ordinarily driven, and are placed at the rear of the main cell, at equal distances on either side of the center.

Running Gear. As already mentioned, the original mounting was on skids only, but since about July, 1910, all of the Wright

Fig. 3. Brookins in Headless Wright Just About to Leave the Ground

machines have been fitted with four pneumatic-tired wheels attached to a rectangular frame. The total weight of the machine described above is 1,050 to 1,150 pounds and the speed 40 miles per hour; 41 pounds are lifted per horse-power of the motor and 2.05 pounds per square foot of supporting surface. The aspect ratio is 6.25 to 1. These figures, however, apply only to this particular machine, as the Wright biplane built for the United States Signal Corps, as well as those constructed by the Aerial Company of France, have a spread of only 36 feet with a total supporting surface of 490 square feet.

French Wright. In the French Wright machines, the aviator sits next to the motor, and when instructing Count Lambert and

M. Tissandier in the winter of 1909 at Pau, Wilbur Wright had fitted to the machine an extra lever to control the elevation rudder on the right side of the passenger who sat next to the motor. The position of the levers for the passenger was, therefore, the reverse of the usual one. Messrs. Tissandier and Lambert, having learned to operate in this manner, have never changed, but as they in turn have become the instructors of many purchasers of Wright machines, their pupils are taught to control in the normal manner.

New Model Wright. The new Wright machine, introduced in the summer of 1910 and first seen in public at the Asbury Park Meet, has no front elevation rudder and was, therefore, popularly dubbed the "headless" Wright, shown in Figs. 3 and 4. The elevation of the machine is controlled by the rear horizontal surface alone. This machine is also smaller and faster, its spread being 39 feet, depth 5.5 feet, and supporting surface 410 square feet. With the 30-horse-power motor employed, the lift is 37 pounds per horse-power, or 2.5 pounds per square foot of surface. The aspect ratio is 7.1 to 1.

Fig. 4. Headless Wright in Flight

Wright Racer. The Wright Racer is officially known as "Model R" by the manufacturers, but owing to its diminutive size was immediately christened the "Baby Wright" on its first appearance at the International Meet at Belmont Park in 1910. It was especially designed for high speed and one of this model with an eight-cylinder motor was entered in the Gordon-Bennett cup race, but owing to an accident it did not take part. This machine is shown in Fig. 5 with Orville Wright driving, Hoxsey holding the machine on the right, and Brookins on the left. As the engine is running, the propellers do not show in the illustration. Sufficient accommodation only for the aviator is provided so that it is a one-man machine. It is said to be the fastest climbing aeroplane ever built,

TYPES OF AEROPLANES

Johnstone's record of 9,714 feet made at Belmont Park having been accomplished on this model.

Frame. This machine is of the same headless type as that brought out in the larger size during the early part of 1910. The construction of the frame throughout is the same as in the latter.

Supporting Planes. The supporting planes are of the same design and construction as in the larger machine, but they have a spread of only 26½ feet by a depth of 3 feet 7 inches, giving a total area of but slightly over 185 square feet. The length fore and aft is 24 feet, while the height from the ground to the top of the upper plane is but 6 feet 10 inches.

Elevation Rudder. The elevation rudder, as well as the direction rudder, is of the same design, construction, and operation as the

Fig. 5. Wright Baby Racer, with Orville Wright at the Wheel

standard Wright flyer, the dimensions merely being made to correspond to its smaller size.

Transverse Control. The regular Wright warping device in connection with the control of the direction rudder is employed, as in the larger machines.

Power Plant. The power plant is an eight-cylinder, V-type, 50- to 60-horse-power motor which is characterized by the same features of design as the standard Wright four-cylinder motor used on the larger machines. It drives two two-bladed wood propellers in opposite directions through the medium of chains and sprockets, and, so far as may be noted by a casual examination, they are identically the same as those employed on the regular Wright machines and are designed to run at the same speed, *i. e.*, about 400 r.p.m., the speed of the motor being 1,300 r.p.m.

General. The seat for the aviator is directly in front of and in line with the motor and there is no provision for carrying a passenger, owing to the extremely small size of the machine. It is, in fact, a "fly-about," to coin a term analogous to that prevalent in the automobile field. The machine is mounted on two pairs of pneumatic-tired wheels straddling each of the skids and placed directly under the center of the machine.

The weight of the machine alone is only 585 pounds, its total weight in flight ranging from 735 to 800 pounds, thus lifting 13.3 pounds per horse-power, taking as a basis the maximum weight of 800 pounds and putting the horse-power of the motor down as 60. On the same basis of total weight, the loading is 4.27 pounds per square foot of surface. The aspect ratio is 7.4 to 1.

Wright Model B. In automobile parlance, this is the standard 1912 Wright Model, and while it shows few or no departures from the principles already established in its predecessors, it is distinguished by a number of refinements. The spread is 39 feet and the chord 6 feet 2 inches, the main planes being built in three sections and covered with Goodyear rubberized fabric in place of the canvas formerly employed. The fabric is laid diagonally and is attached to each section independently, the sections being laced together when the machine is assembled. The main spars are of spruce, as is most of the rest of the woodwork, $1\frac{3}{4} \times 1\frac{1}{4}$ inches, the greatest dimension being vertical in the front spar and horizontal in the rear spar. They are larger in the middle section of the lower plane, ash being used in the rear of the latter. There are 34 ribs to each plane, spaced a foot apart in the center and wider toward the lateral extremities of the planes. The ribs which come near struts are solid between the main spars, the others being built up of an upper and lower strip with blocks spaced about six inches as distance pieces. The two ribs that support the engine and the two seat ribs are the only ones between the spars of the lower main plane in its center section. There are nine pairs of uprights of various sizes, the outer two sets on each end being secured to the planes by the familiar flexible joint, the remainder having a form

TYPES OF AEROPLANES

of socket joint. A few turnbuckles have made their appearance in the center section, doubtless to facilitate replacement of the engine or other parts. All the steel piano wires not fitted with turnbuckles are cut to length and are interchangeable. When setting up the planes, the wires are attached and the struts then sprung into place. These guy wires are cut and the loop bent by a special machine at the factory. As the wire employed has a breaking strength of 800

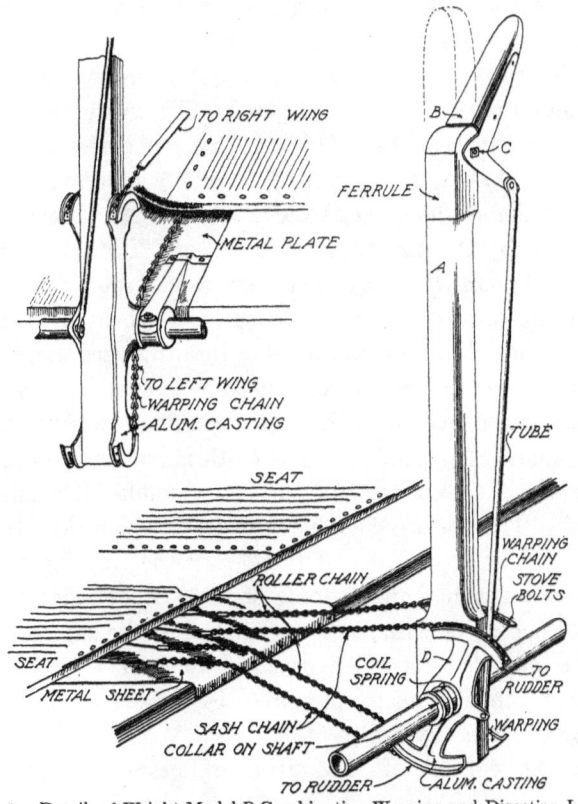

Fig. 6. Details of Wright Model B Combination Warping and Direction Lever

to 2,400 pounds, according to size, there should be no occasion for adjustment on account of stretch. The curve of the planes is 1 in 20, the greatest depth being two fifths of the chord back from the front edge. The aspect ratio is 6.25 to 1.

The small semicircular fins or "blinkers" familiar on the 1910 machine have given place to two sets on the latest machines, due to the fact that greater area is required as the skids have been shortened, thus bringing these surfaces closer to the main planes. Their shape is that of small jibs.

The vertical rudder is, in general, of the same construction as in the earlier models, though somewhat smaller. The rudder is operated by the combination warping and direction lever, Fig. 6. As shown, this lever also warps the wings. By "breaking" the top section B, either to the left or to the right (without moving the rest of the lever from its position), the rudder is moved only to steer left or right, respectively. In making flat turns, without banking, the top section only of the lever is used. The movement is entirely a natural or instinctive one. This separate movement of the rudder is obtained by having the sector D, movably mounted, capable of individual action with respect to lever section A, through the steel tube actuated by the section B of the lever. The wire which goes over the top of sector D must go to the left side of the rudder cross bar.

The front third of the elevator surface is held rigid while the remainder is flexible. This is operated by a forward and backward movement of the elevator lever, the wires being crossed so that pushing out on the lever steers down and pulling toward the operator causes the machine to ascend. The cloth is laid on diagonally and only one surface is used, the ribs and spars running through pockets in the cloth. There is a second elevator lever which can be used by a student passenger, who would then work the warping lever (and rudder) with his right hand. Some of the Wright aviators use the seat next to the engine with the warping lever at the left, while others sit on the outside seat. This second elevator lever has a disk attached, encompassed on its periphery by a flat steel friction band to hold the lever in any set position.

While the control of the machine does not appear to be instinctive, it certainly is very easy to learn and, after having it once impressed upon the mind, is very satisfactory. It would seem that the exertion of moving the warping lever fore and aft is a great deal less than if it were arranged to move sideways as in some other machines. The warping is effected by the lever A, Fig. 6. Pushing forward raises the left wing and depresses the right; the same movement turns the rudder to the left—besides having a lesser angle of incidence, when the lever as a whole is used. The wiring

TYPES OF AEROPLANES 13

for the warping is shown in the diagrammatic sketch, Fig. 7. The rear spars of the two end sections of the planes are hinged to those of the center section, so that warping may be accomplished without flexing the spar. The lever arrangements have varied on many of the machines. Some are flown with the aviator using the left hand for warping. Students taught by these use the right hand for warping, as a rule, and this is now the practice in "breaking in" flyers in order that any passenger or other weight they may carry will occupy a central position on the machine and retain the balance. However, one or two machines have been put out with two warping and two elevating levers, for those who desire to fly together, both having learned the use of the same hand for warping.

Referring to the combination warping and rudder lever, Fig. 6, the lever A is jointed or hinged at the top. The short section B

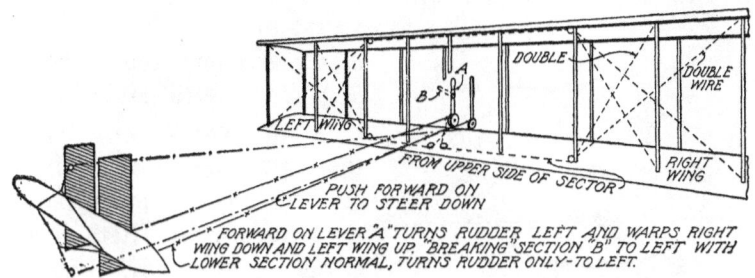

Fig. 7. Diagrammatical Sketch of Wright Control-Mechanism

turns left or right on the axis C for independent rudder action. The lever as a whole moved forward warps the left wing up and the right wing down, at the same time turning the rudder towards the left, to offer resistance to the side having the lesser angle of incidence. The elevator is also warped down to enable the machine to gain speed, and the aeroplane has begun to bank, the right side being the higher. Next, this combination lever as a whole is gradually brought back to normal position, as the aeroplane is now at almost a forty-five degree angle. At this stage with this lever (as one) normal, and the wings straightened out, the top section of the lever is "broken" over to the left, which turns the rudder only to this side. This operation is gone through in making short circles, or spirals, for which the Wright machine is famous. For right spirals, the reverse of the operation just described must be carried out, care being taken to straighten out before the machine has banked at so steep an angle as to make recovery impossible. In Fig. 6 the section B is broken to the left, turning the rudder only in that direction.

The motor on this machine does not differ except in a few details from that which the Wright Brothers have been building for their own machines ever since they began flying. One of the innovations consists of an emergency shut-off of the power, consisting of a wire conveniently placed over the aviator's head. Pulling this raises the exhaust valves and thus cuts off the power of the motor, without bringing it to a sudden and dead stop, as in the case where the switch for short-circuiting the Mea magneto is closed. The power can thus be cut down considerably without bringing the motor to a stop. The same method of feeding the gasoline directly to the inlet manifold by means of a gear pump, and without a carbureter, is still retained. As its speed increases with that of the engine, the amount of fuel fed is always in proportion to the latter's speed. Retarding or advancing the spark is accordingly the only method of controlling the speed of the motor, apart from the exhaust valve control previously mentioned. A pedal in front of the aviator sets the spark back to facilitate safe starting of the motor, and the magneto is provided with a catch to hold it in the retarded position, so that an aviator may start his own machine without danger of having it run away from him before he can get into the seat. The weight of the bare engine is 180 pounds and it consumes about 4 gallons of gasoline per hour, the 12-gallon tank accordingly providing sufficient for a three-hour flight.

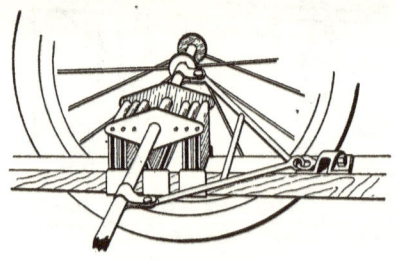

Fig. 8. Wheel Mounting Details, Wright Model B

The engine is mounted at either end of the base on cross members, which in turn rest on the solid engine foundation ribs. Duplicate sprockets, 'which are screwed and locked to the crank shaft back of the flywheel, drive by means of special roller chains the

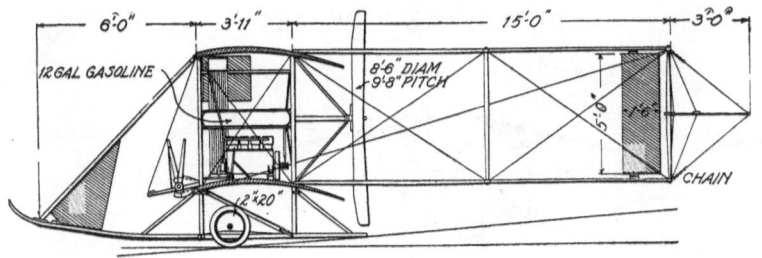

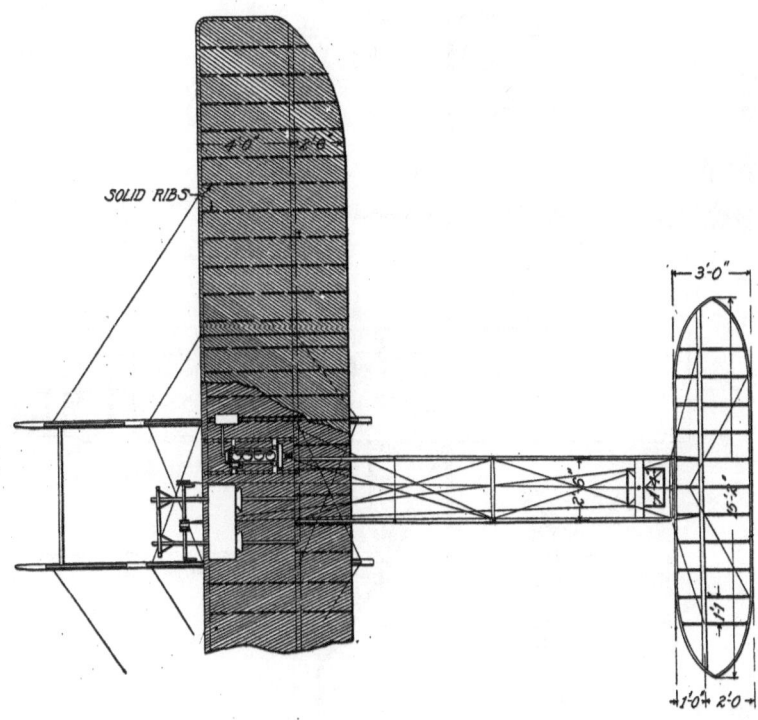

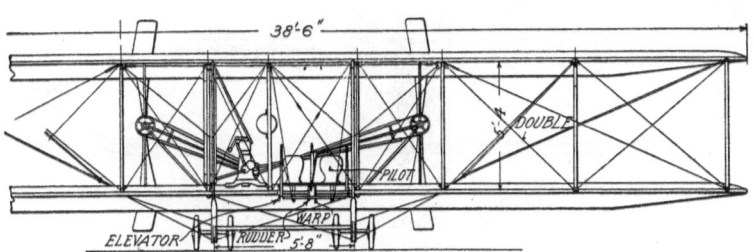

Fig. 9. Detailed Diagrams of Wright Model B

16 TYPES OF AEROPLANES

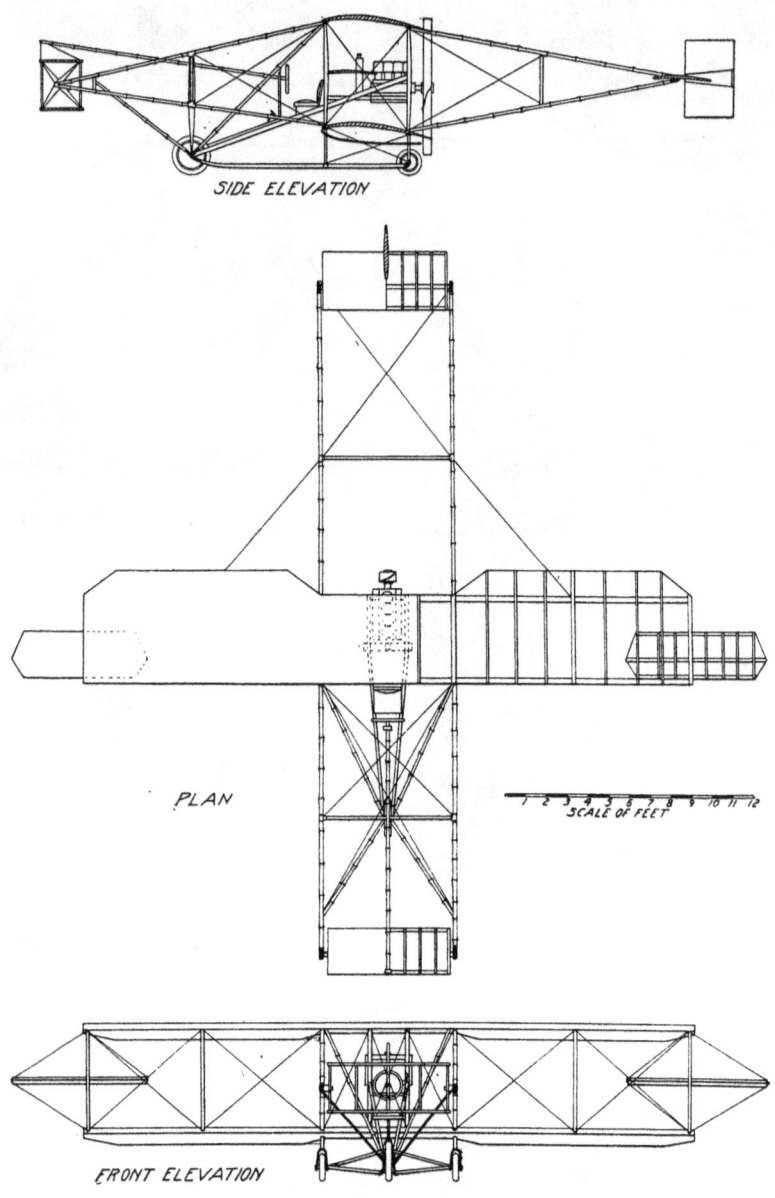

Fig. 10. Detailed Diagram of Curtiss Biplane

SCENE AT AN AVIATION MEET AT ROUEN, FRANCE, SHOWING AN ANTOINETTE MONOPLANE MAKING A TURN
This Photograph Protected by International Copyright

Intentionally blank as was the original edition.

two propellers, their speed being geared down in the ratio of 11 to 34. At an engine speed of 1,325 r.p.m., the propellers turn at

Fig. 11. Curtiss on His Trip from Albany to New York City. Leaving Poughkeepsie

428 r.p.m., giving a flying thrust of about 250 pounds. Adjustable stays are provided for tightening the chains.

TYPES OF AEROPLANES

For the landing gear, wheels are used in combination with the usual skid arrangement, the skids themselves having been very much shortened. The method of mounting the wheels is illustrated in Fig. 8. The complete machine is illustrated in Fig. 9.

With operator and passenger, ready to fly, the machine weighs about 1,250 pounds. The weight thus carried per horse-power is about 40 pounds, while the loading on the above basis figures out at but $2\frac{1}{2}$ pounds per square foot. Lancaster gives the Wright machine an efficiency of 63 per cent, after deducting 5 per cent for loss in the chains. In a book by Eiffel (1911), it is stated that 30

Fig. 12. Curtiss on His Albany to New York Trip. Flying Down the Hudson

horse-power is required to fly the Wright machine, which, in view of the facts, is obviously an erroneous conclusion.

Curtiss. The Curtiss biplane, Fig. 10, embodies in its construction several features that distinguished the aeroplanes built by the Aerial Experiment Association, of which Glenn H. Curtiss was a member. The first flight of this type was made in June, 1909. At Rheims, France, in August of the same year, this miniature biplane captured the Gordon-Bennett trophy as well as several other prizes, under the able guidance of Curtiss. A number of these machines

TYPES OF AEROPLANES

are being flown and have a great many estimable performances to their credit, such as the flight of Curtiss from Albany to New York, illustrated in Figs. 11, 12, and 13, and Ely's flight from the deck of a man-of-war to the shore and back. The Curtiss is one of the fastest biplanes in use.

Frame. The main cell and smaller parts are made of ash and spruce, while the long outriggers are of bamboo, several of the members of the frame meeting at the front wheel of the landing chassis. Small steel cables and wires are employed for bracing.

Supporting Planes. The supporting planes consist of two identical directly-superposed surfaces made of one layer each of Baldwin rubber silk tacked to spruce ribs and laced to the frame, and are of highly-finished construction. A distance of 5 feet separates the two surfaces. Their spread is 26.42 feet, depth 4.5 feet, and total area 220 square feet.

Elevation Rudder. The elevation rudder is a small biplane cell having two similar surfaces of a total area of 24 square feet and mounted on bamboo outriggers on the meeting point of which it is pivoted, Fig. 14. It is controlled by a long, bamboo pole attached to the stanchion on which the steering wheel is mounted. To descend, the operator pushes out on the wheel, and to ascend draws it toward him. In Fig. 14, Curtiss is shown at the wheel.

Fig. 13. Curtiss Rounding the Statue of Liberty

TYPES OF AEROPLANES

Direction Rudder. For steering to right or left, a single, vertical surface of 6.6 square feet of area is pivoted at the meeting point of a similar pair of bamboo outriggers extending to the rear. It is operated from the steering wheel by cables running through the hollow outriggers.

Transverse Control. Transverse control consists of two independent balancing planes, or ailerons, of 12 square feet area each, which are shown very clearly in Fig. 15. They are placed at each end of the main cell and are pivoted midway between the upper and lower main planes. They are designed to preserve the lateral balance and are tipped inversely by means of a brace fitted to the

Fig. 14. Elevation Rudder and Steering Gear on Curtiss Machine

aviator's shoulders and controlled by the movement of his body. If the machine is depressed on the left side, the aviator leans to the right and in doing so shifts the brace, causing the aileron on the left side to turn down and the one on the right to turn up, the two being interconnected by cables, thus righting the machine. By "turning down" in this connection is meant a motion relative to the axis of the aileron itself and not to the line of flight. In other words, it swings on its supporting shaft. When turned down, its incidence, *i. e.*, the angle it makes with the line of flight, is positive

TYPES OF AEROPLANES

and it therefore exerts a greater lifting force. When making a turn to the right, for instance, the aviator by leaning to the right, thus causing the left end to lift, can make a much sharper turn than with the use of the direction rudder alone, while the lateral balance is also preserved.

Keel. A horizontal fixed surface, or keel, is placed in the rear and has an important steadying effect. Its area is 15 square feet. A small, triangular vertical plane is sometimes placed in front and aids in turning.

Power Plant. In the original machine the power plant consisted of a four-cylinder, vertical, four-cycle, air-cooled motor of 25 horsepower, placed well up between the two main planes at the rear. It drives a two-bladed wood propeller direct at 1,200 r. p. m. The

Fig. 15. Curtiss Machine in Flight, Showing Ailerons and Position of Operator

propeller has a diameter of 6 feet and a pitch of 5 feet. In more recent Curtiss machines, an eight-cylinder, V-type, four-cycle, air-cooled motor of 50 horse-power is employed.

General. The seat for the aviator is on the framing in front of the main cell and in line with the motor, Fig. 15. When a passenger is carried, a seat is provided at one side and somewhat below the aviator. The machine runs on three pneumatic-tired wheels, rigidly fixed to the frame, no springs being provided. The total weight is from 530 to 570 pounds, and the speed is 47 m. p. h.; 22 pounds are lifted per horse-power, and 2.5 pounds per square foot of surface. The aspect ratio is 5.65 to 1.

During 1910, Willard, one of the Curtiss aviators, employed a much larger machine of exactly the same type, in which he succeeded in carrying three passengers besides himself. The supporting planes of this machine have a spread of 32 feet, a depth of 5 feet, and a total area of 316 square feet. The elevation rudder is 31 square feet in area, and the direction rudder 7.5 square feet, while the rear horizontal keel has an area of 17.5 square feet and the ailerons are each of 27 square feet area. A Curtiss eight-cylinder, 50-horse-power motor is employed to directly drive a 7-foot propeller at 1,100 r. p. m. The maximum total weight in flight is 1,150 pounds, thus lifting 22.6 pounds per horse-power, and 3.64 pounds per square foot of surface. The aspect ratio is 6.4 to 1. It was in a machine of this type that Curtiss made his flight from Albany to New York.

At the International Meet at Belmont Park, New York, in October, 1910, Curtiss exhibited a radically different type of machine. (See Fig. 49.) This embodied most of the constructional features already described, but instead of two similar planes there was one very large main surface with an extremely small superposed plane directly above the center of the latter. Though termed a biplane, it was practically a monoplane in everything but name. No opportunity was afforded of seeing what it could do in flight.

In a later type of the Curtiss, the ailerons are pivoted from the rear struts instead of the front ones, this doing away with their interference of the lifting power of the upper main plane. Head resistance has been cut down by double surfacing the planes, thus enclosing the ribs and beams, and also by adopting a single surface in place of the former biplane elevator. The axis of the new elevator is placed only 6 feet 9 inches in front of the main planes and has two short stays of bamboo between the wheel and the elevator instead of the elaborate and complicated structure formerly employed for staying. The rear tail flaps work in conjunction with the elevator, being pivoted at a point about 13 feet to the rear of the main planes. Two triangular stabilizing fins are used instead of the usual plane, their angle of incidence being about 2 degrees, which can readily be changed. The vertical rudder is placed between these two flaps and is pivoted back of its front edge, and it is operated by a tiller post or forward extension, instead of attaching the cables directly to the rudder itself. The span is 30 feet, chord 4 feet 2 inches, and the planes are 4 feet 5 inches apart vertically, the

TYPES OF AEROPLANES

camber apparently not having been changed. The dimensions of the front elevator are 2 feet × 6 feet 3½ inches, with a triangular vertical fin attached to it above. A standard eight-cylinder, V-type, 50-horse-power motor of Curtiss make drives a Curtiss two-bladed propeller, the laminated engine base being supported at the rear by steel tubing, which is also used to brace the entire rear section. In front, the base is bolted to two short laminated struts. The height of the base is 14 inches, and above this a triangle of 1-inch oval steel tubing extends to the top plane, where it is secured by a bolt. The

Fig. 16. Delagrange Model of Voisin Biplane

engine is placed 9 inches rearward from the rear beam, and the canvas seat is 8 inches forward of the front beam.

Voisin. The Voisin Brothers began their activity as constructors of aeroplanes as early as 1905, when they built gliders for both M. Archdeacon and M. Bleriot. These gliders were successfully operated over the Seine, being lifted from the surface of the river and towed at high speed by motorboats. In 1906, they built a power-driven machine after the designs of the late M. Delagrange, Fig. 16, and subsequently, after making a few changes in the design,

24   TYPES OF AEROPLANES

built a machine for Henri Farman, Fig. 17, which was the first successful aeroplane of European manufacture. Since that time, the design of this type has remained substantially the same, except for the addition of several keels, Fig. 18. The Voisin biplane has been largely used abroad, over one hundred machines of this type having been built.

Frame. The frame is made of ash with steel joints and several parts of steel tubing. It consists essentially of a large box-cell

Fig. 17. Henri Farman in an Early Type of Voisin Biplane

mounted on a central chassis, while attached to it some distance in the rear is a smaller box-cell of the same form. This central chassis is really a unit in itself, carrying the wheels, the motor, the aviator's seat, and at the front the elevation rudder.

Supporting Planes. Two main supporting planes of similar dimensions and directly superposed are employed, the surfaces consisting of continental cloth (a cotton and rubber fabric) stretched

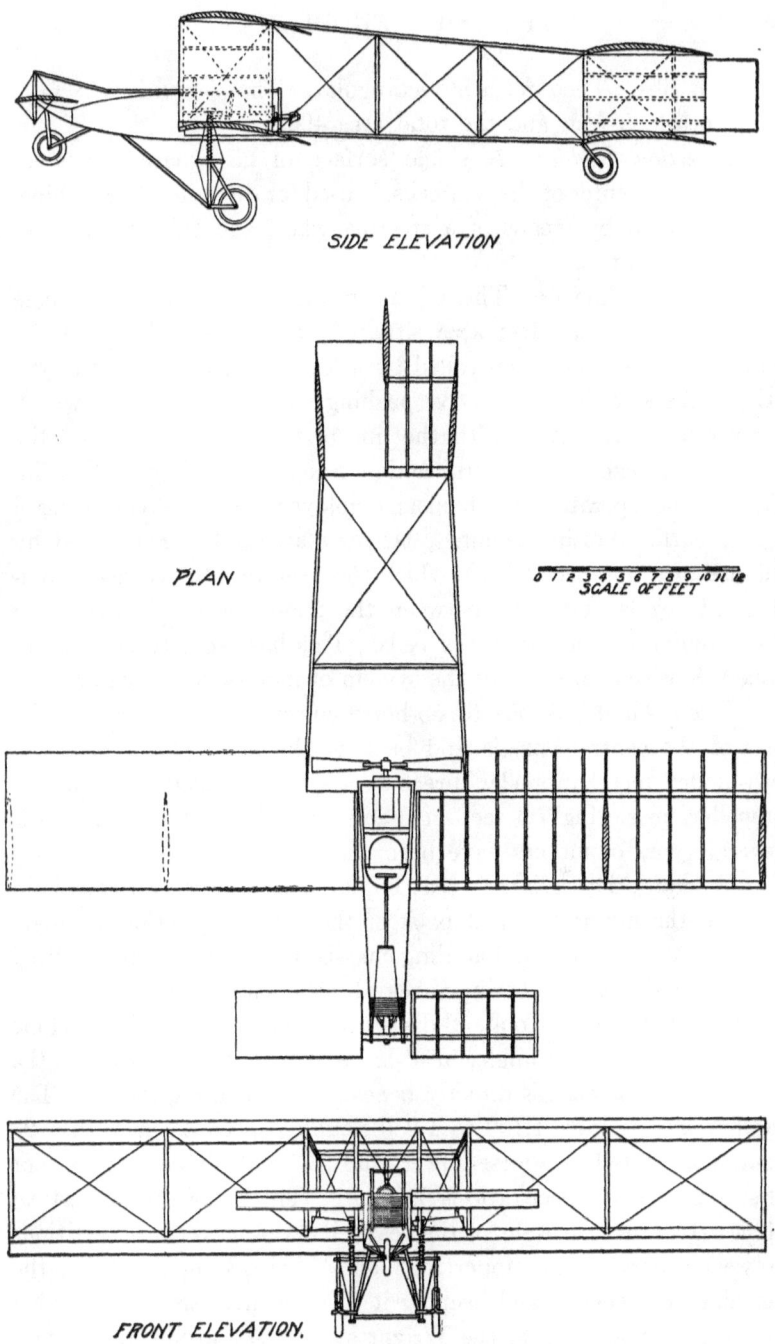

Fig. 18. Voisin Biplane with Vertical Keels

over ash ribs. Their form is rectangular. The spread is 37.8 feet, the depth 6.56 feet, and the total area 496 feet.

Direction Rudder. A single surface of 25 square feet area, placed in the center of the rear cells, is used for directing the machine. It is operated by means of a steering wheel and cables similar to those on a boat.

Elevation Rudder. The elevation rudder consists of a single surface of 41 square feet area situated at the forward end of the central chassis, and is controlled by a lever system attached to the axis of the steering wheel. By pushing out on the steering wheel, the rudder's inclination with the line of flight is reduced and the machine descends, the reverse action being obtained by pulling in. There is no operating mechanism employed for transverse control in the earlier Voisin machines, lateral stability being attained by the use of a number of keels which took the form of vertical partitions at regular intervals between the main planes, thus dividing the machine into a number of cells. This has recently been abandoned, however, in favor of the system of independent ailerons.

Power Plant. A 50- to 55-horse-power motor, placed on the rear of the central chassis and back of the main planes, drives a two-bladed metal propeller direct at a speed of 1,200 r. p. m., the propeller measuring 7.6 feet in diameter with a pitch of 4.6 feet. Several types of motors have been used.

General. The aviator's seat is placed on the central chassis in front of the motor and just back of the forward edge of the main planes. As a starting and landing chassis, two large pneumatic-tired wheels fitted with coil spring shock absorbers are fitted at the front and two at the rear. To avoid disastrous results, should the machine land at too sharp an angle, head-on, a small wheel is fitted to the front end of the chassis directly beneath the elevating rudder. The total weight is from 1,100 to 1,250 pounds, speed 35 m. p. h.; 23 pounds are lifted per horse-power, and 2.37 pounds per square foot of surface. The aspect ratio is 5.75 to 1. The use of the six vertical planes (two vertical walls of the rear cell and four vertical partitions between the two main supporting planes), Fig. 18, for steadying the machine transversely and keeping it to its course, are much lauded by Berget as superior to the Wright system of warping the planes, but experience appears to have proved to the contrary.

TYPES OF AEROPLANES 27

The Voisin type of biplane has recently been modified as follows: The vertical partitions have been done away with and ailerons are employed, together with a single plane, horizontal keel at the rear, instead of two planes. A 60-horse-power E. N. V. motor is employed, the total weight of the machine being about 1,170 pounds, giving a lift of 19.5 pounds per horse-power, and 3.27 pounds per square foot of surface. The aspect ratio is 5.13 to 1. This is a racing type of Voisin and is characterized by the elimination of most of the struts, cross wires, and other parts tending to increase the resistance to flight.

The regular Voisin biplane also has been altered by discarding the vertical partitions altogether, the design otherwise remaining the

Fig. 19. Voisin Biplane in which Paris-Bordeaux Flight was Made

same. This machine has a spread of 36.1 feet, a depth of 6.56 feet, a total area of 430 square feet, and a weight of 1,350 pounds. The motor employed is an eight-cylinder E. N. V. of 60 horse-power, carrying 22.5 pounds per horse-power and 3.14 pounds per square foot of surface. The aspect ratio is 5.5 to 1. In some of the more recent Voisin machines the front elevating rudder also has been discarded, Fig. 19.

Voisin Tractor Screw. This machine, Fig. 20, was first built in the latter part of 1909, and embodies several totally new departures in the construction of biplanes. It did not meet with particular

28   TYPES OF AEROPLANES

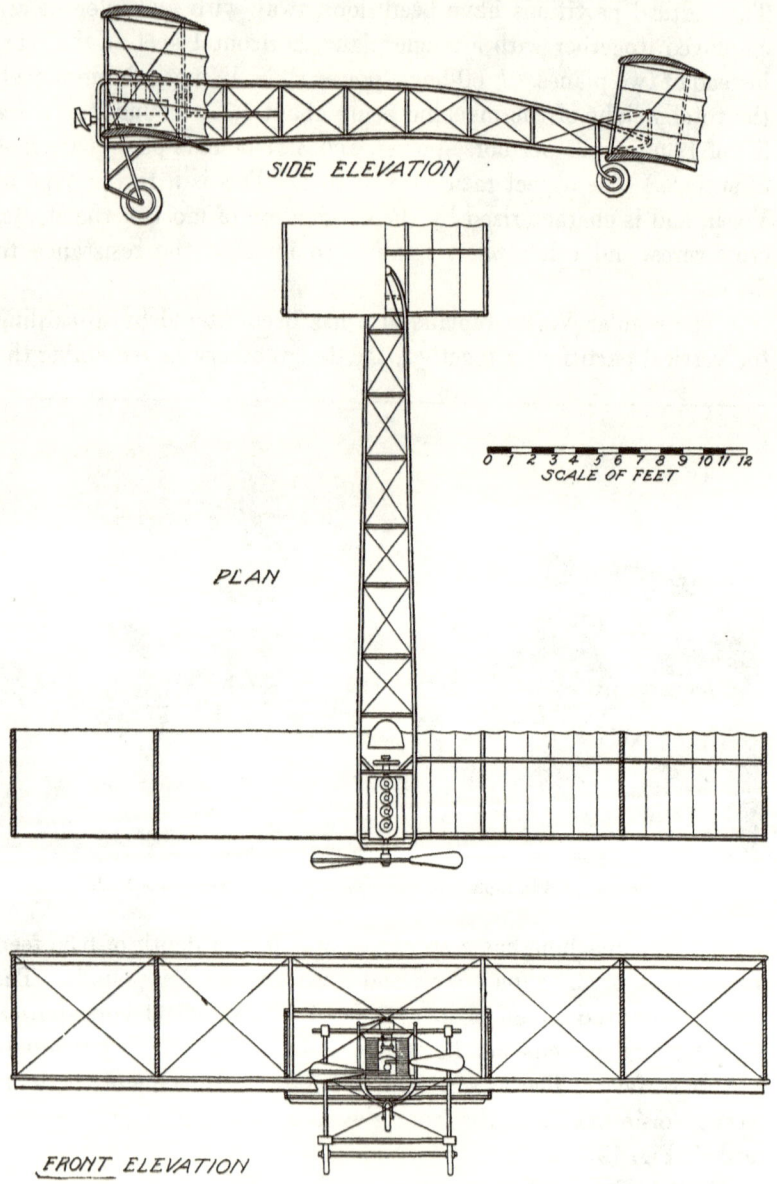

Fig. 20. Voisin Tractor Screw Type

TYPES OF AEROPLANES

success during 1910, although the Goupy and Breguet aeroplanes of the same type have been flown with great ease.

Frame. In this instance, the central chassis is extended a considerable distance to the rear, forming an "appendage." At the front are situated the motor and propeller, while directly behind the propeller is the main cell, with an auxiliary cell at the extreme rear. Ash, steel joints, and steel tubing are used throughout.

Supporting Planes. The supporting planes are two similar, directly-superposed surfaces with a spread of 37 feet, a depth of 5 feet, and an area of 370 square feet. By comparing the side elevations of the Voisin and Wright machines, the slight difference in the curvature of the planes, as well as their thickness, will be noted, though on comparing this feature in all of the machines illustrated, their striking similarity, as well as their close adherence to the pisciform contour of the plane—laid down by Colonel Renard as the most efficient shape for speed and stability—will be at once apparent.

Direction and Elevation Rudder. As these two elements are combined in the actual construction, they are accordingly described together. They are formed by the rear cell, consisting of two horizontal surfaces of about 80 square feet of area, and two vertical surfaces of about 50 square feet, the entire cell being pivoted on a universal joint so that it may be moved in any direction. The movement of the cell is controlled by cables leading to a large steering wheel in front of the aviator, the horizontal surfaces acting to elevate or depress the machine, and the vertical surfaces to change the direction of its travel. To ascend, the inclination of the cell relative to the line of flight is decreased, the leverage desired being the opposite of that necessary with a front elevation rudder. Four vertical partitions are placed between the main planes. There is no transverse control.

Power Plant. The power plant consists of a 40-horse-power, four-cylinder Voisin motor placed at the front end of the chassis and carrying directly on its crank shaft a two-bladed metal propeller 7.2 feet in diameter with a 4-foot pitch, which it drives at 1,300 r. p. m.

General. The chassis is mounted on two large pneumatic-tired wheels forward, fitted with shock-absorbing springs, and a smaller third wheel at the rear, while the aviator's seat is placed on the central frame at the rear of the main cell. The total weight is from

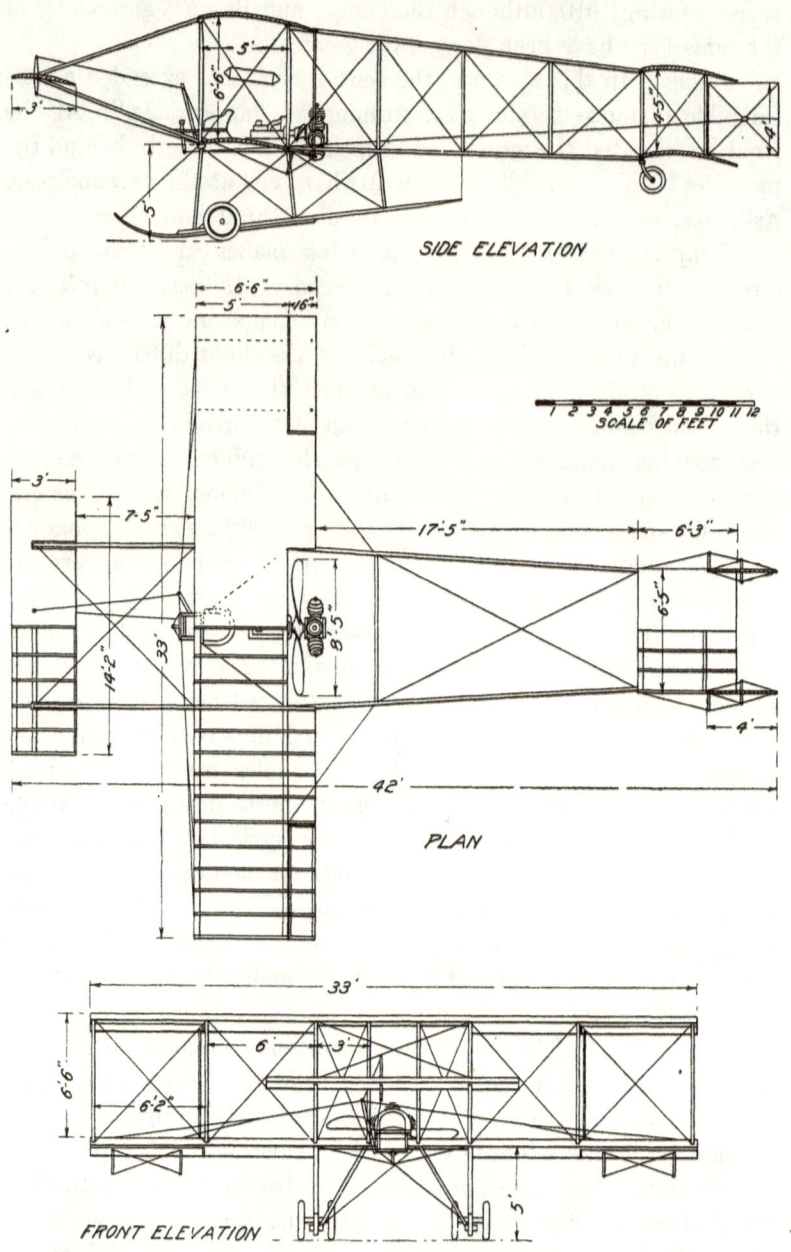

Fig. 21. Details of Farman III Biplane

TYPES OF AEROPLANES

800 to 950 pounds and the speed is said to be 50 miles an hour; 19 pounds per horse-power are lifted and 2.36 pounds carried per square foot of surface. The aspect ratio is 7.4 to 1.

Farman. The Farman machine, Fig. 21, has figured very prominently in the making of records and the winning of prizes, having been employed extensively by such aviators as Paulhan and White, as well as by Farman himself, Fig. 22. More than a hundred of the Farman biplanes had been built and put into use up to the end of 1910. It is a comparatively heavy type, and for a slow-moving, reliable machine it has proved very satisfactory.

Frame. The frame consists essentially of a main box-cell, somewhat similar in design to a Pratt truss, counterbalanced throughout with identical upper and lower chords, uprights of wood acting as compression members and cross wires as tension members, as is the case in all of the biplanes considered in this description of standard types. The supporting surfaces are analogous to the upper and lower decks of such a truss.

Supporting Planes. These supporting planes are practically identical with those of the machines already described, the surfaces themselves being made of continental cloth, stretched tightly over ash ribs. Their spread is 33 feet, depth 6.6 feet, and total area 430 square feet. The distance between the planes is 6.6 feet, which causes the machine to appear very much larger than the others by comparison and also gives it a very cumbrous look, the latter being accentuated by its very deliberate flight.

Elevation Rudder. The elevation rudder consists of a single, horizontal surface having an area of 43 square feet and is placed well out in front. It is hinged and braced to two sets of outriggers, firmly attached to the main cell, and is controlled by a large lever at the aviator's right hand. By pulling on this lever, the rudder is tilted upward and the machine rises, the method of control being almost instinctive and very easily acquired.

Direction Rudder. Two equal surfaces vertically placed, of an aggregate area of 30 feet, serve to control the travel of the machine. These surfaces move together and are operated by a pivoted lever on which the aviator rests his feet. By pressing so as to turn the lever to the left the machine alters its course in the same direction, the movement being transmitted to the rudder itself by cables.

Transverse Control. The control of the lateral equilibrium, *i. e.*, the tipping from side to side, is effected by the use of ailerons or "wing tips" consisting of four flaps constituting the rear ends of each plane. The operation of these wing tips is brought about simultaneously with that of the direction rudder through an arrangement identical with that on the Wright biplane, *i. e.*, a lever which may be moved in any direction, its forward and back motion actuating the rudder, while a sidewise movement operates the wing tips, from which it will be apparent that they are merely a modification of the Wright idea. This lever is connected by wires to the lower flap on each side and they are interconnected in the same manner with the flaps above them. When the machine is standing still the flaps merely hang loose and the wires relax, but when in flight the wind keeps them out and the wires are taut so that they may be controlled by the lever. The extra resistance these flaps or ailerons create is probably responsible in large measure for the decreased speed of the machine.

Keels. Two horizontal surfaces at the rear act as keels. Their combined area is about 80 feet, but as their angle of incidence is low the lift they exert is small, their only function being to steady the machine longitudinally.

Power Plant. The power plant consists of a 50-horse-power, seven-cylinder, air-cooled, rotary Gnome motor, mounted on a shaft at the rear of the lower plane. A two-bladed wood propeller of 8.5 feet in diameter by a 4.62-foot pitch is attached directly to it and revolves with the motor at a speed of 1,200 r. p. m.

General. The machine is mounted on two long skids forming part of the framework, similar to the Wright construction, and upon each of these skids is placed a pair of wheels. The latter are attached to rubber springs so that in starting the machine runs on them, but in alighting they give way, permitting it to slide on the skids. The total weight is from 1,100 to 1,350 pounds, the variation in this, as in every instance, being accounted for by the fact that it includes that of the aviator. The weight lifted per horse-power is 24 pounds, and 2.8 pounds per square foot of surface, while the speed is 37 miles per hour. The aspect ratio is 5 to 1.

New Models. In the foregoing, a description has been given of the original type of Farman biplane, numerous modifications

Intentionally blank as was the original edition.

TWENTY HORSE-POWER NIEUPORT MONOPLANE MAKING A LANDING
This Photograph Protected by International Copyright

Fig. 22. Farman Biplane in Flight

having been made in more recent machines, Fig. 22. The latter, for instance, are fitted with a single-surface direction rudder, instead of the twin surfaces mentioned. The elevation rudder is kept in front, but is made smaller, and in addition the rear end of the upper of the two fixed, horizontal keels at the rear is made movable conjointly with the front rudder to control the elevation of the machine. In some cases, only a single surface is used at the rear. One wheel has been substituted for the two formerly employed, the other characteristics of the machine remaining substantially as described.

The new racing Farman biplane is distinguished by the following features: The spread is reduced to 28 feet and the area to 350 square feet, while the total weight in flight is about 1,050 pounds. The lift is 21 pounds per horse-power, while that per square foot is the unusually high figure of 3 pounds. The aspect ratio is 4.2 to 1.

Another more recent type of Farman is the huge, new passenger-carrying machine which made the first four-passenger record. This has a spread of 47.6 feet and an area of approximately 540 square feet. The maximum total weight is nearly 1,750 pounds, or close to a ton, thus giving a capacity of 34 pounds per horse-power and a loading of 3.15 pounds per square foot of surface. The aspect ratio is 7.1 to 1.

In a still later type of the Farman, the ailerons are let into the wings and while they are hinged they are not permitted to hang down, as was formerly the case, this innovation being responsible for a decided reduction in the head resistance. Another type, brought out at the end of 1911, shows an entirely new form of stabilizing surfaces. These take the form of two pairs of long planes, one at each end of the main planes, and with their narrow edge to the wind, giving them a very small aspect ratio, though they have a comparatively large area. Each pair is held apart by struts and they are mounted on a vertical shaft, which is turned to swing them outward. The construction of the main cell in this machine does not exhibit any departures from the regulation Farman form, but in the machine with the set-in ailerons, which also made its debut at the Paris Salon at the end of 1911, the planes are "staggered," *i. e.*, the lower plane is very much shorter than the upper, and they are connected by diagonal steel struts, thus doing away with the maze of wire braces. A single surface tail is employed in connection with front and rear elevators and twin vertical rudders.

The Maurice Farman biplane differs somewhat from the machines just described (Henri Farman), the two brothers having at first operated independently. It is noteworthy for its remarkable duration performances. It was in one of the Maurice Farman biplanes that Tabuteau broke the 1909 world's duration record of 244 miles in 5 hours 3 minutes 5 seconds, by traveling 290 miles in 6:8:12 (October 28, 1910), which he increased on December 30, 1910, to 365 miles in 7:48:31, thereby winning the Michelin cup. The same machine also won the $20,000 prize for the flight from Paris with a passenger to the Puy de Dome, a mountain 4,800 feet high and 235 miles distant. Numerous attempts had been made to win this during three successive years. The Farman biplane covered the distance in 5:10:46, including a stop of 14 minutes, the time limit in which the prize could be won being six hours, which included circling the Arc de Triomphe in Paris and the steeples of the cathedral at Clermont-Ferrand near the finish as part of the conditions. The machine has a supporting surface of 635 square feet and an aspect ratio of 8 to 1. Its weight is 1,210 pounds and with a 60-horse-power Renault, eight-cylinder, air-cooled motor its speed is 48 miles per hour. The propeller is driven from the cam shaft instead of the crank shaft, so that at a motor speed of 1,800 r. p. m., it makes 900 r. p. m. Maurice Farman was the first to employ a covered body enclosing the seats and the engine, this construction now being considered essential for the comfort of the pilot and passenger on all Continental aeroplanes, though up to the beginning of 1912, it had not been made a feature of any of the American machines. The Farman control is very simple and effective. It consists of a hand wheel on a sliding shaft and a pair of pedals. Forward and backward motion of the wheel controls the angle of the elevator, while rotation of the wheel operates the rudders, the pedals actuating the ailerons. The wheel is vertical, its shaft passing horizontally through an automobile type of dash on which are mounted a clock, a gradient indicator, an aneroid barometer, and a recording barograph.

Sommer. In June, 1909, Roger Sommer purchased a biplane constructed by Henri Farman (the machine of Maurice Farman differs in design) and on July 3 he made his first flight. Scarcely a month later he held what was then the world's record for duration

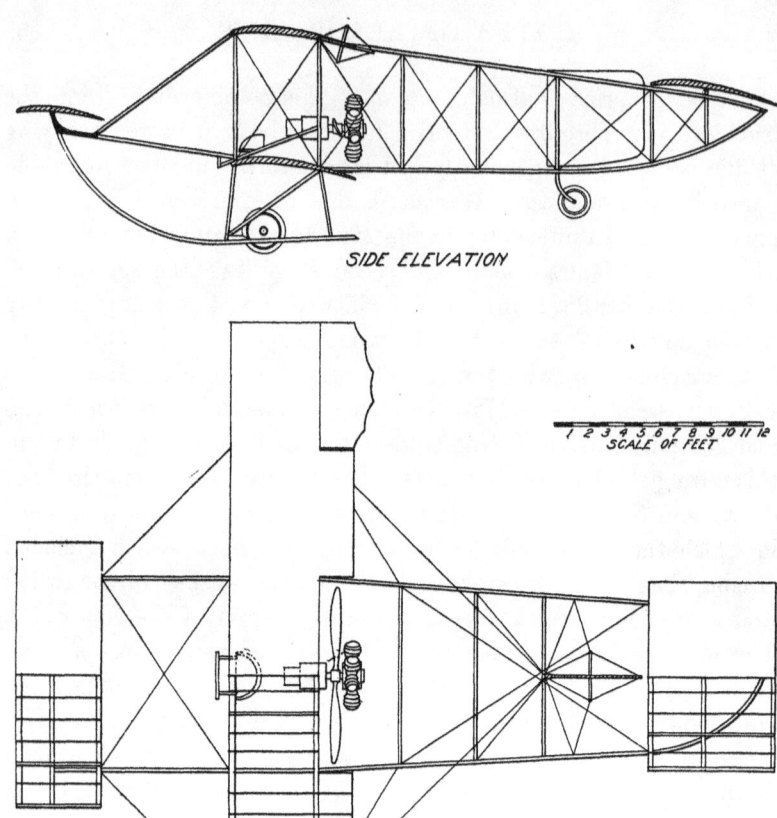
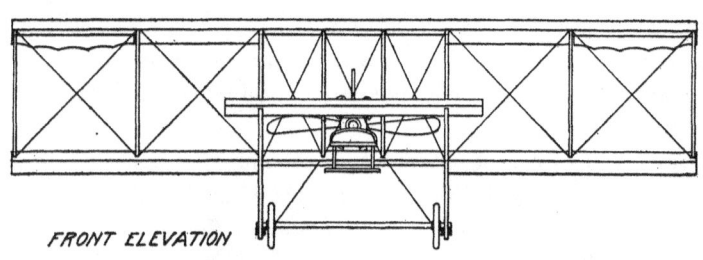
Fig. 23. Details of Sommer Biplane

of flight, having flown continuously for two and one half hours. His sudden jump into the ranks of the great aviators was remarkable and showed that, after all, it is not so hard to learn to fly well. He won many prizes at Rheims and Doncaster in 1909, but shortly afterward gave up flying on the Farman biplane and proceeded to design and build one of his own, Fig. 23. This was first tried out in January, 1910, and after a few days of experimenting he succeeded in making a long cross-country flight. The Sommer biplane is also operated by other prominent French aviators.

Frame. The construction of the frame is chiefly of hickory and ash with steel joints and steel tubing, its general character and appearance being similar to that of the Farman.

Supporting Planes. Two identical and directly-superposed rigid planes carry the machine, the surfaces being made of rubber cloth covering wood ribs. The sectional curvature of the surfaces is not so highly arched as in most other types, being more nearly, as in the Wright machine, a very even and gently sloping curve. The spread of the planes is 33 feet, their depth 5.2 feet, and their area 326 square feet.

Elevation Rudder. At a distance of 8.25 feet in front of the main cell, and supported on framing carried down to the skids, is placed the single-surface elevating rudder. This is governed by a large lever held in the aviator's left hand, which, when pushed out, turns down the rudder and, when pulled in, turns it up; thus, respectively, causing the aeroplane to mount or descend.

Direction Rudder. The direction rudder consists of a single surface of but 10 square feet in area, placed at the rear. It is operated by a pivoted foot lever similar to that of the Farman.

Transverse Control. Lateral equilibrium is secured by two wing tips, one placed at either end of the rear of the upper plane, as shown clearly in Fig. 24, there being no ailerons on the lower main plane as in the Farman. These are controlled by cables leading to a brace attached to the aviator's body. By leaning to the right, the wing tip on the left is pulled down, at the same time pulling up that on the right, causing the left end of the machine to rise and the right end to descend. Though not interconnected, the direction rudder and the transverse control are operated simultaneously by the operator, thus giving the same effect as is obtained in the Wright and

Farman machines by controlling these two elements from the same lever.

Keels. A single horizontal plane of 55 square feet area and of very light construction is placed at the rear and steadies the machine longitudinally. This plane is movable though it does not act as a rudder. A lever at the right hand of the operator, which automatically locks in place, enables the angle of incidence of this surface to be varied at will, thus increasing the attainable stability.

Power Plant. The power plant consists of the same type of rotary, air-cooled, seven-cylinder Gnome motor as employed on the Farman. It is placed at the rear of the main cell and is attached

Fig. 24. Sommer Biplane Equipped with Gnome Seven-Cylinder Motor

to a two-bladed wood propeller of 7.2 diameter by a 5.2-foot pitch, which it revolves at 1,200 r. p. m.

General. Two large wheels are attached forward and two small wheels at the rear of the chassis, the front wheels being held by rubber springs to two skids, built under the frame. The skids themselves are attached to the main frame by uprights, the joints being made of a springy sheet of metal bolted to the framing. This adds still further to the resilient character of the mounting. The seat for the aviator is placed on the front of the lower main plane at the center and is fitted more comfortably than on most other biplanes which had been built up to that time.

In more recent machines for racing purposes the two end panels

TYPES OF AEROPLANES 39

of the lower surface of the Sommer have been eliminated, reducing the spread and cutting the area down to 256 square feet. The loading is 3.25 pounds per square foot.

Cody. Colonel Cody, an American, for a long time resident in England, is doubtless best known in this field through his connection with the successful operation of man-carrying kites several years ago. His work in this line for military scouting attracted considerable attention in England. In 1907, he commenced work on an aeroplane

Fig. 25. Cody Biplane Ready for Flight

of huge dimensions, Fig. 25. At first, the tests of this machine were very disappointing, but by his remarkable perseverance Colonel Cody turned failures into successes and finally, in the late summer of 1909, accomplished a superb flight of over an hour, establishing what was then the world's record for cross-country flight. The machine has been altered a number of times, and in its form as settled upon in the spring of 1910, Fig. 26, was the largest successful aeroplane in use.

Frame. Bamboo is employed extensively throughout the frame but all joints are wound with steel wire. In addition, there are a number of upright members of ash. At the center several members

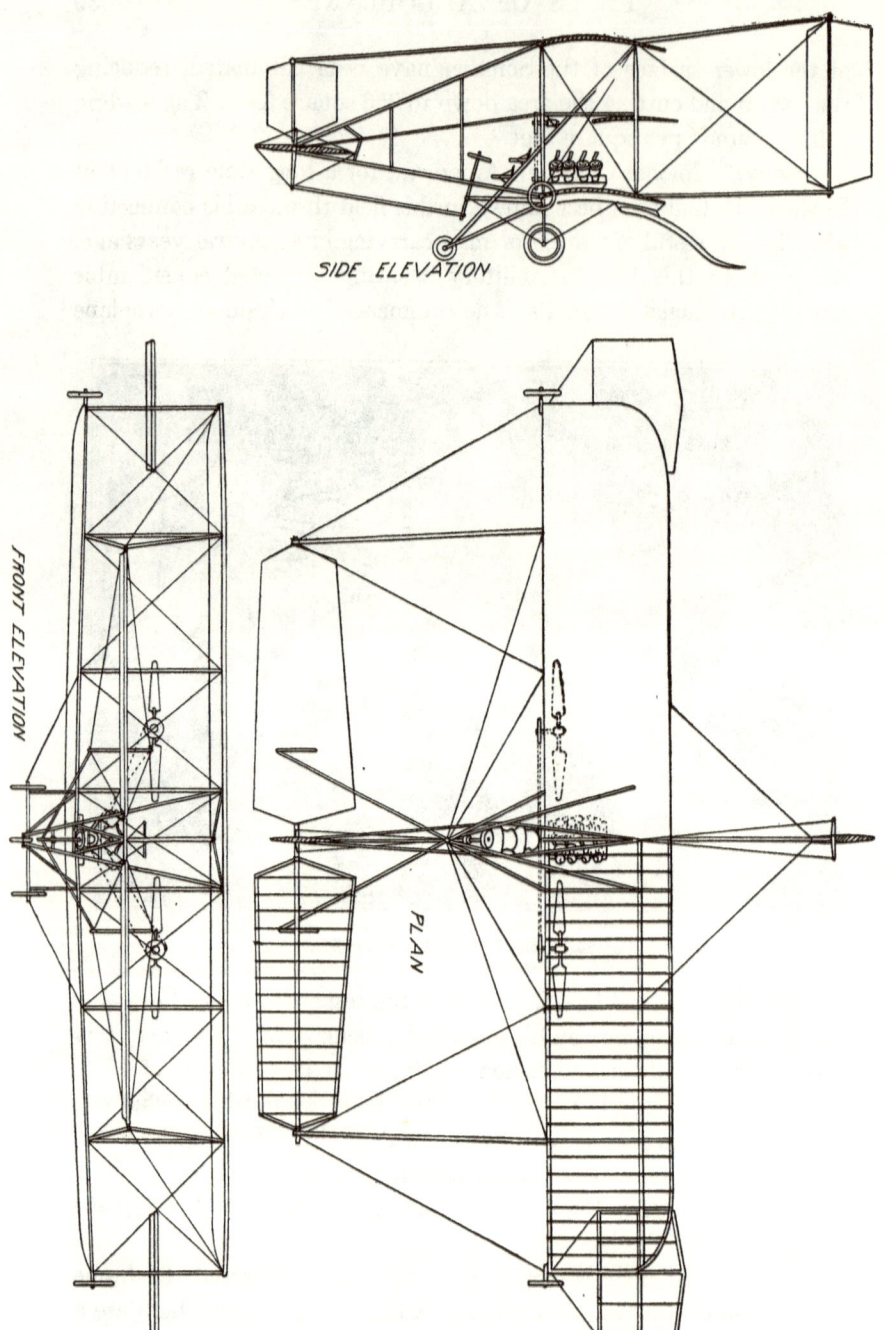

Fig. 26. Details of Cody Biplane

TYPES OF AEROPLANES

meet in the supporting chassis which is very heavily built. Steel wire is used for bracing.

Supporting Planes. The main planes are of rectangular form with rounded rear edges. They are identical and directly superposed, the surfaces being made of canvas tightly stretched over wood ribs. At the center, the distance between them is 9 feet, but they converge slightly toward either end where they are separated by only 8 feet. The spread is 52 feet, the depth 7.5 feet, and the area 780 square feet.

Elevation Rudder. At the front of the machine, supported by large bamboo outriggers from the central cell, are two equal surfaces placed on either side of the center. They are jointly movable and serve to control the elevation of the machine. They are governed by the forward or backward movement of the stanchion to which the steering wheel is attached, in the same manner as on the Curtiss. If the aviator wishes to rise, he pulls the wheel toward him. This motion, by means of a lever system, causes the elevating rudder surfaces to be tilted upward to the line of flight and the machine ascends.

Direction Rudders. Two direction rudders are employed, a large one at the rear and a small one in front, the former constituting the main rudder. These rudders are moved together by a steering wheel and cables as in a motorboat. Their combined area is about 40 square feet.

Transverse Control. Two balancing planes of 30 square feet area, one placed at either end of the main cell, control the transverse inclination of the machine. They are moved inversely by cables leading from the steering gear and operate in the same manner as the ailerons of the Curtiss machine and the wing tips of the Farman and Sommer biplanes, one balancing plane being turned up while the other is turned down. Lateral stability is also controlled by the inverse movement of the two halves of the elevation rudder, the one on the depressed side being elevated while the other is turned down. There are no keels on the Cody biplane, all surfaces serving either to lift or direct the machine.

Power Plant. The power plant is an eight-cylinder, 80-horsepower E. N. V. motor placed near the forward edge of the lower main plane and directly back of the aviator. It drives two two-bladed wood propellers mounted on shafts located at their front end half way between the main planes. These are driven in opposite directions by means of chains, as in the Wright biplane. These propellers have a diameter of 8.25 feet and a pitch of 6 feet; and are revolved at 600 r. p. m.

General. The mounting consists of a large pair of wheels which carry most of the weight, a small wheel in front and a skid at the rear. Wheels are also attached to the outer ends of the lower plane to carry the machine easily over the ground should it alight on end. The total weight is from 1,900 to 2,100 pounds; speed 37 miles per hour; 25 pounds per horse-power are lifted and 2.57 pounds per square foot of supporting surface. The aspect ratio is high—7 to 1. Seats are provided for the aviator and for one passenger, both being placed low at the center of the front of the main cell, that for the passenger being higher than that for the aviator, as it is designed for the use of an observer in war time.

Since the machine was first built, the E. N. V. motor has been replaced by two 50-horse-power, four-cylinder Green motors, both driving a single propeller instead of the twin propellers formerly used. Either motor can be operated independently, the advantage of this arrangement being that if one motor breaks down while in flight the other can still be used to drive the machine.

MONOPLANES

Antoinette. Up to the time of the present writing, the Antoinette, Fig. 27, is the largest monoplane in use and its construction is distinguished by a number of features not found on others. Levavasseur, designer of the Antoinette motor and motorboats, is credited with the design of this type. After building some experimental machines, notably the Gastambide-Mengin monoplane, the Antoinette IV was built for Hubert Latham. This machine was at first controlled transversely by means of wing tips, but the warpable surface, or Wright control, has since been adopted. The Antoinette is remarkably well built from an engineering standpoint and has been successfully operated by M. Latham in high winds, though not as strong as the gale in which the two Wright biplanes were blown backward 30 and 40 miles from Belmont Park at the International Meet, despite all they could do. The Antoinette is also flown by other prominent French aviators and several of the machines have been purchased by the French War Department.

TYPES OF AEROPLANES

Frame. The frame is of long, narrow, girder-like construction, Fig. 28, of cedar, ash, and aluminum, carrying at its forward part the main plane, the "nacelle" or car for the aviator, and at its extreme front end the propeller, while at the opposite end are placed the rudders, the longitudinal dimensions of the machine being in excess of 36 feet, or almost three fourths as much as its spread. The arrangement of the planes and rudder, as well as the location of the motor, is similar to that in all the monoplanes described here with the exception of the Pfitzner.

Supporting Plane. The supporting plane consists of a single surface divided in half, the two sections being of trapezoidal shape, placed at a slight dihedral angle to each other. They are constructed

Fig. 27. Two Antoinette Monoplanes Competing at Belmont Park, 1910

of rigid trussing, nearly a foot thick at the center and covered over and under with a smooth, finely-pumiced silk. The plane is also braced from a central mast. The spread is 46 feet, the average depth 8.2 feet, and the surface area 370 square feet.

Direction Rudder. The direction rudder consists of two vertical triangular surfaces at the rear and measures 10 square feet in area. These surfaces are moved jointly by means of wiring cables worked by a lever operated by the aviator's feet. When this lever, which moves in a horizontal plane, is turned to the left, the machine will change its course in the same direction.

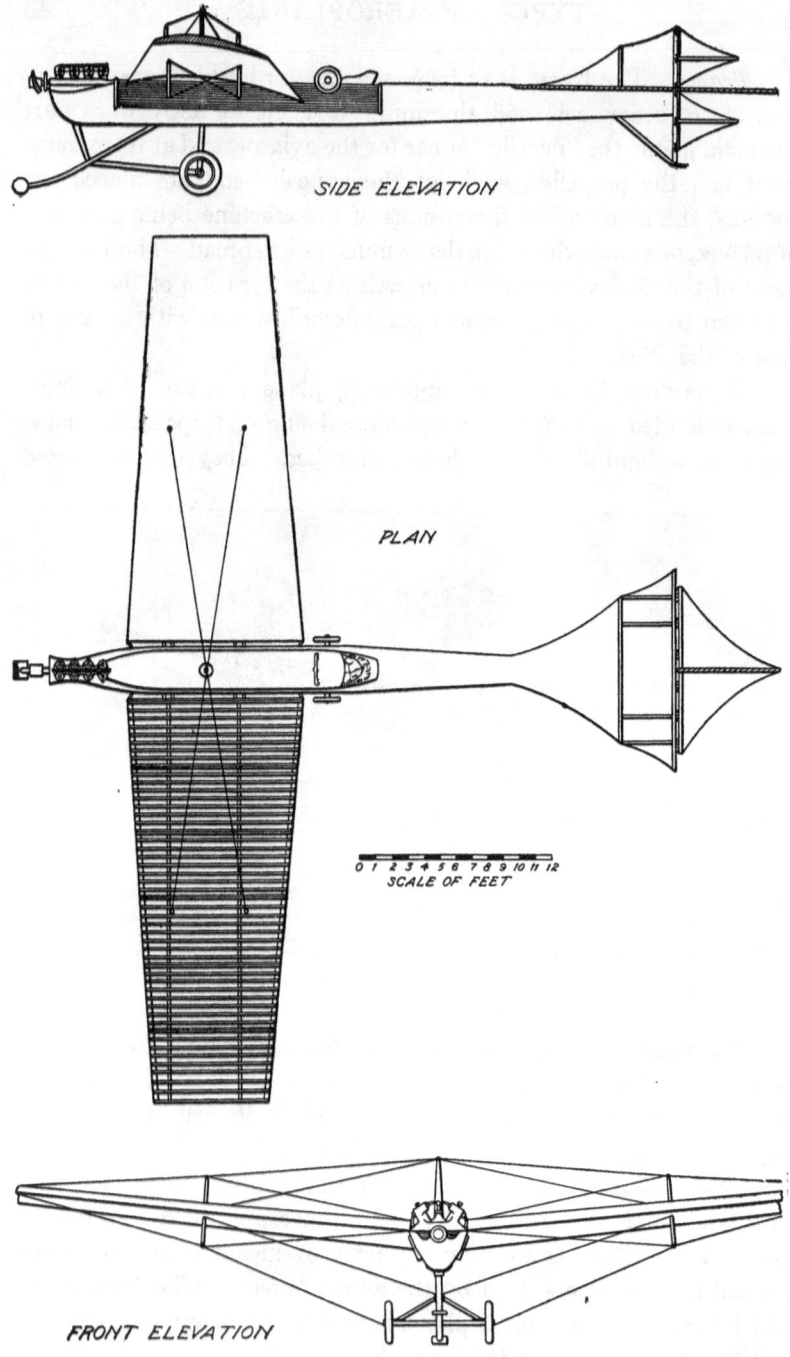

Fig. 28. Details of Antoinette Monoplane

TYPES OF AEROPLANES 45

Elevation Rudder. The elevation rudder has an area of 20 square feet and is also triangular. It is placed at the extreme rear in order to provide the maximum leverage, and is controlled by cables leading round a drum attached to a wheel at the aviator's right hand. To ascend, the wheel is turned up. This causes the inclination of the elevating rudder with regard to the line of flight to decrease, and the machine, therefore, rises.

Transverse Control. Lateral stability is maintained by warping the outer ends of the main plane in much the same manner as in the Wright machine, except that the front ends of the plane are movable and the rear ends are rigid throughout in the Antoinette, the reverse being the case in the Wright. Through cables and a sprocket placed at the lower end of the central mast, the warping is controlled by a wheel at the aviator's left hand. To correct a downward inclination at the right, the right end of the wing is turned up and at the same time the left end is turned down, restoring the balance.

Keels. At the rear, leading up to the rudders, are tapered keels, both horizontal and vertical, that add greatly to the bird-like appearance of the Antoinette in flight.

Power Plant. The power plant is an eight-cylinder, V-type, four-cycle, water-cooled Antoinette motor of 50 horse-power, the radiator taking the form of two banks of tubes placed along either side of the car. The motor carries on the forward end of its crank shaft a two-bladed, metal propeller, 7.25 feet in diameter by 4.3 feet pitch, which it drives at 1,100 r. p. m.

General. The chassis is mounted on a pair of pneumatic-tired wheels attached to the central mast by a pneumatic spring. In addition, a single skid is placed forward to protect the propeller in landing, and another at the rear. The seat for the aviator is placed in the frame back of the main plane and about 8 feet directly behind the motor, a seat for a passenger being provided in front of and slightly lower than that for the aviator. The sides of the space are walled with canvas, affording the aviator and passenger more protection than is usually provided. The total weight is 1,040 to 1,120 pounds, the speed 43 miles per hour. Thirty pounds are lifted per horse-power and 3.96 pounds per square foot of supporting surface. The aspect ratio is 6 to 1.

TYPES OF AEROPLANES

In a later machine, the spread is 49.3 feet, the area 405 square feet, and the total weight 1,200 to 1,350 pounds, 27 pounds being lifted per horse-power, and 3.33 pounds per square foot of surface. The aspect ratio is 6 to 1. A new 100-horse-power type is also employed for racing, this machine being fitted with the Antoinette sixteen-cylinder, V-type motor. The newer models of the Antoinette differ so radically that they have been described in the article devoted to special types.

Santos=Dumont. The first sustained flight of a motor-driven aeroplane in Europe was made by M. Santos-Dumont on November

Fig. 29. Santos-Dumont's Earliest Aeroplane with Which He Made the First Power Flight in Europe

12, 1906, in a biplane of his own design, Fig. 29. In 1907 he began work on a monoplane and after a great deal of experimenting succeeded in evolving the Demoiselle, Fig. 30, so-called owing to its diminutive size, as it is the smallest aeroplane in use up to the present writing. It is extremely simple and compact and many of them are flown abroad. Some of Santos-Dumont's earlier attempts were based on principles attractive in theory, but which experience has

TYPES OF AEROPLANES

shown to be erroneous. Chief among these are the use of a sharp dihedral angle for the supporting surfaces and a very low center of gravity to simulate a pendulum. As shown by the Wright Brothers' experiments, while a pendulum may give a certain stability in a state of perfect rest or when flying straightaway in a dead calm, it exaggerates oscillation, once the latter is set up, and is entirely destructive of stability. Planes set at a dihedral angle give neither the same lifting power nor an amount of stability equal to a surface of the same dimensions that is made perfectly flat laterally. This is the case in all the biplanes described here and some of the monoplanes, the supporting surfaces of the Bleriot and Antoinette being set at a slight dihedral angle, however. This characteristic is still

Fig. 30. Santos-Dumont Demoiselle, the Smallest Man-Carrying Aeroplane

strongly marked in the Santos-Dumont monoplane, but the motor has been placed on a level with the supporting surfaces. The lack of stability of this machine was very marked as compared with both the biplanes and monoplanes taking part in the International Meet near New York, both its pitching and rocking reaching extreme angles and continuing throughout the flight. When compared with the larger machines in the air, it appeared almost like a sparrow among eagles, and the difference in the character of their action in flight was also similar. At no time did Audemars or Garros leave the ground more than 30 or 40 feet below, when flying the Demoiselle monoplanes on the occasion in question.

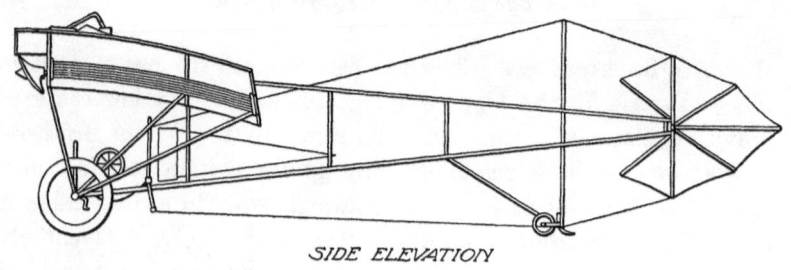

SIDE ELEVATION

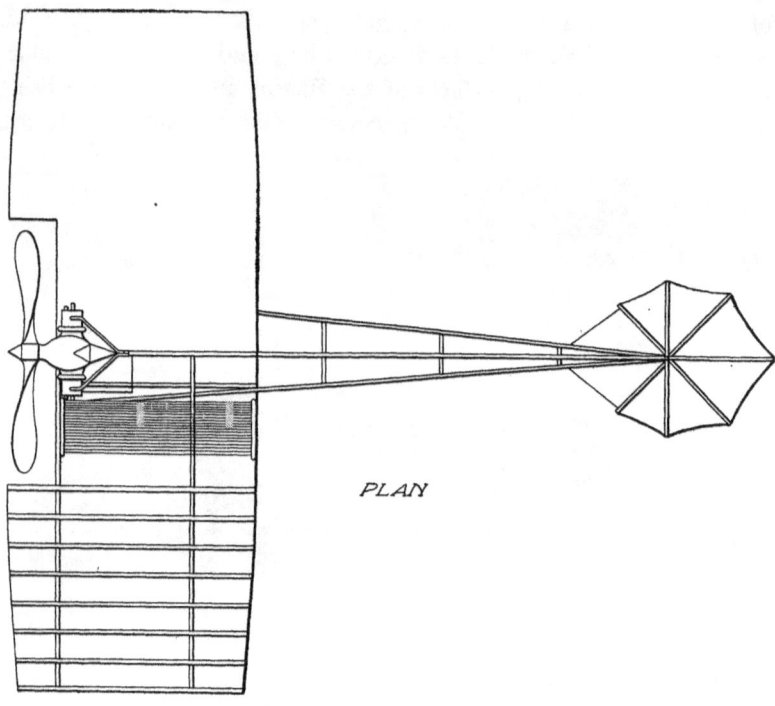

PLAN

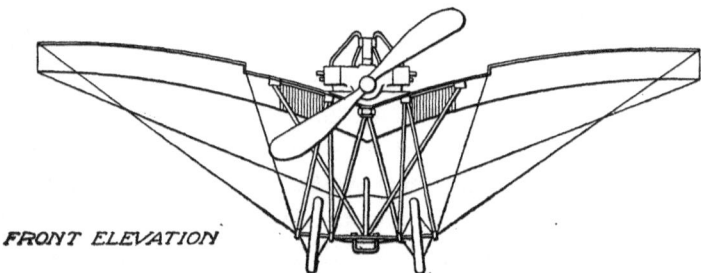

FRONT ELEVATION

Fig. 31. Details of Santos-Dumont Demoiselle

TYPES OF AEROPLANES

Frame. The frame is triangular in form, Fig. 31, with its apex at the rear and is composed of bamboo with steel joints and several members of steel tubing.

Supporting Planes. Owing to the curvature of the supporting surfaces closely approximating the arc of a circle, there are really two planes joined at their inner ends. They consist of a double layer of silk tightly stretched over bamboo ribs, the whole being braced by steel wires led to the central frame. The spread is 18 feet, the depth 6.56 feet, and the area 113 square feet.

Direction and Elevation Rudders. The direction and elevation rudders are combined at the rear in the form of two fan-shaped surfaces, one vertical and the other horizontal, swung on a universal joint at the point of the triangular frame. The elevating rudder has an area of 21 square feet, while the direction rudder is somewhat smaller. A lever at the aviator's right hand controls the elevating rudder, while a wheel at the left operates the direction rudder. To ascend, the tail is moved up and to the right, to alter the line of travel in that direction. There are no keels.

Transverse Control. Transverse control is accomplished by warping the main planes, their operation being governed by a lever at the back of the aviator which fits into a pocket sewed into his coat. If the machine should suddenly tip up on the left, the aviator, by moving quickly in that direction, could pull down the plane on the right and increase the angle of incidence on that side. It will be seen from the foregoing that in flight he is kept pretty busy. The flexibility of the ribs of the planes permits them to warp without any special constructional details for that purpose.

Power Plant. A 30-horse-power, two-cylinder, horizontal-opposed water-cooled Darracq motor drives a two-bladed Chauviere wood propeller 6.9 feet in diameter by 6-foot pitch at 1,400 r. p. m., although Clement-Bayard and Panhard motors are also used on this machine.

General. The machine is mounted on two rigidly attached pneumatic-tired wheels at the front and a single small skid at the rear, the aviator's seat consisting of a strip of canvas placed across the frame and located directly beneath the motor. The propeller, instead of extending forward beyond the main planes, revolves in a rectangular opening cut in the latter. The total weight is from 330 to 370 pounds, speed 52 miles per hour. Twelve pounds are lifted

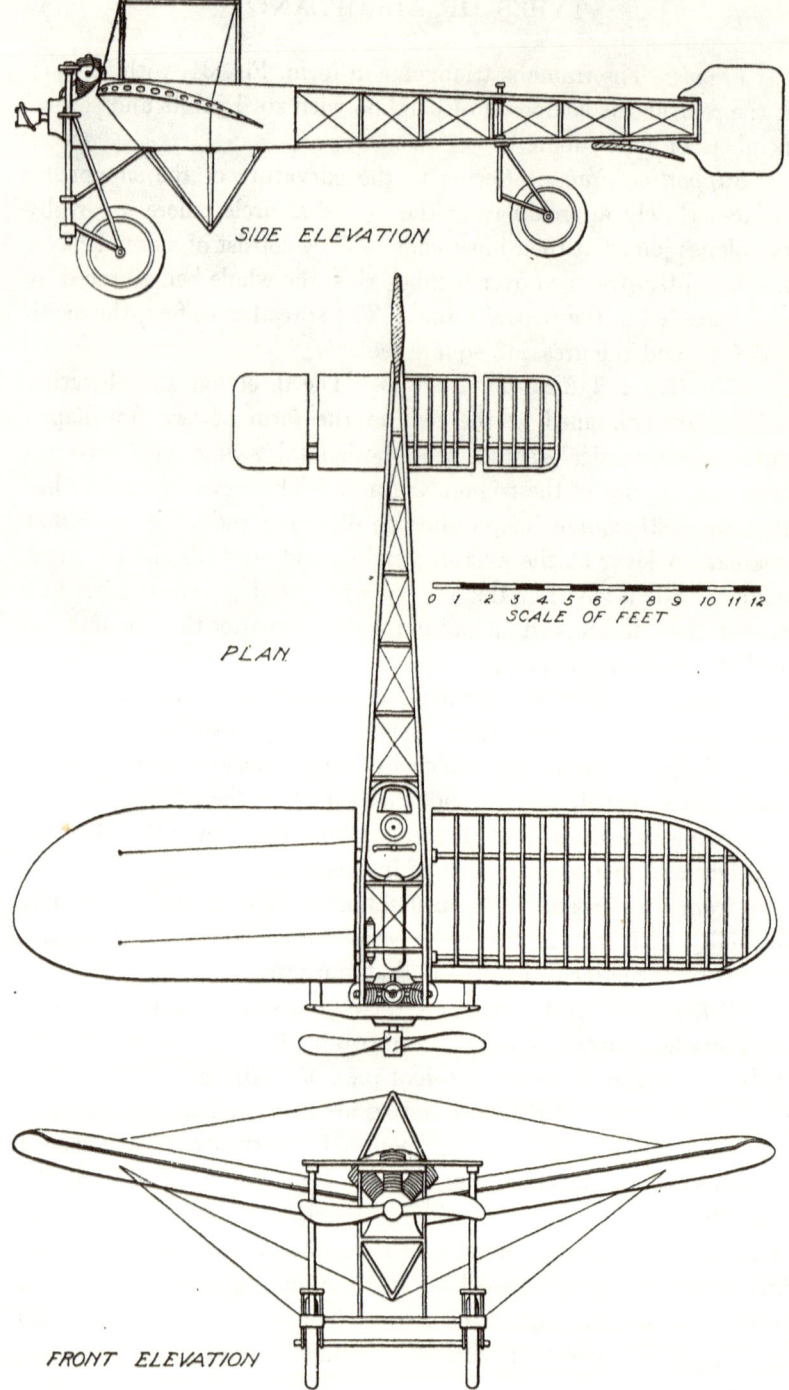

Fig. 32. Details of Bleriot XI Monoplane

per horse-power and 3.1 pounds per square foot of surface. The aspect ratio is 2.7 to 1.

Bleriot XI. In 1906, M. Louis Bleriot constructed and flew the first successful monoplane built. The two years following were devoted to experimental work, during which period a number of various modifications of the original were built until, in 1908, Bleriot succeeded in making a number of extended flights in his large monoplane, No. 8 Bis. In July, 1910, he made his sensational cross-channel trip, starting from Calais and landing near Dover. This flight was accomplished in the No. XI type machine, Fig. 32, a small one-passenger monoplane which is very simple and has come into widespread use abroad. Delagrange, Le Blanc, De Lesseps, Le Blon, Balsan, and Guyot are among some of the noted French aviators who have flown Bleriot monoplanes, two of whom have been killed in their operation. More than one hundred and forty of these machines were manufactured and sold during the year ending with August, 1910.

Frame. The frame consists essentially of a long central body of tapering construction to which the planes and rudder are attached. The framework is very lightly but strongly built of wood and is cross braced with steel wires throughout.

Supporting Plane. The main plane is placed at the forward part of the central frame and is divided in half, each section being mounted on either side of the central frame by socket joints. The halves are thus readily detachable at that point and when not in use are dismounted and placed in a vertical position along the frame so as to make the machine as a whole occupy very little room. The surfaces consist of wood ribs covered both above and below by Continental rubber fabric. The curvature is more pronounced than in most other types, with the exception of the Demoiselle, and a sharp front edge is obtained by the use of aluminum sheathing at that point. The two halves of the main plane are set at a slight dihedral angle. Their spread is 28.2 feet, depth 6.5 feet, and surface area 151 square feet. They are braced both above and below by steel wires led to the central frame.

Direction Rudder. The direction rudder consists of a very small plane having only 4.5 square feet of area and is placed at the extreme rear. It is controlled by a foot in the manner already described in some of the foregoing machines.

Elevation Rudder. The elevation rudder is divided into two parts, one half being mounted at each extremity of a fixed horizontal keel. It has 16 square feet of surface and is operated by the longitudinal movement of a bell crank device. This takes the form of a universally-pivoted lever placed in front of the operator, and is normally vertical. At the lower extremity of the lever is fixed a dome or hood-shaped piece of metal to which the wires are attached, at the same time protecting them from entanglement in the aviator's feet. To ascend the aviator pulls the lever toward him, and to descend pushes it from him.

Transverse Control. Lateral equilibrium is maintained by warping the main planes, the structure of the latter enabling them to be twisted as in the Wright machine, though in this case they warp about the bases which are rigidly attached to the main frame by the socket joints mentioned. The two halves are warped inversely by the side to side motion of the bell crank, *i. e.*, if the machine should tip up on the right, then the bell crank would be moved to the right. This would increase the incidence of the lowered side and at the same time decrease that of the raised side, thus righting the machine. The combination of this side to side movement of the bell crank with the movement of the foot lever controlling the direction rudder is used in turning.

Keels. To preserve the longitudinal stability, a single, fixed, horizontal keel is placed at the rear. Its area is 17 square feet.

Power Plant. The power plant is a three-cylinder, fan-shaped Anzani motor, developing 23 horse-power. It is of the air-cooled type and is placed at the forward end of the central frame. It drives a two-bladed wood propeller of 6.87 feet in diameter by 2.7-foot pitch direct at 1,350 r. p. m. Most of the more recent Bleriot monoplanes have been fitted with 50-horse-power Gnome, seven-cylinder, rotary, air-cooled motor.

General. The machine is mounted on an elastic chassis with two large rubber-tired wheels forward and a small wheel rear. The springs are made of thick rubber rope, affording great elasticity and strength with small weight. The aviator's seat is back of the main plane.

The total weight is from 650 to 720 pounds and the speed is 36 miles per hour with the Anzani motor and 48 miles per hour with the

TYPES OF AEROPLANES

Gnome motor; 29 pounds are lifted per horse-power and 4.5 pounds per square foot of surface, this ratio being unusually high. The aspect ratio is 4.35 to 1.

Later Types. In the later Bleriot machines, the elevating rudder is of different form, being attached at the rear edge of a tapering keel much larger than that formerly used. The small wheel at the rear has been replaced by a skid and the overall length of the central frame has been shortened considerably. The regular one-passenger type of this monoplane has further been altered to the new No. XI Bis, in which the sectional curvature of the planes has been made very nearly flat on the under side. This change has been found to

Fig. 33. Bleriot Two-Passenger Monoplane

greatly decrease the dynamic resistance of the machine without seriously impairing its lift. There are two new models of this machine which have been very successful. They are the No. XI 2 Bis, a two- or three-passenger machine, Fig. 33, and the No. XI racing model, Figs. 34 and 35. The former has a spread of 36 feet, a depth of 7.6 feet, a surface of 270 square feet, and a weight in flight of about 990 pounds. In other respects it resembles the No. XI Bis. 19.8 pounds are carried per horse-power and 3.68 pounds per square foot of surface. The aspect ratio is 4.75 to 1. The *type de course*, or No. XI racing model, is the machine on which Morane established the record of almost 69 miles per hour. It has a very short body, flat planes, and a reinforced frame. The surface has been reduced to 129 square feet and it is equipped with one of the new 100-horse-power,

Fig. 34. Bleriot Racing Model in Fl'ght

fourteen-cylinder Gnome, rotary, air-cooled motors. The total weight is about 750 pounds; only 7.5 pounds are carried per horsepower and as much as 5.76 pounds are lifted per square foot of surface.

Fig. 35. Bleriot Rounding a Pylon in International Race for Gordon-Bennett Cup

Bleriot XII. The Bleriot XII is a passenger-carrying type which differs in construction from those just described. With one of these large machines, M. Bleriot made the first flight in an aeroplane carrying three passengers. It has since come into general use, more than thirty of them having been built.

Frame. The long central frame of wood, Fig. 36, braced in every panel by steel cross wires, is very deep forward and tapers gracefully to a point at the rear.

Supporting Plane. On the upper deck of the central frame at the front is placed the main plane which is continuous and perfectly horizontal. Its structure is similar to that of the No. XI and it is braced by a number of wires from the frame. The spread is 30.2 feet, the depth 7.6 feet, and the total area 228 square feet.

Direction Rudder. A single surface placed at the rear extremity of the vertical keel is used for this purpose. Its area is only 9 square feet and it is operated in the same manner as on the No. XI.

Elevation Rudder. The elevation rudder also consists of a single surface of 20 square feet area and placed at the extreme rear. It is operated by the movement of a bell crank, as already described.

Transverse Control. The main surfaces are warped inversely, exactly as in the No. XI, a small surface under the aviator's seat also assisting in the lateral balancing. A horizontal keel of 21 square feet area is placed on the framework at the rear, but somewhat forward of the elevating rudder.

Power Plant. The power plant consists of a 60-horse-power, eight-cylinder E. N. V., air-cooled motor, placed on the frame under the main plane. By means of a chain transmission it drives an 8.8-foot propeller mounted on a shaft at the edge of the main plane. The propeller has an unusually long pitch—9 feet—and turns at only 600 r. p. m.

General. The mounting is similar to that of No. XI, while the seat or bench for three persons is placed under the main plane and back of the motor. The total weight is from 1,150 to 1,300 pounds; speed 48 miles per hour; 21 pounds are lifted per horsepower and 5.3 pounds per square foot of surface. The aspect ratio is 4 to 1. Bleriot is one of the most prolific designers of monoplanes, and it would require a volume to describe them. The Bleriot Limousine or "aerial taxi" is described under special types.

Grade. Herr Grade has the distinction of being one of the first German aviators to design and build an aeroplane. In the fall of

56 TYPES OF AEROPLANES

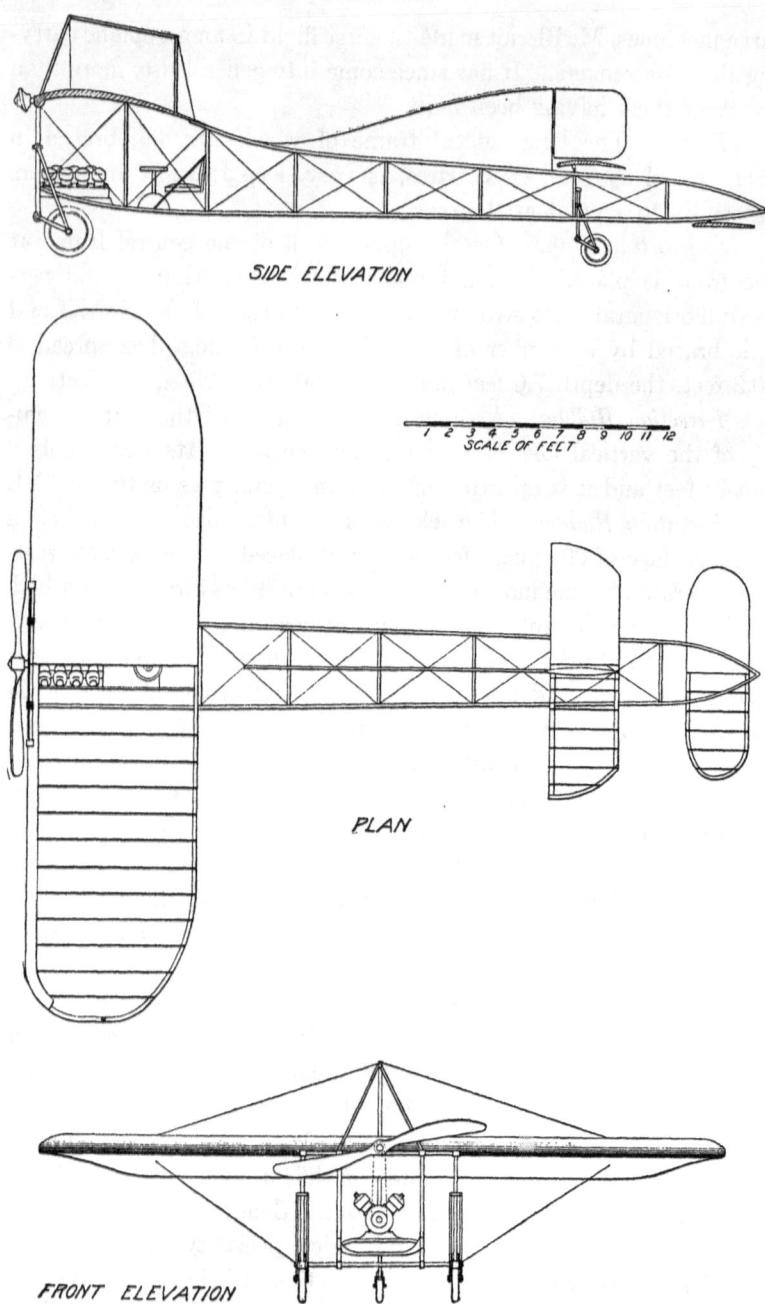

Fig. 36. Details of Bleriot XII Monoplane

TYPES OF AEROPLANES

1909, he began flights on his interesting monoplane, Fig. 37, and on October 30, 1909, won the Lanz $10,000 prize for a German-built

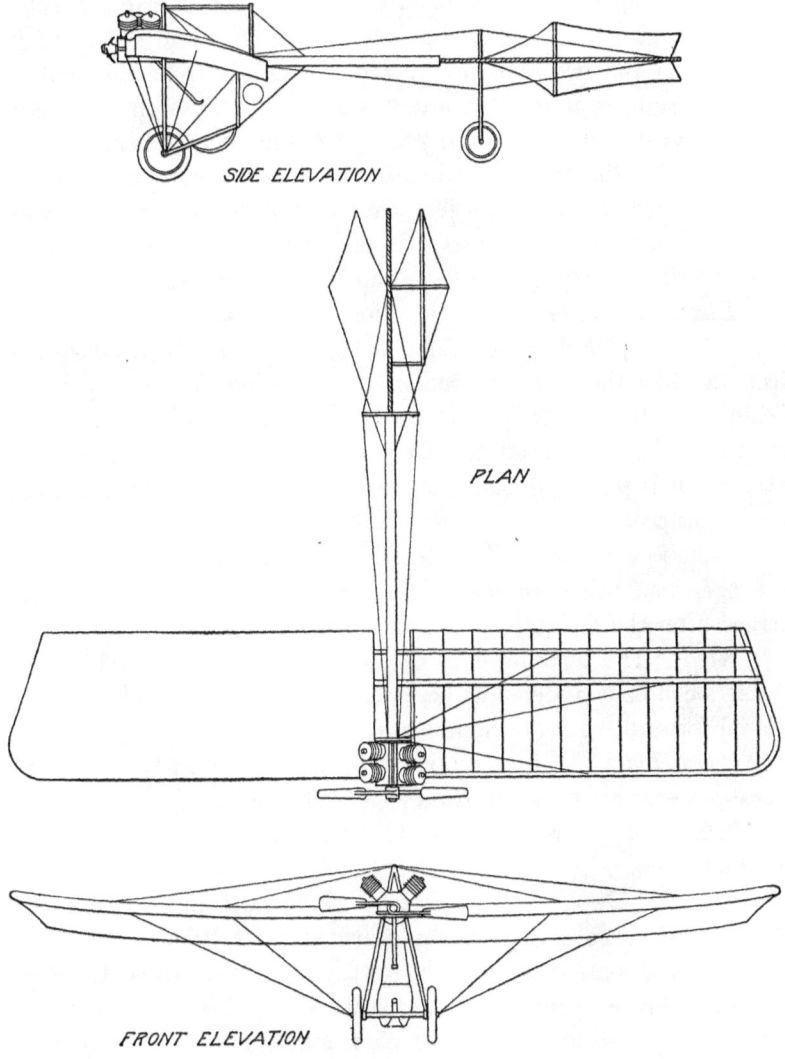

Fig. 37. Grade Monoplane, One of the Few German Aeroplane Designs

machine. The machine is simple and flies easily. A number of them have already been built and sold in Germany.

Frame. The frame is remarkable for the simplicity of its construction, consisting of a main metal tube chassis at the front from which a long thick member supporting the rudders is run out to the rear.

Supporting Plane. The main surface is made of Metzler rubber fabric stretched over a bamboo frame. The surface is very flexible and the two ends are turned up slightly from the center. The curvature is almost the arc of a circle and the section is very thin. The spread is 30 feet, depth 7 feet, and area 208 square feet.

Direction Rudder. The direction rudder consists of a single, flexible surface of 16 square feet area, carried at the rear and controlled by a lever. The surface itself is not hinged, but is bent in the direction desired by the lever and wire connections.

Elevation Rudder. The elevation rudder also consists of a single surface placed at the rear. It has an area of about 20 square feet and like the direction rudder its operation depends upon its flexibility. It is controlled by a large lever universally pivoted on the frame above the aviator. To rise, this lever is pulled up, and to descend, it is pushed down, thus bending up or down the rear horizontal surface.

Transverse Control. Warping the main planes is resorted to, the operation being similar to the Bleriot, which, in turn, is patterned after the Wright.

Keels. The tapering ends of both the direction and elevating rudders can be considered as keels, an additional vertical keel being placed forward, both above and below the main plane.

Power Plant. A four-cylinder, V-type, air-cooled motor of 24 horse-power is placed at the front edge of the plane. It drives direct at 1,000 r. p. m. a two-bladed metal propeller 6 feet in diameter by a 4-foot pitch.

General. Two wheels are employed forward and one rear for the mounting, no springs being provided. The front wheels are provided with a brake to bring the machine to a quick standstill after alighting, this being an important feature where the space is limited. The seat is placed under the main plane and consists of a hammock-like piece of cloth which is very light and very comfortable. The total weight is from 350 to 450 pounds and the speed approximately 44 miles per hour; 17 pounds are lifted per horse-power, and 1.9 pounds per square foot of surface. The aspect ratio is 3.2 to 1.

TYPES OF AEROPLANES 59

Pelterie. By many, the Pelterie monoplane, Fig. 38, is considered to be one of the most perfect types of aeroplane. Great

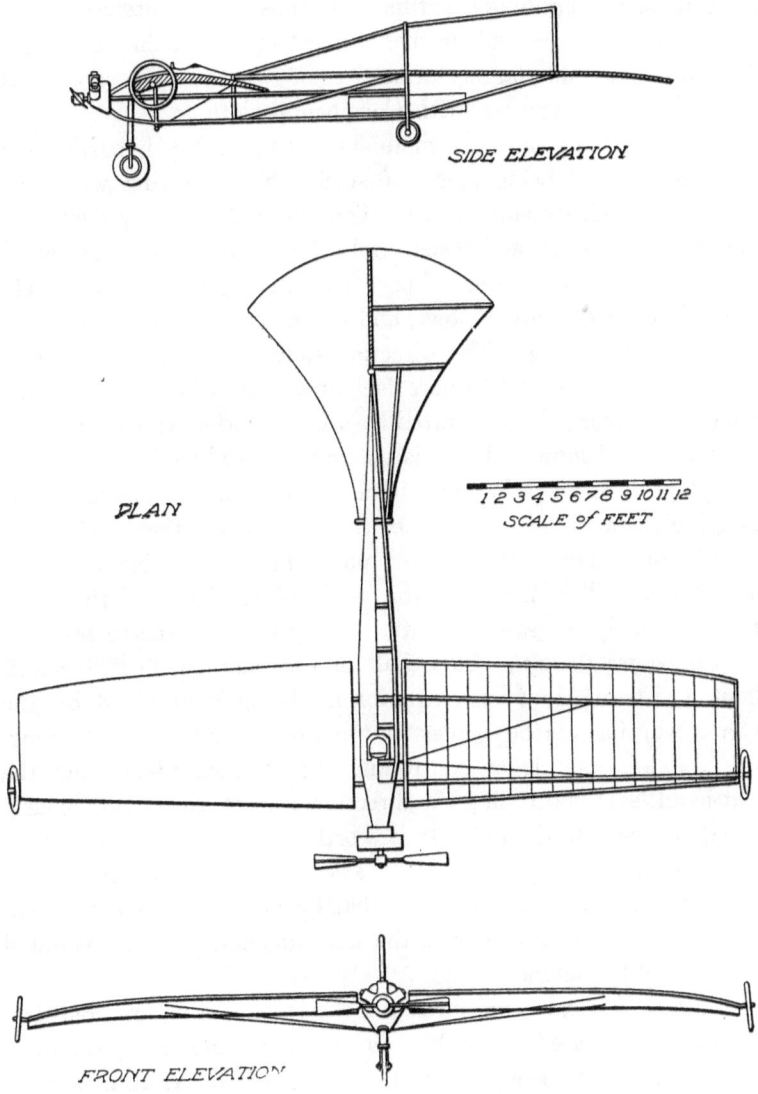

Fig. 38. Pelterie Monoplane

care is shown in its construction and finish, but owing to motor troubles, it has never flown for any length of time. Its designer,

Robert Esnault Pelterie, is one of the foremost French aviation scientists, and previous to building this machine, he conducted a lengthy series of gliding experiments of considerable interest.

Frame. The central frame, somewhat similar in form to a bird's body, is made largely of steel tubing and is quite short. All exposed parts are covered with Continental cloth.

Supporting Plane. The main supporting surface is particularly strong and solid, being made of steel tubing carrying wood ribs covered with Continental cloth. The curvature is very similar to that of a bird's wing, and transversely the surface curves downward, dihedrally from the center. Very little bracing is necessary. The spread is 35 feet, depth 6.1 feet, and the area 214 square feet.

Direction Rudder. The direction rudder consists of a vertical rectangular surface of 8 square feet area placed below the central frame at the rear. It is operated by a lever at the aviator's right.

Elevation Control. There is no elevation rudder in the Pelterie monoplane, the elevation of the machine being accomplished by changing the angle of incidence of the main planes themselves. To ascend, for instance, the aviator pulls the lever in his left hand toward him. This increases the angle of incidence of the plane and accordingly increases the lift, causing the machine to rise.

Transverse Control. Each half of the main plane is warpable about its base, transverse equilibrium being maintained by the inverse warping of the planes in the usual manner. In turning, both the left-hand lever controlling the warping planes and the right-hand lever controlling the direction rudder are simultaneously moved to the side desired. It is worthy of note here, that of all aeroplanes employing the Wright system for maintaining lateral stability—and there are very few that do not—none of them combines the control in one lever in the same ingenious manner as found in the Wright machine.

Keels. Vertical and horizontal keels consisting of gradually tapering surfaces are fixed to the frame and aid in preserving stability. The rear horizontal keel, shaped like a bird's tail, has an area of 20 square feet.

Power Plant. The power plant consists of a seven-cylinder, fan-shaped, air-cooled R. E. P. (Robert Esnault Pelterie) motor of very ingenious design. It is placed at the front and drives direct a four-bladed aluminum and steel propeller at 900 r. p. m. Its diameter is 6.6 feet and its pitch 5 feet.

General. The mounting consists of a large single wheel carried on a combined hydraulic and pneumatic spring at the center of the front, with a smaller wheel on the same center line at the rear. Wheels are also placed at the outer ends, or tips, of the supporting planes, so that when first starting to run along the ground, the machine is inclined. The seat is placed in the frame, and protected on all sides, the aviator's shoulders coming flush with the supporting surfaces. The total weight is from 900 to 970 pounds; speed 39 miles per hour; 27 pounds are lifted per horse-power and 4.4 pounds carried per square foot of surface. The aspect ratio is 5.75 to 1.

In a later model of the R. E. P. the fuselage is entirely of steel tubing connected by welded joints and the whole strongly trussed. Each wing is composed of two ash spars covered by red Continental rubberized fabric. The method of attaching the wings to the fuselage is a distinctive feature. In most monoplanes the ends of the spars are let into the fuselage, but in this case they are attached to the body by means of joints. This prevents the portions of the wings near the fuselage from having to endure abnormal stresses due to their attachment in case the supporting stays should become slack. This arrangement also permits the dihedral angle between the wings to be varied slightly. The lower stays of the rear spar are attached to an oscillating lever mounted on ball bearings and controlled by the wing-warping lever, while the lower stays attached to the front spar and supporting the wings in flight are steel cables covered with cloth. The tail fins, elevator, and rudder are demountable, being composed simply of steel tubing covered with fabric. The well-developed horizontal tail fins, being distant from the center of gravity, give great longitudinal stability to the machine. The elevator, which forms the prolongation of the horizontal empennage or tail, is divided into two parts by the rudder, forward of which is the vertical keel.

Pfitzner. The Pfitzner machine, Fig. 39, represents a radical departure from all other aeroplanes in some of its features, while it differs from other monoplanes in the placing of the aviator, motor, and rudders. It was built in the early part of January, 1910, by A. L. Pfitzner at the Curtiss factory in Hammondsport, New York.

TYPES OF AEROPLANES

It was the first to employ the comparatively simple and efficient method of transverse control by means of sliding surfaces, and while

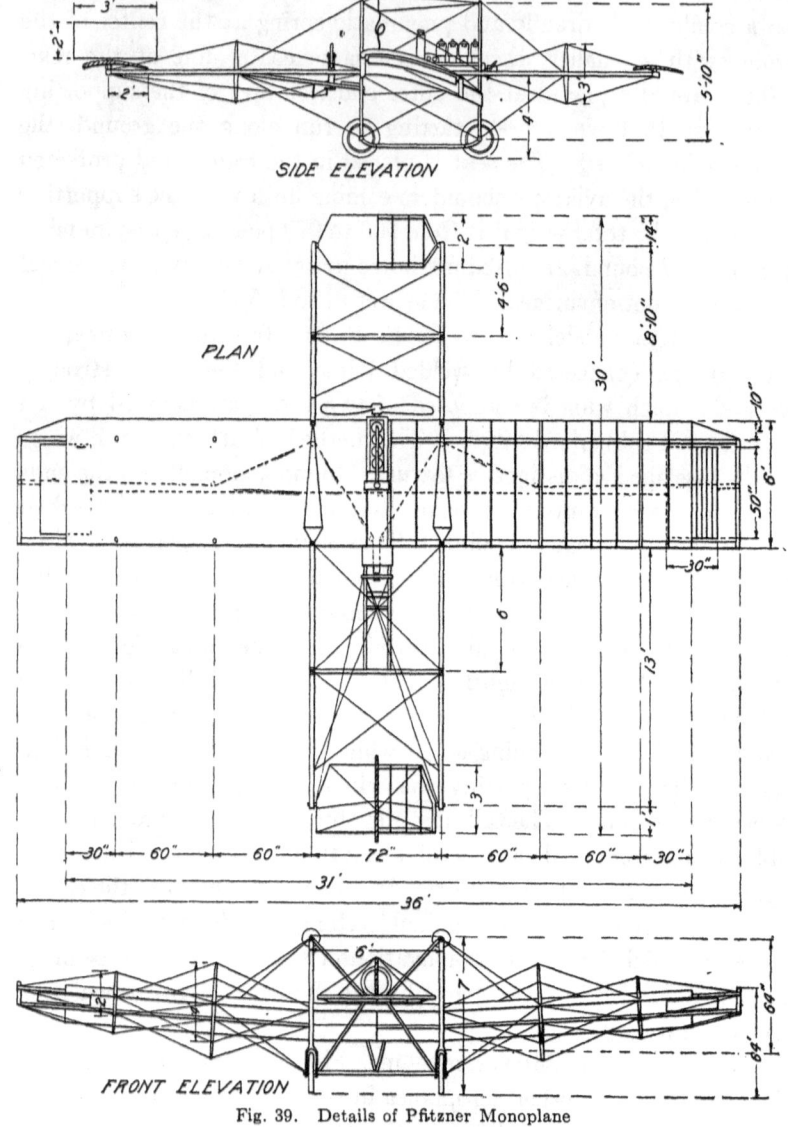

Fig. 39. Details of Pfitzner Monoplane

the first flights were short, largely due to the inexperience of the aviator, it is considered by many to be a very promising type, par-

TYPES OF AEROPLANES

ticularly as it does not conflict with the Wright system in any way.

Frame. The framework is largely a combination of numerous king-post trusses with spruce compression members and wire tension members. The framework is open throughout, enabling quick inspection and easy repairs. At the center, the chassis is mainly composed of steel tubing.

Supporting Plane. The main supporting plane, a 5-degree dihedral angle, consists of two main beams, across which are placed spruce ribs. The surface is made of Baldwin vulcanized silk of jet-black color tacked to the top of the ribs and laced to the frame. The curvature of the surface is slight and is designed for high speed. The spread is 31 feet, depth 6 feet, and surface area 186 square feet.

Direction Rudder. The direction rudder is a rectangular surface of but 6 square feet in area and is placed at the front. It is operated by wires leading to the bracket underneath the controlling column. Turning this column to either side causes the machine to turn to that side.

Elevation Rudder. The elevation rudder is likewise placed at the front and is also a single surface of 17 square feet in area. It is operated by wires leading to a lever at the side of the controlling column. Moving the column forward or backward causes the elevation rudder to turn down or up, respectively.

Transverse Control. The framework of the main plane is carried out 30 inches beyond the end of the surface on either side and affords a place for a rail on which the auxiliary sliding surfaces move. These sliding surfaces, or equalizers, are each $12\frac{1}{2}$ square feet in area and when "normal" project 15 inches beyond the end of the fixed surface on either side. They are interconnected by wires, and a long cable running to each end through a pulley connects them to the steering wheel. The control is as follows: If the right end of the aeroplane is tipped down, the wheel supported on the controlling column is turned away from the lowered side. This causes the equalizer on the raised end to be pulled in under the main surface, or "reefed," while at the same time the one on the other end is pulled out. This action merely decreases the surface on the raised end and increases it on the lowered end, thus righting the machine.

Keels. A horizontal surface placed at the rear acts as a longitudinal stabilizer. It is 10.5 square feet in area and is fixed firmly to the supporting framework, 10 feet to the rear of the main surface.

Power Plant. The power plant consists of a four-cylinder, air-cooled, 25-horse-power Curtiss motor placed on the framework above the plane and to the rear of it. The motor drives direct a two-bladed wood propeller 6 feet in diameter by 4.5 feet pitch at 1,200 r. p. m. This propeller is of original design and is said to be very efficient.

General. The machine is mounted on four small, rubber-tired wheels placed at the lower ends of the four main vertical posts of the chassis. They are spaced by steel tubing and are fitted with brakes, but have no springs. The seat for the aviator is placed out in front of the main plane and directly in the center line. The total weight in flight is from 560 to 600 pounds, while the speed is estimated at 42 miles per hour; 24 pounds are lifted per horse-power, and 3.2 pounds carried per square foot of surface. The aspect ratio is 5.7 to 1.

COMPARISON OF STANDARD TYPES

From the foregoing description of what has been termed standard types, it will be apparent that, while all have many features in common, no two are exactly alike in either design, constructional detail, or efficiency. Some that are less desirable from certain points of view than other types belonging to the same class, show an unusually high degree of efficiency; others have advantages of greater stability. All, however, have proved successful in operation and some to a far greater degree than others. It will accordingly be both interesting and profitable to note the contrasts and distinctions that may be drawn. From these it will be possible to arrive at conclusions as to what particular features are most desirable at present, as well as to note what the trend of the future may be. For this purpose the aeroplanes already described are compared according to the following essential features, which are given as nearly as possible in the order of their importance, where their influence on the result aimed at—flight—is concerned: (1) transverse control; (2) aspect ratio; (3) incident angle; (4) propellers; (5) rudders; (6) keels; (7) mounting; (8) speed; (9) flight; (10) efficiency.

The object of placing the factor of efficiency last in order of importance is not to indicate that as its actual position from the

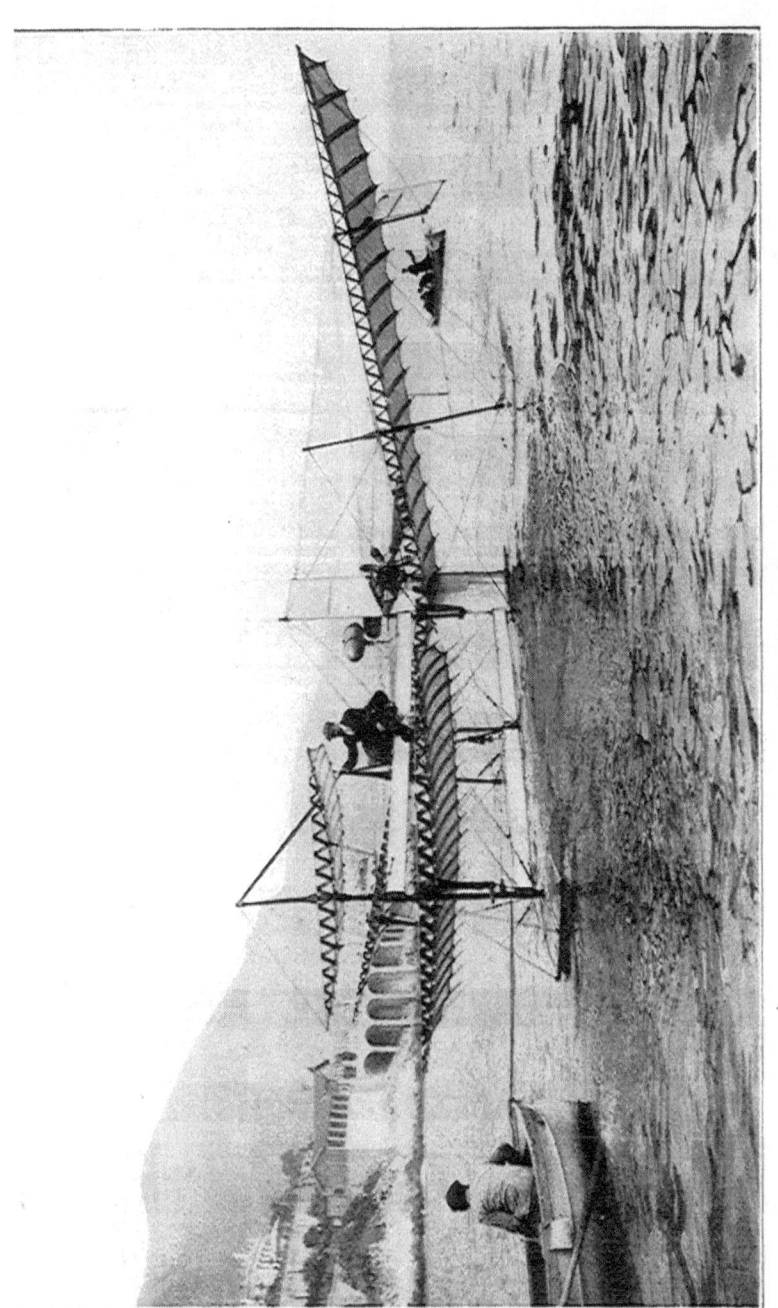

THE HYDROAEROPLANE INVENTED BY FABRE OF FRANCE, BEING THE FIRST AEROPLANE TO FLY FROM AND ALIGHT UPON THE WATER
This Photograph Protected by International Copyright

practical viewpoint, as this is the one thing that designers are now striving hardest to attain, but more because it represents the best opportunity to sum up generally the performances of the different machines. Motors are compared at the conclusion of the chapter on that subject.

Transverse Control. In practice, the lateral stability of aeroplanes is maintained by four different methods: (1) automatically; (2) by warping; (3) by balancing planes, *i. e.*, wing tips or ailerons; (4) by "reefing," or the employment of supplementary sliding planes or equalizers.

At present, warping the planes is the most generally employed and most practical method, but it is expected that a simple method of automatically preserving the lateral equilibrium will be the ultimate development, and many designers, including the Wright Brothers, are striving for that end, so that it is given precedence here.

The Voisin is the only type for which automatic stability has been claimed, but it is noticeable that in later types of this machine, wing tips have been employed. The rear box-cell and the vertical keels or partitions between the surfaces of the main planes exert such a forcible "hold" on the air that to displace the machine is difficult and, in all ordinary turmoils of the air, it displays exceptional stability. In fact, a well-known aviator amusingly stated at Rheims that, were a Voisin tipped completely over on one end, it would still be aerodynamically supported, so great is the expanse of vertical surface.

Without such keels, however, the lateral balance of an aeroplane is so precarious that some form of control is absolutely necessary. The method of warping the planes in connection with the operation of the vertical or direction rudder is the chief claim of the Wright patents, and all machines employing it are essentially the same as the Wright device, even though the operating connections do not control the main planes and the rudder simultaneously. In addition to the biplanes employing it, all the successful monoplane types, except the Pfitzner, depend upon warping the main planes for this control.

Because of the structural difficulty of rigidly bracing the surface of a monoplane, warping is an ideal form of control. But the rigid structure of the biplane permits auxiliary planes to be more easily provided. This is done in the Curtiss, Farman, Sommer, the recent

Voisin, and the Cody. Both these methods of transverse control are very efficacious, but the additional resistance, unaccompanied by any increase of lift, which is produced by balancing planes, renders them less desirable than warping. On the other hand, there are objections to weakening the structure of the main surfaces by making them movable.

There is a further distinction between these two methods of control, which, although not thoroughly understood in a general sense, appears to be borne out in practice, viz, when a plane is warped the action tends not only to tip the machine up on one side but also, due to the helical form thus assumed, to turn, which can be counteracted only by the vertical rudder. In the case of wing tips, however, due to the equal but contrary position in which they are placed, both sides of the machine are equally retarded and, in addition, since the main surfaces preserve the same shape and the same angle of incidence, this tendency to turn appears to be absent. Curtiss states that to correct for tipping alone, he makes no use of the vertical rudder.

Sliding panels, or "equalizers," as applied to the Pfitzner monoplane, represent one of the recently-designed methods of transverse control which are considered not to infringe the Wright patents. This system has not been adequately tried out as yet, but there appears to be no reason why it should not be as effective as either the system of warping or the use of wing tips. There are many other methods designed to give transverse control and it seems at present that they are all equally reliable. Structural individualities of the types of aeroplanes will persist, in all likelihood, so that we can not picture the machine of the future with any one form of transverse controlling apparatus. Balancing planes and wing tips, or ailerons, are widely used at present, but further progress in aerodynamics is likely to show that warping is better, particularly as the development of improved forms of construction and more suitable materials eliminate the objection of weakening the main structure as now built.

Aspect Ratio. It is at once observable from the values given that the ratio of spread to depth (aspect ratio) of the monoplanes is generally less than that of the biplanes. This interesting fact is due very likely to the structural difficulty of making the wing of a monoplane long and narrow, and at the same time providing the necessary strength without involving undue weight. The Antoinette monoplane has recently shown a departure from this standard by decreasing the depth and increasing the spread, thus increasing the aspect ratio, but the framework had to be greatly strengthened. The new model Voisin has the highest aspect ratio of the types considered here, but exhibits no remarkable qualities therefrom.

Both theoretically and experimentally the value of this quality is considered to have much to do with the ratio of lift to drift; but whether or not in actual practice those machines like the Santos-Dumont, having as low an aspect ratio as 3 to 1, are really inferior in their qualities of dynamic support to a machine like the Cody with as high an aspect ratio as 7 to 1, is difficult to determine, since so many other factors, such as the loading and velocity, are involved. It is interesting to note here that some of the large soaring birds, such as the albatross, may be considered as aeroplanes of very high aspect ratio. The effect of aspect ratio upon speed is not discernible upon comparing the types.

Greater stability, however, is commonly supposed to result from a high aspect ratio, because of the decreased proportionate movement of the center of pressure. A further advantage is that the higher the aspect ratio of a plane, the lower is the angle giving the maximum ratio of lift to drift, and consequently for given speed and loading less power is necessary. There appears to be little question but that the development of aeroplane construction of the near future will tend toward an increase in the aspect ratio to as high, possibly, as 12 to 1.

Incident Angle. The angle that the main supporting surfaces of an aeroplane make with the horizontal line of flight is termed the incident angle, and it is something that at present varies greatly in the different types. The Wright biplane is notable for its very low angle of incidence in flight, rarely exceeding two degrees.

Renard, after deductions from the experiments of Borda, Langley, and other investigators, has enunciated the principle that, *as the incident angle diminishes, the driving power expended in sustaining a given plane in the air also diminishes.* Wilbur Wright states that, *the angle of incidence is fixed by the area, weight, and speed alone. It varies directly as the weight, and inversely as the area and speed, although not in exact ratio.* Faraud concludes that small angles are the most efficient for all aeroplanes. There is for each type a most efficient angle of incidence, or point where the power expended for flight is least. In flying, the incidence should be kept constant at this angle in order to obtain the highest speed.

The Farman, Voisin, Bleriot XI, Grade, and Sommer have an angle of incidence when first starting much greater than when in flight. Since this involves greater drift resistance and consequently more power necessary to attain the velocity of levitation and, furthermore, as aeroplanes with as heavy a loading but without an excessive angle are able to rise after a reasonably short run, it would appear as if this provision were unnecessary.

Recent experiments in aerodynamics indicate that the ratio of lift to drift, with a surface of the shape now so generally used, varies little between the values of 2 degrees and 6 degrees, a maximum value being reached in the neighborhood of 3 degrees. This explains in a measure the wide variations in this angle as observed and recorded for the different types, and also that many of the present machines preserve their equilibrium during comparatively large changes of their longitudinal inclination.

In general, the incident angle of the monoplanes is greater than that of the biplanes. The most common angle is in the neighborhood of 5 to 7 degrees. But in the Bleriot XII, an incident angle of 12 to 13 degrees is often used in flight. Incidence will very likely be established purely by the lift-drift ratio of a plane, and the angle kept as constant as possible to give this its highest value.

Propellers. With one or two exceptions, aeroplanes of all types are driven by a single, high-speed screw. The Wright and the Cody are the only instances of machines provided with two propellers rotating in opposite directions. The greater efficiency of a propeller of large diameter revolving at a slow speed over one of small diameter and high rotative speed has attracted much attention. This seems to be borne out especially in the case of the Wright machine, in which more thrust is obtained per unit of power than in any other type. The limit of rotative speed in practice is approximately 1,500 r. p. m., and in all types excepting the Wright, Cody, and Bleriot XII, the r. p. m. rate exceeds 1,000. Many of the aeroplanes, more particularly those of foreign design, use the Chauviere

TYPES OF AEROPLANES

wood propellers, for which an efficiency of 80 per cent is claimed. The Antoinette, Grade, and Voisin, use metal screws.

The thrust and efficiency of the various propellers are about the same for equal sizes, and although the theory of propeller design is very little understood as yet, the experimental methods used have resulted in the design of propellers of as good efficiency or higher efficiency than those used in marine practice. The position of the propeller in front in most of the monoplanes is largely a matter of convenience of design, although it has an advantage in that the swiftly moving mass of air thrown backward by the screw also exerts an added lift when thrown back on the plane. At the same time, however, this action also increases the resistance, but as the frame resistance of the monoplane is much less than that of the biplane, the propeller may be placed in front without any very serious consequences. The Voisin (tractor type) biplane has the screw in front, but the results obtained indicate that this is detrimental to the speed.

It is generally believed by aviators that much better results could be obtained by the use of propellers 15 to 20 feet in diameter, rotating slowly. But there are two disadvantages involved in this feature of construction which make its adoption in the machines of the future rather doubtful. The first is the greatly added weight of so large a propeller and the second is that of building a good chassis high enough to permit of the propeller rotating freely.

Rudders. The direction rudder in all types, except the Pfitzner, is placed at the rear. The Cody biplane has an additional direction rudder in front. All the monoplanes, with the exception of the Pfitzner, have their elevating rudders at the rear, while in all the biplanes, except the new Wright and more recent Voisin models, this rudder is placed out in front. Rudders placed at the rear are advantageous in that they act at the same time as keels. But, in general, the placing of the elevating rudder in front seems to offer more exact control of the longitudinal stability.

The elevating rudder almost always exerts some supporting power. Therefore, when placed in front and turned up for ascent, the support is increased, as it naturally should be. But when this rudder is placed at the rear, the movement for ascent is such that the supporting power of the rudder is decreased, making it of negative value, so that instead of causing the front of the machine to rise, it causes the rear to sink. Following the same theory shows that when the elevating rudder is out in front, in starting, the front of the machine lifts off the ground and is strongly followed by the body; while if this rudder be in the rear, when turned to give ascent the rear merely sinks more, and not only is the run greatly increased, but the power required and the risks incurred are greater. That it is generally so used on the monoplanes is the result of necessity due to the propeller being at the front.

In the Wright biplane the elevating rudder is so constructed that when elevated it is automatically warped concavely on the under side, and when depressed, curved in the opposite way. This materially adds to the rudder's force due to the peculiar law of aerodynamics whereby a curved surface, under the same conditions as a flat surface, has a greater ratio of lift to drift. The reduction in the size of the rudder is thus made possible and its flat shape when normal greatly reduces the head resistance. In so far as a biplane is usually supposed to cause interference of the two surfaces and greater head resistance, it would appear as if the biplane rudders as used on the Wright and the Curtiss were not as efficient as single planes, but the structural advantages of this arrangement are important.

The method employed by Grade of merely bending flexible surfaces, instead of turning rigid movable planes, has a great advantage in that the rudders, after being used, spring back to their normal position. This method has not been adopted on any other type, however, although it has many considerations of safety favoring it.

In almost all of the successful aeroplanes, with the possible exception of the Wright and Antoinette, it is conceded that the size of the rudders is much too great. This is clearly indicated by the remarkably small change of inclination usually necessary for a change of direction. This ultra sensitiveness where, as in some machines, a movement of a few hundredths of an inch will considerably alter the state of equilibrium of the machine, is certainly undesirable. To begin with, it need hardly be pointed out that oversensitiveness of a rudder usually invites dangerous situations. Furthermore, if a rudder be extremely sensitive, it is a good indication that it is too large, in which case it is absorbing considerable power that could be put to better use elsewhere. It is quite likely, therefore, that a great decrease in the size of the rudders will be a development of the near future.

Keels. Keels on aeroplanes, like keels on a boat, add greatly to the stability. But on an aeroplane they are "dead surfaces" and, as such, have the disadvantage of offering greater expanse of surface for wind disturbance to act upon. They unquestionably decrease the speed. Tapering keels, such as those employed on the Antoinette, the Pelterie, and the latest Bleriot XI, offer a maximum of "entering edge" with a minimum of area, and for that reason are more advantageous than those of rectangular form. Keels are entirely lacking in the original Wright, Santos-Dumont, and Cody, but in the later "headless" Wright two small, vertical keels of semi-circular form are placed in the angles made by the meeting of the skids with the braces from the latter to the upper main plane, while a horizontal keel of considerable area is employed in the rear of the Short Wright (English manufacture).

In the Voisin, use is made of several vertical keels of large area, really partitions, placed not only in the rear cell but also between the main planes themselves. That these have not proved entirely satisfactory is indicated by the adoption of ailerons to maintain transverse stability in the more recent Voisin machines. Keels add greatly to the resistance of a machine, the head resistance and skin friction with their consequent power absorption being considerable. It is generally conceded now that control by rudders is becoming so perfected that any inherent stability to be obtained by the use of keels at the expense of power is hardly worth while. No special form or combination of keels, so far designed and tried, have really succeeded in giving any kind of complete inherent stability.

Actual practice, however, demonstrates that they do increase stability, tending to hold the machine to its course, and keels at the rear of a machine somewhat on the order of a bird's tail are found advantageous, so that it is quite unlikely that they will disappear as a feature of aeroplane design for years to come.

Mounting. This is the only remaining detail of construction that need be considered in this connection. There is probably no other single feature in which the various machines differ more widely, nor any other in which such totally different provision, or the absence of it, for absorbing the shocks of landing, proves so uniformly successful. When an aeroplane drops as a dead weight for even a short distance, it suffers considerable damage regardless of the presence of shock absorbers or otherwise, whereas, in ordinary use, it appears to be as easy to land lightly with a machine having a rigid chassis, as with one in which elaborate precaution is taken to guard against shocks.

There is another factor to be guarded against, however, and that is the gyroscopic action developed by the swiftly revolving propeller, which tends to resist a sudden change of its plane of rotation, as well as all vibration. If, therefore, when running over the ground the machine be suddenly jarred, the propeller is likely to snap off. This has been experienced by M. Bleriot on more than one occasion, and he emphasizes the necessity of providing springs on a heavy machine mounted on wheels.

Three distinctive methods of mounting have been employed to date:

(1) Using skids only, as in the original Wright machine. This is already obsolete, as it involved the use of special starting apparatus.
(2) Wheels only, as in the Curtiss, Voisin (both types), Bleriot (both types), Pelterie, Grade, and Pfitzner.
(3) Wheels and skids combined — Farman, Antoinette, Santos-Dumont, Cody, Sommer, and later Wright machines.

Details of some of the most important designs are given in Fig. 40.

The relative merits of mounting on wheels only or skids and wheels constitute a subject of wide discussion. Where the former are employed independently, the addition of a brake is almost indispensable to bring the machine to a quick stop where the landing area is restricted; whereas, with a skid forming part of the support, as in the Antoinette, the latter acts as a brake. Of course, it performs the same office in starting, to the detriment of a quick rise from the ground. The extra power required on that account, however, is not very great, as the skid, supporting only the tail, does not carry any great weight. It is consequently not very efficient as a brake either, so that provision of the latter class on all types should be made.

TYPES OF AEROPLANES

Fig. 40. Types of Landing Skids for Aeroplanes

A number of combinations of skids and wheels have been tried, such as that of the new Wright which starts on its four wheels, and lands on the skids to which they are attached. The Sommer and Farman are typical examples of this combined form of mounting, and experience in their use appears to demonstrate that they are the most effective for heavy machines. On light aeroplanes, such as the Curtiss and the Grade, where the loading is reasonably light, spring mountings have been found unnecessary, the wheels alone taking the shock of landing. No skids are employed. The more recent Curtiss machines are provided with an efficient brake. It is quite likely, however, that the high speed aeroplane of the future will not only be provided with an elastic mounting, but when regular stations are established, means will be employed for projecting it from some ingenious starting device at high velocity, so that it may be quickly launched into the air.

Speed. It is generally conceded that the chief object of the aeroplane designer at present is to increase the speed, prophecies of 100 miles per hour, and considerably more, being not at all uncommon. Whether this can be attained or not is a question that only the future can solve, but a comparison of the speeds prevailing in January, 1910, and December, 1910, shows such a marked increase for the development of a single year that this does not appear to be beyond the possibilities of the future, by any means. It must be borne in mind, of course, that while resistance increases as the square of the speed, the power to overcome it must increase as the cube. This would seem to make the attainment of the 100-mile mark something that would involve considerable modification of the present type of aeroplane, in order to attain increased efficiency, as the goal in view is not to be won by a mere increase of power.

The speed shows no direct variation with aspect ratio or loading, and higher speeds seem to be merely attained by an excess of power, a decrease of head resistance, and a small supporting surface. In Table I are given the speeds of the various types described, *i. e.*, those of which they had been shown capable up to January, 1910.

Flight. In the manner of flight of the different types, pronounced distinctions may be drawn. Probably the widest variation in this respect exists between the Wright and the earlier Voisin

TYPES OF AEROPLANES

TABLE I

Speed Data

Type	Miles per hour	Type	Miles per hour
Bleriot XI (Racing Type)	63	Farman (Racing Type)	44
Santos-Dumont	55	Sommer (1910 Model)	44
Bleriot XI Bis (1910 Model)	51	Wright (Rear Control)	43
Antoinette (1910 Model)	50	Wright (1910 Model)	41
Voisin (Racing Type)	49	Farman (1910 Model)	41
Curtiss	48	Voisin (1910 Model)	40
Bleriot XII (1910 Model)	48	Farman (Passenger Type)	39
Bleriot XI 2 Bis	48	Pelterie	39
Pfitzner	45	Cody	37
Grade	44		

with numerous vertical keels. The flight of the latter may be best described as "sluggish." The enormous resistance of this machine appears to hold it back very perceptibly, while in making turns its action is slow and "deadened." In sharp contrast to this is the strikingly active flight of the Wright machine. Its resistance is very small for a biplane and its movement through the air is quick and precise, particularly when compared with the flight of the Farman biplane, the sluggish movements of which at the International Meet near New York earned for it the sobriquet of "the ice-wagon." In changing direction or warping to maintain lateral stability, the action of the Wright is precise and almost instantaneous, the Wright biplane answering its helm in a remarkably quick and effective manner.

In grace of form and swiftness of flight the Antoinette and Bleriot monoplanes are a delight to the eye. They appear to move through the air without the slightest effort and at the distance of a mile or so give the impression of being huge, soaring birds, so steady and perfectly under control is their every movement. Due to the smooth whirring of their multi-cylindered motors, this is accentuated when close at hand, in comparison with the clattering exhaust of the four-cylinder Wright engine, which many uninitiated spectators mistake for a noise made by the propellers, the turning of which is plainly visible owing to their low speed.

The Curtiss in flight is noticeable for its constant rising and

TABLE II
Characteristics of Different Types

Machine	Pounds per h. p.	Pounds per sq. ft.	Speed in Still Air, m. p. h.
Wright	41	2.05	41
Wright (r. c.)	37	2.50	43
Farman (pssgr)	34	3.15	39
Bleriot XI	29	4.50	51
Antoinette	27	3.33	50
Pelterie	27	4.40	39
Cody	25	2.57	37
Farman ('10)	24	2.80	41
Pfitzner	24	3.20	45
Curtiss (pssgr)	22.6	3.64	..
Voisin ('10)	22.5	3.14	40
Curtiss	22	2.50	48
Farman (rcg)	21	3.00	44
Bleriot XII	21	5.30	48
Bleriot XI 2	19.8	3.68	48
Voisin (rcg)	19.5	3.27	49
Voisin (tractor)	19	2.36	40
Grade	17	2.00	44
Sommer	16	2.76	44
Sommer (rcg)	15	3.25	..
Santos-Dumont	12	3.10	55
Bleriot XI (rcg)	7.5	5.76	63

falling, tracing a sinuous, vertical path through the air, in contrast with the perfectly even and level keel maintained by most of the other machines. In making any comparison of flight, however, the personal equation also must be considered, as the action of the machine is largely governed by the skill of the aviator. In the present instance, however, the impressions recorded were of the different machines in the hands of skillful pilots, all of whom had been flying for a year or more and had made a great many flights. The Santos-Dumont was early dubbed the "clown" of the International Meet and its appearance was invariably the signal for a roar of amused applause. Despite its speed, its erratic action marked by continual dips and violent rocking, always seemed to have it on the verge of tumbling to the ground. Because of its light loading, the Grade seems especially buoyant in the air. The other types mentioned show characteristics between the extreme sluggishness of the Voisin and Farman and the remarkable preciseness of the Wright.

TYPES OF AEROPLANES

As the question of duration of flight depends much more upon the skill of the aviator, the endurance of the motor, and the amount of fuel carried than it does on the machine itself, a comparison of the longest flights made by each type would be valueless.

Efficiency. One of the best indications of the general efficiency of an aeroplane is the amount of weight carried per horse-power, but it will be apparent that this must also be considered in connection with the weight lifted per square foot of lifting surface, its speed, and similar factors. The first of these mentioned is usually termed "pounds per horse-power" and is obtained by dividing the total weight of the machine in flight by the horse-power of the motor. This is a variable owing to the different weights of the aviators, but not one of sufficient importance to record in the case of a one-man machine. At the time Table II was compiled (January, 1910), the Bleriot XI (racing model) appeared to be the most wasteful of power, while the Wright was the most efficient, this still being true of the latter. It must also be borne in mind that the Bleriot is a very much faster machine than the Wright. Table II summarizes the various characteristics of the different types.

AIRSHIP CROSSING ONE OF THE NATIONAL ROADS IN RURAL FRANCE
This Photograph Protected by International Copyright

TYPES OF AEROPLANES
PART II

SPECIAL TYPES

As explained under the head of "Standard Types," this designation is not intended to cover aeroplanes that can properly be regarded as standardized in the usual acceptance of that term, although with one or two exceptions they are built along essentially the same lines in their respective classes. In addition to the machines described in that category, there are hundreds of others which do not differ sufficiently from these types to merit reference. Besides these, however, there are some aeroplanes which are distinguished by radical departures from the accepted standards in question, or which have been designed for some special form of service, and no work on the the subject would be complete without at least a brief description of their distinctive features. All of these machines are of more recent construction and, as they are being brought out in rapid succession as the art develops, those given here naturally include only a limited number.

Paulhan Trussed Type. The most radical departure noted up to the present writing is a machine constructed for Paulhan, Fig. 41, in which by reason of utilizing tetrahedral surfaces similar to those of the well-known kites invented by Alexander Graham Bell, neither warping nor ailerons are required to maintain lateral stability. The planes of the Paulhan machine are built upon a form of trussed girder made up of two long, thin ash planks about 8 inches wide near their central section, and about $\frac{1}{4}$ inch thick, the general plan upon which the biplane is constructed being similar to the Curtiss machine. There is a central section containing the motor and the aviator's seat, the outer sections being attached to this central section in a novel manner. The planks in question are spaced about 8 inches apart and the lower one curves upward toward its ends until it meets the upper one. These two planks are tied together by a series of flat, steel plates forming a series of **V**'s, thus forming a very

Copyright, 1912, by American School of Correspondence.

rigid trussed girder that eliminates the necessity of using the numerous guy wires ordinarily employed. The ribs are attached to the lower members of these main girders by means of clamps passing over an armored wood fillet that lies within the base of every other **V**. The ribs are cut out of solid wood and are arched to the proper curve. The cloth is provided with pockets which enable it to be slipped on the ribs and laced in place. As the ribs are attached to the girders at their front ends only, they have a certain amount of spring or flexibility which, it is claimed, gives the machine a high degree of inherent stability.

Both the lower and upper girders are divided into sections and connected by uprights. The uprights of adjoining sections are placed side by side and fastened together by **S**-shaped leather straps which wrap around them and are drawn taut by a special fastener.

Fig. 41. Paulhan-Fabre Biplane with Tetrahedral Cell Girder Framing

Leather straps are also used to connect the uprights of the center cell to the chassis as well as in most other parts of the machine where joints must be made. Except for its tendency to stretch, leather affords a very strong and tough material for this purpose, while its use avoids the necessity of piercing holes in the struts. It is ideal for a machine like the Paulhan biplane here described and the Fabre monoplane, along the lines of which the former is constructed, as both are intended to be demountable in order to make them readily portable.

There are two long, trussed girders running from the front of the lower plane out to the rear, where they support the single-surface

EDOUARD NIEUPORT AT THE HELM OF HIS MONOPLANE, THE SPEED AND EFFICIENCY OF WHICH ARE DUE TO THE DEEP STREAM-LINE BODY

This Photograph Protected by International Copyright

tail and the vertical rudder in front of it, while at the front they carry the monoplane horizontal rudder, or elevator. The motor is on a frame back of the pilot's seat which is located in a torpedo-shaped aluminum car secured to the lower plane simply by crossed guy wires that run through it at the front. The car and frame are one and besides the 50-horse-power Gnome motor they carry a large tank for gasoline just behind the aviator and passenger's seats which are in tandem. The aluminum car is employed to protect the aviator and to reduce head resistance, the fore-and-aft girders having their sides covered with cloth for the same purpose. The machine is mounted on two skids placed beneath these two fore-and-aft girders, each skid being carried on a pair of pneumatic-tired wheels connected by a short axle which is attached to the skid by a rubber band and is guyed fore and aft to keep it from twisting.

In place of the single-control lever to which he has become accustomed in piloting the Farman machine, Paulhan uses a vertical steering wheel similar to that originated by Curtiss. Pushing or pulling on this wheel turns the horizontal rudder downward or upward, while turning the wheel operates the vertical rudder at the rear. No method of warping the wings or other device for correcting side tipping was shown on this machine when it was exhibited at the 1910 Paris show, and it is claimed that the flexible ribs in connection with the zigzag-girder construction give the machine sufficient transverse stability to make any provision of this nature unnecessary. The machine has been flown successfully and proved remarkably steady in flight, from which it is evident that the means at present in use of maintaining lateral stability mark only the first steps toward what may be eventually accomplished in this direction.

In addition to this important feature, the chief claim made for the machine is the rapidity with which it may be assembled or demounted. The end cells may be detached by taking out three bolts at the top and bottom of the uprights, an operation that requires only a minute or two at the outside, while the whole machine may be taken apart and packed in a case $15\frac{1}{2}$ feet long by $3\frac{1}{4}$ feet square, within an hour. The ready detachability of the end cells makes it possible to store the machine in an ordinary shed, as the total spread of 38 feet is reduced to 12 or 15 feet when these sections have been removed. The fore-and-aft length of this new biplane is $25\frac{1}{2}$ feet and, including the horizontal rudder and the tail, the area is 300 square feet. The total weight of the machine itself is 800 pounds, which is low, considering its size and heavy construction.

M. Fabre, designer of the hydroaeroplane described later, is also responsible for the construction of this Paulhan biplane, and makes the following claims for his system: Great strength and rigidity; small head resistance; absence of trussing wires with their liability to loosen or break and their considerable head resistance; automatic transverse stability due to the zigzag girders resembling tetrahedral cells—the most stable form of supporting surface; and its ready portability.

In view of the supporting power and stabilizing effect of the trussed girders, it is interesting to note that, assuming the machine's critical speed to be 45 miles an hour with the cloth planes in place, the girders would support its 800 pounds of weight alone were the speed increased to 120 miles an hour. If it were possible to reef the cloth of the wings while in flight, it would, therefore, be possible to keep diminishing the supporting surface until this consisted of the girders alone, while the speed would increase to 120 miles an hour, or more.

Three years ago, Santos-Dumont constructed a small biplane having its supporting surfaces set at a sharp dihedral angle. Wood was used for the aeroplane surfaces, and it was thought the machine would be very speedy. However, the supporting surface was so small in proportion to the weight that it was difficult to attain sufficient speed for a sustained flight, and almost at the first attempt the machine was smashed and abandoned. The Paulhan biplane with reefed surfaces would be an almost direct descendant of Santos-Dumont's wood-surfaced flyer, and the possibility of a machine flying under bare poles, so to speak, would give an idea of what might be accomplished in the future. The promise of the "reefing aeroplane," as it may be termed, is being seriously considered and will be treated later in this article.

Nieuport Monoplane. More than ordinary interest attaches to the Nieuport monoplane, as, while it does not differ radically in design from the majority of French monoplanes, it is not only the simplest but likewise the most efficient type thus far produced and it is to be greatly regretted that its creator, Edouard Nieuport, should

TYPES OF AEROPLANES

have met an untimely death in an accident, as the great success of his efforts in the two years that he devoted himself to aviation presaged greater and more important developments. During 1911, the Nieuport monoplane earned for itself the title of the "fastest aeroplane." Weyman's 100-horse-power Nieuport made an average of 78 miles per hour in the Gordon-Bennett, winning the trophy for America, while a 30-horse-power machine of the same make made 58.9 miles per hour in the same event. What this means may best be realized from the fact that the original Wright biplane with a motor of the same rating could not do better than 40 miles per hour. A 70-horse-power Nieuport has made 74.8 miles per hour, as compared with the speed of 61 miles per hour made with the 100-horse-power Bleriot which won the 1910 Gordon-Bennett. In the French military competition, Weyman's 100-horse-power Nieuport averaged 72.6 miles per hour for 186 miles with three people.

The construction of the Nieuport type for two persons, fitted with a Gnome 50-horse-power revolving motor is as follows:

The wings are built up on two main spars of ash, while between these spars are run three light battens merely to tie the ribs together. The ribs, of which there are 13, are of I-section, built in the usual manner and with the webs perforated to save weight, while the box ribs are built up by using two webs and larger top and bottom flanges. The rib curve varies in each rib, decreasing toward the wing tips and going down to a flat bow. The wing section given in the sketch, Fig. 42, might be taken as the standard curve, allowance being made for the different chord at various places, and also for the different thicknesses of the spar, which tapers both ways from a straight central portion. It will be noted that there is a slight reverse curve on the under surface at the trailing edge, while it is very pronounced on the upper surface. Each wing is trussed with two heavy standard cables, top and bottom, to each spar, and they are set at a slight dihedral angle. The fuselage longitudinals are also of ash, rectangular in section, and channeled out between the struts to achieve lightness. Rectangular ash struts are also employed, except those for the skids, which are steel tubing. Connection between struts and longitudinal members is made by aluminum castings to which the wire bracing is anchored. The entire structure is covered with fabric.

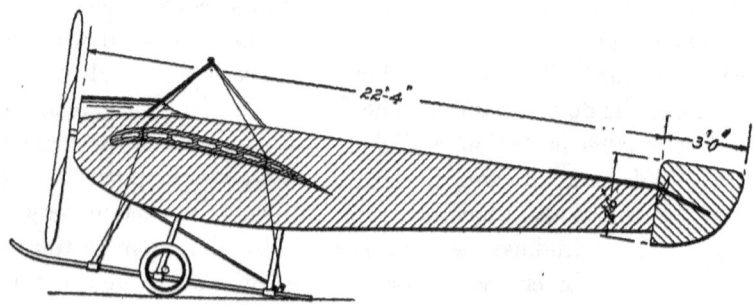

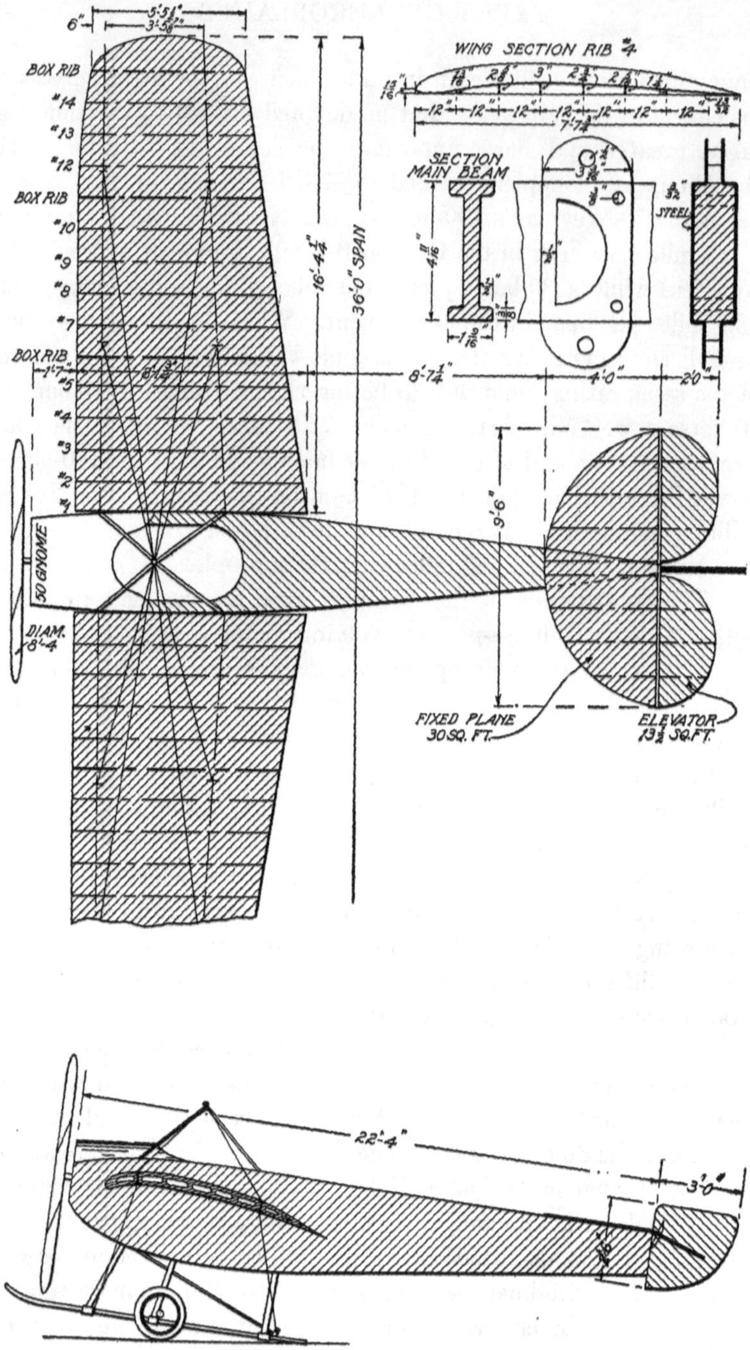

Fig. 42. Details of Nieuport Monoplane

TYPES OF AEROPLANES

Control is by means of a single hand lever, operating the rudder and elevating plane, while a bar for the feet works the warping mechanism. This single hand lever is mounted by a swivel joint on a short shaft lying along the floor inside the body. A forward and backward movement of this lever operates the elevator by wires passing around pulleys mounted at the ends of the rocking shaft, while a lateral movement of the lever actuates the rudder wires through a crank formed by an extension of the rear pulley sheave which is fixed to the rock shaft. The elevators are semicircular in plan, and are constructed of steel tubing frames covered with fabric on both sides, the tail or fixed plane also being built of steel tubing, while nothing but steel is employed in the construction of the running gear, the central skid, the axle which is made of a single,

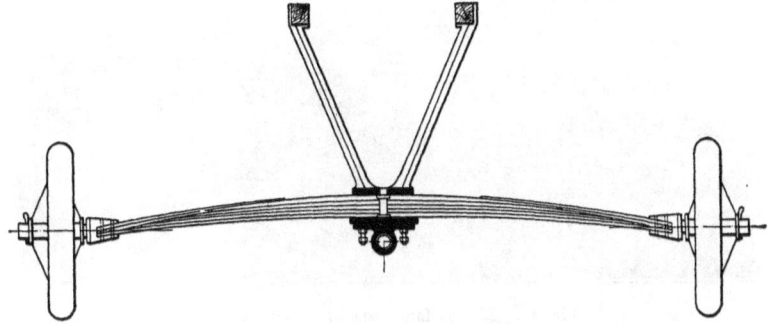

Fig. 43. Nieuport Running Gear

five-leaf spring, and the oval skid struts. The V-members are made up as a unit and can be slipped over the skid and put in place in a short time should repairs be necessary. The extreme simplicity of this running gear is apparent at a glance, Fig. 43. The power plant is a 50-horse-power Gnome motor, driving a two-bladed propeller 8 feet 4 inches in diameter. The span is 36 feet, the wings having an extreme width of 8 feet $1\frac{3}{4}$ inches, where they are joined to the fuselage, and tapering to 5 feet $5\frac{1}{2}$ inches at their outer ends, the total area of the main planes being 221 square feet, while the tail or fixed rear plane of semicircular form, placed 8 feet $7\frac{1}{4}$ inches back of the wings, has an area of 30 feet, and the elevators, which are practically part of the tail, being hinged to it, have a spread of $13\frac{1}{2}$ square feet. This makes a total area of $274\frac{1}{2}$ square feet, which on a total weight of 715 pounds, exclusive of the aviator, gives a loading of 2½ pounds, or of 3⅕ pounds with the pilot, assuming the latter's weight to be 170 pounds, as is customary. The overall length, exclusive of the propeller shaft, is 25 feet 4 inches.

Bleriot Limousine. The Bleriot Limousine, Fig. 44, is a novel aeroplane that marks an advance in development, as it is the first to appear with a closed body for the passengers. The aviator sits forward and outside of the body, the resemblance to a cab thus caused having also earned for it the name of the "aerial taxi." This machine was built by Bleriot to the order of M. Henri Deutsch, who has probably done more for aviation in France than any other single individual. In general design, this machine somewhat resembles

Fig. 44. Bleriot Limousine or Aerial Taxicab

the original Bleriot XII and, like the first passenger-carrying machines turned out by this maker, the passengers are seated in the center below the main plane. In all other respects, however, it is different, and appears to constitute more or less of a reversion to the original Wright type, the horizontal being placed some distance out in front, while a stabilizing plane and the direction rudder mounted over it, are carried some distance behind the main planes. The power plant is a 100-horse-power, fourteen-cylinder Gnome revolving motor, and it is mounted at the rear of the main plane, instead of at the front, the fuel being carried in a torpedo-shaped tank above the roof of the cab and just in front of the motor. Control is by the usual Bleriot method, consisting of a universally-mounted post having an aluminum bell at the bottom to which the control cables are fastened. Complete, but without any passengers or the aviator, the machine weighs 1,540 pounds, and it has a supporting surface of $430\frac{1}{2}$ square feet, triple heavy rubber bands being employed as shock absorbers on the chassis, to sustain the unusual weight. The spread of the main plane is 43 feet, and the overall length of the machine is 46 feet. Although it would seem that the twenty odd square feet of surface presented head to the wind by the front wall of the body would cause a seriously detrimental head resistance, the machine has flown very successfully, showing itself to be capable of carrying two passengers, besides the aviator, at a rate of 50 miles per hour. The seats in the body are fitted with pneumatic cushions to take up the shock in case the machine alights heavily. A speaking tube is provided, so that the passengers can communicate with the aviator. This is the first time that a machine has been built and flown in which special care was taken to construct it with a comfortable body for the carrying of passengers, and it is doubtless the forerunner of many more of a similar type that will make their appearance in the next few years.

Tatin=Paulhan Aerial Torpedo. M. Victor Tatin, who is responsible for the design of this extremely novel-looking aeroplane, has waited twenty years to see his ideals realized. He originally designed the machine about 1890, and has argued for the correctness of its lines in several brochures and books published in the interval, though the machine itself was not built until the latter part of 1911. The body is completely enclosed from end to end and reveals a fine example of the pisciform shape recommended by Renard for the dirigible. The propeller is placed at the extreme rear and the direction rudder is placed just above the elevator, a few feet forward of the propeller, so that without the wings the resemblance to a fish is striking, while the upturned outer ends of the main planes give it the appearance of a large soaring bird. This upcurving of the wings is said to provide stability to an extent that makes wing warping unnecessary, while the torpedo-shaped body cuts the head resistance down to a minimum. The machine is provided with a flat tail, the rear part of which is movable and forms the horizontal rudder. The pilot's seat is located in the body just forward of the wings, and the 50-horse-power Gnome motor is placed just back of the pilot in a special compartment. The chief peculiarity of the design is the placing of the propeller at the extreme rear, instead of forward as is usual in monoplanes. Drive is by means of a long, universally-jointed shaft running back from the motor and carried in five bearings supported by piano-wire guys. The chassis consists of two wood beams bent in semi-elliptic form and connected at the lower part by an axle fitted with shock absorbers and carrying two pneumatic-tired wheels.

Bleriot Racer. That increased speed is largely a matter of refinement of detail based upon experience is evident from the 1911 Bleriot racer, which has developed a speed of 81 miles per hour with 50 horse-power, its designer having taken advantage of the lessons taught by the several long-distance European aeroplane races, most of which were won by Bleriot machines. To reduce head resistance, the upper flat cross member of the usual Bleriot chassis has been placed below instead of on top of the body. This results in shortening the steel tube uprights. The body has been made extremely narrow at the front, while at the rear it flattens completely, terminating in an absolutely flat horizontal rudder. The extreme front end narrows down to not quite a foot in width, though ample space is allowed for the aviator, while a long aluminum hood covers the tanks and motor and prevents the usual spray of oil in the aviator's face. The usual running gear and shock absorbers are placed forward, while the bamboo skid is at the extreme rear end of the fuselage. Beside the usual simple V-shaped support for attaching the bracing wires of the wings, the bracing tubes below are employed and they have been made considerably longer besides being well guyed to the body. They carry the warping mechanism at their lower ends and this has been modified in some ways. The vertical rudder has the outline of a shark's fin and is carried on top of the tail, as in the Bleriot XII.

This is the twenty-seventh different model that Bleriot has constructed. It has a span of 23 feet, an overall length of 29 feet, and a supporting surface of only 129 square feet, while its weight complete is 948 pounds, which gives the unusually high loading of 7 pounds per square foot.

Bleriot Canard. In contrast with the Voisin canard, or duck, as an aeroplane with the aviator in front in a covered body and the motor behind has come to be known in France, this machine is a

TYPES OF AEROPLANES

monoplane, Fig. 45, and instead of being new is a revival of one of Bleriot's earliest attempts. Santos-Dumont was really the inventor of this type of machine and with its aid he was the first man to leave the ground in a power-driven aeroplane in Europe. The new Bleriot canard is much shorter than the Voisin, its thick, short body projecting forward of the monoplane wings but a small distance, the horizontal rudder being placed at the tip end of the bow, while two tiny vertical rudders on top of the main plane at each end serve to steer. The wings are guyed to an inclined rod beneath, which extends forward from a shoe on the bottom of a vertical post. Generous-sized, hinged ailerons are employed instead of warping the wings. The running gear is the same as that of the Nieuport, while the span and area of the machine are identical with those of the Bleriot racer

Fig. 45. Bleriot Canard Showing Unique Position of Engine and Propeller

just described, the total overall length being but 18 feet, while the weight complete with a 50-horse-power Gnome motor is only 882 pounds. The aviator's seat is so far forward that it would seem as if he ran very little risk of being injured by the motor in case of a fall, since there are five or six feet of stout framing between the engine and the pilot. A peculiarity of this type of machine is that in flight it appears to be going backward.

Antoinette Armored Monoplane. Excess weight appears to have lost all its terrors for the designer of aeroplanes, as where every effort has been made previously to reduce this to the absolute working minimum, the builders of the Antoinette have brought out a machine in which the most vulnerable parts, such as the motor and chassis, are protected by armor plate. This machine was designed especially to take part in the French military competition, and by far its most important feature is the total elimination of all cross wires, struts, and the like. Every part is enclosed, even the wheels and the skids, with the result that the head resistance is greatly decreased, but the weight increased still further, at the same time giving the machine a most peculiar appearance. In addition, a peculiar wing section is used, flat on the under side and curved on the upper. Aerodynamical experiments have shown this type of wing section to have a very bad drift resistance at low angles of incidence and a very uniform rate of change of the ratio of lift to drift under the same conditions. The center of pressure does not move back as rapidly as on other shapes, as the angle of incidence decreases below 10 degrees. This type of wing is, therefore, more stable and of smaller resistance. The distribution of pressure, however, is very uneven, but because of the great strength of the planes themselves at all points, this is not a disadvantage. The wings are immensely thick, being braced entirely from the inside and measuring over two feet in section where they join the body—something altogether without precedent in aeroplane design. Their section decreases to 8 inches at the wing tips. The shape of each wing is trapezoidal and they are placed at an extreme dihedral angle. This adds to the stability of the machine in a calm, but in gusty winds conditions arise where a large dihedral angle is considered by many to be extremely dangerous. The boat-like body is completely enclosed and is very capacious. The motor of the regular eight-cylinder Antoinette V-type, of 100 horse-power, direct connected to a Normale two-bladed propeller, is placed at the extreme forward end, while the aviator's seat is in the body at a point between the wings. Though equipped with a 100-horse-power motor, the machine is said to be capable of flying with but 60 horse-power. The oddest feature of this type is the landing gear, which is entirely enclosed to within a few inches of the ground. There are six landing wheels forward, three on each side of the center and enclosed in what is termed a "skirt." Two smaller wheels are placed at the rear. The dimensions are: Spread $52\frac{1}{2}$ feet, length overall 36 feet, width of wings at body 13 feet, at tips 9 feet, area of supporting surface 602 square feet, total weight, including aviator and fuel,

2,400 pounds. The aviator obtains a view below the machine through the glass floor of the body under his seat. To reduce resistance to a minimum, even the exhaust pipes of the motor are covered with a stream-line design shield. This type is of an immense size as compared with its predecessors and is very bird-like in flight, several successful trials having been made with it. But whether the great sacrifices made to eliminate projecting spars and wires are wise, remains to be seen. The machine has an unusually large expanse of vertical surface which makes it difficult to handle in a gusty wind.

Short Two=Motor Biplane. Although the Gould *Scientific American* prize of $15,000 for a successful two-motor aeroplane in which either motor can be used independently, and the second started in mid air in case of the accidental stoppage of the other, has now been open for almost two years, there have been few attempts to win it. A Queen monoplane was built during the summer of 1911 for this purpose and fitted with two 50-horse-power Gnome motors, but on the occasion of its first trial it came to grief. M. Legrand, the French engineer, has brought out a racing biplane equipped with two 100-horse-power, fourteen-cylinder Gnome motors, and this machine was flown successfully by Guillaume at Juvisy in October, 1911. The Coanda biplane, entered in the French military competition, was also provided with two motors driving the propellers through shafts and bevel gearing. The Short biplane, equipped with two motors, has made duration flights exceeding one hour, so that it is capable of fulfilling the conditions of the Gould prize, though not eligible for the latter as it is a foreign built machine.

In general outline it is a biplane of the Farman 1910 type, equipped with two 50-horse-power Gnome revolving motors, placed centrally and one in front of the other in the rear of the lower main plane at either end of a nacelle or enclosed body. The front motor drives two propellers in opposite directions by means of chains, precisely as on the Wright biplane. The propellers are of high pitch, similar to the Wright type, but are placed in front of the main cell, instead of behind it. The rear motor drives a single low-pitch propeller at high speed as on the Farman machines. It is possible to operate either motor separately or both together, and the feasibility of the arrangement has been well proved in actual flights. The rudder and aileron controls are of the usual Farman type, the landing chassis and all details of the construction having been made specially strong owing to the extra weight. The aviator sits in the enclosed body and there is a seat for a passenger beside him. With the immense extra power available, one motor sufficing for flight, this type has the ability to go fast or slow, and with its full 100 horsepower can climb very rapidly. The axes of the front propellers and the rear one are not on the same level, this being done to counterbalance the effect on the tail caused by the draft from the rear propeller. As soon as the latter ceases to operate the lifting tail sinks, but the higher position of the axis of thrust of the forward propellers at once overcomes this. The dimensions are: Spread 34 feet, chord $6\frac{1}{2}$ feet, supporting area 435 square feet, weight in flight 2,000 pounds. The speeds are said to range from 35 to 50 miles an hour depending on whether one or both motors are operated.

Dunne Biplane. This is a machine of unusually novel type for which a great deal is claimed, but unlike the thousand and one machines that are built around claims and do not get much further, the Dunne has given evidence of its ability to do what its inventor claims for it. However, it is put forward as a machine in which automatic stability has been achieved, where, as a matter of fact, the design is one possessed of an unusually high degree of inherent stability, there being no devices or mechanism to give automatic stability in the sense that that term has come to be understood. Instead of having the main planes in a line with one another, they are in the form of a large **V** with its apex forward, so that while the machine is tailless in that there are no supplementary surfaces of the class termed tails or stabilizers, the ends of the **V** extend so far back that it actually has two tails instead of one, and upon this fact is based much of its ability to maintain equilibrium. The official report of a test of the Dunne witnessed by Orville Wright and Griffith Brewer in December, 1911, is in substance as follows:

> The first flight was over a distance of about three miles, the machine being turned at a height of about 100 feet and making a good landing near the starting point. During the second flight of 2 minutes 29 seconds, Mr. Dunne made notes on a piece of paper (involving use of both hands). In both cases, the engine was cut off in the air before landing and the machine came down without materially altering its angle of incidence.

A resumé of Dunne's patent will serve to show most clearly what

TYPES OF AEROPLANES

his aims are and how he achieved them, reading "inherent" instead of "automatic" stability. The patent was granted early in 1910 in England and covers the "curvature and shape of surfaces."

The object of the invention is to obtain a form of aeroplane which shall possess, solely by the form and arrangement of its surfaces, automatic stability in still and agitated air, and freedom from oscillation. The inventor has found that twisting the wings of an aeroplane involves the disadvantage that sections, either longitudinal or transverse, taken across the wing tip, give curves that are more or less concave on their upper sides, thus failing to give large pressure reactions, and that when such wings are twisted, the changes brought about in the pressures by the concave portions are so abrupt as to produce unsteadiness, and that the similar concavity on the transverse section produces lateral instability. The two essential conditions to be observed are to decrease gradually the angles of the fore-and-aft cross sections of the wings from root to tip, without producing points of inflection in the surfaces; and secondly, to maintain considerable differences in the angles of the inner and outer portions without too much loss of pressure under the outer portions. The present invention consists in constructing each of the main surfaces as a rearwardly projecting wing whose angle of incidence decreases from the root to the tip, and by shaping the wings so as to compress air between the positively-inclined portion of the wing near the root to the negatively-inclined portion near the tip. The wings must be so sloped backward along their leading edges that the wing tips lie behind the center of gravity of the whole aeroplane. Further, each wing is so constructed that its upper face is formed as a portion of a cone or a cylinder, the angle of incidence of the wings decreasing toward the tips, and in some cases changing sign, *i. e.*, negative to positive angle, or *vice versa*.

The principle is applicable to the monoplane quite as readily as the biplane, one of the former type of Dunne machines having been exhibited at the Olympia show in 1911. Like its prototype, it is designed to possess natural stability, and it is tailless in the ordinary sense of the term. In principle, however, the V-plan of its wings gives it two tails instead of one, and the hinged flaps on the trailing extremities of its wings give it two elevators instead of one. These flaps are under independent control, and serve the purpose of steering the machine horizontally and vertically. The special formation of the wings already referred to in the case of the biplane, is likewise generated on the surface of a cone, but the apex of the cone is an entirely different place, being situated, on the monoplane, a short distance behind the trailing extremity of the wing and more or less directly in line with the outside edge. This formation of the wing gives a variable angle of incidence from shoulder to tip, which, in conjunction with the V-plan form, confers on the machine the principles of the fore-and-aft dihedral angle, which is one of the accepted methods of obtaining natural stability and is a characteristic feature in the design of all successful aeroplanes. Owing to the wing extremities being situated in an exposed region and not sheltered behind the middle portion of the plane, as is more or less the case with the tail of an ordinary aeroplane, Dunne claims that their tail effect is enhanced. Also the same argument applies to the efficacy of the dihedral angle, because, owing to the formation and continuity of the wings, it is impossible to define what part constitutes main plane and what part tail. In fact the relative functions of these members are performed by different parts of the wings in accordance with the requirements of the moment.

Lateral stability in the Dunne monoplane is somewhat more difficult to explain, but the most significant feature of the design is unquestionably the fact that the wing formation provides down-turned wing tips, as distinct from the upturned wing tips on several other monoplanes, all of which are designed more or less with a view to natural stability. It will be noticed, of course, that it is the leading edge of the Dunne monoplane that is turned down, whereas in the Hadley, Page, and Weiss monoplanes, it is turned up, so that the relative positions of the leading and trailing edges in all three machines are identical. On the other hand, there is a very material and fundamental difference in principle between the two methods, for whereas the upturned trailing edge represents the lateral dihedral angle, the down-turned leading edge represents the gull's wing, which is an accepted method of obtaining lateral stability in side gusts. The general action is as follows:

A side gust ordinarily lifts that side of the machine against which it first strikes, because of the aeroplane action of the planes considered in their attitude toward the gust and the consequent travel of the center of pressure toward the leading edge facing the gust, which involves an actual travel of the center of pressure laterally from the real center of gravity of the machine. Thus the machine cants over and the upset is emphasized with the dihedral angle, because the upturned wing offers an increasing surface for normal pressure. In the gull's wing method, the remoter down-turned wing tip presents the more effective surface to the gust and tends to counteract the lift due to the travel of the center of pressure on the remainder of the plane. It is, in principle, little more or less than the idea which was tried by the Wright Brothers in some of their early gliding experiments. Like most things of this kind, however, there was all the difference between the broad principle, and the detail of carrying it into effect on a practical machine. It is the latter that makes the Dunne monoplane such an original monoplane.

De Marcay=Mooney Monoplane. In this machine there has been materialized, for the first time, a practical form of folding-wing construction. Taking advantage of the system of construction developed by Bleriot and other French designers in their monoplanes, each wing has been made integral together with its supports and bracing guys, the design otherwise being the same as the Bleriot except as necessarily modified to meet the purpose in view. Each wing is pivoted at its point of attachment to the body, to an outward-sloping metal upright that serves as a mast or strut from which the bracing wires are strung, in addition to its functions as a hinge. A wheel alongside the driver's seat controls the position of these wings, and by turning it the change is effected from the usual full spread for flying to the closed position over the body, in which form the machine bears a most striking resemblance to a huge beetle. In both positions, there is provision for securely locking the wings in place. No attempt has been made to permit of altering the position of the wings in flight, the novel design having for its sole purpose the more compact stowing of the wings while the machine is on the ground, to facilitate storage and to permit of its being driven along narrow roads or across other than clear fields. To facilitate the latter operation, the wheels of the landing chassis are movable and can be controlled by a steering gear provided for the purpose. This running gear suggests that of the Breguet, which is similarly steerable on the ground, and, in fact, apart from the folding wing feature, the machine is along conventional French lines. Lateral stability is obtained by warping the wings in the usual manner, while the tail is apparently a blending of the Nieuport and Bleriot fan-tailed designs. The fuselage is a characteristic four-car, tapered-box girder, covered with fabric and providing seating accommodation for the driver between the wings. Though there has been no attempt on the part of its makers to embody this improvement in the present machine, it has been pointed out by several authorities that folding the wings in this manner undoubtedly approximates the means employed by the birds for varying speed, and that when it is discovered how to apply these in a practical way, without longitudinal shifting of the center of gravity, the long-desired variable speed aeroplane will have become a reality.

Variable Speed Aeroplanes. As at present designed, every aeroplane has what is termed its critical speed, *i. e.*, the rate of its travel through the air at which it sustains and propels itself most efficiently. In many designs this is almost a fixed factor, *i. e.*, the aeroplane can not sustain itself in the air in case its speed falls to any extent below this critical point. Take the old type Wright biplane as an example. This had a speed of 40 miles per hour, but its stability became precarious at 35 miles per hour, or a drop of slightly over 10 per cent, while at 30 miles per hour, it probably could not keep to the air except by making dives and thus taking advantage of the acceleration of gravity. With the greatly-increased speeds that have been obtained with the aeroplane, a variable-speed type is more to be desired than ever, as a landing, to be safe, must be made at low speed. Probably one of the greatest variations in speed shown by an aeroplane thus far is that of Bleriot's 100-horse-power racer which won the Gordon-Bennett trophy at Belmont Park in 1910, at an average speed of practically 70 miles per hour, but which started and alighted at 50 miles per hour. It is not always possible to select safe landing places, particularly when compelled to alight, and the danger of landing increases with the velocity. A substantial prize has accordingly been offered by the Marquis de Dion, through *L'Auto* (Paris) for aeroplanes which can travel over a given course with the greatest variation in speed. To a degree, the Breguet monoplane meets these conditions, as it can vary its speed greatly by changing the angle of incidence of its sustaining surfaces. As yet, however, this has not been developed to a point where the change can be made during a flight, so that unless the Breguet is permitted to change its angle of incidence between trials, it will not possess any advantage over the machines with fixed wings. According to aeroplane constructors, the minimum speed on striking the ground with the motor stopped, is three fourths of the starting velocity. For the Bleriot this would be 37 miles per hour. The disastrous effects of striking a slight elevation of ground at such a speed and with a vertical velocity

A FRENCH DEVELOPMENT OF THE WRIGHT MACHINE BUILT UNDER THE WRIGHT PATENTS
There is Little Resemblance to the Original Except in Wing Form and Warping

Intentionally blank as was the original edition.

of 10 or 12 feet per second, may easily be imagined, and the danger increases with the size of the machine. The further development of the aeroplane depends largely upon the successful provision of a factor of safety in this respect. There is, of course, a great temptation to employ a water surface for landing, if possible, as this is not only level but it forms an admirable buffer against shocks. Moreover, a large aeroplane can be mounted more conveniently on rigidly connected floats than on wheels and springs. But with this construction it would be also necessary to rise from the water, starting at the low speed at which the propeller could drive the craft when afloat.

In order to combine high maximum speed with low speed in starting and landing, and for emergencies, the inclination of the sustaining surfaces must be capable of variation, so that the speed can be varied greatly while the axis of the machine remains horizontal, and the propeller must be designed to work with maximum power and efficiency, using the full power of the motor at all speeds of the aeroplane, for in starting, especially from the water, full power must be employed. An aeroplane propeller driven by a constant speed motor exerts a maximum thrust when its blades have a definite inclination, which varies with the speed of the aeroplane. For the purpose of automatically adjusting the propeller blades to the angle of maximum thrust at every speed, flexible blades are employed by Breguet, a centrifugal governor by Capon, and an electric regulator by Reister-Picard. The devices of Breguet and Capon are simple, but only approximately solve the problem; while that of Reister-Picard is perfect in theory, but complicated and delicate in practice.

Breguet. Breguet's original flexible blade was formed of rubber cloth stretched over a series of flat steel springs, which were attached at one end to the rigid front edge of the blade, but the construction was afterward simplified by adopting a rigid blade, capable of motion around its edge, and controlled by a single spring. Breguet has carried six persons in an aeroplane fitted with a propeller of this type, driven by a 50-horse-power motor, and has since developed a three-bladed, flexible type which promises even better results. In this, each blade is attached to the shaft by an arm, and is free to oscillate, under the control of springs, about three axes. At starting the blade turns on its axis so as to strike the air at a very small angle and produce a maximum thrust. As the aeroplane gains speed the blade returns toward its normal position, and thereafter automatically adapts its inclination approximately to the speed of the aeroplane. The blade protects itself against the irregularities of the motor by turning slightly in its plane of rotation about its point of attachment to the arm, and also by rocking backward and forward.

Capon. Capon's system of regulating the inclination of the propeller blades by means of a centrifugal governor is very simple in theory and construction; but the inclination of the blades is controlled entirely by the speed of the motor, and is not affected by the speed of the aeroplane, unless the former is made to depend upon the latter by another regulator. This is not the usual practice, nor is it desirable, as the efficiency of the internal combustion motor is impaired by alterations of its normal speed.

Reister-Picard. In Reister-Picard's system, each of the two blades of the propeller is attached to an arm which can be turned on its axis by a crank connected through a linkage to a spring-controlled sliding collar on the propeller shaft. This collar is in turn connected to a hand lever by means of which the pilot can alter the angle of inclination of the propeller blades to give the maximum thrust, as determined by the reading of a pressure gauge in front of him. This gauge communicates with a small annular vessel filled with lubricating oil and fitted with a piston so as to put pressure on the oil. This vessel is directly back of a bearing next to the collar, so that it gives a visible indication of what the propeller is doing at any moment. The same result can also be obtained automatically by means of an electric solenoid and plunger, the circuit of which is made and broken by a spring piston in a small oil cylinder communicating with the main oil chamber already referred to. In action, the coil of the solenoid would be intermittently energized by currents traversing it first in one direction and then the other, which would tend to maintain the thrust at its maximum value, but, like automatic stability devices of a similar nature, the apparatus is too delicate to form a practical adjunct to the aeroplane in its present state of development. Reister-Picard has also designed an aeroplane in which the inclination of the sustaining surfaces can be varied. This is practically a double biplane, Fig. 46, having a biplane elevator E forward and a vertical rudder G at the stern. The two biplanes are connected by a braced girder P, which serves to support the

TYPES OF AEROPLANES

power plant and its accessories. The four slightly arched sustaining surfaces X are capable of rotation on transverse horizontal axes Y. M is the motor, R the fuel tank, and C the mechanic's seat, L being the lever by which he can control the inclination of the propeller blades if their automatic regulation becomes deranged. S is the seat of the pilot who operates the rudders and also varies the inclination of the sustaining surfaces by turning the wheel T. The mean inclination of these surfaces to the horizon, as they are drawn in the figure, is about 15 degrees, but their inclination can be diminished to 5 degrees as indicated by the dotted line w, for soaring at very high speed, and increased to 30 degrees, as indicated by K, for landing. In starting from rest on the ground or water, the surfaces are set as nearly level as possible. When sufficient velocity has been attained, the angle is suddenly shifted to 15 degrees, and the aero-

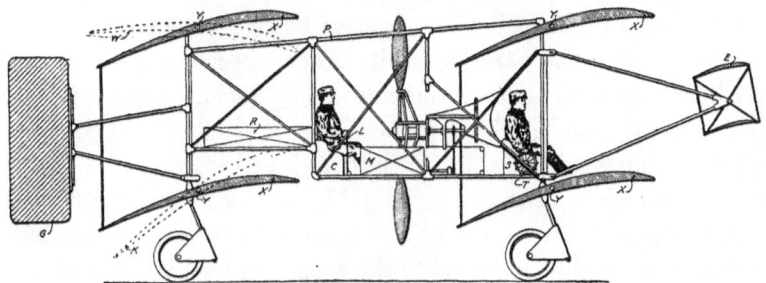

Fig. 46. Reister-Picard Double Biplane with Provision for Inclining the Supporting Planes

plane rises without calling upon the full power of its motor, as is the usual practice. The inclination of the sustaining surfaces is then gradually diminished and the power increased by operating the throttle until the maximum power is being developed. At this time, the inclination of the sustaining surfaces is about 7 degrees and the aeroplane has attained its normal speed. In landing, the inclination is gradually increased to 15 degrees, while the power is diminished, the motor being stopped just before the ground is struck and the inclination is then suddenly increased to the full 30 degrees, enormously increasing the head resistance and bringing the aeroplane to a stop in a very short distance.

Etrich Bird=Wing Monoplane. The Etrich monoplane is the result of a lengthy study of bird-wing structure, Etrich beginning his experiments in 1898 by acquiring the Lilienthal glider. He made extensive studies of the propulsive organs of every form of flying animal, birds, insects, bats, the flying fish, even extending his investigations to the vegetable kingdom by studying the various forms of flying seeds, such as those of the sycamore and the pine.

The wings of the Etrich monoplane are what he terms of the "zanonia" form, and were previously tried out very thoroughly in a glider, the experiments with the latter dating from 1904. As will be apparent in Fig. 47, the front part of each wing is rigidly constructed of webbed ribs, built over three longitudinal spars, of w' ich the forward one forms the leading edge. These sections are double surfaced, *i. e.*, covered on both sides with a rubberized fabric. Behind the rear beam extend bamboo continuations of the ribs which are covered with a single surface of fabric and form a flexible trailing edge. The flexible wing tips are turned up at the rear within and so give both wings an effective negative angle of incidence. It is to this feature that the Etrich owes its pronounced degree of inherent stability. Lateral balance is maintained by raising either wing tip by means of a cable, which, passing over a pulley situated at the top of the king post, divides up into eight wires connected to the flexible extremities of the wing. A cable passing over the lower end of the king-post lowers the opposite tip a corresponding amount. Enormous strength is imparted to the wing by a bridge-like structure of steel tubing, which embraces the middle-wing spar and is attached below the under surface, which renders the wings capable of withstanding strains many times in excess of those they are likely to be called upon to bear in flight.

A small wheel mounted at the lower extremity of the king-post protects the wing tip from contact with the ground. The bird tail pivots in one unit about a horizontal axis, the rear portion of this tail forming the elevator, which is controlled by warping the horizontal tail plane. Two small, triangular vertical rudders, one above and the other below the horizontal tail plane, are hinged to the rear edges of two triangular stabilizing fins and are operated by pedals in front of the pilot's seat, these being plainly apparent in the plan view of the machine, Fig. 47. Elevation and lateral balance are controlled by a rotable hand wheel placed on the top of a vertical column. The chassis is similar to that of the Bleriot with the addition of a movable,

TYPES OF AEROPLANES

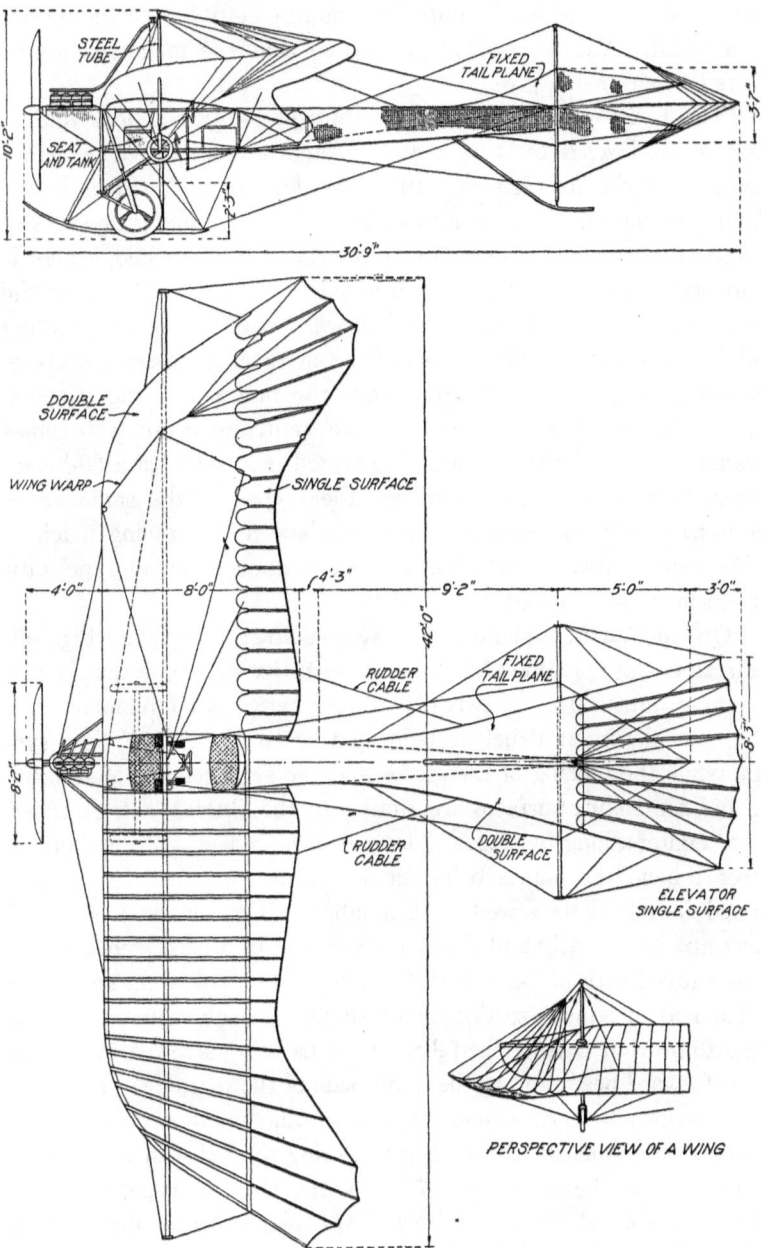

Fig. 47. Diagram of Etrich Bird-Wing Monoplane

central, ash skid which is controlled simultaneously with the rudder by a pedal. The wheels are pivoted so that the machine may be steered when on the ground.

The body is a fish-shaped structure of four wood longitudinal spars, cross braced by wire guys. From the engine bed, which is mounted at the forward end, the body deepens and widens in the vicinity of the pilot's seat, from which point it gradually tapers, still preserving its triangular section, until the tail is reached, where it terminates in a vertical line. To avoid internal disturbance in the air discharge, the body is covered forward with aluminum sheeting and aft with fabric. The radiator is an inverted V suspended above the passenger's seat, its height above the motor securing effective thermo-siphon circulation in case the centrifugal pump becomes deranged. The Etrich machine illustrated is fitted with a 60-horsepower, four-cylinder motor, while other types of the same are a 120-horse-power, three-passenger monoplane and a racing machine of 60 horse-power. Etrich has also built another novel type with bird-form wings termed the "swallow."

Queen=Martin Biplane. The Queen-Martin biplane, Fig. 48, is an American machine and is a representative of a type that is now becoming numerous. It is really a cross between a monoplane and a biplane, the main structure being patterned after the Wright system, while the placing of the motor and the arrangement of stabilizing and controlling surfaces are similar to the Bleriot, being carried on the end of a long fuselage. The spread is 30 feet, with a chord of 5 feet 1 inch, the planes being single-surfaced and having the ribs slipped into pockets sewed in the fabric. The planes are spaced 5 feet apart vertically and the struts are held in brazed steel sockets, double guyed with nickel-plated, flexible cable. The main beams are of ash and of square section, with simply enough rounding of the edges to prevent cutting the fabric, the ribs being screwed to the top of the forward beam and to the under side of the rear one. There are three sections to each plane, the ribs at the junction points being of square box construction with intervening solid ribs of rectangular section. Near the center is a T-rib of the Farman type, while the outermost ones at the extremities of the planes are of the usual L design. Spruce is used for the struts, except in the center section, and also for the small ribs, the box ribs being elm. The sections are

TYPES OF AEROPLANES 103

joined by lengths of square steel tubing fitting over the ends of the beams and bolted. The fuselage is in two sections joined by square

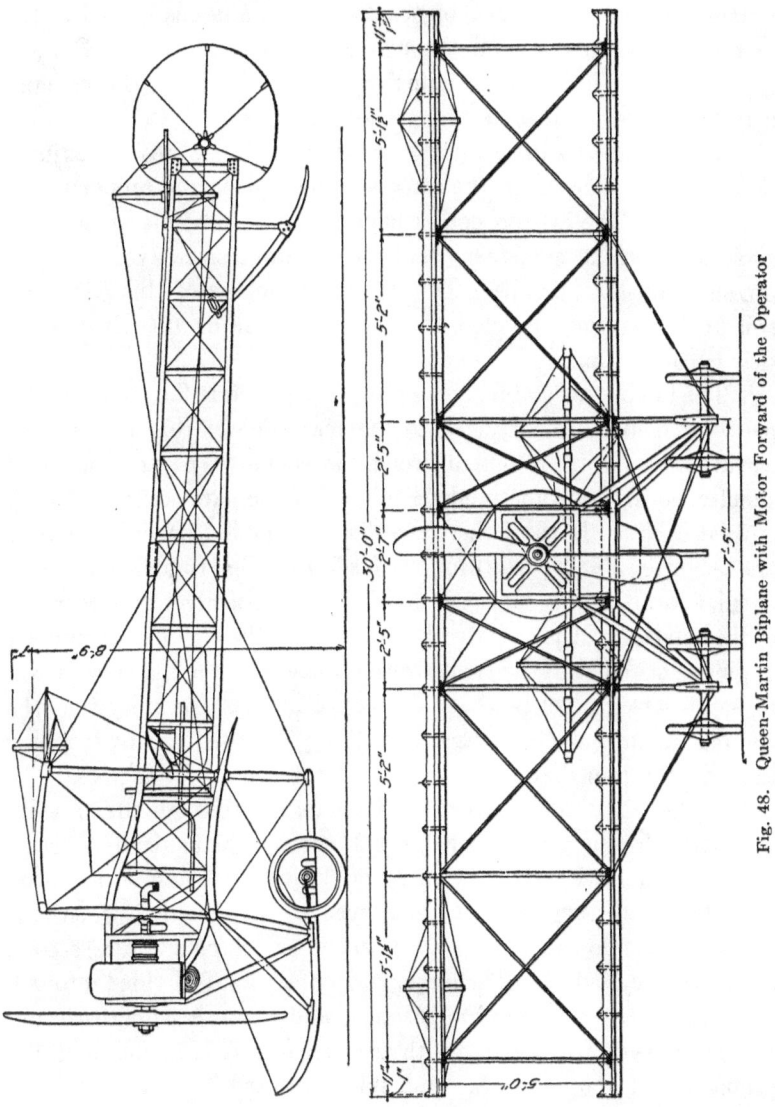

Fig. 48. Queen-Martin Biplane with Motor Forward of the Operator

steel sleeves, the aviator's seat being in the forward section just at the trailing edge of the lower plane. Under this seat is placed a large supplementary gasoline tank, from which fuel can be transferred by the aviator to the gravity tank in front of him. The aviator has to look over the gravity tank as is the case in a monoplane. Lateral control is by means of positive acting ailerons hinged to the rear upper beam operated through a gate control of the Burgess type, as shown in the longitudinal elevation, Fig. 48. Either hand may be used when it is desired to rest the other.

The elevator is in two parts and each half operates in conjunction with the ailerons on the same side, though in the proportion of but 1 to 6. The aileron cables have a certain amount of slack to avoid any turning movement of the aeroplane, also to avoid unequal pressures on the ailerons. The vertical members of this gate control are universally pivoted to permit of working the elevator in that capacity alone.

The tail or rear stabilizing surface is a perfectly flat, semicircular plane fixed in place. Hinged to the rear edge of this are the two elevators which are also semicircular in shape. They are operated simultaneously by a fore-and-aft motion of the gate control through crossed cables. Both of the elevators are double surfaced and they are separated by the width of the fuselage. The rudder is of semicircular form, double surfaced, and is hinged directly to the rear end of the fuselage. It is operated by a foot yoke through cables running in guides fastened to the struts of the fuselage. The machine is said to be possessed of such a high degrees of inherent stability that the ailerons do not have to be used in ordinary weather, and by stopping the motor it immediately assumes its gliding angle of 5 degrees. The power plant is a 100-horse-power Gnome, fourteen-cylinder revolving motor driving a propeller 8 feet 3 inches in diameter by 7 feet 6 inches in pitch, the ignition wiring of the motor being so arranged that the aviator may short-circuit seven of the cylinders when it is desired to cut down the power. A second switch cuts out the second set of seven cylinders. The large, horizontal tank is divided into two equal compartments, one for gasoline, and the other for castor oil, the latter being fed directly with the fuel to a Gnome motor in the proportion of about 1 to 5. Ash skids are used in connection with the usual rubber, spring-mounted wheels on the running gear, a hickory skid being placed under the tail. The weight with fuel and oil is 950 pounds, sufficient of the latter being carried for a 5-hour flight. Instead of being designed to fly at a certain angle of incidence, the Queen-Martin biplane depends entirely upon the camber of its surfaces for its lift, which is very small, not exceeding $2\frac{1}{2}$ inches.

Albatross Biplane. As its name indicates, the design of this machine is somewhat similar to that of the Etrich monoplane, in that it has flexible surfaces patterned after a bird's wings, but the idea is carried further by extending the same principle to the tail. Like the Queen-Martin, it has a monoplane body and a single tractor screw forward, but the fuselage, instead of taking the usual form of a rearward-tapering box girder of lattice construction, is flattened and broadened out just behind the lower main plane to form a support for the tail which is a horizontal triangle, similar to that of a bird. The vertical rudder, in the shape of an elongated fin, is placed directly above the center of the tail, while the flexible rear end of the latter serves as an elevator, exactly as it does in nature. The use of a flattened fuselage at the rear with a rudder above the tail and the elevator at its extremity was inaugurated by Bleriot in his racing machines in the summer of 1911. It has proved so efficient that it has since been adopted by a number of the leading foreign manufacturers and is a feature of the Bleriot French army machines. In the Albatross, which is of German manufacture, the lower plane is very much smaller than the upper, while the struts between them are placed diagonally, thus eliminating the use of the usual numerous stays and wire braces. The ends of the upper main plane taper to a point in the form of a bird's wing and for several feet from the end they are flexible, this use of flexible wing and tail surfaces doing away with all supplementary stabilizing planes, the area of the tail being unusually large, while its supporting effort, instead of being utilized merely at the end of the lever, is extended to a point just back of the lower main plane. More than twenty of the Albatross biplanes have been made for the German army.

Breguet Biplane. Breguet was one of the first French constructors to adopt the arrangement originated by the Wrights of running a large diameter propeller at low speed, and he was also a pioneer in the introduction of the biplane with a monoplane type of body and placing of the power plant. The unusually high efficiency gained is evidenced from the fact that with an ordinary two-passenger biplane he has carried six persons of a total weight of 924 pounds, which is very close to that of the weight of the machine itself—1,045 pounds—while his racing machines have also proved unusually speedy. The span is 43.3 feet, but the lower plane is only 32.5 feet wide, with a chord of 5.6 feet. A five-cylinder, semi-radial R. E. P. motor of 50 to 60 horse-power drives a two-bladed propeller 9.5 feet in diameter and of variable pitch through reduction gearing. The entire fuselage is enclosed with fabric, and the combined rudder and elevating plane in the form of a cross are hung from its after end on a universal joint. Control is by means of a wheel placed on a column, as in the Curtiss, revolving the wheel causing the rudder to turn, while pushing or pulling on it moves the column back and forth and actuates the elevator. Pushing the wheel from side to side flexes the wings, thus centering the control on a single lever. With the motor in question, its speed is 53 miles per hour, but a special racing type with only 280 square feet of supporting surface and a higher-powered motor is also made.

Tubavion Monoplane. Very radical departures from accepted standards of monoplane construction are found in this machine. A long steel tube forms the backbone and replaces the usual monoplane body, while converging, upward-curving skids are attached to this tube at the front and rear, thus making what is practically an "underslung" type, the motor being placed forward under a bonnet closed in front by the radiator, as on an automobile. The propeller is mounted on the main steel tube forming the backbone, just back of the main plane, and is chain driven from an extension of the engine shaft which runs back beneath the pilot's seat, thus giving an arrangement of the motor in front and the propeller at the rear. In fact, the power plant has been brought right up to date by providing the motor with a self-starter, so that it may be re-started in the air in case of accidental stoppage. The pilot sits directly behind the motor. Several machines built on this general principle, *i. e.*, monoplanes with a small underslung car in place of the usual monoplane body, made their appearance at the Paris aeroplane show late in the winter of 1911.

Morane Monoplane. While this machine is in general based upon Bleriot lines, Morane having been an associate of Bleriot's for some time, it is noticeable for the entire suppression of the dihedral angle between the two wings and their flatness on the under side,

TYPES OF AEROPLANES 107

this having been planned to increase the speed. The shape of the ends of the wings has also been radically altered and their point of maximum camber placed very close to the leading edge. The mast carrying the upper wing stays is pyramidal and is so arranged that the support at the front is more at right angles to the wings and so better protects the spars from over stress. The rudder is divided into two sections by the stabilizing tail, just forward of which is a light double skid. The pilot sits behind a long bonnet enclosing the tanks and extending over the engine, in the type employed in the long-distance races in the summer of 1911, but at the Paris salon in December of the same year, Morane exhibited a strikingly novel machine of all steel construction. The body is made of pressed steel in torpedo shape, $i.\ e.$, ovoid forward and tapering to a sharp point aft with a perfectly smooth finish outside, and as bracing is done on the interior this cuts the head resistance to the minimum. The Gnome revolving motor is completely enclosed with a comparatively small number of openings for cooling it, the propeller being the only part of the power plant that is visible from the outside. The use of steel tubing for the beams and ribs of the wings also does away with practically all braces and guys, so that the machine should prove exceptionally fast, even as compared with its immediate predecessor, which showed an average of 70 miles an hour on a closed circuit with a 50-horse-power motor. The chief dimensions are: Span 31 feet 6 inches; length 22 feet 6 inches; supporting area 188 square feet, of which 151 square feet are in the wings and the remainder in the stabilizing tail. Some idea of the care that has been taken to reduce weight is evident from the fact that the complete machine empty weighs but 440 pounds, and this has not been attained at the sacrifice of strength, as the machine is very solid. Among the speed performances of the Morane are the covering of 210 miles in 2:12, or at the rate of 90 miles an hour with a 20-mile favoring wind; 500 miles in 6:55, or 72.28 miles for the entire distance, and the winning of the Paris-Madrid race, the start of which was marked by the killing of two aviators and two French officials of prominence. In this race the Morane driven by Vedrines was the only aeroplane to finish, capturing the prize of $20,000.

Deperdussin Monoplane. While apparently a small machine, the Deperdussin has unusual carrying capacity and high speed with heavy loads, holding all world's records up to the end of 1911 for 4 and 5 passengers for distances up to 30 miles. Two of these monoplanes were brought to this country in the summer of 1911 and have made an excellent showing at various aviation meets. It is said to be one of the easiest machines for the beginner in which to master the difficult art of flying, and for this reason they have been employed to a great extent by schools on the other side. The wings are similar in shape to those of the Antoinette and, in fact, the entire machine resembles the latter to some extent. In the regular passenger and school machines, the wings are set at a slight dihedral angle and there is a perfectly flat triangular tail plane; but in the racing machines the planes are flat and the tail is of the lifting type. As there is every reason to believe that the non-lifting tail is the more efficient for a machine of this kind, the precise reason for the employment of a lifting tail is rather obscure. The elevator is hinged to the rear of the tail plane, while forward of the rudder extends a small stabilizing fin. The control is one of the best points of the machine, giving the greatest possible amount of freedom to the pilot. Instead of the usual arrangement of a vertical lever between the pilot's knees, the Deperdussin has two side levers connected by a pinned crosspiece on which is mounted a hand wheel. The rotation of this wheel corrects the lateral balance, while a to-and-fro movement controls the elevator, steering being effected by a foot lever in the manner common to French monoplanes. The cables from the warping control are carried down to a T-shaped lever mounted on the rear cross-member of the chassis and, after passing over pulleys on the skids, branch out into two wires each and proceed to two points on the spar of each wing. By rotating the wheel to the right, therefore, the whole of the rear spar of the left wing is pulled down, while the similar spar on the right wing rises a corresponding distance, and *vice versa*. Very little wire bracing is used on the landing chassis, rigidity being given to the structure by two wood diagonal struts in compression, the forward portion of the skids being an extension of these struts, and is connected to the skid proper by a thin band of steel to prevent the upturned front part of the skid from letting the machine down too heavily in the event of a sudden landing. A peculiar feature noticeable on the racing type is that the big tractor screw comes below the skids when in the vertical position, so that it is almost certain to be smashed in the event of a rough landing. Two Deperdussin monoplanes shared the honors with the Nieuport by being the only three monoplanes to meet the severe conditions imposed by the French military authorities in the 1911 competition.

Valkyrie Monoplane. The Valkyrie is one of the few English machines of this type. It is a peculiar combination of monoplane and biplane features, resembling in one respect the Voisin canard type, by having the elevator and a pair of stabilizing fins way forward of the main planes, and in another, the original Wright machine, in that the elevator is forward and the vertical rudder aft of the main planes, though structurally it does not resemble either of these types particularly. The main planes are in three sections, the center one being given a shorter chord than the other to allow room for the propeller, while the two outer sections are set at a pronounced dihedral angle. There is also a longitudinal dihedral angle between the main planes and the forward fixed plane, which is placed above the elevator and is given an angle of incidence of 9 degrees, while that of the wings is 13 degrees. The front fixed plane is placed 11 feet 9 inches forward of the main planes and its angle may be varied to compensate for changes in the loading. The elevator, which is below and at the rear of the forward fixed plane, is characterized by a slightly upturned trailing edge. All planes are of the single surface type and of Farman construction. Lateral stability is secured by the use of flaps at the extremities of the wings, but warping can be used. Twin vertical rudders some distance apart and placed three feet back of the main planes are employed. It has been found necessary to fit "blinkers," or small vertical fins similar to those used between the forward braces on the Wright, as without them, when making a short turn, the machine was likely to turn completely about its radius of gyration and come to the ground in a heap. The running gear is of the Farman type.

Hanriot Monoplane. The Hanriot is another French monoplane that has made such a favorable name for itself abroad that plans have been made to produce it in this country, the monoplane being a type that has not been particularly developed in America, unfortunately. There are many points of distinct originality in the Hanriot design and construction. Chief among these is the wood, boat-shaped hull, supported on three A-frames from the chassis, which makes a remarkably simple and strong construction, while the boat-like body dispenses with the usual great amount of wire necessary to brace a girder or box frame. This body is almost a replica of the usual racing scull, being entirely decked in except for a small cockpit to accommodate the aviator and the controls, this deck being made strong enough for the aviator to stand upon. Three steel ribbons form a support for the body on the **A**-type chassis frame, and steel tapes are also employed for lashing the main spars of the wings to the body. These spars are laminated, a form of construction that overcomes the usual tendency of the monoplane spars to buckle. The E. N. V. eight-cylinder, **V**-type, 40-horse-power motor is carried well forward of the main planes, where it is mounted on the bow of the boat body, and is also partly supported by the struts of the **A**-framing of the chassis. An unusually large rear stabilizing plane is employed, measuring 9 feet 3 inches in depth by 8 feet in width, in the form of a triangle. Two elevating planes are hinged to the rear edge of this fixed plane, with a space for the rudder between them. The span of the main planes is 30 feet and the chord 7 feet and they are set at a dihedral angle of 1 in 25; their total area is 184 square feet. This fixed tail plane is quite flat and consists of a single surface stretched tightly by the aid of two transverse spars. Its rear portion is deflected a little below the line of the leading edge, to which it has a relative though small angle of inclination.

Curtiss Racing Machine. In developing a racing machine, the Wright Brothers have proceeded along exactly the same lines as in their regular type of machine, high speed being obtained by cutting down the supporting surface and increasing the power. The Curtiss racing machine, however, is a special type, in that it is not exactly either a biplane or a monoplane. As will be apparent from the photograph, Fig. 49, it is a cross between the two and is accordingly in a class of its own. So far as its main supporting surface is concerned, it is a monoplane; but, placed centrally above this main plane, is another but very much smaller plane which resembles a canopy more than anything else. This small upper surface is not employed merely for the purpose of obtaining additional supporting area, but simply to take advantage of the support afforded by the tubular, vertical struts for the attachment of the guy wires. The elevating plane is placed in front but quite close to the main plane,

TYPES OF AEROPLANES

and it is a single surface instead of the usual biplane cell employed on the regular Curtiss machine. There is also a rear plane, but instead of arranging this to move, its rear edge is made flexible and it also acts as an elevator, thus providing the machine with an elevating rudder both front and rear. The running gear, as will be apparent, is closely modeled after the customary Curtiss standards, but the framework, instead of being of bamboo or light wood, is largely composed of steel tubing.

The usual balanced vertical rudder is placed at the rear and small vertical keels are used forward to offset the effect of side winds on the rudder. The wings are rigid and are fitted with hinged ailerons as in the Farman type. These ailerons have a spread of 6 feet 2 inches by a depth of 20 inches and are operated by means of cables attached to a shoulder brace as in the regular Curtiss machine.

Fig. 49. Curtiss Racing Machine. This is Practically a Monoplane

The main planes have a spread of 29 feet and a depth of 4 feet 6 inches, giving an area of 120.5 square feet. The front elevator measures 6 feet 2 inches by 2 feet 8 inches, while the rear elevator has a spread of 8 feet 2 inches and a depth of 2 feet 10 inches, the rear edge, which can be flexed, having a depth of 20 inches. This makes the total supporting area of the machine 160 square feet, exclusive of the small upper plane.

The mottor is an eight-cylinder, four-cycle V-type, water- instead of air-cooled, the valves being placed in the heads of the cylinders. The cylinder dimensions are, bore 4 inches, stroke $4\frac{1}{2}$ inches. It weighs 250 pounds all told and develops 70 horse-power. Lubrication is by means of a rotating vein oil pump, the supply being carried in a wedge-shaped tank below the motor. The radiator is placed forward of the motor and just behind the aviator. Mounting is on three 12-inch wheels shod with heavy pneumatic tires, while instead of the spoon brake employed on the front wheel of the regular Curtiss machine, two sprags are attached to the main axle. It was found that the front wheel bore such a small part of the weight that a brake was not effective. These sprags are brought into operation by an extreme forward movement of the vertical steering wheel, the remainder of the control consisting of a foot-operated throttle for the motor, and the working of the ailerons by the shoulder braces, the turning of the steering wheel governing the vertical rudder. The propeller is of laminated spruce, 8 feet in diameter by a 6-foot pitch, and is attached directly to the crank shaft of the motor.

The front control is placed 8 feet forward of the main plane, while the rear control is 14 feet back of it, giving the machine a total depth of 26 feet overall. Very little wood is used in the construction of the framework, thin steel tubing predominating, while the surfaces of the planes are composed of the thinnest racing yacht sail cloth. This is the Curtiss machine that was designed and built to compete in the Gordon-Bennett contest at Belmont Park in the fall of 1910, but which was finally not entered.

Multiplanes. It will be noted that neither in the article on "Standard Types," nor in the present one, has any mention been made of machines with more than two independent surfaces. In fact, all of the machines that have been successfully flown to any great extent thus far, have either been biplanes or monoplanes. One reason for not attempting to use more than two planes is to be found in the greater complication involved in the construction, as well as the introduction of a new factor brought about by the increase in the height of the machine—that of vertical stability. With good control of the lateral stability by warping or ailerons, and of longitudinal stability by means of the tail and elevating rudder, the aviator can safely disregard this third factor. Unless something happens to the machine it is in no danger of assuming an angle of inclination to the horizontal that would tend to rob it of supporting power to an extent that would make a fall imminent through the aeroplane "standing on its head," or the reverse. With the towering structure represented by three or more superimposed planes, it appears as if a sudden gust

Intentionally blank as was the original edition.

UNIQUE VIEW OF THE BLERIOT "TYPE POPULAIRE" WITH ONE WING AND ONE SIDE OF BODY REMOVED SHOWING THE INTERIOR ACCOMMODATION AND MECHANISM

TYPES OF AEROPLANES

of wind—a sharp puff that happened to strike the upper planes and not the lower ones, as is quite possible, or a strong slant of wind that exerted considerably more pressure upon the upper part of the machine than it did on the lower—would be quite likely to cause this result. It will be recalled that the Wright Brothers give it as their opinion that no advantage is to be gained by increasing the number of planes above two.

Roe. However, so many obvious theories that apparently can not fail to hold good in practice have been upset by the results obtained in flights with various types of machines, that it is difficult to put any of them down as entirely untenable until this has been

Fig. 50. Roe Multiplane

demonstrated by experiment. Unfortunately, most of the experiments with multiplanes so far have not resulted successfully. Some, on the other hand, have given considerable promise but have been carried out only on a small scale. The first public appearance of a triplane was at the Harvard Aviation Meet, in September, 1910. The machine was designed and built by A. V. Roe, an Englishman, who also attempted to fly the machine. As will be apparent from the photograph of this machine, Fig. 50, it is practically a Farman biplane, with the addition of a third plane of smaller dimensions placed below the other two. The tail is likewise a triplane. Control of lateral stability is attained in the same manner as in the Farman, *i. e.*,

114 TYPES OF AEROPLANES

by ailerons or wing tips, but these are attached to the rear surfaces of the middle plane instead of to the upper plane as in the French machine. The motor is mounted at the forward edge of this central plane with the direct-connected propeller placed in front, while the aviator's seat is placed in the framework about on a level with the third or lowest plane. The construction of this frame is somewhat similar to that of the Bleriot. The machine is mounted on two pairs of pneumatic-tired wheels attached to long skids, as in the Farman, while a third small skid is placed under the elevating rudder. On the only occasion on which the Roe triplane was used at the Harvard Meet, it made a short flight, Fig. 51, and then dove to the ground,

Fig. 51. Roe Multiplane in Flight

wrecking itself. As many successful machines have performed in a similar manner in the hands of unskilled aviators, this does not necessarily imply a fault in the design, nor for that matter a lack of skill, as something may have gone wrong with the control.

Roe has been a persistent experimenter with the triplane and worked at the problem for a long while, developing his first machine in which he succeeded in getting off the ground. This was practically a Langley aerodrome in triplicate and not the machine used at Boston. The three planes were of the same area and were attached to three similar but smaller planes, forming the tail by means of a triangular frame. It was mounted on two wheels forward under the main planes and a skid at the rear, the aviator sitting in the body or enclosed frame about midway between the main planes and the tail. The forward or main supporting surfaces measured 20 feet in spread by a depth of 3 feet 7 inches, while the rear planes were of the same depth with exactly half the spread, or 10 feet, giving a total area of 320 square feet. The motor of but 10 horse-power was mounted originally at the forward end of the framing and carried a three-bladed propeller directly on its crank shaft. With this motor the total weight of the machine itself was but 200 pounds, or with the aviator, about 350 pounds, thus lifting 35 pounds per horse-power. Subsequently, a 20-horse-power motor was installed and the weight of the machine considerably increased. The body is constructed of deal (spruce) and is covered with oiled paper backed with muslin. Instead of the usual elevating rudder, the machine is caused to ascend or descend by altering the angle of incidence of the main planes themselves, all three being pivoted for this purpose. The transverse control consisted of warping the rear edges of the main planes in the usual manner and at the same time employing the vertical rudder at the rear. With this machine, a number of short flights in a straight line were made, the most striking feature being the low power necessary.

Sellers. From similar experiments made in this country, the possibility of greatly increasing the efficiency as represented by the present-day standard appears to be the chief promise held out by the multiplane. M. B. Sellers, a Kentuckian, has made extended experiments in this direction with a quadruplane and has made a number of flights, using a Bates two-cylinder opposed motor rated at but 10 horse-power. The four planes are not placed directly above one another, but are joined in the form of a parallelogram with a forward inclination from the vertical in the direction of the machine's flight, thus bringing each surface slightly in advance of the one below.

Zerber. Another type, the Zerber, is shown in Fig. 52.

Paulhan Triplane. Paulhan has brought out a triplane of the same construction as the box-girder type already described, but trials made with it during the summer of 1911 were not successful.

Maxim. A machine that probably conforms less to the standards already set forth than any other is the new Maxim aeroplane, about the construction of which considerable secrecy has been maintained. It is, in fact, the Maxim flying machine of almost twenty years ago brought down to date, every part of it, even including the motor and propellers, being made by the inventor himself, in accordance with his own theories. His first care was to reduce the proportions of the machine as compared with the gigantic apparatus built at a cost of $100,000 in 1894. The spread of the new aeroplane is but 44 feet—large in comparison with most standard

Fig. 52. Zerber Multiplane

machines, but not when compared with the spread of over 100 feet of the original Maxim. Like its prototype, the new aeroplane is of the multiplane type and is, in effect, made up of six aeroplanes, each being 6 feet 6 inches in depth, giving it an aspect ratio of 6.77. The planes are noticeably thin and consist of waterproof silk, very tightly laced on. From the central plane spring out two superposed wings, raised well above it, and so curved as to produce inherent lateral stability to a very high degree.

There are balanced rudders fore and aft and a horizontal steering rudder, the Maxim patent device for altering the pitch of the

TYPES OF AEROPLANES

planes when in flight being utilized. This differs from the Wright warping device in that the wings are moved in one direction by a lever worked by hand, while a spring controls them in the reverse direction.

The engine is mounted between the planes and behind the pilot, who sits in a low, metal-covered compartment, with the steering and control levers directly in front of him. One of the most novel features of the machine is its power plant and drive. On the engine shaft is one small propeller, mounted at the rear of the planes. This screw turns at the same rate as the engine shaft and also serves as a flywheel. In addition, there are two large propellers, 11 feet in diameter, mounted higher up between the planes and driven by steel cables kept taut by idler pulleys. The small screw and one of the large ones rotate in the same direction, while the other large one turns in the opposite direction. This screw is also given a finer pitch and a higher velocity than its companion and in this way its gyroscopic action balances the joint gyroscopic action of the other two propellers, rotating in the reverse direction.

The motor is a four-cylinder, vertical, water-cooled type of 60 horse-power, built throughout of a special grade of Vickers steel, making it amply strong but very light. Special attention has been paid to the valve and carbureter design and a greater degree of reliability is claimed for the engine than those usually employed in aviation. An ingenious force-feed system of lubrication is employed which carries oil to every working part of the motor in a very effective manner. The radiator is mounted under the upper plane in a manner somewhat similar to that employed on Santos-Dumont's Demoiselle.

The whole machine is mounted on wheels and shock absorbers. There is a noticeable absence of the complication of stays, guy wires, and framework common to the usual biplane construction, and which causes so much head resistance. The grouping of the various members has been skillfully carried out, those parts creating the greatest resistance being set as far as possible in line behind one another. Like its predecessor, it has also been experimented with in a captive state, but instead of the tracks on which the first Maxim machine ran, an apparatus similar to that designed by Captain Ferber is employed. This consists of a mast with a huge revolving arm, permitting the aeroplane to fly in a circle round its support. When so many other new machines are experimented with in free flight by aviators of litt'e or no experience, the Maxim method scarcely appears necessary, though it at least has the virtue of greater safety.

Steel Tube Construction. That there is likewise ample room for improvement in constructional details will be obvious upon a consideration of the methods and materials employed in building the standard types of aeroplanes already described. Crudity was to be looked for at first—many successful experimenters had neither the means nor the facilities to employ special materials or construction. They were in much the same position as early experimenters

Fig. 53. Fairchild Monoplane with Frame of Steel-Tube Construction

in the automobile field. But now that so much has been done in the development of steels and light alloys of tremendous strength for automobile construction, there appears to be no reason why they should not be taken advantage of to replace the more cumbrous and none too safe wood or bamboo framing. Two instances of this are shown in Figs. 53, 54, and 55. Many of the new machines produced during 1911 employ steel tubing to a greater or less extent.

Fairchild Monoplane. The Fairchild (American) is one of the few types of monoplanes extant, employing two propellers. It is, in fact, a model of mechanical construction, and if its flying capabilities are in any way commensurate with the intelligence and resourcefulness displayed in the working out of its design, it would seem to presage the advent of the eminently successful American monoplane.

Fig. 54. Henri Farman in His New Monoplane. The Frame is of Steel-Tube Construction

The frame is of graduated steel tubing, lightness with maximum strength having been obtained through the use of different diameters and thickness of tubes, the necessary strength of each part having been carefully calculated in detail. Wherever special strength is required, the tubes are forced over elm poles. In the trussing of the frame, steel tape and cable are employed in place of the usual

Fig. 55. Front View of Farman Monoplane

piano wire, which, though very strong, is an uncertain factor and likely to give way unexpectedly.

The wings are of the usual monoplane type and are built up of 14 double ribs over transverse 1-inch steel tubes. They have flexible curved tips which are balanced for a certain lifting effect, but which can not be controlled by the aviator. The tail is similar to the flat type of the Antoinette and is employed solely as a stabilizer, its lifting capacity alone being equal to sustaining itself and the weight of the framework attaching it to the body. Vertical and horizontal changes of direction are obtained through rear rudders of the Antoinette type, except that a further vertical rudder in front of the hinge, in prolongation of the rear one, occupies the position of the French machine's fixed, vertical fin. Efficient lateral control is expected from a novel and very radical device, the construction of which the builder did not wish to reveal at the time.

Like the Bleriot XII, the Demoiselle, and the Grade, the Fairchild monoplane has its center of gravity comparatively low, but unlike these machines, the aviator sits above. It is anticipated that any tendency toward oscillation produced by thus placing the center of gravity low will be overcome by a large, vertical fin placed directly over the center of the machine between the main planes, as well as the fact that two propellers are employed for propulsion, or rather traction, as both will draw the machine, and both are designed to revolve in the same direction—contrary to all precedent in this field. Fairchild holds that if the gyroscopic effect of a single propeller can be deemed negligible in the monoplane, that of two is even more so. These propellers have a 7-foot diameter and a 6-foot pitch.

The motor is a six-cylinder, two-cycle Emerson rated at 100 to 125 horse-power. It is of a special four-port type and is said to show great efficiency, having developed in excess of 134 horse-power on a brake test. It is mounted at the lowest point of the main frame below the center of the wings and just above the landing chassis which is exceptionally wide and strong. A pair of pneumatic-tired wheels support the fore part of the machine when on the ground, the supporting columns, which are double, forming part of the frame; the forks carrying the wheels are hinged to the lower ends of the tubes and the wheel hubs are stayed independently to loose collars that ride upon a portion of the upper ends of the columns. These collars are anchored to the lower ends of the columns by a pair of powerful compression springs. Skids, normally 3 inches off the ground, are depended upon to absorb any excess shock, while light double skids support the tail.

TYPES OF AEROPLANES

The wings have a spread of 37 feet and a depth of 8 feet 4 inches where they join the body, giving it the low aspect ratio of but 4.45 to 1. The supporting surface measures 280 square feet, but despite these large dimensions the total weight of the machine scarcely exceeds 700 pounds, which is a tribute to its construction. The curve of the wings is a composite one, worked out from calculations by the designer. The length overall of the machine is also 37 feet; the area of the fixed tail is 60 square feet and that of the horizontal rudder, or elevator, 22 square feet. The greatest care has been taken in the construction of this remarkable monoplane and the engineering skill of its builder is discernible in the many ingenious details it displays, many of them never having been employed in aeroplane construction. This machine was wrecked through an unfortunate accident that had no bearing on its design or construction. It was rebuilt late in 1911 with numerous detailed improvements.

H. Farman Monoplane. A radical departure from current methods of construction is also to be found in the new H. Farman monoplane, Figs. 54 and 55. The frame is a triangular structure united at the forward end by steel girder construction in the form of a cross, the center of which serves as the support for the shaft of the seven-cylinder revolving Gnome motor. The four main frame members are connected by suitable stanchions and are trussed with piano wire; they are not joined at the rear. The wings are not mounted directly on this framework but are carried almost 2 feet above it. This places the power plant and its accessories, as well as the aviator, on a lower level than the supporting surface. The wings are mounted on another triangular structure which also serves for the attachment of the running gear. At right angles to the longitudinal frame members are two vertical members, attached to the steel girder construction on the forward end of the frame, and mounting above the level of the wings and descending considerably below the level of the frame. From the lowest point of these two uprights are two similar members inclined toward the rear, attached to the two longitudinal members of the frame and receiving on their upper extremities the rear transverse girder of the wing. This, as can be seen readily from the illustration, forms a triangle, or really two triangles, one at each side of the frame, the apex of each being near the ground and forming the support for the axle of the running gear.

The rear plane is mounted directly on the frame with the rear portion overhanging to allow free movement, while the rudder and vertical fin are mounted above the frame, and consequently above the horizontal rudder. There are neither shock absorbers nor main skids, the aeroplane landing on two small-diameter, pneumatic-tired wheels carried on a rigid steel axle passing through the two ends of the triangles already described. A simple skid is used at the rear to prevent the tail dragging on the ground. The aviator's seat is placed in the main frame, slightly more than a third of the length of the machine from its forward end. Placed below the level of the wings, the pilot is more advantageously situated to correctly estimate his distances for landing than when seated above the wing level. This advantage is obtained without any loss of protection in case of a rough landing, as almost half the machine must take the shock before the aviator can be reached.

Lateral stability is obtained by the usual Farman wing tips, or hinged surfaces attached to the rear outer ends of the main planes, the Farman being the only successful French monoplane to employ them. The Antoinette was originally built this way, but later abandoned wing tips in favor of warping, while Bleriot, Tellier, and Hanriot never used them. The spread is 23 feet 6 inches; depth, 6 feet 6 inches; aspect ratio, 3.6 to 1, which is extremely low. The tail has about 30 square feet of surface, making the total about 190 square feet. The overall length is 26 feet 2 inches, and the total weight of the machine alone, 660 pounds. So far as can be gathered from examination, the wing curvature is the same as for the standard biplanes.

Types with Fixed Stabilizing Plane. *Herring Biplane.* As is naturally to be expected, many of the special types of aeroplanes built are designed with a view to providing automatic stability, thus circumventing the Wright patents. In the Herring machine, the modification takes the form of a number of vertical, triangular fins mounted on the upper plane, Fig. 56. Each of these vertical keels has about 2 square feet of surface and there are six of them all told, two being equally spaced on either side of the center and quite close to it, while the other two are near the opposite ends of the upper main plane. When an aeroplane tips to one side, it has a tendency to slide to the ground endwise, but as the weight is low and the keels offer resistance to this sidewise motion, the upper part of the machine

TYPES OF AEROPLANES

is retarded, while the lower part swings over like a pendulum and equilibrium is regained.

Fig. 56. Herring-Burgess Biplane Ready for Flight—Herring in the Operator's Seat

In the first test, made in the spring of 1910, the special paraffine-coated silk surfaces were very loose, owing to the dampness and fog, and when the machine was in the air it was necessary for the aviator to sit well to the left to counterbalance a difference in the lifting power of the two sides of the machine. The biplane rose readily after a run of 85 feet and is said to have taken to the air at a speed as low as 22 miles an hour. The elevating rudder was turned too abruptly and the machine shot 40 feet in the air at an angle of almost 30 degrees from the horizontal. After flying straightaway about 300 feet, the machine made a successful turn, tilting at an angle of about 20 degrees, and making a 40-degree turn. The machine weighed only 400 pounds, while the aviator weighed 190 pounds, and according to the inventor, it rose with a propeller thrust of only 140 pounds, while he believes that a thrust of 80 to 85 pounds is sufficient to fly it. On its trial flight, the motor was not run at full throttle and was thought to have developed only 9 horse-power, which would give the machine as a whole an unusually high efficiency. The method of maintaining automatic lateral stability appeared to work fairly well and is an improvement over the Voisin in that the head resistance due to the vertical keels is reduced to a minimum, owing to their form and location.

The spread of this Herring biplane is only 28 feet; depth, 4 feet; aspect ratio, 7 to 1; total supporting surface, 220 square feet. A 25-horse-power, four-cylinder Curtiss, air-cooled motor is mounted on the lower plane at the rear and carries on its crank shaft a four-bladed, 6-foot propeller of 5-foot pitch, designed especially for the machine by Mr. Herring. The total weight is about 400 pounds, or with its inventor 590 pounds, giving it a pounds-per-horse-power factor of 2.36, and a loading of 2.6 pounds per square foot of surface. The thrust obtained from the propeller at 1,200 r. p. m. is said to approximate 200 pounds. A double-surfaced elevating rudder is carried upon hollow, inclined extensions 12 feet in front, while the single-surface steering rudder is similarly placed at the rear. The machine is mounted upon a central runner having two smaller skids at each side, there also being another skid at each end of the lower plane. The aviator sits in a small seat located in front of the lower plane, and clings to two inclined braces running out in front to vertical struts connecting the poles that support the elevating rudder. The latter is operated by a foot lever, while a small lever at the right controls the steering rudder.

TYPES OF AEROPLANES

Baldwin Biplane. Another modification of the same scheme is incorporated in a machine built by Captain Baldwin, the dean of American aviators. This consists of the use of a single, rectangular stabilizing plane placed vertically at the center and above the upper main plane, as the Baldwin is also a biplane. This rudder may be turned about its vertical axis by means of a yoke fitting around the aviator's shoulders as in the Curtiss machine. When the machine tips, the aviator leans to the high side and sets the stabilizing rudder at an angle to the line of advance. This exerts sufficient force to bring the machine back to an even keel. The new stabilizing rudder is the result of experiments carried out by the Aerial Experiment Association several years ago and has been tried by Curtiss, who claims that it worked satisfactorily on his machine.

The Baldwin biplane has a spread of 28 feet and a depth of 5 feet; aspect ratio, 5.6 to 1; total area of main planes, 280 square feet. A small, horizontal biplane tail is carried on a triangular frame extending back of the main planes and mounted on a skid. The vertical or direction rudder is placed in the center of the horizontal rudder, or tail. The arrangement of the power plant and aviator's seat is along monoplane lines, the motor being placed at the front edge of the lower plane and the aviator's seat above the rear edge of the same plane. The flywheel of the motor extends above and below this plane. The propeller is placed half way between the main planes and is driven by a chain and sprockets. It is about $8\frac{1}{2}$ feet in diameter and of high pitch. The regular Curtiss single wheel control is employed, while the mounting consists of a pair of pneumatic-tired wheels in front and a single skid at the rear. The machine has had a number of successful tests at Hammondsport, New York.

Waldon-Dyett Monoplane. Another variation of the idea of utilizing stationary keels to attain lateral stability is found in the Waldon-Dyett monoplane, a machine of American design and construction. In this case, the keels are somewhat similar in form to an old-time kite—a triangle with a spherical instead of a flat base. These keels are about 18 to 20 inches across their widest part and taper back sharply to a point, having a length equivalent to the depth of the main plane of the machine. Two of them are employed, one at each outer edge of the main plane, but contrary to the examples already described, they are set at an angle of about 45 degrees from the vertical as measured from the tip of the main plane to the keel. In other words, they both lean outward at the same angle. It will be obvious that as these keels are rigidly fixed in place, they form what may be termed "pockets" at each end of the main supporting surface. The method of their operation, or rather the rôle they are designed to play, will be equally apparent. When flying straight ahead, whether on an even keel, ascending, or descending, they are neutral. Should the machine incline to the right, it will be evident that as it goes downward on that side the lower surface of the right keel approaches more and more closely to the horizontal and interposes a correspondingly increased resistance to further inclination. At the same time the upper surface of the left keel presents a similarly increased resistance, tending to hold that end down. There is no manual control of these surfaces by the aviator.

HYDROAEROPLANES

Advantages. Ability to alight upon and rise from the water as well as from the land is a feature that the aeroplane must possess before it can be said to completely fulfill its mission. Contrary to the general impression, water is quite as hard and unyielding as solid ground when struck sharply at right angles, and the destructive effects of a vertical fall from any height would scarcely be less in striking the former than the latter, but when struck at an angle by a properly-designed surface the force of the impact is very greatly reduced as compared with a ground landing, the shock of which must be absorbed by the springs of the chassis. It is, accordingly, considered much safer to alight upon the surface of the water than it is upon the ground. But the ability to do both of these things carries with it numerous other advantages. There are few parts of the country where flights of any duration would not carry the aviator over lakes and streams, and in making long flights one of the chief concerns of the aviator is to be able to select safe landing places, so that the number available would be more than doubled. Any stretch of water, short of a swift running slant of rapids, affords an infinitely better surface than the most carefully leveled field, and when alighting in strange country, the aviator always can be certain that the surface of a lake does not hide any dangerous pitfalls in the form of grass-covered holes, rocks, and ditches that are seldom lacking in the ordinary field, and which prove so destructive to the chassis. Obstructions of a serious nature all appear perfectly flat when viewed from above so that a field which may have the appearance of a velvety lawn from a point several hundred feet over it, is quite the reverse when seen from the ground, and quick work is necessary to effect a safe landing on it. Another and even greater advantage is to be found in the fact that the wind blowing over a surface of water is much more uniform, usually being free from the uncertain puffs and gusts that characterize the same wind blowing over the adjacent land. It was doubtless for this reason that Langley selected the Potomac River as the site of the first flights of his aerodrome.

The added weight of both a landing chassis and a hydroplane float for alighting on the water naturally forms a disadvantage, but with the results of laboratory experiments now being carried out at command it will doubtless be possible to construct an aerocurve or aerfoil, as it is variously termed, *i.e.*, a supporting surface that will have such a greatly increased efficiency for the same area, that the addition of a hundred pounds or more will call for no appreciable increase in area. Constructional difficulties are also involved as the hydroplane floats must be so arranged as not to be damaged by the yielding of the springs of the chassis when landing on the ground. To a certain extent, there always will be a demand for a machine adapted to rise from and alight upon the water alone, such as the hydroaeroplanes designed for naval use, and the experiments of the past few years have been centered on the development of a machine for this purpose.

Early Attempts. While the credit for constructing the first practical hydroaeroplane belongs to a Frenchman, M. Fabre, who brought out his first machine only a few years ago, the subject was investigated in this country several years previous. This was at a time when the only motors available were unreliable automobile types, and the difficulty encountered in keeping the engine working for any length of time caused the abandonment of the experiments. Although numerous practical flights had been made over water prior to the summer of 1910, some of them of quite considerable distance, the precautions taken to insure the floating of the aeroplane in case it should drop into the water, were always of a makeshift nature, intended merely for the particular occasion. For instance,

Wilbur Wright in preparing for his flight up the Hudson from Governor's Island, lashed a canoe beneath the biplane. Curtiss in his flight of 148 miles down the Hudson from Albany to New York, made use of pontoons, while in other cases air cylinders have been secured under the machine to insure sufficient buoyancy. The only instance in which the precautions proved necessary was in the case of Latham's first attempt to cross the English Channel in an Antoinette monoplane.

Fabre Hydroaeroplane. To meet conditions of this nature, Fabre designed a novel monoplane, Fig. 57, capable of starting from

Fig. 57. Fabre Hydroaeroplane in Flight

and alighting on the water. It can also navigate the surface in calm weather in case of damage to its supporting planes. In its construction, the Fabre hydroaeroplane differs radically from any of the other designs, in fact, it is thus far the only monoplane of its kind. The construction consists of a vertical chassis, analogous to that of a bicycle, and to which the single main supporting plane is fastened at the extreme rear. This plane is in two sections set at a slight angle, the under side of the left-hand section being shown in the figure. The motor is mounted on its after edge. Forward a biplane elevating rudder, of which the lower plane is the larger, is also attached to this frame. Immediately above the biplane rudder forward are

HARRY ATWOOD IN HIS BURGESS HYDROAEROPLANE SKIMMING OVER THE SURFACE OF MARBLEHEAD BAY

Intentionally blank as was the original edition.

TYPES OF AEROPLANES

two twin vertical keels, the direction rudder being placed at the center of the main plane, just where the sections join and immediately forward of the propeller, where its leverage is greatly increased by the rush of air to the latter. The aviator's seat is placed directly in the center of the frame. The cylindrical gasoline tank is placed directly behind the aviator's seat and is suspended between the guy wires of the direction rudder aft and the main longitudinal beam. Reference to the figure shows that there is less framing and less bracing on this monoplane than on any other of equal size.

The complete machine rests upon three hydroplane floats, one at the forward end of the chassis and the two others under the main plane half way between the center and the two ends. These hydroplanes are of the Ricochet-Bonnemaison type in which the bottom forms a hydroplane surface. But while, in the ricochet boats of Bonnemaison, longitudinal stability is obtained by placing one surface in front of another, and joining the two by a vertical surface forming a notch, in this case the front plane has been completely separated from the rear plane, each forming the bottom of a separate float. This arrangement has the advantage of giving both longitudinal and lateral stability, while the fact of the rear plane being divided and its halves placed some distance apart takes them out of the disturbing influence of the wake of the forward float. In addition, as each float is made up of but a single continuous surface, it has a form offering slight resistance to the air. It resembles the shape of the Antoinette monoplane wing. The resistance to the air that the notch would give is thus avoided, and the float performs a third function, since it acts as an auxiliary supporting surface when in the air. This form of float with the plane surface below and a cylindrical surface on top has the further advantage of acting like a hydroplane even though it be completely submerged. It accordingly does not offer any great resistance when engulfed by a wave, but because of its speed receives a more energetic upward impulse than ever.

The chief disadvantage of this type of hydroplane is the terrific pounding it receives when moving rapidly over water that is only slightly disturbed. The portion of the lifting plane in contact with the water, which is a strip of only a few square inches along its rear edge when the plane is moving rapidly, is instantly increased tenfold the moment the surface is no longer perfectly smooth and level, because of the slight inclination of the plane to the horizontal. The float then receives upward vertical accelerations equal to ten times its weight. To absorb these dangerous shocks, the Fabre hydroaeroplane floats have a flexible under surface. This is made up of thin veneered wood, which acts in the same way as the head of a drum. By this means, even the framework of the monoplane is protected from the shocks of the waves, in the same manner as an automobile is protected from jolting of the road through its pneumatic tires. Moreover, very great flexibility is attained between the body of the float and the heavy parts of the apparatus. As may be seen by referring to the illustration, Fig. 57, the elasticity of nearly every part of the machine comes into play to absorb the upward thrust of the waves before reaching the motor or the aviator. When at rest on the surface, the Fabre hydroaeroplane has a very slight draft, not exceeding 25 centimeters (9.8 inches), decreasing to nothing when in motion.

The tapering form of the bottom of the floats permits them to pass over weeds, ropes, and other floating bodies, or to skim over shoals without danger, even at high speed. No motor boat has such ease of evolution in shallow water as a hydroplane driven by an aerial propeller. This is true to an extent where it holds good even if there be *no water*. If the Fabre marine aeroplane should land on a meadow it would not be injured as the floats are sufficiently solid to act as skids. A device is being perfected to permit it to land or start either on the water or on the ground. The floats are capable of resisting the action of salt water, as a test, one having remained afloat for two months without damage.

The wings of this aeroplane are stretched upon a special steel truss of the same form that Fabre has employed in the Paulhan biplane just described, and the wings themselves are capable of being reefed or folded when the machine is at rest on the water as the machine might otherwise be damaged by the wind. The wing itself is composed of four parts, somewhat analogous to a bird's wing:

(1) A trussed longitudinal girder is placed along the front edge in the position which the bones occupy in a bird's wing. This is the only longitudinal support of the wing and it is depended upon to give rigidity to the whole construction so that it is very strongly reinforced. The uprights to which the floats are fastened are attached directly to it. This zigzag form of girder, which is a newly patented

TYPES OF AEROPLANES 131

construction, is used not only for the wings and horizontal rudders, but also for the members of the chassis, and for the framework of the hydroplanes; in a word, the whole apparatus is essentially a Fabre reinforced beam.

(2) The ribs which correspond to the quill feathers of a bird's wing, consist of thin strips of wood superposed and glued together. They fit into sockets on the bottom of the single longitudinal girder.

(3) The covering of the wing consists of "simili-silk," such as is used for the light sails of racing yachts. This is hemmed and reinforced at the edges and provided with eyelets and grummets, permitting it to be laced on, so that it may be quickly removed without dismounting any part of the skeleton of the wing. Pockets corresponding to the position of the ribs are sewed into the cloth and the latter is drawn on over them and then laced to the main girder, wood eyelets being employed for this purpose, while at the rear it is held taut by ingenious spring clamps.

(4) Suitable braces are provided for holding the main beams of the wings against turning in their sockets when the machine is in flight. Steel cables fastened to the lower ends of these braces serve to regulate the angle of incidence of the wings or to warp them. The wings themselves are also trussed with similar braces.

The spread is approximately 47 feet, depth 6 feet, aspect ratio 7.4 to 1, total area about 280 square feet, pounds per horse-power 5.6. The total weight in flight is about 950 pounds, giving it a loading of 3.4 pounds per square foot. The power plant consists of a 50-horse-power, seven-cylinder revolving Gnome motor, directly attached to an $8\frac{1}{2}$-foot, two-bladed wood propeller which it drives at 1,100 r. p. m.

The Fabre hydroaeroplane made its first flight at Martigues, France, March 28, 1910. It attained a speed of 34.2 miles (55 kilometers) an hour on the surface, and then flew about 7 feet above the water for a third of a mile. Later it made a longer flight at a height of about 10 feet above the surface. On May 17, a series of flights were made by Henri Fabre before Paulhan. The machine rose easily and gracefully from the water and made a splendid flight of about 4 miles at a height of 65 feet. In coming down, however, the aviator volplaned at too great an angle and landed with a terrific splash, throwing Fabre head first out of his seat but not injuring him.

132 TYPES OF AEROPLANES

Under similar conditions on land, such a descent would have meant not only the total wreck of the machine but in all probability the death of the aviator. As it was, the only damage suffered was a ducking and the breakage of one end of a wing and one of the floats.

Curtiss Hydroaeroplane. The most persistent as well as the most successful experimenter in this field in America has been Glenn H. Curtiss. He first began his investigations in the early part of 1910 by attaching floats to one of his standard type biplanes, but did not find it possible to attain a speed in excess of 20 miles per hour, which was not sufficient to permit the machine to rise from the surface. Winter cut short these experiments which were carried out at Hammondsport, New York, the site of the Curtiss factory, and they were shortly after transferred to San Diego, where he was engaged at the time in instructing several army and navy officers in flying.

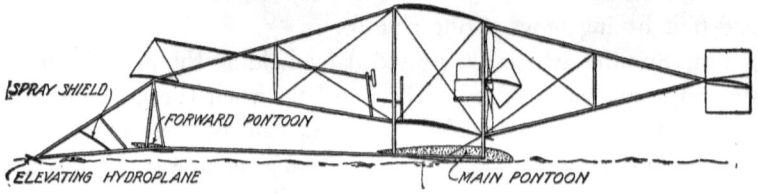

Fig. 58. Side Elevation of Early Curtiss Hydroaeroplane

First Flights. In his first experiments on the Pacific Coast Curtiss followed the Fabre design, so far as the form of the floats was concerned. One large float, or hydroplane, 6 feet wide, 5 feet from front to rear, and 1 foot thick at its central section, was constructed and placed under the center of the machine. The bottom of this float was perfectly flat and was fixed at an angle of 10 to 12 degrees. Some distance forward of the main float, at about the same position as the front wheel of the chassis of the land machine, another float 6 feet wide, 1 foot from front to rear, and 6 inches deep, was placed; while at the extreme forward end of the biplane there was mounted a small elevating hydroplane measuring 6 feet wide by 8 inches fore and aft and 1½ inches thick. This hydroplane was carried on a special outrigger and was fixed at an angle of about 25 degrees, in order to lift the forward end of the machine, a spray shield being fitted just behind it to keep the aviator dry when skimming over the surface. The location of these three hydroplanes, as well as their

TYPES OF AEROPLANES

relative angles of incidence, are plainly shown in the side elevation, Fig. 58.

It was found that while these floats caused considerable disturbance of the water, especially at low speed, there was no difficulty in attaining a speed of 45 miles an hour on the surface. At as low a rate of travel as 10 miles an hour, the hydroplanes, which are normally submerged when the machine is at rest, rose to the surface, and as the speed increased, only the rear edges of the two main floats were required to support the machine. The aeroplane readily attained sufficient speed to rise in the air, for, as the speed increased and the floats emerged from the water, their head resistance diminished,

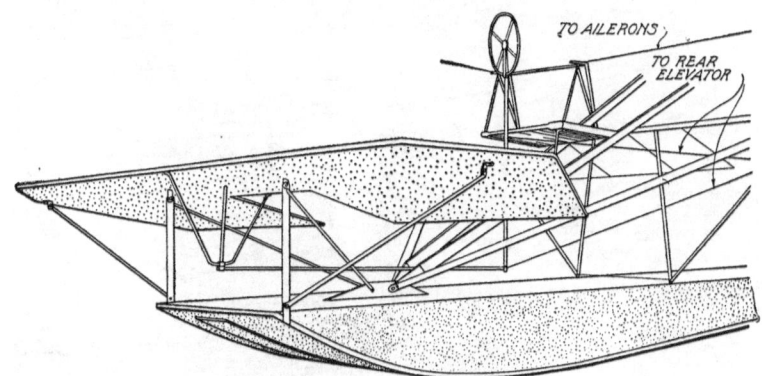

Fig. 59. Diagram of Pontoon on Curtiss' Latest Hydroaeroplane

and there were only the skin friction of the water on a very small area, plus the air resistance, to be overcome.

At the first try-out, while traveling over the water at a high rate of speed, Curtiss found himself approaching the land, and to avoid running ashore, he turned the horizontal rudder sharply upward, with the result that the machine rose from the water with perfect ease. Succeeding flights demonstrated that there was no difficulty in arising from the water and alighting upon it as often as desired. The machine developed a maximum speed of 50 miles an hour in the air, as compared with 45 miles per hour on the surface of the bay. But the great fuss stirred up by these original floats as the machine got under way preparatory to rising, and the fact that they were not suited to anything but a calm surface, caused them to be discarded shortly afterward. They were replaced by a large single float, 12 feet long by 2 feet wide and 12 inches deep, Fig. 59. This was built entirely of wood and resembles a common flat-bottomed boat or scow, the top being covered with canvas to prevent the entrance of water. Three feet from the forward end, the bottom curved upward sharply, forming a smooth bow the entire width of the float, while at the rear it was inclined downward in a similar manner. This single float is placed under the biplane in such a position that the major portion of the weight of the machine and the aviator is slightly aft of the center of

Fig. 60. Curtiss Hydroaeroplane About to Rise from the Water

the float, which causes the latter to rise slightly forward when resting normally on the surface, thus providing the necessary angle for hydroplaning. The weight of the new float is but 50 pounds, or less than half that of the two large floats previously employed. Trials of the biplane fitted with the new floats showed an astonishing difference in the amount of disturbance, practically no commotion being caused even when the machine was just getting under way, while the aeroplane rose from the surface even more readily than before. Fig. 60 shows one of this type just getting under way. Besides being much more compact and creating less resistance, this new float can also be employed for carrying articles or a passenger.

TYPES OF AEROPLANES

In order to prevent the aeroplane from listing, or tilting to one side or the other, an inclined brace 4 feet long by 3 inches wide, is fastened to the front edge of the lower plane at each end. Attached to each of these braces is an inflated rubber tube to give extra buoyancy to the ends of the machine, should it be tilted sufficiently to submerge them when skimming over the surface. By the use of these "water props" the aeroplane is prevented from wabbling from side to side, even though the main supporting plane is but two feet in width. A number of flights made with this arrangement demonstrated the necessity of altering the balance of the biplane, and the motor and

Fig. 61. Latest Model of Curtiss Hydroaeroplane Showing Two Propellers and Engine Ahead of Operator

propeller were accordingly placed forward while the aviator's seat was located at the rear of the main plane, just the reverse of the standard Curtiss machine.

All of Curtiss' experimenting with the hydroaeroplane was carried out with what was practically a standard biplane of his own make, mounted upon floats. As the result of the experience thus gained, he subsequently designed a machine specially for this service. This is shown in Fig. 61, and the radical departure it represents from the standard Curtiss type will be apparent at a glance. Instead of the single propeller at the rear, two tractor screws are employed. These are carried in bearings mounted on twin steel tubular struts and are driven through chains running in steel tubes by an eight-cylinder, V-type, water-cooled motor placed in the forward part of the boat or hydroplane float. Twin steel tubular struts are also employed to reinforce the structure just back of the propeller supports. The lower plane is cut away at the center and the aviator's seat is placed in the boat, bringing the center of gravity of the biplane very low. Tubular braces are run from each side of the boat to points on the under side of the lower plane, and fastened to the steel plates holding the propeller supporting struts, while bamboo braces run from the upper plane to the bow of the boat on either side, thus stiffening the entire structure. Both the elevator and the direction rudder are placed at the rear, the remainder of the construction not differing particularly from the standard Curtiss machine. Some very successful flights have been made with this hydroaeroplane.

Naval Trials with Improved Type. A great many very successful flights were made with this Curtiss hydroaeroplane as redesigned, the chief of these being the flight made by Curtiss over San Diego Bay from North Island to the U. S. S. Pennsylvania. He alighted upon the surface alongside the cruiser and the machine was hoisted aboard by means of one of the launch cranes. In addition to the reversed positions of the motor and aviator, numerous other changes were made, so that the machine is really a special type in itself. The front horizontal or elevating rudder of the Curtiss machine was removed entirely, and a special twin V-finned tail with a vertical fin in the center placed at the after end of a tail frame, similar in appearance to the *fuselage* framing of the French monoplanes. Stabilizing fins running from the lower main plane to the props already described, were also added. Special balancing planes were also placed at the rear of the main planes, half way between them and the float underneath. The removal of the forward elevating rudder made it possible to hoist the aeroplane aboard the vessel so that the aviator could climb on the deck, the modified design of the machine making it particularly adaptable for naval work, though Mr. Curtiss did not like the arrangement owing to the blast of air from the propeller constantly striking his face and the interference with his view forward caused by the new location of the motor. The demonstration so favorably impressed the naval authorities that a new machine of this type has since been purchased from the Curtiss factory and a number of naval officers were trained in its handling at Hammondsport during the summer of 1911. On one trial Lieutenant Ellyson, the navy's first qualified aviator, carried Captain Chambers, in charge af the aeronautical work of the navy, on a flight the length of Lake Keuka, a distance of 40 miles, while on a measured course the machine covered 16 miles in 18 minutes, carrying the two officers. Trials were later transferred to the Chesapeake, where Lieutenants Ellyson and Towers, of the Naval Aviation Corps, flew 140 miles from Annapolis to Fortress Monroe in two hours twenty-seven minutes, or at the rate of close to 60 miles an hour. For most of the distance an elevation of 1,000 feet was maintained. The machine was fitted with a new device brought out during the summer of 1911, which permits either the pilot or the aviator to assume control of the machine as desired. During the flight in question, the officers frequently shifted the control wheel from one to the other, demonstrating the rapidity and effectiveness with which the change could be made.

In order to utilize the advantages of the aeroplane for naval service to the fullest extent, a simple and rapid method of launching the machine from the vessel, without the necessity of encumbering the deck with special contrivances for that purpose, is essential, so that the later experiments carried out at Hammondsport with this end in view were of far greater importance than the most successful flights. Lieutenant Ellyson has devised a method by which a hydro-aeroplane may be launched at sea directly from the vessel, without the loss of time necessary to put it overboard and permit it to rise from the surface of the water. Heavy seas often continue for some time after the wind occasioning them has subsided, and under such conditions, it would not be safe to launch an aeroplane from the side of the vessel, though it might be quite feasible for the machine to return alongside and be hoisted aboard, after having taken flight directly from the vessel itself. The new method simply calls for the use of cables stretched from the boat deck or superstructure of the ship, to the bow. One of these is a main wire cable down which the aeroplane slides to gather momentum for rising, while the others are merely auxiliary wires at the sides and parallel to the main cable, to maintain the machine in balance on the latter during its downward slide. These auxiliary wires support the outer ends of the wings until the machine acquires sufficient headway to maintain its own equilibrium by means of its balancing planes. This rigging does not interfere in any way with the working of the armament and is arranged so that it can either be left permanently in place ready for immediate use, or may be quickly stowed away, the cables simply being hooked in heavy eye bolts and stretched taut to make them ready for use. This system enables the machine to be launched when a high sea would make it impossible to arise directly from the surface after being lowered overboard. The experiments carried out at San Diego in connection with the U. S. S. Pennsylvania demonstrated that the hydroaeroplane could be landed alongside and hoisted aboard in a wind of 10 knots and with a 4-knot tide running, the sea conditions being too rough for successful launching. Ability to get away from the ship at the crucial moment is regarded as being by far the most important point in the practical use of the aeroplane by the navy, since the wrecking or even the loss of the machine after the desired information had been obtained would be considered of minor importance. With the new launching apparatus, it is also possible for the ship to steam head into the wind at any desired speed, thus securing the necessary conditions for quick launching.

To thoroughly test this method, a platform was erected 150 feet from the shore of Lake Keuka and the necessary cables stretched from it to the water. The main cable was a $\frac{3}{4}$-inch steel rope made fast to a pile driven in the lake 250 feet distant and submerged so that the aeroplane could pass over it without damage. The machine employed was the regulation navy type of Curtiss hydroaeroplane, equipped with a 75-horse-power motor, fitted with the new Curtiss double control system and capable of carrying two persons at high speed. Its total weight is 1,200 pounds. The bottom of the pontoon under the hydroaeroplane carries a grooved runner, 1 inch wide by $1\frac{3}{4}$ inches deep, lined with sheet iron throughout its length and reinforced with iron bands at each end to form a durable bearing surface, while the outer ends of each lower plane were equipped with light irons, forming a bearing surface to engage the balancing wires strung on either side of the main supporting cable. The main cable was passed over a pair of shears 16 feet high, and fitted with a small platform from which the motor of the machine could be started. The grade was about 10 per cent. A simple releasing device was provided to start the machine on its downward slide, this consisting of a short length of rope fastened to the bow of the pontoon (also variously termed the float or hydroplane) and fitted with an eye through which passes a toggle pin connecting this short piece with a rope made fast to the legs of the shears. A sharp jerk on this rope pulled the toggle pin and released the machine, which quickly gathers headway under the combined force of gravity and the thrust of the propeller. During the trials, the machine was first floated on the lake and then hauled up on the cable. The prevailing wind was about 10 miles an hour, its direction slightly quartering against the line of flight, the trial apparatus naturally not possessing the mobility of a vessel at sea, as the latter could always be headed directly into the wind. In the first trials, two men held lines running to the outer ends of each wing to make certain that the machine would maintain its balance until sufficient headway was gained, but this assistance was found unnecessary. The machine rose easily from the cable after having traveled a distance of about 150 feet, attaining a speed of 30 miles an hour just before lifting. Numerous trials were carried out with unvarying success, demonstrating that the length of cable required is so short as to make the fitting of the new launching apparatus possible even on the smallest cruisers, as with the advantage of the head wind created by the speed of the vessel, the aeroplane could rise almost directly from the cable without having to take advantage of the full force of gravity by gliding down its entire length before beginning its flight. In the opinion of Captain Chambers, another year will see the hydroaeroplane developed to such an extent that each battleship of the American navy may have its own flying machine.

Combination Land and Water Type. Since bringing out the type of hydroaeroplane purchased by the navy, Curtiss has been experimenting with still further improvements, the new machine being equipped with wheels in addition to the large float. There are only two of these wheels, one at either side of the float about under the center of the lower main plane, the forward third wheel of the standard machine having been discarded. These wheels are pulled up out of the way by means of a hinged brace which runs from the wheel hubs to the front beam. The elevating rudder has been placed extremely low, at a level about midway between the lower main plane and the deck of the pontoon, while there is also a small auxiliary hydro-surface just forward of the pontoon and under its bow. A Curtiss standard eight-cylinder, V-type, 50-horse-power motor supplies the energy and drives the machine at a speed of 45 to 50 miles an hour over the water.

Curtiss Family Hydroaeroplane. As the result of his success in developing the hydroaeroplane for naval use, Mr. Curtiss has brought out a type designed for pleasure flying. Owing to the fact that it is intended to carry several passengers, this has been dubbed the "family hydro." It consists of a standard Curtiss biplane mounted directly on a single open boat of unusual size without any intermediate framing, so that the lower plane rests directly on top of the boat amidships. The passengers are seated in the bow of the boat just forward of the main lower plane, while the motor is mounted just underneath the upper plane, so as to allow the propeller sufficient clearance over the back of the boat and keep it out of the spray thrown up when the machine is skimming the surface rapidly. The side floats, or inflated tubes, employed on the previous machines to maintain them in lateral balance when skimming, are also a feature of the new passenger-carrying hydroaeroplane, which is said to handle as easily and safely as a fast motorboat, while having the advantage of the latter in that its lifting ability permits it to travel over rough water or to rise above it entirely. It is also capable of rising from and alighting upon the ground as well as on the water, as it is equipped with the folding two-wheel chassis just described in connection with another type of Curtiss hydroaeroplane.

Burgess Hydroaeroplane. It was only natural that W. S. Burgess, the well-known yacht designer, who some time ago forsook that field to take up the building of the Burgess-Wright biplanes, should also devote attention to the development of the hydroaeroplane. So far as the machine itself is concerned, it is of the usual Burgess-Wright two-propeller headless type, driven by a four-cylinder motor. The water supporting surface consists of two hydroaeroplanes 14 feet wide by 2 feet long and having a draft of 10 inches at their deepest point. They are designed to meet the water so as to create the minimum of head resistance or disturbance and are fastened comparatively close together under the center of the machine. They are of the single-step hydroplane type much used in racing motor-boat design and are heavily trussed and reinforced to give them a high factor of safety. The first trials of the new machine showed it to be very speedy on the surface and with ample lifting power to raise the boats from the water. During one trial, Mrs. F. G. Macomber, Jr., was carried, she being the first woman to make a flight in a hydroaeroplane over the Atlantic. Flights were made under varying conditions ranging from a perfect calm to a 25-mile wind, and it was noticeable that the winds which would bother a skilled aviator over the uneven ground gave the novice no concern in the new hydroaeroplane over the water. In fact, the advantage is so great that doubtless most of the teaching henceforth at the Burgess school will take the form of over-water flights, as one of the greatest difficulties that both the manufacturer and the instructor have had to encounter is that of impressing upon the untrained novice, the importance of attempting to fly only in the most favorable weather.

Brown Hydroaeroplane. A departure from either of the foregoing types is found in the Brown hydroaeroplane which was built on the Chesapeake and has been successfully flown there. The aeroplane itself is of the original Henri Farman type, having ailerons attached to the outer rear trailing edges of both main planes, direction rudder at the rear, elevator of the single-plane type in front, and the propeller at the rear edge of the lower main plane, the aviator sitting just forward of the motor. The spread is 32 feet and the length 31 feet, the planes themselves being $3\frac{1}{2}$ feet wide, while the distance between them is $4\frac{1}{2}$ feet, this also representing the chord. The main planes are constructed in five sections and can be removed or replaced without the necessity of rebuilding an entirely new upper or lower main plane, as is usually the case. The camber of the curve is 3 inches and it is located one third of the distance back from the forward edge. Power is supplied by a 45-horse-power motor directly driving a 7-foot 6-inch propeller with a 5.9-foot pitch. The power plant, fuel, and water weigh about 450 pounds, and the hydroplanes and their braces 175 pounds, the complete weight being 1,000 pounds. There are three supporting hydroplanes with a total displacement of 27 cubic feet. They are designed with such an easy bow curve that they would skim the surface after the machine had not gone more than 50 feet, and would leave the water the moment the machine

142 TYPES OF AEROPLANES

attained a good speed. The first hydroplanes employed were of sheet metal and of crude construction, but in spite of this drawback the machine showed itself capable of 40 to 50 miles an hour on the surface and 52 miles an hour in the air.

Detroit Flying Fish. A type of machine that is part hydroplane and part aeroplane is that recently placed on the market by a Detroit manufacturer, Fig. 62. It is aptly termed the "flying fish", as it is designed to do most of its travel by skimming over the water, seldom, if ever, rising more than 8 or 10 feet above the surface. It consists of a water-tight steel and aluminum tank, 2 feet deep, 5

Fig. 62. Detroit Flying Fish

feet 7 inches wide, and 7 feet 2 inches long. This tank, or pontoon, has a sloping bow, but is otherwise square. Mounted on this pontoon on steel tubing supports, about 6 feet high, are monoplane wings, or rather a single plane of 26 feet spread by 6 feet 6 inch depth. The supporting surface is of oil-treated canvas. The horizontal and vertical rudders are combined, the four-vaned plane of canvas being mounted at the end of a steel tube frame. This is the machine's aerial tail. Extending back of the hull and connected with the frame above it by tubing, is the marine tail. It consists of two steel arms and a wood transverse member a foot wide. On this flat board, 5 feet 7 inches in length by 1 foot wide, and $\frac{1}{2}$ inch thick, the machine is expected to fly, or rather travel. When the speed is sufficient—

and the machine is expected to attain a rate of 65 to 70 miles an hour —the plane is designed to lift the hull out of water entirely, only the wood and steel tail touching at intervals to steady the flight. A powerful eight-cylinder, V-type, water-cooled motor drives a 6-foot two-bladed wood propeller through a chain. At the rear of the hull is placed a cane seat with a high back, the cockpit being directly in front of it. The control levers are mounted at either side. Complete, the machine weighs only 750 pounds. The first model made 65 miles an hour over the ice of Lake Michigan, scarcely touching the surface, although equipped with a much smaller motor. Though having every appearance of being a marine aeroplane, the machine is really more a hydroplane equipped with wings.

Transatlantic Hydroaeroplane. As the result of his long-continued and successful experiments with the hydroaeroplane, Glenn H. Curtiss who believes that the crossing of the Atlantic in one of these machines would be quite possible is ready to build a special aeroplane for the purpose, and Roger K. Wallace, chairman of the Royal Aero Club, London, is making efforts to raise £20,000 ($100,000) as a prize for the first America-to-England flight. H. N. Atwood, who made the first long-distance, cross-country flight in America—St. Louis to Boston—in 1911, has seriously proposed the undertaking, as has also James V. Martin, who is a master mariner, as well as a licensed aviation pilot. Mr. Martin gives the following data regarding the trip:

The two chief difficulties are the carrying of sufficient fuel for the 2,000-mile flight, and the question of navigation; the latter is more serious than it may at first appear as no great error would be necessary to divert the aeroplane from its course to such an extent as to largely increase the distance and risk a shortage of fuel. On this point, Prof. R. W. Willson, of Harvard, who has made a life study of the problems of nautical astronomy and aerial navigation, is authority for the following:

> Given an engine which can be absolutely relied on, a properly constructed aeroplane, and favorable weather, I see no reason why the transatlantic passage of less than 2,000 miles might not be successfully made. Assuming that the mechanical difficulties of keeping the aeroplane in motion can be successfully overcome, the navigating officer would first have to select the course to be followed, and by taking the ocean steamship "lane," the chances of loss in case of disaster would be materially lessened. The distance

144 TYPES OF AEROPLANES

from Newfoundland to England is the minimum. But the problem of navigating an aeroplane is a peculiar one. The path of a ship through the water is determined with considerable accuracy by the course and distance sailed as determined by the compass and the log, while astronomical observations are used to check this "dead reckoning" at stated intervals, unless prevented by clouds or fog. The aeroplane, on the contrary, may often be at a sufficient altitude to allow of an accurate determination of its position by observation, when a low-lying fog would cut off from a ship below the sight of the horizon necessary for the usual observation of the sun's altitude. The difficulty with the aeroplane is to keep account of its speed and its direction of motion, which is, of course, more dependent on the motion of the body of air in which it flies than the course of the ship is dependent on the ocean current or its leeway caused by the wind and sea. Since there is no treatise published on the sub-

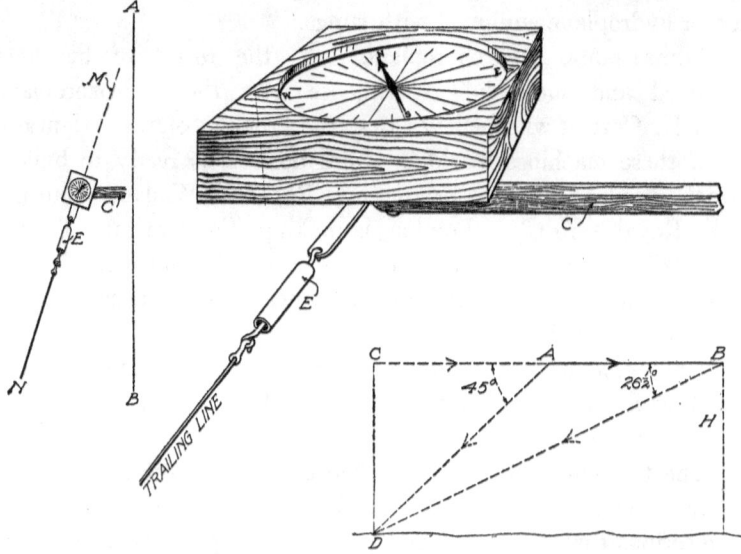

Fig. 63. Device for Determining Direction and Speed of an Aeroplane in Flight

ject, I would venture the following suggestions, which should naturally be thoroughly tested on the preliminary trials that should certainly precede any well-advised attempt to make the journey.

In the first place, it should be definitely ascertained if, in good weather, the sea horizon is sufficiently defined for sextant observations at the height at which the passage would be made, remembering, of course, that the height could be decreased, if desired, merely for the purpose of making observations. On the occasions on which I have had an opportunity to observe the horizon at elevations of 2,000 to 5,000 feet, the uncertainty has been so great that I should estimate the error at 20 miles. Special refraction tables might be necessary at the height of a mile, though it is true that an uncertainty of 20 miles is of far less importance to the airman than to the seaman, and that his problem of a land fall is in some respects simpler. There should be no diffi-

Intentionally blank as was the original edition.

VIEW OF A VOISIN HYDROAEROPLANE JUST RISING FROM THE SURFACE OF THE SEINE NEAR PARIS

TYPES OF AEROPLANES 145

culty in making observations of the altitudes of the heavenly bodies if the development of the science of aviation makes it necessary. For determining the course and distance, it would be possible to learn something at any time when the aeroplane could be made to pass nearly over some well-marked point in the water beneath—how conspicuous such objects would have to be and how frequently they would be visible is uncertain. Patches and streaks of smooth water and perhaps other objects easily visible at a mile or two away, and sufficiently stationary to be used from a rapidly moving aeroplane for the observations of a four-point bearing, are not uncommon. By observing the time when the object D, Fig. 63, is directly beneath and again when it is left behind and depressed 45 degrees below the horizon, the distance traveled in the observed interval of time is equal to the height of the aeroplane, hence the speed may be determined while a compass bearing of the object taken at the same observation gives the course. Of course, all the methods of using two bearings and the elapsed time, which are useful at sea, may be modified in a similar way, the problem being the reverse of the nautical, the distance of the aeroplane from the water being used to find the speed, instead of the speed being used to find an unknown distance. Of course, it is necessary to know the height and for this purpose a reliable barometer should be carried, and it has been suggested that the often unreliable aneroid be checked by finding the dip of the horizon and then computing the height; this would be possible with a fair degree of accuracy at moderate heights and with a clear horizon by means of the navigator's prism. As proposed by Vaniman, the white caps can be employed as points of observation, while a steamer might also serve for this purpose, by making allowance for its speed. Doubtless, a method that would prove of great assistance involves no observations at all: This would be simply to obtain "positions" by wireless from passing steamers, and there are so many of the latter in the transatlantic lane that communication would always be easy. To ascertain direction and speed, a light line N with a float might be trailed in the water, and it is probable that only a very small float would be necessary, the large amount of line dragging furnishing the necessary friction. If the direction and force of the wind were constant at all levels from the aeroplane to the water's surface, or if conditions were such that all points of the line lay in the same plane, this plane would indicate pretty accurately the direction of flight, while conditions could be so arranged that the vertical angle at which the line left the aeroplane would give a measure of the speed. The latter might also be ascertained by the use of a small patent log at the end of a line, or by measuring the comparative tension of a spring inserted in the line where it left the aeroplane, as shown at E, Fig. 63. This line would be about 2 miles long and the aeroplane would be maintained at a height of 3,000 feet during the observation.

Probable Features of Design. The special difficulty in such an extended trip by aeroplane is that of sustaining the weight of oil and fuel necessary to keep the engines running during the period required for the aeroplane to travel from St. Johns, Newfoundland, to the coast of Ireland, a distance of approximately 1,800 miles. Opinion varies as to the type of machine best adapted to make such a trip, some believing that extreme speed should be the chief consideration in the design, since a speedy machine would lessen the time and require less fuel on that account. Others believe that a slow, large-surface machine would be more reliable, since it would carry more weight per horse-power than the fast machine. Doubtless, a design between these two extremes would lend itself best to the purpose, that is, a machine sufficiently powerful, relative to its area, to have a speed of 50 miles per hour in order to afford control in gusty winds. In attempting to increase the speed beyond this, the resist-

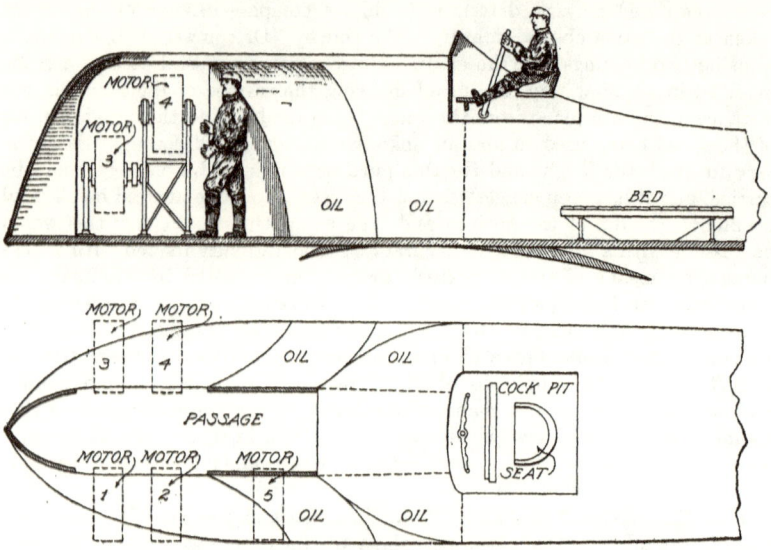

Fig. 64. Design of Transatlantic Hydroaeroplane

ance increases so disproportionately that a very substantial increase in the size and weight of every part of the aeroplane would be necessary. On the other hand, a large surface machine may be relatively inefficient by reason of its slowness and very dangerous on account of its sluggishness in control. The machine proposed is a biplane with a span of 100 feet by a chord of 10 feet, or an aspect ratio of 10 to 1, and it could be propelled by five 50-horse-power revolving motors, geared down to two tractor screws. This would give it a speed of 50 miles an hour and a weight-carrying capacity of 7,500 pounds, 4,500 pounds of which would be useful load, an allowance that would provide for the carrying of two pilots, one engineer, and sufficient fuel and oil to drive the aeroplane at 50 miles per hour for 36 hours. Each of the engines would be fitted with a friction clutch, enabling it to be cut out at any time for inspection or adjustment. All five motors would be used to attain the necessary altitude and speed with full load, but as the fuel was consumed and the machine lightened, one after the other could be stopped, thus utilizing the fuel and oil to the greatest advantage. It might be possible to sustain the machine with only two of the motors running after most of the fuel and oil had been consumed.

The sketch, Fig. 64, shows a portion of the enclosed fuselage which is directly under the normal center of pressure. Sufficient fuel and oil could be stored here in tanks so arranged as to leave a 2-foot passage fore and aft from the cabin, just under the pilot's cockpit, to the engine room. The extreme width of the fuselage is 8 feet and it affords 6 feet clear headroom, the engines being placed on both sides of the enclosed central passage, making every one of them accessible. They would all be working in free air and would drive to a central transmission shaft, from which the tractor screws are driven by encased silent chains. The clutches would permit of throwing any one of the engines in or out of operation at will, so that the cleaning of the valves and spark plugs should be as simple a matter during the passage as at rest, though for that matter, experience has shown that a 36-hour run of a Gnome revolving motor that is clean and otherwise in good condition does not involve any particular need for inspection or adjustment. In a machine as large as that proposed, the passage fore and aft of the engine attendant would hardly be perceptible to the control of the operator. The resistance of such a machine should be quite low, since it has an enclosed streamline form throughout and since the single row of struts in the normal center of pressure of the planes greatly reduces the wire and strut resistance common to most biplanes. Though large, the controls are all of the balanced type, so there would be no difficulty in their handling by one man in gusty winds. Two boats would be employed as floats, the flat-bottom hydroplane principle being superfluous where the aeroplane has excess lifting capacity to raise them from the water. While light, these would be made so as to serve as lifeboats in case of emergency. If it became necessary to alight on the water in midocean, this could be accomplished in a comparatively smooth sea without great risk, and unless the seas were new and short, the aeroplane could take to the air again with little trouble.

It is practically certain that were this aeroplane to travel at its normal speed in the right direction for 30 hours at an altitude of about 5,000 feet, the passage of the Atlantic would be accomplished. A height of 5,000 feet would furnish an atmosphere comparatively free from the gusty surface winds and clear of all fog, so that, with a polaris instrument and a special azimuth table, it would not be necessary to depend on the compass for direction. This height would also give a greatly extended horizon (80-mile radius at 4,900 feet) so that there would hardly be a time on the passage over on the steamship route to Europe when some vessel would not be within the 160-mile range of vision. Noting the course followed by these vessels would also afford a check on the other methods of navigation employed. A glance at the pilot chart of the North Atlantic for July and August shows that there is a very dependable westerly movement of the upper air currents, so that it would be possible to rely upon a greatly increased speed of the aeroplane due solely to the wind.

AERONAUTICAL MOTOR

Early Types. In the general acclaim that has greeted man's final conquest of the air, the chief contributing factor that has made it possible has to a great extent been overlooked. Power in sufficiently concentrated form appears to have been the only thing lacking for at least half a century past to have made possible for two or three generations what has been the reality of less than a decade. Not that a perfected light-weight power unit was sufficient in itself, as there are numerous principles governing flight that have been discovered only in recent years, but it was the one thing needed to lift a heavier-than-air machine from the ground and to keep it in the air. With its aid, it appears to be more than probable that the problem of the sustaining plane and the difficulties of equilibrium would have found a solution at a much earlier date. That at least one far-sighted investigator had realized the possibilities of the monoplane is shown by Henson's machine of 1843. Henson's steam engine was justly considered a marvel for its anticipated numerous features that are generally considered as the development of but very recent years in this form of prime mover.

But despite the great improvements it embodied and the fact that it could be operated continuously on but 20 gallons of water, its output was but 20 horse-power for a total weight of 600 pounds. Compare this low limit of 30 pounds per horse-power, of sixty years ago, with the 1.75 pounds per horse-power of the 140-horse-power Gnome motor and the advance that has been achieved will be appreciated. "Continuously" in this connection meant just what it does today—as long as the fuel holds out—and as coal is not only excessively heavy but likewise very inefficient for its weight when burned under a boiler, as compared with gasoline used directly in an internal combustion motor, it is evident that even with the great supporting power afforded by the 4,500 square feet of surface of the main planes, Henson's craft could not have carried sufficient coal to permit of much of a flight.

Copyright, 1912, by American School of Correspondence.

That extremely light weight was not the only desideratum is shown by Maxim's engine of 1892, which totaled only 600 pounds for an output of more than 360 horse-power, or actually less than 2 pounds per horse-power by an ample margin. The boiler weighed in the neighborhood of 1,800 pounds. The engines were compound and by an ingenious regulating device the high-pressure steam passed direct to the low-pressure cylinders when the boiler pressure exceeded 300 pounds per square inch, for which it was designed. This increased the output to 400 horse-power, the piston speed being 750 feet per minute, or more than a third less than what is now common practice with the internal combustion motor. While Maxim's engine, boiler plant, and equipment were extremely light for the power output, they had to work under the great disadvantage inseparable from the use of steam—that is, the low thermal efficiency of burning fuel under a boiler and the consequently increased amount that has to be carried. While ample sustaining area had been provided for this and similar purposes (4,500 square feet) the weight of the fuel necessary for a comparatively short flight would easily have exceeded that of the entire power plant. Apart from this the space *required* for the machinery was out of all proportion to the total space *available*, particularly as it would have been more or less essential to be able to get at the various parts of the plant during a flight.

In this case, the saving in weight was accomplished only at the expense of other disadvantages that would have rendered the final result immature had the machine been developed to a point where it could be actually employed in flight. But in looking back over the history of attempts at power-driven airships, it will be apparent that weight has been by far the greatest deterrent to success. For instance, Giffard's steam engine and boiler employed for driving a dirigible, in 1852, weighed 350 pounds, including coal and water, for an output of 3 horse-power. Dupuy De Lôme's dirigible of about twenty years later was a step backward in this respect, in that human power was employed. This meant a weight of close to 2,000 pounds per horse-power, while the maximum power would naturally be available only for short periods. The Tissandier electric power plant of 1882 had inherent limitations of so serious a nature where weight and restricted traveling radius were concerned that it can scarcely be considered as more than a freak. No one conversant with the drawbacks inseparable from electric power for this purpose would have made the attempt. The 1½-horse-power motor and its battery of primary cells weighed 500 pounds and the type employed (bichromate cells) was such that the power was available only for a very limited period. Despite these disadvantages the first dirigible to attain any measure of success was driven by electricity. This was the La France of 1884, equipped with an 8-horse-power motor, which has been referred to already in the earlier part of the work.

To Santos-Dumont doubtless belongs the credit of being the first to realize the great possibilities of the gasoline motor for aerial navigation. How he derived his inspiration from the motorcycle engine and the numerous attempts he made with dirigibles have already been dwelt upon. His first motor weighed between 15 and 20 pounds to the horse-power and, like everything he has been responsible for in connection with aeronautics, was designed on a very small scale, its total output not exceeding 4 horse-power. Although a pioneer in the field, Santos-Dumont has not been responsible for the subsequent development of the gasoline motor. At the time he took it up, the first stages of its evolution for automobile propulsion were being passed through and the difficulties encountered were so numerous and, in many instances, of such a puzzling nature, that it is easy to realize why attention was concentrated on perfecting it for a purpose that did not involve the further problems of successful flight. The history of the past twenty years shows that the development of the automobile motor was no small task in itself. With this fairly accomplished, the next step was principally one of refinement and adaptation.

GENERAL MOTOR REQUIREMENTS

To bring about its required refinement and adaptation in the aeronautic motor seems a comparatively simple matter, but that it has not proven so in fact will be realized upon reviewing the innumerable expedients that have been adopted by different builders to meet the conditions, and the many departures that these have involved from what may be termed automobile practice. In fact, in the few years devoted to its design, practically a new type of motor has been evolved. In order to obtain a clear understanding of how this has been brought about, it is first necessary to realize how exacting the requirements are and of just what they consist. Following this with a study of some of the more representative types that are now built for aeronautical use will reveal how the various principles laid down have been applied in each case. Before taking this up in detail, it may make matters a little clearer to briefly compare the automobile and the aeronautic motor.

Automobile vs. Aeronautical Motor. Generally speaking, the trend of the past few years, where the automobile motor is concerned, has been to develop a power unit of more uniform torque and of increased efficiency. The more general adoption of the six-cylinder motor and the increase in the length of the stroke, as compared with the bore, afford evidence of this. Little or no attention is now given to the question of weight saving, apart from any reduction that the use of integrally cast inlet manifolds, more direct water circulation, and similar efforts at cutting down the length of piping, may have been responsible for. Weights have reached a point where any substantial reduction could be brought about only by a more or less radical change in methods of construction, as well as the use of much more expensive materials. There would be little to warrant the increased cost of a much lighter motor, besides which it would involve the use of a higher speed to develop the same power with less weight. More important than any of these considerations is the fact that reliability suffers as the weight decreases.

Consequently, the tendency in the development of the automobile motor during the past few years has been mainly along the line of increased efficiency with practically no regard for the matter of weight, while the chief aim of the builder of aeronautical motors has been to get the latter down to the minimum. But that weight saving is not the sole governing factor in the design of a successful motor for flying is amply evidenced by the fact that the first aeroplane ever to make a flight—that of the Wright Brothers—was equipped with a comparatively heavy motor. Nor has this motor undergone any radical changes since it was first adopted several years ago. Like the Wright biplane of standard type, it is not only heavier but develops less power than many other experimenters have thought necessary for the purpose. But in it efficiency and reliability have been developed to a high degree and these vastly important qualities are very largely responsible for the numerous successful flights and for the high standing which the Wright machines enjoy in the field of aviation.

It did not take long, however, to reach a point in the development of the aeroplane where the speed of 40 miles an hour of which the Wright biplane was capable, was considered slow. The demand was accordingly for more and more power—the greater the driving force available, the smaller the sustaining surface needed, with a consequent reduction in the wind resistance. To meet this demand and still keep the weight down, every imaginable expedient has been resorted to by designers.

It has been said that the most important problem in the design of a light motor is the correct choice of type, but when what has already been accomplished in this field is passed in review, it will be found that there are aeronautical motors of every type ever tried on the automobile and many for which the latter was not responsible. Not all of them are successful, of course, but many of such widely differing types have attained such a measure of success that there is no telling what the advances of the next five years may be.

Fundamental Features of Design. *Short Stroke.* As an aeronautical motor of small bore and long stroke is much heavier in comparison to its power output than one in which these two dimensions are more nearly the same, design in this field has naturally gone back to automobile standards of several years ago when it was customary to build what are known as *square* motors, *i. e.*, those in which the bore and stroke are the same. In fact, it was nothing unusual for the bore to exceed the stroke. The advantages of a long stroke are increased efficiency and somewhat smoother running, the greater fuel economy and reduced vibration compensating for its inferior weight efficiency on the automobile. The majority of aeronautical motors are accordingly of the short stroke type, as the weight decreases very rapidly with a reduction in the length of the stroke. This was strikingly illustrated in the case of a large motor built for the Vanderbilt Cup race a few years ago. Its original dimensions were 7-inch bore by 7-inch stroke. In re-designing this motor, it was made 7 by 6 inches, the 1-inch reduction in the stroke being responsible for a saving of almost 200 pounds. The short-stroke motor has the further advantage of a low center of gravity.

Cost No Object. While compelled to reconcile numerous conflicting requirements, such as that of maximum reliability with the minimum weight, the designer of the aeronautical motor is not hampered so much by questions of cost. Consequently, many refinements of construction are available that could not be indulged in on the automobile motor. For instance, pistons are finished all over, inside and outside, and in some cases, the cylinders themselves are machined direct from a bar of solid steel at a cost many times greater than that of casting them of iron. Pistons in some cases are made of steel in order to attain the minimum thickness of wall, and every possible opportunity is taken advantage of to reduce weight, such as making the piston extremely short—even shorter than the stroke in some instances. Pressed steel is resorted to in the making of the connecting rods, or, where forgings are employed, they are simply riddled with holes to get rid of every ounce of metal.

Low Weight per Horse-Power. It must be borne in mind that, even at this early day, there are radically different standards among builders of aeroplanes. Some are constructed for purely sporting purposes. There are racing machines and touring machines, if the latter appellation be permissible. In the case of the former, the motor must develop a great amount of power for a comparatively short period. The fact that its construction is not particularly durable makes it possible to practically eliminate the question of any factor of safety in its parts. The latter are shaved down to the last fraction of an ounce and reliability is sacrificed in consequence, but before going into action the motor will be tuned up to its highest pitch, and if it will run long enough to cover a certain distance, that is all that is necessary.

Even aluminum has been employed for cylinders in rare instances, the bearing surface for the piston consisting of a thin cast-iron bushing forced into the aluminum casting. This has the great disadvantage of providing an aluminum explosion chamber and this metal loses its strength very rapidly as the temperature increases above a certain degree. It likewise involves the most expensive form of construction in that harder seats must also be employed for the valves, aluminum being entirely too soft for this purpose. Aluminum cylinder heads have also been employed with cast-iron or steel cylinders, but considerable trouble has been experienced with them owing to the great difference in the ratio of heat expansion between aluminum and cast iron or steel. Consequently, aluminum is no longer employed for such important parts.*

In addition to drilling the connecting rods, they are usually made very much shorter than in automobile practice, this being as low as 1.5 to 1.75 times the length of the stroke in motors of a type which are inherently well balanced by reason of their design, such as the six-cylinder vertical or the three-cylinder radial. It will seldom be found to exceed 2 to 2.25 times the stroke, the evil of increased friction of the piston against the cylinder walls due to the greater angularity of the short connecting rod being partly compensated for by offsetting the crank shaft with respect to the cylinder center. By this means, the pressure between the piston and cylinder wall are practically equalized on the compression and power strokes. The crank shaft, cam shaft, and even the valve lifters are drilled to reduce weight, the passages thus made eliminating every bit of unnecessary material, and affording convenient means of lubrication.

Automatically-Operated Inlet Valves. In this connection, a further reversion to what is now obsolete in the automobile motor is to be considered. This is the employment of automatically-operated inlet valves. In view of the fact that the aeronautical motor is seldom called upon in service, to vary its speed much, the high degree of flexibility to which the automobile motor has been developed is of no particular advantage and the shortcomings of the automatic type of valve are not a serious drawback. Probably no better instance of the employment of the automatic valve could be mentioned than the Gnome revolving-cylinder motors.

As is the case with most other important parts of the aeronautic motor, experience with the automobile has been drawn upon

---

*In general, however, aluminum or aluminum alloys have been used wherever it is possible to substitute these alloys for the heavier metals, such as iron or steel. The attempt to use them for casting the cylinders is not new, but aluminum itself is not suitable and difficulty has been found in making a proper alloy. But within the past year (1911) magnalium has been successfully employed for this purpose. This consists of pure aluminum with a slight percentage of the metal magnesium and the resulting alloy is not only denser but is about $12\frac{1}{2}$ per cent lighter than No. 12 aluminum, which consists of 93 per cent aluminum and 7 per cent copper, and has a specific gravity of 2.82. Magnalium accordingly weighs about one third as much as cast iron, while its thermal conductivity is seven to eight times greater, which greatly facilitates the cooling, especially of air-cooled engines. Unlike other aluminum alloys that have been employed for cylinders, tests have demonstrated that it gives better service than iron under the same conditions, as the bore of a magnalium cylinder takes on a mirror polish after only a few hours running, while the surface becomes very hard, as has been shown by the piston and rings of a poorly-bored cylinder becoming scored instead of the cylinder walls, as would usually be the case. Owing to its greater strength as well as reduced weight, it is also being employed for crank cases and other motor parts. The expense, however, would be prohibitive for anything but an aeronautical motor.

in the placing of the valves. The high-speed automobile motor has shown that the most advantageous valve arrangements are those in which the valves are in the head, and the so-called De Dion arrangement in which the valves are in line with each other. The reasons for this will be obvious when it is borne in mind that power is obtainable only with high speed where the valves are very liberally proportioned with regard to the cylinder bore. The combined inlet and exhaust valve, as developed on the Franklin air-cooled motor, has also been successfully applied to the aeronautic motor. Placing the valves in the head makes possible a very simple form of explosion chamber with a minimum of wall surface, with consequently increased thermal efficiency as compared with a form of cylinder head involving the use of valve pockets. The absence of the latter prevents the retention of spent gases, which gives increased power and fuel efficiency by reducing the tendency to premature ignition and by the use of higher compression pressures, which mean higher temperatures. The importance of this is obvious in view of the close weight limitations, and it is accordingly customary to employ higher compression pressures and speeds than in the automobile motor. Considerable interest at present attaches to the development of motors with rotary valves, or sliding sleeves and ports instead of valves, as in the Silent-Knight motor. So far little definite progress appears to have been made with the adaptation of this type of motor to the aeroplane, but numerous attempts are being made to evolve a practical form of rotary valve. The Knight motor itself does not offer any advantages of either simplicity or reduced weight so that the solution does not lie in that direction. An interesting development where the valves are concerned is found in the Adams-Farwell rotary motor in which the fuel is injected directly into the cylinder so that only one valve is necessary for each cylinder, and this can accordingly be made of very liberal diameter.

Standard Forms. The foregoing will suffice to give some idea of the difference in design and requirements between the aeronautic and the automobile motor, as well as those features of the latter which have been found advantageous in the new field. But so far, merely the parts themselves have been touched upon. It is in their assembly that the greatest divergence between the two standards is found. A glance over the numerous types that are sufficiently successful to remove them from the class of freaks, or mere proposed forms of construction that have not yet got beyond the paper stage, reveals the fact that every form of automobile motor that has ever been devised, has its counterpart among the newcomers, besides many which were never thought of in that connection. At one end of the list, there is the single-cylinder, air-cooled, motorcycle engine with which Santos-Dumont made his first attempts at dirigible propulsion, and at the other the highly refined and extremely ingenious fourteen-cylinder revolving Gnome motor, and the sixteen-cylinder **V**-shaped Antoinette. Between these two there is every form imaginable, even the two-cylinder horizontal opposed—that hybrid type of purely American origin and development, which foreign designers have always affected to despise, now being built by some French makers.

V-Form. The **V**-form, or 90-degree arrangement in which each pair of cylinders acts upon the same crank pin is very largely employed, both the Wright Brothers and Curtiss using this type in their more powerful machines. This arrangement permits of using a crank shaft of practically the same dimensions as a four-cylinder motor of the same size and is accordingly a great saving of weight. It also makes it possible to actuate all the valves from a single cam shaft, placed in the point of the **V**. From this arrangement, developments have led to the placing of three cylinders round a common crank case in the same vertical plane, also seven cylinders, three in one plane and four in another, as in the Esnault-Pelterie motor. Motors of this and similar arrangement are popularly referred to as "fan" and "star" types, and as all the cylinders act on the same crank pin, and the valve gear is reduced to its very simplest form, the saving in the weight of the crank shaft and crank case thus effected may readily be appreciated. When first attempted such motors did not give much promise of being practical, but as they have proved such a success in actual use, they are now one of the most popular forms of light-weight motors. Their chief disadvantage lies in the amount of space occupied in the direction across the cylinders, making them awkward for use in a dirigible for which a specially designed basket or car of greater weight is necessary.

Revolving Cylinder. Of even less promise at the outset was the revolving-cylinder motor, in spite of the fact that this type had been developed to a high degree of reliability and efficiency in the Adams-Farwell car. In addition to the other difficulties of design, the gyroscopic effect of the revolving mass had to be taken into consideration. It is well known that a large flywheel, revolving rapidly, forcibly resists any attempt to change its plane of rotation, advantage having been taken of this principle to balance a mono-rail car on its single support, and to keep torpedo boats steady in a seaway. While the revolving-cylinder motor dispenses with a flywheel, its revolving mass acts in the same rôle and plays the part of a gyroscope. Placing the latter horizontally would tend to increase the stability of an aeroplane without appreciably affecting its steering, but it was thought that where run in a vertical plane, as is necessary in order to obtain direct driving of the propeller, it would interfere with rounding curves of short radius. In the case of the Bleriot monoplanes with a revolving-cylinder Gnome motor right up forward, this does not appear to have been the case.

The chief advantage of this form of motor is its ability to dispense with a flywheel of any kind and its highly efficient air cooling. The latter has proved effective even with motors of comparatively large size, using an initial compression as high as 75 pounds to the square inch. One thing that the aeronautic engine designer does not have to contend with is dust and grit, so that in some instances all provisions for excluding it have been omitted.

Correspondingly greater difficulties are found, however, in the very important essential of lubrication and in the disposition of the piping. Special means have to be resorted to in order to insure the oiling of every moving part, particularly where centrifugal force enters to complicate the problem, as in the revolving cylinder motor. The lubricating system employed on the most representative type of the latter—the Gnome—is very effective but likewise very wasteful, as the oil is merely pumped through the motor and out into the air. But even in the V- and fan-shaped motors, where the cylinders stand directly over a crank case, as on an automobile motor, splash lubrication can not be employed. The last cylinders in the direction of the motor's rotation would receive very little oil. Fewer difficulties are encountered with the lubrication of motors having their cylinders placed horizontally and provided with a vertical crank shaft, as in the case of the Farcot and Clement engines.

The problem of properly arranging the piping is one that has led to numerous ingenious expedients, such as the employment of independent feed pumps for each cylinder on the eight- and sixteen-cylinder Antoinette, instead of a carbureter and the usual complicated inlet manifold. The latter is even more cleverly dispensed with in the case of the Gnome revolving motor, in which the mixture of air and gas is led through the hollow stationary crank shaft, the different cylinders receiving their supply through automatic inlet valves placed in the heads of the pistons. Where the flying machine is concerned the question of piping has one redeeming feature in that it is permissible to exhaust directly into the air. No one but the pilot of the aeroplane is inconvenienced by this, but the roar is such that it is quite likely a muffler will be a feature of the aeroplane motor before very long. On the dirigible, it would naturally be very dangerous to permit the escape of the exhaust anywhere near the gas bag, and accordingly a muffler is not only employed, but in some cases both the exhaust and the muffler are water cooled to make certain of reducing the temperature of the exhaust to a safe limit.

Flywheel. One other advantage enjoyed by the aeronautic motor is the fact that it is possible in most instances either to dispense with the use of a flywheel altogether, or reduce its weight to an almost negligible factor. But just as early investigators in the automobile field did not appreciate the full value of a heavy flywheel, so some designers of aeronautic motors do not consider it as important as it really is, in view of the particular types of motors they employ. Naturally, the conditions are quite different, as the propeller, though very light, is of large diameter and where directly attached to the crank shaft, does away with the necessity for a flywheel. In reviewing the large number of aeronautic motors now on the market, which is done more in detail a little further along, all shades of opinion will be found represented where this ordinarily important essential is concerned. They range from the conventional cast-iron flywheel of automobile type found on the Wright motor to a perforated-steel stamping, as in the Vivinus, or none at all, this being the case even on two-cylinder, horizontal-opposed motors in which the impulses are very intermittent. Examples of this are found in the Darracq and the Deuthil-Chalmers, both of French make.

Number of Cylinders and Weight Saving. Mention has already been made of the fact that there is a great diversity of opinion among aeroplane motor designers regarding the number of cylinders. As the weight of an engine may be roughly divided into cylinders and pistons on one hand, and the crank case and crank shaft on the other, assuming the conventional type it will be evident that the number of cylinders has a direct bearing on a most important factor—that of weight. In the numerous "spider" types of motors—if they may be so called—those in which the cylinders radiate from a very much abbreviated crank case with a correspondingly reduced crank shaft, this proportion naturally does not hold good. There are, of course, many other factors to be considered in the selection of the proper number of cylinders and it will be apparent from a study of the examples illustrated and described that designers have become very largely divided into three general classes: Those favoring what may be termed the conventional type, through its familiarity on the automobile—that is, the vertical or V-arrangement of cylinders; those who favor variations of the radial arrangement; and those who pin their faith to the revolving motor, this really being a subdivision of the second class.

Assuming a constant r. p. m. rate, both the power output and the weight of a cylinder increase as the product of D^2L, D denoting the diameter of cylinder, L the length of stroke; but if a constant piston speed be assumed, such as the standard of 1,000 feet per minute adopted by the Association of Licensed Automobile Manufacturers, on which to base motor ratings, the power, only, increases as the square, while the weight still increases as the product of D^2L. For moderate powers, the actual weight of the cylinders themselves appears to be but little influenced by their number, but it will be obvious that with any substantial increase in power, the weight of a smaller number of comparatively large cylinders should be less owing to the difficulty of reducing the thickness of the cylinders in proportion to their reduced dimensions. Experience has also shown that an engine with a few large cylinders has a very much higher factor of reliability and is easier to maintain, than one with a large number of small cylinders. While exceedingly fast time has been made over short stretches by an eight-cylinder V-type automobile motor—the 200-horse-power Benz—the fastest time in road races over long distances has thus far always been to the credit of the four- or six-cylinder motor of conventional design.

In addition to almost eliminating the crank case, the small multi-cylinder radial type also dispenses with the flywheel. This last, of course, is equally true of any motor employing six or more cylinders, as the multi-cylinder motor has the great advantage of producing a much more even turning moment. The drive is not continuous in a four-cylinder motor and, theoretically, it will not run at all without a flywheel. However, as the motor is directly connected to the propeller in the majority of instances, the latter is frequently found an efficient substitute. The more uniform torque of the motor with the greater number of cylinders is an added advantage in not imposing such severe stresses on connections as is the case where a smaller number of power units is employed. But the question of reliability enters here again, and as there is always the possibility of one or more cylinders of the multi-cylinder motor ceasing to fire, the reversal of stresses is then quite as great as with fewer cylinders.

Coming back to the question of weight saving—and at the present time it is evident that this is the chief controlling factor—let us see what are the steps leading up to the extremely light-weight modern motor. With the conventional arrangement, *i. e.*, cylinders vertically in a row, the weight of the crank case and crank shaft naturally increase in proportion to the cylinder capacity. By placing two rows of cylinders on the same crank case, as in the usual V-arrangement, the size of the crank case and crank shaft are but slightly larger than for the single row and the weight is cut almost in half. With eight cylinders at 90 degrees, the impulses are evenly spaced throughout the revolution, each pair of opposite cylinders being connected to one crank. But both impulse and mechanical balance are obtainable with as small a number as two cylinders, where the latter are arranged in what is known as the horizontal-opposed motor. The cylinders are slightly offset on opposite sides of a very short crank case and they act upon oppositely-disposed cranks—in other words, a two-throw crank shaft with the pins placed 180 degrees apart. This gives a very smooth running motor where two or any multiple of two cylinders are employed.

The advantages of this type are mentioned at greater length

here as they have only recently received that measure of appreciation which they deserve, as will be noted later in the successful motors of this type that are now in use. While the crank case and crank shaft of the horizontal-opposed motor increase in proportion to the increase in cylinder capacity, as compared with the diagonal or "spider" motor, the impulses are more even and the balance better than in the latter when using less than four cylinders.

In order to give the student a clearer idea of the manner in which the crank case and crank shaft are affected by the arrangement of the cylinders, with a corresponding reduction in the weight, the accompanying illustrations may be referred to. In these sketches the details have been intentionally omitted to

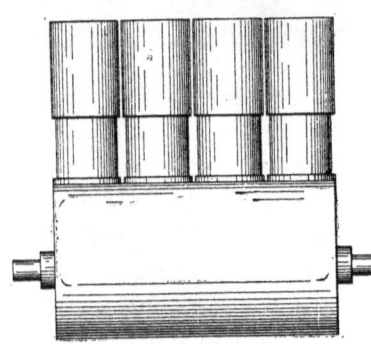
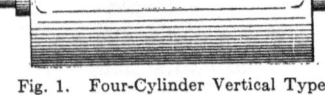
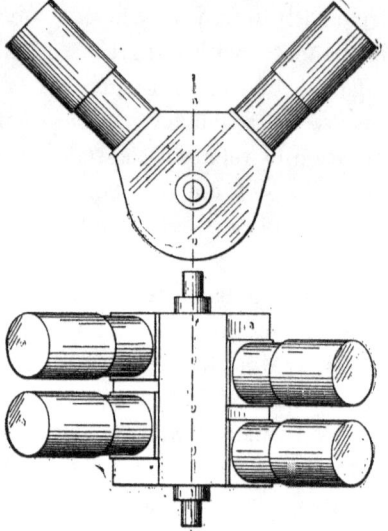

Fig. 1. Four-Cylinder Vertical Type   Fig. 2. V-Type of 2 to 16 Cylinders

prevent confusion; in actual practice, the space between the open ends of the cylinders on the crank case would be very much less than is here indicated. Fig. 1 is the conventional four-cylinder vertical motor as employed on the automobile. In this case the crank case must necessarily be slightly longer than that of the combined length of all the cylinders. The first step away from this is the V or 90-degree arrangement, as shown by Fig. 2, which illustrates the elevation and the plan. A similarly great reduction in the size of the crank case is effected by the horizontal-opposed arrangement, Fig. 3. Either the diagonal or opposed arrangement lends itself readily to two, four, six, eight, ten, or more cylinders, motors of the diagonal type being built with as many as sixteen cylinders. The first step away from this type is what has previously been referred to as the fan or radial arrangement as shown by Fig. 4, also as carried further by the addition of an extra pair of cylinders, as in Fig. 5.

This type naturally does not lend itself as well to water cooling as the first, second, and third arrangements illustrated, owing to the necessity of providing an independent jacket for every cylinder with the attendant complication in the piping. But for air cooling this type is ideal, as the cylinders are so spaced that each one re-

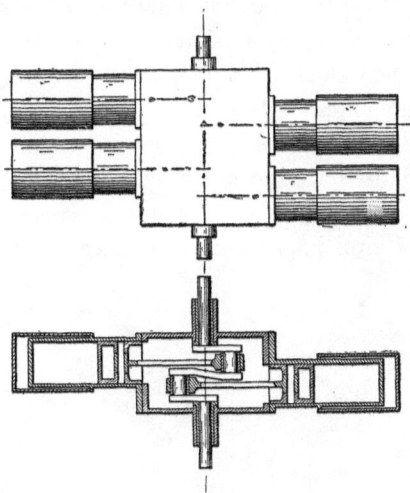

Fig. 3. Horizontal-Opposed Type

ceives an equal amount of air and none can radiate its heat directly to any of the others. The question of water versus air cooling is naturally again to the fore in this field, but under very different conditions for the latter than where the automobile is concerned. Whether directly

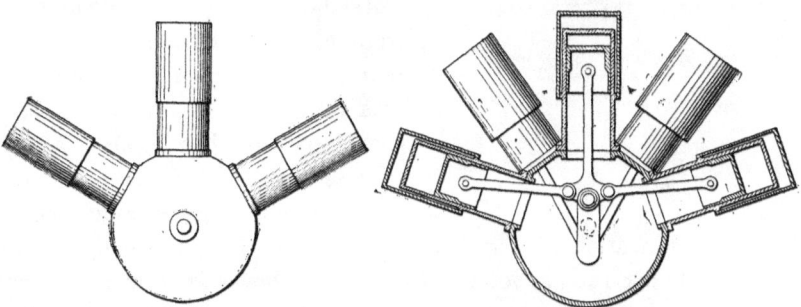

Fig. 4. Three-Cylinder Fan Type   Fig. 5. Five-Cylinder Fan Type

connected to the propeller or used to drive the latter through a transmission system, the motor itself is always completely exposed to the air and is cooled by a current averaging 40 to 60 miles an hour, or even greater. There would appear to be no possibility of ever working an air-cooled motor so hard, even on a warm summer day, as to cause it to be any less reliable on the score of danger of overheating, where the conditions are so favorable. On the other hand, with a multi-cylinder motor of the radial type, the complications of the piping system and connections would be a source of danger in themselves. For numerous reasons, none of which appears to have the slightest bearing on its efficiency or reliability as judged from a purely engineering viewpoint, the air-cooled motor has a rather limited use in the automobile field.

Where the aeroplane is concerned, however, weight saving is of vital importance and space is also a factor which must be closely considered. The designer of aeroplane motors is neither hampered by restriction of style nor by a commercial demand. He does not have to cater to a buying public that has to a great extent conventionalized automobile design, by refusing to aid the manufacturer whose designs in any way departed from the conventional. It accordingly seems quite probable that the question of air cooling will be worked out on the aeroplane motor from a purely engineering viewpoint. Even where the cylinders of a radial type of motor, such as that shown by Fig. 5, are placed so close together there should be no difficulty in properly cooling them.

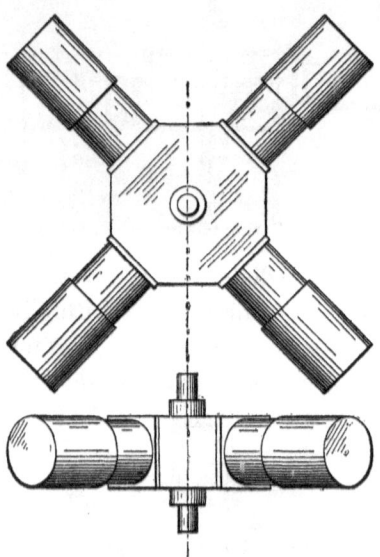

Fig. 6. Four-Cylinder Star Type

A modification of Fig. 4 is illustrated in Fig. 6, which shows a four-cylinder radial motor. In practice, however, four is not a good number for this type, as the impulses can not be evenly divided, which accounts for the general use of an odd number of cylinders in a radial arrangement. Such a motor can be satisfactorily balanced where the cylinders are evenly spaced about the circumference of the crank case, as all the connecting rods are attached to a common crank pin, and, therefore, form one revolving mass, which can be balanced by a suitable balance weight. But as the number of cylinders increases, the difficulty arises of attaching all the big ends of the connecting rod to one crank pin, without making the ends of the connecting rods unusually narrow or the pin itself over long. This is obviated by the arrangement shown in Fig. 118, one connecting rod, the upper one in the sketch, being formed with a disk to which the others are attached by means of bosses, or short pins.

In balance, this engine is naturally superior to either of the arrangements shown in Figs. 4 and 5. In the case of Fig. 4, the placing of all the cylinders on top of the crank case makes it impossible to divide the impulses evenly, and this motor has to be built with heavy inside flywheels, similar to a motorcycle engine. With this addition, such a motor runs well, but it is a question whether the advantage of greater accessibility gained by placing the cylinders in this position, is not more than offset by the extra weight of the flywheels that could be saved by disposing the cylinders equidistant around the crank case, so that the impulses would come 120 degrees apart.

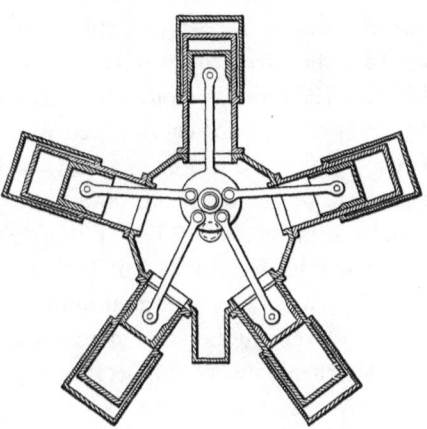

Fig. 7. Five-Cylinder Radial or Star Type

Fig. 5 is really a five-cylinder radial engine with the two cylinders shown below in Fig. 7 placed on top of the crank case. In this case, three of the pistons actuate one crank and the remaining two another, the cranks themselves being opposed or 180 degrees apart. The division of the impulses is the same as in the complete radial engine, Fig. 7, and the balancing almost as good, but the crank shaft has to be of a larger diameter owing to its weaker form, and as both it and the crank case are longer, there will be an increase in the weight. Take Fig. 7 and assume that its crank shaft is held stationary, and we have the usual revolving type of radial motor which has proven so successful in service. It does not require any great amount of study to show that whether the cylinders revolve or remain stationary, the total weight of the motor will be the same, assuming the accessories and fittings in each case to be similar. This being the case, the only manner in which the revolving cylinders can be of any advantage is either to make the crank case and the cylinders themselves lighter, or to obtain more power for the same sized cylinder when revolved.

The chief advantages of the revolving motor are that it dispenses with a flywheel and makes air cooling more positive. Under the conditions obtaining on an aeroplane soaring at any considerable height, it may be questioned whether this is not really too much so, the great reduction in the temperature of the motor very unfavorably affecting its efficiency and unduly increasing its fuel consumption. That this is quite likely to be the case will be apparent from the fact that in a revolving motor in which the ends of the cylinders are 15 inches from the crank shaft, the former will be moving through the air at 95 miles an hour when the motor is running at 1,200 r. p. m. In practice, the power obtained per cubic inch of cylinder capacity from the Gnome motor is small, and it seems quite probable that the same power could be obtained by employing fixed cylinders of smaller dimensions. That it is extremely light for its size will be seen from its weight of but 0.35 pound per cubic inch of cylinder capacity, but this is undoubtedly due to the high-grade materials used and the methods of machining employed in its construction.

Another point of importance in the comparison of these various arrangements that is quite as vital as that of weight, or will be as soon as durability in an aeroplane motor is given proper consideration, is their effect on the bearings. By grouping the cylinders the crank case is shortened but the work put on the bearings is increased, without, in most cases, any proportionate increase in the amount of bearing surface. For instance, in the diagonal or V-type, each main bearing has to take the load of two cylinders, instead of one. This is aggravated still further by placing three cylinders on top of the crank case and in the radial type matters are still worse, though in the latter, various expedients to overcome this, such as that illustrated by Fig. 7, are adopted.

The difficulty of lubricating the radial type of engine has already been mentioned and need not be repeated here. Just how each maker has solved this extremely important part of the problem of his design, will be referred to in connection with the descriptions of a number of prominent American and European aeronautical motors that follow.

AMERICAN MOTOR TYPES

Wright. As the Wright motor was the first to leave the ground in a man-controlled aeroplane, it is natural that it should be given prominence in this connection. When the Wright Brothers attacked the problem of using power for their flights they searched the market for a suitable motor but were unable to find anything that met their requirements. It will be recalled that the automobile motor was not a very highly developed power unit in 1902. They were accordingly compelled to develop a design by study and experiment, as in the case of the aeroplane and the propellers. The result is an exceedingly simple and efficient motor of the four-cycle type which at first glance resembles the present-day automobile motor of light cars, particularly since the practice of making an oil tank an integral part of the crank case has come into vogue. The Wright motor is of the four-cycle type, the cylinders being cast independently of gray iron, while the crank case, of unusual depth, is of aluminum alloy, as are also the water jackets of the cylinders. The exhaust valves are in cages opening directly to the air and are operated by means of rocker arms, as they are placed in the head, alongside of the automatic inlet valves. The crank shaft is of nickel steel and in accordance with the practice that obtained in the automobile field seven or eight years ago, it is *whittled* out of a solid block, the cam shaft also being machined from the bar in the same manner. Oil is carried in a special tank forming the bottom of the 1-piece crank-case casting, lubrication being insured by a small gear type of pump driven from the cam shaft. A second small gear pump driven in the same manner and located beside the oil pump, shown in the illustration of the right side of the motor, Fig. 8, is for the purpose of supplying the fuel to the engine, a carbureter being dispensed with in view of the extreme variations of altitude under which the motor must operate. As will be apparent from the photo, this pump delivers the gasoline direct to a mixing chamber located at an elbow of the intake manifold, the end of which is open to the air. An injector controls the amount of gasoline supplied to each cylinder in direct proportion to the speed of the engine. By comparison with the highly developed type of carbureter now employed on the automobile, this device appears to be a reversion to the old stationary engine type of mixer, but it must be borne in mind that an aeroplane motor constantly operates at its normal or even maximum output, so that provision which would be totally

Fig. 8. Right Side of Wright Four-Cylinder Aeronautical Motor

unsuited to automobile use in view of the demand for the greatest possible range of speed and power output, is undoubtedly far more reliable under such ideal conditions of operation.

Ignition is provided by a "Mea" high-tension magneto driven by a two to one gear on the end of the cam shaft but outside of the crank case, the magneto being set on a bed cast integral with the latter. In this type of magneto, the entire field magnet is arranged to oscillate about the armature, so that regardless of the position of "advance" or "retard" for which the spark control is set, the spark

AERONAUTICAL MOTOR

always occurs at what is known as the "peak of the curve," *i. e.*, the point of greatest current flux, giving a spark of the maximum value for ignition purposes. The cooling water is circulated by means of a centrifugal pump attached directly to the end of the crank shaft, as shown by the view of the left side of the motor, Fig. 9, which also illustrates the magneto and its drive. The radiator consists of a small group of flat, vertical, copper tubes, several feet in

Fig. 9. Left Side of Wright Four-Cylinder Motor Showing Magneto and Its Drive

height, and with small aluminum headers at each end. Unlike many designers of aeronautic motors, the Wright Brothers have not attempted to reduce weight at the expense of safety, as will be very apparent from the liberal flywheel provided. Where not more than four cylinders are employed, there is no single feature that adds so greatly to the reliability of a motor and the uniform delivery of its power output, as a flywheel of ample weight. This essential is of web pattern and is of cast iron, instead of the usual spoked wheel commonly employed. The cylinder dimensions are $4\frac{3}{8}$-inch bore by 4-inch stroke, the power output being 30 to 35 horse-power at about 1,200 r. p. m. The total weight, not including the radiator or water supply, is 180 pounds, or 5½ to 6 pounds per horse-power, which is very high as compared with the weights of the majority of aeronautic motors. The power is transmitted to the propellers through the two sprockets shown on the crank shaft at the flywheel end, and nickel steel roller chains, one of the latter being crossed to reverse the motion of its screw. The propeller shafts are of chrome nickel steel and are carried on annular ball-bearings. The high

Fig. 10. Complete Power Plant and Transmission of Wright "Baby" Biplane

degree of reliability shown by the Wright motor in service affords a striking illustration of the fact that extremely light weight is far from being the chief thing to be desired in an aeroplane motor. For the "baby" Wright machine and the "racer," an eight-cylinder, V-type motor, Fig. 10, which is characterized throughout by the same features of design, is employed. This is rated at 60 horse-power, and is designed to drive the propellers at a much higher rate of speed than in the standard machine in which they turn at 400 r. p. m.

Curtiss. On the early Curtiss aeroplanes, a four-cylinder, vertical, four-cycle, air-cooled motor, which was practically the same in most respects as the standard automobile type, was employed.

This developed about 25 horse-power. It soon gave way, however, to an eight-cylinder, V-type motor of the same general design rated at 50 horse-power, and it has been with this motor that Curtiss has made all of his flights of note. The new Curtiss racer is provided with a water-cooled motor, Fig. 11, something which serves to accentuate the difference in the conditions between land and air travel. It would appear that in view of the high wind blowing on the motor and the low temperature of the air blast, that air cooling

Fig. 11. Curtiss Water-Cooled V-Type Motor

would present no difficulties whatever. As already mentioned, however, an aeroplane motor operates constantly under full-load conditions, and the rear cylinders of a longitudinally-arranged motor are apt to become overheated despite the constant supply of cold air blowing on them. This, in addition to involving the risk of stopping the motor without warning, also cuts down the power of these cylinders due to the rarefaction of the fuel mixture at a high temperature, makes lubrication difficult, and greatly increases the consumption of lubricating oil. Tabuteau's 8-hour flight in France with a Renault air-cooled motor shows the efficiency of air-blast cooling.

The amazing rapidity with which aviation has progressed during the past few years has been responsible for the entrance of a number of motor manufacturers into the field, many of whom are already building automobile or marine motors, while others undertook the making of special aeronautic motors from the start. As is naturally to be expected, the majority of the motors turned out by the former class are more or less conventional in their design, though distinguished by special features in some instances, yet not as a whole of sufficient interest to merit detailed description of more than a few that may be regarded as representative of a class.

Four=Cylinder Water=Cooled Type. The first of these is the four-cylinder four-cycle vertical water-cooled motor. This, in brief, is nothing more nor less than a light type of automobile motor, and in some cases no great attempt has been made at weight-saving, as there are several in which the water jackets are of cast iron, integral with the cylinders as in automobile practice.

Harriman. In the Harriman, these were at first replaced by copper jackets and more recently by light sheet-steel jackets autogenously welded in place, thus insuring against leakage. A novel feature of this motor is the fact that the lower ends of the cylinders are threaded and screw directly into the crank case and lock, the usual flange and bolt fastening being done away with. Both valves are placed side by side in the head and are operated by a superimposed cam shaft placed between them and driven by a vertical shaft and bevel gears from the crank shaft. The same cam operates both the inlet and exhaust valve in each case. The water jacket of the cylinder head, and the valve ports are cast with the cylinder, the jacket of the barrel being of sheet steel as mentioned. An auxiliary exhaust port in the form of a series of holes drilled in the cylinder castings and uncovered by the piston at the lowest point of its stroke aids in quickly scavenging the cylinders. The Harriman is one of the few aviation motors on which the option of battery ignition is offered, the Atwater-Kent system being employed. These motors are built in two sizes, 30 and 50 horse-power and are designed to run at 1,400 r. p. m. Their weight is four pounds per horse-power.

Horizontal=Opposed Type. On one hand there has been a demand for a simpler and lighter motor to give the same power as the type just mentioned, and on the other for greatly increased power. The former has been met by the horizontal-opposed type.

Detroit Aero. An example of this is the Detroit Aero, which with cylinders of 5½-inch bore by 5-inch stroke is rated 25 to 30 horsepower at 1,500 r. p. m. The valves are located in the head and actuated by tappet rods and rocker arms. Cooling is by air direct, the arrangement of the cylinders lending itself with great advantage to this. Quite a number of this type of motor are now being used

Fig. 12. Call Aviation Motor Fitted with Mufflers

in France where they were never regarded favorably for automobile work.

Call. A specially-designed horizontal-opposed type is the Call aviation engine, Fig. 12. This has four cylinders opposed in two pairs, the dimensions being, bore 6 inches, stroke 5¼ inches, and rated at 90 horse-power. It is also built as a two-cylinder opposed rated at 45 horse-power. The cylinders are of a vanadium alloy iron, machined inside and outside and pressed into magnalium (a very strong and light aluminum alloy) water jackets. To save weight, the cylinders are cast of the usual thickness at the combustion chamber, extending down as far as the stroke of the piston, and from there on to the crank case are only half as thick. It is claimed that this construction in connection with the unusually light jackets gives a weight per horse-power equal to that for the cylinders of the customary construction. Ribs extend inwardly from the magnalium jacket and press tightly against the machined outer surface of the cylinder, thus reinforcing the combustion chamber. The cylinder heads are of the same construction as the cylinders, the main portion

Fig. 13. 65-Horse-Power Indian Aeromotor, Hendee Manufacturing Company

being of magnalium which is lined with a circular plate of iron over the combustion chamber. Both valves are mechanically operated and are in cages in the head. The valve seats are water cooled while the cages are air cooled to save weight. These cages are cast very thin and have cooling flanges to protect the valve stem bearings. The pistons, cast of the same iron as the cylinders, are provided with internal cooling flanges on the heads. Magnalium is also employed for casting the crank case, numerous internal ribs amply reinforcing it. Lubrication is by the splash system, the supply being maintained by individual oilers in the form of large cups on the tops of the cylinders. A quick exhaust is insured by the use of large valves with a full lift of approximately one-fourth the valve diameter, supplemented by auxiliary exhaust ports at the end of the stroke. The Call engine is the first aeronautical motor to be fitted with a muffler. Silencers of special design without the usual tubes or baffle plates are fitted directly to the exhaust valves and auxiliary exhaust ports of every cylinder, extending straight downward. The weight of the 45-horse-power motor is 135 pounds, and of the 90-horse-power type, 225 pounds, or 3 and 2.5 pounds per horse-power, respectively.

Fig. 14. Hamilton Eight-Cylinder V-Type Motor

Eight=Cylinder V=Type. *Hendee.* The Hendee aviation motor may be cited as an example of the eight-cylinder V-type, Fig. 13. No attempt has been made to achieve extreme lightness, the object being rather to provide a motor that will carry full load for long periods. The cylinders and heads are cast separately, the former having a light brass water jacket spun into grooves and the joint brazed. The heads have separate jackets connected to the cylinder jackets by a flexible joint. Both valves are placed in an out-board port on the inner sides of the cylinders, the inlet valve being placed on top and operated by a rocker arm while the exhaust is operated direct. The inlet valve is carried in a cage held in place by a breech-block lock; its removal exposes the exhaust valve and permits its withdrawal. The cylinder dimensions are 4-inch bore by $4\frac{1}{2}$-inch stroke, the output being 60 to 65 horse-power, and the weight 260 pounds, or 4.3 pounds per horse-power. Curtiss used one of these motors in the long-distance flights at the Harvard Aviation Meet.

Hamilton. The Hamilton motor, Fig. 14, is of the conventional eight-cylinder V-type, but is distinguished by an unusual valve operating mechanism most of the details of which will be apparent from the photograph. Both valves are placed in the cylinder heads, and the entire valve-operating mechanism is superimposed on them. The vertical tube visible in the foreground between the cylinders is a crank-case "breather" or vent.

Two-Cycle Motors. *Roberts.* As already mentioned, the aeroplane affords an excellent field for the two-cycle motor in view of the constant power requirements, similar to the condition obtaining in marine work. A representative motor of this type is the Roberts, designed by E. W. Roberts, whose experience in the field of aviation dates back to 1894 and 1895 when he served as assistant to Hiram S. Maxim in his experiments at that time. The Roberts two-cycle aviation motor is of the customary three-port type except that instead of opening the admission and exhaust by means of the piston, a special tubular rotary valve is employed, it being claimed that this effects better control of the opening to the crank case and greater economy. The cellular by-pass fitted to Roberts marine motors is also employed to prevent back firing or explosions in the crank case. The cylinders are of hardened steel, their dimensions being $4\frac{1}{2}$-inch bore by 5-inch stroke. Part of the water jacket is cored out of the cylinder casting while the remainder is covered with an aluminum jacket caulked into a groove in the cylinder itself. The pistons and rings are of cast iron and the crank case of magnalium. Ignition is by means of a Bosch magneto with a special advance device as it is impractical to operate the two-cycle motor with a fixed ignition point, it being necessary to retard the explosion timing considerably in order to start without danger of the motor kicking back. To effect this a helical gear is employed to turn the armature of the magneto with relation to the drive. The four-cylinder Roberts

VIEW OF THE R. E. P. MOTOR AND LANDING GEAR
This Machine is the Work of One of the Cleverest Aeroplane Designers in Europe

Intentionally blank as was the original edition.

motor with carbureter and magneto weighs 165 pounds and develops 52 horse-power at 1,400 r. p. m., while the six-cylinder weighs 220 pounds and develops 78 horse-power at 1,500 r. p. m,. or 3.17 and 2.8 pounds per horse-power, respectively.

Fox. The Fox aero motor is another two-cycle type that is distinguished by the use of a special fourth port. Apart from this, the motor is of practically the conventional three-port type. This fourth port, known as an *accelerator*, is an opening placed below the third port and is designed to admit air alone, which goes through a by-pass on the side of the cylinder, where the fourth port is uncovered by the upward stroke of the piston immediately after the opening of the third port. The incoming fuel charge through the latter is deflected toward the bottom of the crank case, while the air entering through the fourth part is deflected upward and is pocketed under the piston until the opening of the intake port, entering the explosion chamber in advance of the fuel charge. It accordingly serves to drive out the exploded gases in advance of the entrance of the fresh fuel, thus increasing the power and making the motor more economical. The external opening of this fourth port is directly controlled by the operator through a lever, so that it may be closed entirely, when the motor will operate as the usual three-port type; or it may be opened full when greater speed and power are required, which accounts for the name given it. These motors are built in sizes ranging from 36 horse-power, weighing 150 pounds, up to 200 horse-power, weighing 850 pounds, the cylinder dimensions of the smallest size (four cylinders) being $3\frac{1}{2}$ by $3\frac{1}{2}$ inches, and the largest (eight cylinders) 6×6 inches, the average weight per horse-power being about 4 pounds. The cylinders are placed in line in all the sizes.

Elbridge. A two-cycle motor with which a number of successful flights were made by amateur aviators during 1910, is the Elbridge aero special. This is a four-cylinder, vertical, three-port type and it is claimed by the makers that it will carry almost its maximum load up to as high a speed as 2,000 r. p. m. Without the magneto it weighs slightly less than 150 pounds and delivers 50 to 60 horse-power.

Rotary Type. *Adams-Farwell.* The Adams-Farwell, Fig. 15, which is the prototype in this field, was first used for automobiles

AERONAUTICAL MOTOR

in 1898 and has recently been redesigned for aviation purposes. In some respects this motor is very similar to the five-cylinder revolving motors used in the Adams-Farwell automobile, having the same number of cylinders, the same single throw crank, the same positive oiler, and the same crank construction. In other respects, however, it is quite different, being designed solely for aviation purposes, and revolving in a vertical plane, so that it may be direct connected to propeller shaft or have the propeller mounted directly upon the motor for aeroplane work.

The most interesting improvement found on this motor and, no

Fig. 15. Adams-Farwell Revolving Aeronautical Motor

doubt, the most important advance made in the construction of aviation motors since the introduction of the revolving cylinder type, is the elimination of the carbureter and employment of fuel injection with a means for regulating the amount of gasoline injected into each cylinder, and insuring that all cylinders will receive exactly the same mixture. This also makes it possible to do away with the inlet valve, and employ one valve for both inlet and exhaust, as only air is drawn in by the suction stroke of the piston, while the gasoline is sprayed within the cylinder where it is mixed with the charge of air before compression. Having but one valve in the head of the cylinder it can be made amply large to insure a full charge and a free exhaust.

AERONAUTICAL MOTOR

In order to relieve the cam controlling the action of all five valves from the heavy load of opening a large valve against the high pressure at the time exhaust takes place, the cylinders are provided with auxiliary exhaust ports, which are uncovered by the piston on its downward stroke. No check valves are required over these auxiliary ports, as, on the suction stroke, pure air and not a mixture of gas is drawn in, so what air is drawn in through the auxiliary ports on the suction stroke becomes a part of the explosive mixture in the cylinder, and being a constant quantity does not affect the operation of the motor.

The control of the motor is entirely taken care of by regulating the amount of gasoline used, and the only adjustment that might be construed as belonging to the carburetion system, is the valve by means of which this control is accomplished. The motor is not sensitive to adjustment, and the speed may be regulated through quite a wide range by this simple means.

The lubrication system mentioned consists of a simple and ingenious oiling device that is a patented feature of the motor and represents a great advance over the present wasteful method of lubricating rotary motors. This oiler consists of a single rotary member much resembling in form the cylinder of a revolver, with longitudinal chambers bored therein. Each of these chambers carries a plunger which, as the cylinder revolves, is driven from end to end by two stationary cams, causing a small amount of oil to be drawn in to each of the chambers at the bottom and ejected into a corresponding tube at the top. This oiler supplies cylinder oil of an extra heavy grade to the various bearings and to the cylinders, doing away with the necessity for splash lubrication, which calls for the flooding of other revolving cylinder motors with a great quantity of oil that dirties the valves and soots up the spark plugs.

There are two spark plugs in each cylinder of this motor, and two independent ignition systems are employed, so that either or both of the set of plugs may be used, thus insuring against the accidental stoppage of the motor from a broken wire.

Something over ten years ago, the Adams Company conducted a series of experiments to determine the action of the air in circulating about the cylinder of a revolving cylinder motor, and, as a result, established beyond question the fact that longitudinal ribs are much more efficient than the circular type. The air coming in contact with the cylinder walls is thrown off radially, circulating lengthwise of the cylinders, so the only logical arrangement of cooling ribs is lengthwise of the cylinders. The placing of ribs in this way has the further advantage of strengthening the cylinder against tensile strain caused by the action of centrifugal force, and the explosion.

This new motor operates satisfactorily on low-grade fuels, but when these grades are employed, it is desirable to have a small tank of gasoline of higher specific gravity to facilitate starting. Reliability has been considered above extreme light weight, as evidenced by the large connecting-rod bearings, the liberal size of the crank shaft, and the fact that four rings are employed on the piston where some builders of aviation motors are using only a single ring. Vanadium chrome nickel steel is used wherever practicable. The dimensions are 6-inch bore and stroke, and at 1,000 r. p. m. the motor is rated at 72 horse-power. It drives a 9-foot 6-inch propeller of 6-foot pitch at 900 to 1,000 r. p. m., developing a thrust of 440 to 460 pounds, which can be maintained indefinitely without overheating the motor.

Brooke "Non-Gyro" Motor. This is another American motor of the rotary type of recent development. It is made in Chicago and is distinguished by several new features that should make it of value for aeronautical purposes, and particularly for aeroplane work. The Type "E" Brooke motor, which lists at $2,500, has 10 cylinders, arranged in two units of five each, either of which may be run independently of the other when desired. With all 10 cylinders working, the motor is rated at 85 horse-power. The cylinders are offset slightly on the crank case and measure $4\frac{1}{4}$ by $4\frac{1}{4}$ inches. Two Stromberg carbureters are employed, one for each unit, while a two-cylinder type of magneto takes care of the ignition of all 10 cylinders, there being but one foot of high-tension cable necessary and no moving contacts, making a very simple and positive ignition system that should prove of great value, as the ignition is a weak point in even the best of motors and its failure through trivial causes is hard to guard against where a number of small parts and a great deal of wiring is necessary. Another improvement is the elimination of the wasteful method of "shooting" oil through the motor for lubrication, as in the Gnome, a nine-tube, force-feed oiler being employed instead. The intake valves are placed in the piston heads, while the exhaust valves are in the cylinder heads. Light springs are used to keep the valves in place when the motor is idle, but they have no function to perform when it is in operation.

Weinberg. An interesting development of this kind is the Weinberg, two-cylinder, horizontal-opposed, air-cooled motor, a Detroit product. The crank shaft is stationary while the cylinders revolve about it, centrifugal force being taken advantage of to draw in the charge through the hollow shaft and to exhaust it. During the outward stroke of the pistons a vacuum is created in the crank case, drawing in the mixture of fuel and lubricating oil, a check valve between the carbureter and crank case preventing its escape on the return stroke. When the piston reaches the lower limit of its stroke, the charge enters the combustion chamber through a by-pass, the motor accordingly being in reality a two-cycle type with an independent exhaust valve. The latter is mechanically opened by means of a rocker arm. This valve is located in the cylinder head and is very large—almost two-thirds the cylinder diameter. Centrifugal force keeps it closed between explosions so that no valve spring is required. The cylinders and pistons are cast iron machined all over, while the crank case is a one-piece casting of aluminum alloy. The magneto is gear driven at the same speed at which the cylinders revolve, the current being distributed to the spark plugs through a revolving sector. Both cylinders fire simultaneously.

Metz. The Metz is a four-cycle, seven-cylinder revolving motor of unusually large size, Fig. 16, the cylinders having a bore and stroke of $6\frac{3}{4}$ inches. It develops 125 horse-power at 800 r. p. m. and weighs 375 pounds, or exactly 3 pounds per horse-power. The cylinders are of chrome steel machined direct from hollow forgings with very thin integral flanges for air cooling. They are attached to a drum-shaped crank case cast of alvanum, another aluminum alloy of great strength and lightness, mounted on large annular ball bearings. The stationary crank shaft and crank pin are of chrome nickel steel. Both valves are placed in the cylinder heads and are mechanically operated. The valves themselves are nickel steel while the push rods for operating them are light tubes of the same metal. Instead of feeding the mixture up through the pistons as in the Gnome revolving motor, it is led from the crank case to each of the inlet valves through light copper pipes. The fuel and lubricating oil enter the crank case through the hollow crank shaft, centrifugal force being relied upon to distribute the lubricant. The pistons are very light and are fitted with a novel type of floating piston ring.

Weight per Horse-Power Hour. It will be noted that in very few of the cases mentioned does the weight of the motor exceed four

Fig. 16. Metz Seven-Cylinder Revolving Motor with Nickel-Steel Cylinders

pounds per horse-power; in the majority it is between two and a fraction of this figure, or say an average of three pounds. This, of course, refers to the motor alone; in the case of water-cooled motors the addition of the radiator, water supply, gasoline tank, and similar fittings will usually increase the weight by almost a pound per horse-power. Even at that it will be evident that improvements in construction and a disregard for the cost of the finished product have accomplished wonders where the reduction of the weight is concerned. It is not too much to say that even the heaviest of the motors in question is a remarkably light power unit. But there is a factor that is of greater importance in the result than that of the weight per horse-power. This is the weight per horse-power hour as explained in Dirigible Balloons, page 25.

FOREIGN MOTOR TYPES

As with the automobile, the French took up the aeroplane and its motive power with all the energy and enthusiasm they possess, right from the start. Even before the Wrights made their first public flights in France, interest was widespread and much had been accomplished. The same spirit was not infused into the art on this side of the Atlantic until 1910 and even then the number

Fig. 17. Deuthil-Chalmers Two-Cylinder Air-Cooled Motor

of investigators devoting their attention to it, the number of machines in existence, and the number of men who could actually fly, were but a small fraction of those engaged in the pursuit of aviation in France. This briefly explains why so much attention has been devoted to the development of the aeroplane motor abroad, as shown by the following examples, the majority of which are of French construction.

Horizontal=Opposed Type. *Deuthil-Chalmers.* There is, however, an American *note* in this development, if it may be so called, and that is the adoption of the two-cylinder, horizontal-opposed motor—a purely American type—for very light units. The best representative of this class is the Deuthil-Chalmers 20-horse-power, air-cooled motor used to drive Santos-Dumont's Demoiselle. Following the precedent of so many other makers, later models of this motor are water cooled, Fig. 17. The first air-cooled, two-cylinder type weighed but 48.5 pounds, or $2\frac{1}{2}$ to $2\frac{3}{4}$ pounds per horse-power, while the later model, and particularly the four-cylinder type, weighs 4 pounds per horse-power. The connecting rods of each pair of cylinders are attached to a common crank, while instead of the usual flywheel, a wire spoke wheel resembling bicycle construction, is employed. Cylindrical valves, both of which are mechanically operated, are placed in the heads, the cylinders being attached to the drum-shaped

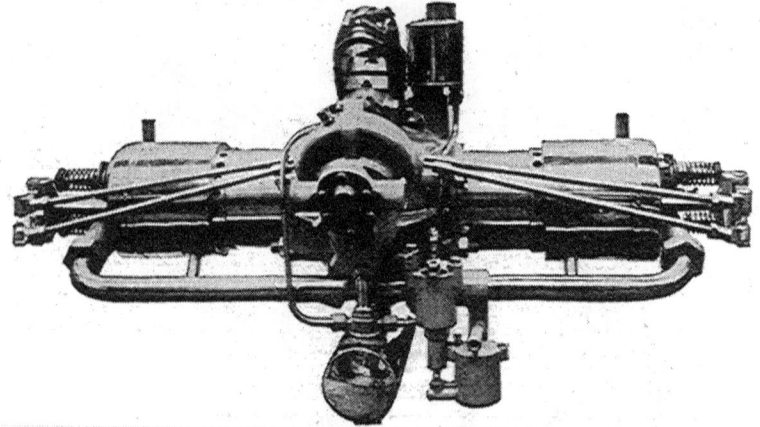

Fig. 18. Darracq Two-Cylinder Motor

crank case by means of long stay rods which pass through clamps over the cylindrical heads. The spark plugs are placed in the upper sides of the heads with the water outlets close to them, the water intake being on the under side. Special oil feeds are run to the cylinders to lubricate the pistons, splash not being depended upon for this purpose. The complete motor is attached to the aeroplane by two bolts passing through lugs cast in the crank case.

Darracq. Another motor of this type is the Darracq, shown in Fig. 18. This is also a water-cooled motor, most of the constructional details of which are apparent in the photograph. Both valves are mechanically operated by rocker arms and push rods actuated

AERONAUTICAL MOTOR

by a pair of eccentrics completely housed in, this being a distinction from the general practice in aviation motors, the timing gears usually being exposed as in the original automobile motors. The magneto is mounted at an angle on top of the crank case, while both the carbureter and the oil tank are suspended below it, a pump immersed in the tank itself distributing the lubricant.

Clement. In the Clement motor of this type, both the oil and water tanks are combined and are mounted over the crank case,

Fig. 19. Clement Two-Cylinder Water-Cooled Motor

as shown by Fig. 19. A similar valve action and arrangement of the carbureter and intake piping are employed as in the Darracq, while the magneto is mounted alongside the gear type water pump at the back of the motor.

The next class in what may be termed the order of development is the conventional four-cylinder vertical type, many of which, however, are distinguished by unusual features.

Conventional Four=Cylinder Type. *Wright-Barriquand.* Of the more conventional types, the Wright-Barriquand (French Wright motor) differs from its American prototype only in slight detail, the principal feature being the use of mechanically-operated inlet valves. (See Fig. 20.)

Panhard and Primi-Berthand. The Panhard and Primi-Berthand, Figs. 21 and 22, are similar in so far as their cooling arrange-

Fig. 20. Wright-Barriquand (French Wright) Motor

ments are concerned. That is, both have light sheet-copper jackets of corrugated section to increase the radiating surface. But the former is a four-cycle type with the valves in the head operated by rocker arms, while the latter is a two-cycle engine, as will be apparent from the photo, which illustrates the carbureter and the method of drawing the fuel mixture into two outside chambers, which communicate with the cylinders through the ports shown, these being opened by the pistons at the lower end of the stroke.

Vivinus. The Vivinus, Fig. 23, is another aviation motor that has been directly developed from the automobile type of the same make. No attempt has been made to achieve lightness, the motor weighing 300 pounds for an output of only 50 horse-power, or 6 pounds per horse-power. But trials have shown it to be capable of sustained operation without power losses, it having been employed successfully on a Farman biplane in England. As the illustration shows, a pressed-steel flywheel is employed.

Other Vertical Cylinder Types. Motors of a generally similar type, the chief features of which are evident from the illustrations, are the De Dietrich, Fig. 24; M. A. B., Fig. 25; Aster, Fig. 26, and the Buchet six-cylinder, which is shown mounted on the framing of a Bleriot monoplane in Fig. 27. It will be noted that the propeller in this case is depended upon to take the place of the flywheel. Practice shows this to be permissible when six or more cylin-

Fig. 21. Panhard Aviation Motor

Fig. 22. Primi-Berthand Water-Cooled Motor

ders are employed, although its omission is not infrequent even on a four-cylinder motor, as will be noted by reference to the Gregoire, mentioned farther along. The flywheel also has been eliminated even when no more than two cylinders are employed as in the Deuthil-Chalmers horizontal-opposed type already described. To say the least, it is not good engineering practice, particularly in two- and four-

Fig. 23. Vivinus Aviation Motor

cylinder types, as there is a well-defined interval between the impulses in both of these. In the six- and eight-cylinder types in which the impulses always overlap, giving a continuous torque, even the slight weight of the wood propeller blades revolving at such a great distance from the hub is sufficient to compensate for the lack of a flywheel,

AERONAUTICAL MOTOR 41

Fig. 24. De Dietrich Motor

Fig. 25. M. A. B. Aviation Motor

Fig. 26. Aster Aviation Motor

Fig. 27. Buchet Six-Cylinder Mounted on a Bleriot Frame

but it is safe to say that the operation of all these motors would be improved by the use of a flywheel, which would add but very slightly to their total weight.

Fig. 28. Green Motor with Superimposed Cam Shaft

An instance of the employment of a superimposed cam shaft is found in the Green, Fig. 28, a motor of English design, while the Gregoire, already referred to, and illustrated by Fig. 29, shows the use of an integral radiator which permits of greatly reducing the weight by cutting down the amount of water required to a fraction

44 AERONAUTICAL MOTOR

of that ordinarily necessary. This radiator consists of four banks of light copper tubes of small diameter the forward sections of which have two rows of tubes while the after ones have but one row. These tubes terminate in headers at top and bottom on much the same principle as the water-tube boiler, the upper or main headers being of considerably greater diameter than the lower ones. These headers

Fig. 29. Gregoire Motor with Directly Attached Radiator

extend entirely across the cylinder heads and outboard for some distance and are connected with the water jackets at the valves, or hottest part. The lower headers are in two parts, directly attached to the lowest part of the jacket at right angles. As the water heats it rises in the large, vertical, uptake tubes, spreads across the upper headers and drops through the banks of small tubes which are cooled by the wind, the circulation being entirely on the thermo-syphon

Intentionally blank as was the original edition.

A FRENCH MONOPLANE TRAVELING SIXTY-FIVE MILES AN HOUR
This Photograph Protected by International Copyright

principle. The four-cylinder motor shown in Fig. 30 is noteworthy chiefly owing to the fact that the very radical departure of

Fig. 30. Four-Cylinder Type with Gear Drive to Propeller Shaft

incorporating a gear drive between the crank shaft and propeller connection as an integral part of the motor has been tried.

Fig. 31. 100-Horse-Power Sixteen-Cylinder Antoinette Motor

V-Type. *Antoinette.* From the four-cylinder to the eight-cylinder V-type motor is a logical step in the problem of weight saving as this type permits of the use of the same form of crank shaft of scarcely greater diameter, each opposite pair of cylinders having the big ends of its connecting rods attached to a common crank pin. The Antoinette is the most prominent instance of this, a sixteen-cylinder motor of this class rated at 100 horse-power being shown in Fig. 31. One or two of these have been employed in the Antoinette racing monoplanes, but the eight-cylinder engine shown by Fig. 32, is more commonly employed. This is rated at 55 horse-power and is a later model than the sixteen-cylinder motor shown, having the cylinder heads and valve seats made in one piece from light steel drop forgings, instead of being cast separately as heretofore. The

Fig. 32. Eight-Cylinder Antoinette Motor

cylinders are machined inside and outside and the valves are placed one above the other in chambers, the inlet valves being automatic, individual plunger pumps being employed to inject the fuel directly into the valve opening. These pumps are operated by variable throw eccentrics, the travel of which may be adjusted by means of the hand wheel back of the motor which is within reach of the aviator. This controls the amount of power developed by adding or decreasing the amount of gasoline in the mixture, instead of throttling the latter as is ordinarily done. The water jackets are of pure copper and are deposited directly in place on the cylinders by an electrolytic or plating process. There are thus no joints whatever and the jackets are very light and strong, the method of attaching them to the cylinders being patented.

The water pump is placed at the rear end of the crank shaft in a special casing, a pulley on an extension of the pump shaft carrying a belt which drives a smaller water pump placed at the bottom of the panel of condenser tubes which form part of the triangular forward

Fig. 33. Fiat Eight-Cylinder Air-Cooled Motor

part of the body of the Antoinette monoplane. These tubes are less than one-half inch in diameter and are extremely light and flexible, their weight forming four-fifths of the complete weight of the condenser, while the headers connecting the tubes constitute the remainder. Horizontally mounted back of the motor is a cylindrical tank employed to separate the steam and water coming from the jackets. At the top of this tank is a pipe leading to the condenser, to carry off the steam collecting in the upper part of the tank. Upon being retransformed into water, it is returned to the tank by the smaller pump mentioned. This arrangement makes it possible to cool the 55-horse-power motor shown when running constantly under full load, with but three gallons of water. The motor converts one-fourth gallon of water into steam per minute, the con-

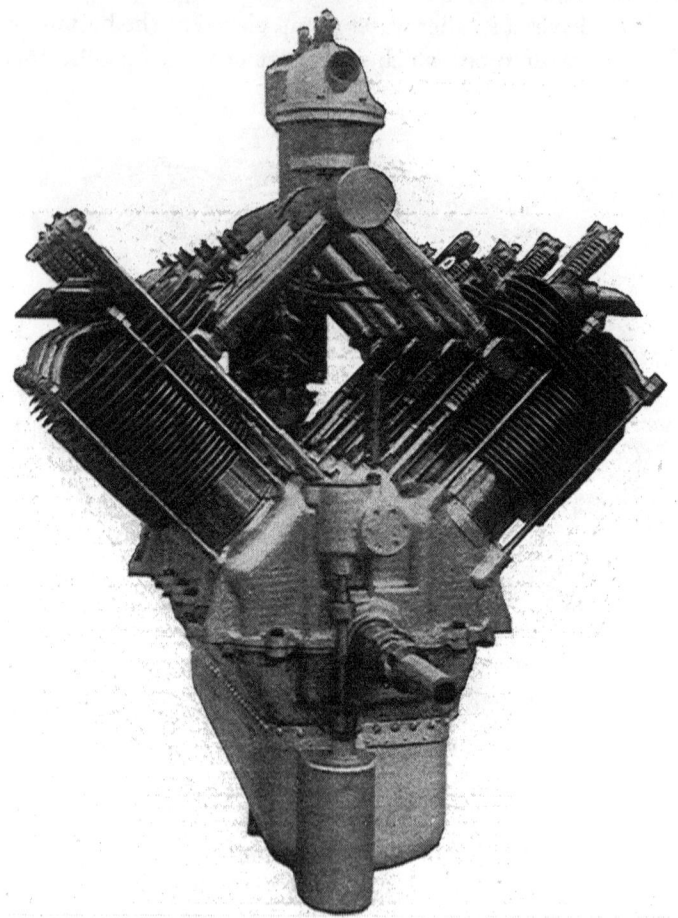

Fig. 34. Renault Air-Cooled Eight-Cylinder Motor. Fan Housing Removed

denser having ample radiating surface to take care of this. As mounted along the body of the monoplane, this condenser does not add perceptibly to the head resistance. Owing to the flexibility of the tubes, it could be mounted on the aeroplane surfaces if desired, though the location already adopted is preferable for many reasons.

AERONAUTICAL MOTOR 49

Fiat. Fig. 33 shows the Fiat eight-cylinder, V-type, air-cooled motor, in which the valve chambers are placed horizontally despite the 45-degree angle of the cylinders. All the valves are mechanically operated from a single cam shaft through adjustable rods and levers. A separate high-tension magneto is employed for igniting each group of four cylinders, the two magnetos being placed on either side of the crank case at the rear and at an angle of 45

Fig. 35. Renault Air-Cooled Motor with Fan Housing in Place

degrees. They are driven by external timing gears but are protected from below by the sheet aluminum pan shown, the latter forming one-half of the complete housing of the motor, the upper part having been removed to expose its details. A single carbureter placed between the cylinders supplies them all with fuel. The normal r. p. m. rate is very high—1,700 to 2,000 r. p. m., at which the motor develops 35 to 40 horse-power, its maximum being 50 horse-power. The cylinder dimensions are 4.3-inch bore by 4.1-inch stroke.

50   AERONAUTICAL MOTOR

Renault. Though of smaller dimensions, 3.5-inch bore by 4.7-inch stroke, the Renault air-cooled motor of this type, shown in Fig. 34, is rated at 45 to 55 horse-power with 1,500 to 1,800 r. p. m., the former being its normal speed. In this view it is shown with the air-cooling apparatus removed. All valves are mechanically operated from a single cam shaft, the exhaust being placed directly over the inlet valves, the inlet manifold being so arranged as to obtain the maximum heating effect from the cylinders. An auto-

Fig. 36.   Pipe Air-Jacketed V-Type Motor

mobile type, automatic carbureter, entirely of aluminum, vaporizes the fuel, and a high-tension magneto is employed to fire the charge. As will be noted, this carbureter is mounted on the upper side of the center of the inlet manifold. Oil is carried in a large tank beneath the crank case to which it is raised by a pump driven through bevel gearings. The motor is designed so that the propeller of the aeroplane may be mounted either on the crank shaft or on the cam shaft, the turning speed being reduced to one-half that of the normal r. p. m. rate of the motor, in the latter case, or 750 r. p. m. This motor has developed as high as 58 horse-power on a dynamometer test. To

AERONAUTICAL MOTOR

cool it a centrifugal fan of large diameter is mounted in a housing at one end, as shown by Fig. 35. The cold air from the periphery of this fan is led between the cylinders by means of the extended housing shown, finding an outlet at the side between the cooling flanges on the cylinders. Complete with magneto, carbureter, and air-cooling equipment, it weighs 374 pounds, or $6\frac{1}{2}$ pounds per horse-power. It was with one of these motors that Tabuteau won the Michelin prize of $20,000 in 1910 by flying for more than eight hours without a stop, covering close to 400 miles.

Pipe. Another motor of the same type which is air cooled on the same principle as the Renault is the Pipe, of Belgian manufacture, illustrated by Fig. 36. The cylinders are 100 millimeters square, *i. e.*, 3.9 inches bore and stroke. The crank shaft is mounted on three large ball bearings with a ball thrust bearing at one end, the cam shaft also being similarly mounted, with the exception of the provision against thrust. One of the chief features of this motor, apart from the cooling, is the combined inlet and exhaust valve, on the same principle as the Pelterie (French) and the Franklin (American) motors.

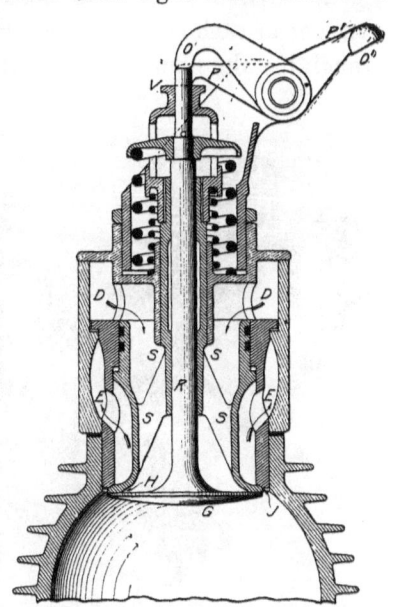

Fig. 37. Combined Inlet and Exhaust Valve of Pipe Motor

It consists of a sliding sleeve, bell mouthed at its lower end to form the exhaust valve, and the seat for the inlet valve as well. This is illustrated in section by Fig. 37. The inlet valve G is concentric with the sleeve S, its stem R passing through the hollow stem of S, and it seats upon it at H. The seat for S in the cylinder head is at J. The two valves thus formed are provided with suitable retaining springs and are operated by the levers OO' and PP'. P is forked to surround R and bear upon the cap V surmounting S. S forms a piston and is provided with two piston rings just below the inlet ports DD, to prevent the exhaust gases from leaking into the inlet pipe when being expelled through the exhaust ports EE. When G is opened by the rocker arm O, gas is drawn from the carbureter through DD and down through the hollow sleeve S. At the end of the working stroke, the sleeve S is moved downward from its seat at J by the forked rocker arm P, the exhaust gases then being expelled through the ports EE. The passage of the cool gases through the center of S prevents both the inlet and exhaust valves from warping due to the heat and is thus of great advantage on an air-cooled motor. Two blowers of special form, one at each end of the crank shaft, force a large volume of air through the aluminum jackets and over the cooling flanges of the cyl-

Fig. 38. Bruhot Eight-Cylinder Water-Cooled Motor

inders similar to the American Frayer-Miller engine. The Pipe motor complete weighs 288.8 pounds, or about $5\frac{3}{4}$ pounds per horse-power.

Water=Cooled Types. Examples of water-cooled, eight-cylinder, V-type motors are illustrated in the Bruhot (French), Fig. 38, and the Wolseley (English), Fig. 39, two of the latter of 200 horse-power each being used on the ill-fated British airship Mayfly.

Fan and Star Types. *Anzani.* It will be noted that few, if any, of the four-cylinder or eight-cylinder motors just described, whether air- or water-cooled, weigh less than 5 pounds per horse-power, while most of them exceed this. To considerably reduce this figure, the fan or star arrangement of the cylinders has been resorted to. In its simplest form this is shown by the Anzani two-cylinder,

Fig. 39. Wolseley Eight-Cylinder Water-Cooled Aviation Motor

air-cooled motor, Fig. 40. In reality, this is nothing more or less than a section of the usual eight-cylinder V-type. Cooling is by means of sheet-metal, perforated flanges pressed on the cylinders.

M. A. B. A closer approach to the fan formation is seen in the

Fig. 40. Anzani Two-Cylinder V-Type Motor

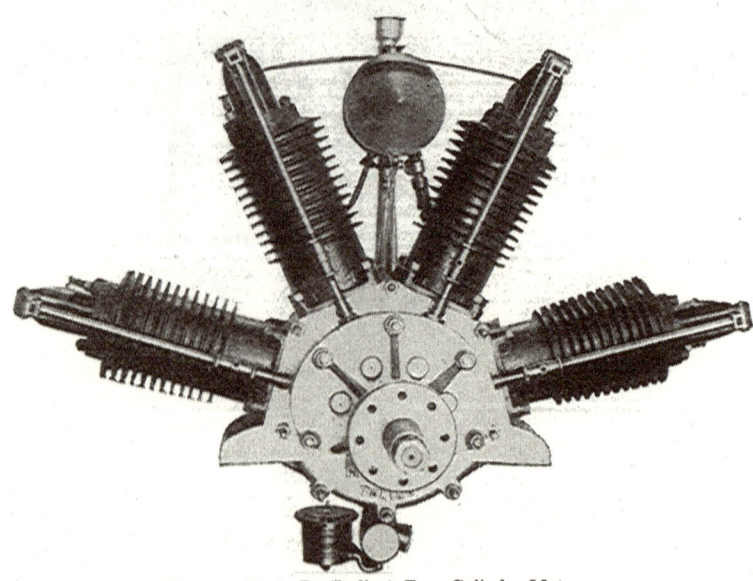

Fig. 41. M. A. B. (Italian) Four-Cylinder Motor

AERONAUTICAL MOTOR 55

M. A. B. (Italian) four-cylinder motor, Fig. 41. In this case, as in those following, the flanges are cast integral with the cylinders.

Farcot. A further extension of the same principle is shown in the Farcot (French), Fig. 42, this having six air-cooled cylinders. The same makers also manufacture a motor in which the cylinders are mounted radially around a circular crank case, the latter with its cylinders lying horizontally, the crank shaft running vertically. On its upper end it carries a seven-bladed horizontal fan to cool them.

Fig. 42. Farcot Fan Type Air-Cooled Motor

This arrangement of cylinders grouped symmetrically around a central crank case is not new, Forest having employed it in 1888, and Manley in 1900 for aeronautic motors, the former building a 50-horse-power, eight-cylinder motor of this type with the then light weight of 11 pounds to the horse-power. Manley produced a 52-horse-power, five-cylinder motor with a weight of but 2.4 pounds per horse-power, or 125 pounds total weight. It developed full power for ten hours under constant load and was subsequently employed by Professor Langley in his full-sized aerodrome. The number of cylinders and their arrangement in a motor of this type have much to do with the balance, regularity of cycle, lack of vibration, and smoothness of running. A four-cylinder motor of this type is nearly in perfect balance so far as centrifugal force is concerned, a suitable counterweight making up for any deficiency. With two sets of four cylinders working on two cranks at 180 degrees, the balance is better still—the more so the nearer together the planes

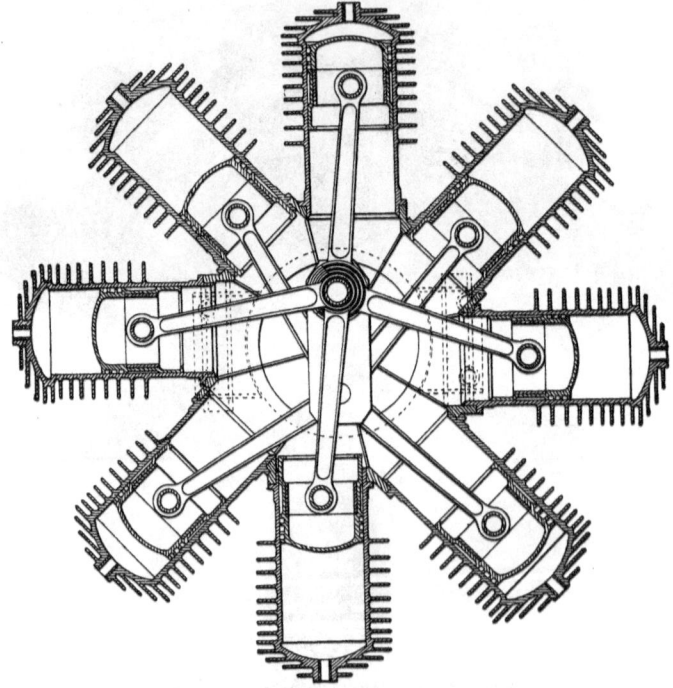

Fig. 43. Cross-Section of Farcot 50-Horse-Power Air-Cooled Motor

of the two sets of cylinders. The relative positions of the pistons, connecting rods, and cranks in an eight-cylinder Farcot motor of this type is shown in section, Fig. 43.

Each group of four cylinders is necessarily in a different plane to permit of attaching the different connecting rods to the two cranks, but by offsetting the rods, the distance between the planes of the two groups has been reduced to one inch. The cranks are at

180 degrees and alternate cylinders are in different planes. As the crank shaft is vertical, a horizontal shaft driven through bevel gears

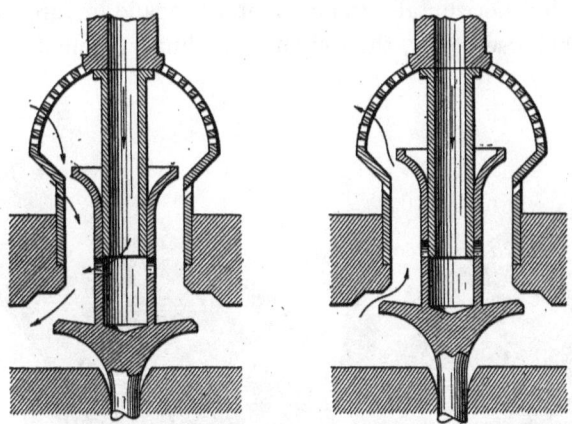

Fig. 44. Farcot Combined Valves, Inlet and Exhaust Positions

at a lower speed is provided for attaching the propeller. A combined exhaust and inlet valve similar to that of the Pipe is employed,

Fig. 45. R. E. P. (Pelterie) Five-Cylinder Motor

Fig. 44. Lubrication is by means of a gear pump forcing oil through the hollow crank shaft and the perforations in the latter leading up through the connecting rods. Two small, high-tension magnetos, one set a quarter turn behind the other, provide ignition. The Farcot eight-cylinder, horizontal, circular motor is made in three sizes, 30, 50, and 100 horse-power, the weight being but 2.2 pounds per horse-

Fig. 46. Gobron-Brillé Eight-Cylinder X-Type Motor

power. Both magnetos weigh only 15 pounds, whereas the ordinary high-tension magneto alone weighs 25 to 30 pounds. It is claimed that the 50-horse-power Farcot motor may be made to develop as high as 70 horse-power for a short period.

AERONAUTICAL MOTOR

Clement. The new Clement aeronautic motor resembles the Farcot in general arrangement, but differs considerably in detail. It has seven water-cooled cylinders, all in the same plane, the connecting rods of which are attached to a single crank. A double counterweight, acting as a flywheel, gives almost perfect balance. The normal r. p. m. rate of the motor is 1,200, but the propeller is driven at 800 r. p. m. by means of a second horizontal shaft operated through bevel gearing, as in the Farcot. The cylinders are of specially heat-treated steel, while the heads are cast steel, screw threaded

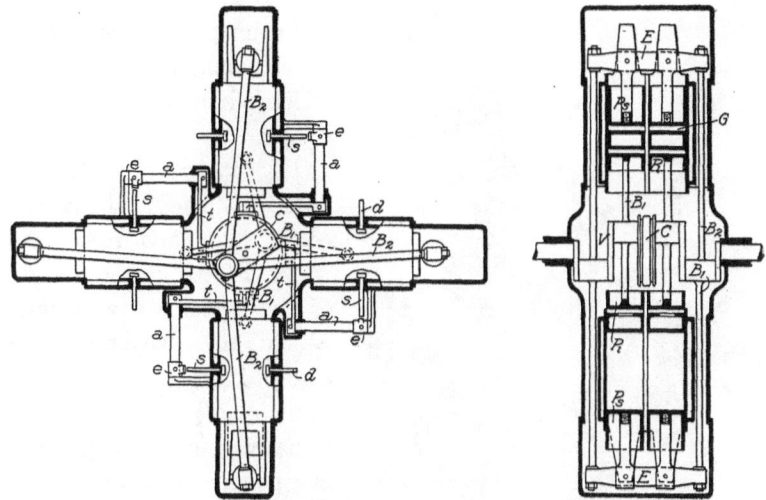

Fig. 47. Side and Edge-On Sections of Gobron-Brillé Motor

and turned onto the cylinders, after which they are solidly welded in place, thus eliminating many small fastenings. The valves are in the heads and are held on their seats by small flat springs, the rocker arms having the usual helical springs. The pistons are of pressed steel, with convex heads, giving a combustion chamber whose general shape is ellipsoidal. The valves are operated by a single cam revolving in the same direction as the crank shaft and at but one-eighth its speed through gearing. There are four high points and four depressions in this large cam, corresponding, respectively, to the opening of the exhaust and inlet valves, the slow speed putting very little wear on the valve-operating mechanism, while the occurrence of the impulses regularly, two-sevenths of a revolution

60 AERONAUTICAL MOTOR

apart, gives very smooth running. There are three principal connecting rods, to which the other four are attached. These three principal rods are carried upon two sets of balls, one upon the inner two rings and the third on the intermediate pair. The crank pin is removable to permit of slipping into place the sleeve to which the connecting rods are attached. This sleeve carries the two counterweights. The high-tension magneto for ignition is driven directly from the crank shaft while a separate distributor runs at half its speed. The carbureter is located beside the crank case and connects by a short pipe to a common chamber in which all the inlet pipes terminate.

The water-circulating pump is placed about the crank shaft and forces the water directly to the bottom of the copper water jackets, which are soldered and clamped in place. The radiator of $32\frac{1}{4}$ square feet of radiating surface weighs but $26\frac{1}{2}$ pounds with its tank of water. The cylinder bore is 4.3 and the stroke 4.5 inches, the motor developing 50 horse-power at 1,200 r. p. m. The diameter of the motor overall is 3 feet and its total weight in working order is only 154.3 pounds, or 3.8 pounds per horse-power. In general design and arrangement it resembles the Manley motor of 1900 built for Langley's aeroplane. The first of these Clement motors is mounted on the Clement monoplane.

Fig. 48. Gnome Seven-Cylinder Revolving Motor

Pelterie. The Pelterie (R. E. P.) is a representative fan type which attracted considerable attention by reason of its ingenious design when first placed on the market. It is built in five-, seven-,

A FRENCH AEROBUS WITH A TAXI BODY ACCOMMODATING FOUR PASSENGERS BESIDES THE DRIVER
Excellent Flights Have Been Made with This Machine

Intentionally blank as was the original edition.

and ten-cylinder models, one of the first being shown by Fig. 45. They are of 25, 35, and 50 horse-power, respectively, the 25-horsepower model being the one illustrated. The cylinders are of the same size in all and are very small, 2.8-inch bore by 3.7-inch stroke.

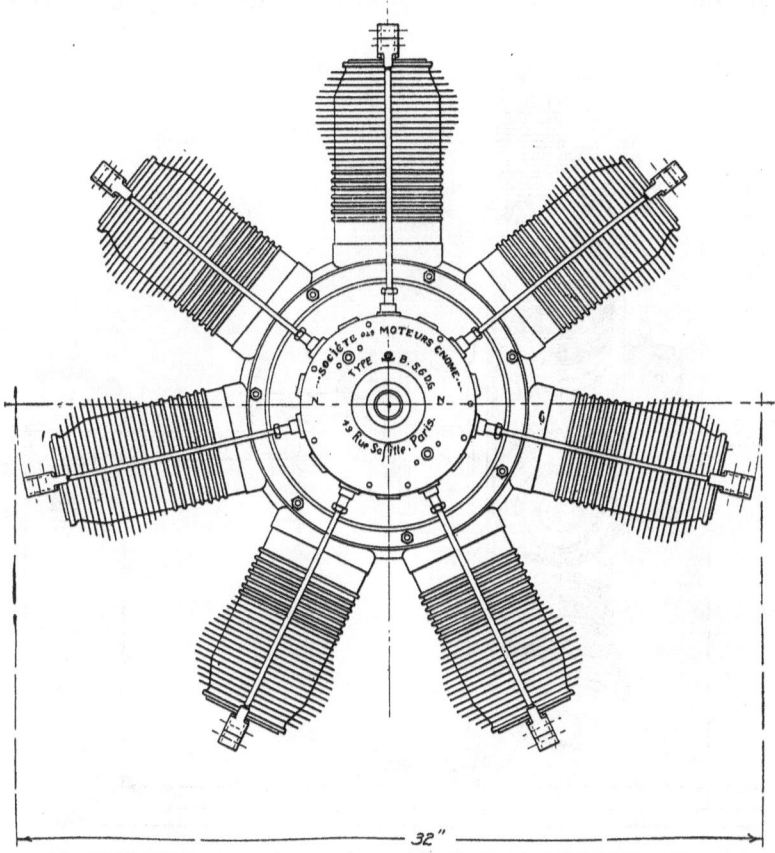

Fig. 49. Detailed Side View of Seven-Cylinder Gnome Motor

In the five-cylinder type, all the cylinders are in the same plane, while in the seven-cylinder, they are staggered, all the connecting rods being attached to a common crank pin by offsetting. The ten-cylinder motor is really two fives placed side by side and very close together. Combined inlet and exhaust valves of the form already described are employed. Two carburetors are employed on the ten-cylinder motor, with a double magneto.

62 AERONAUTICAL MOTOR

Gobron=Brillé X=Form. One of the most radical departures from current practice is found in the Gobron-Brillé, Fig. 46, which has eight cylinders arranged in **X**-form, each cylinder having two pistons. The explosion takes place between the pistons which are thus driven apart, the connecting rods of the inner pistons being

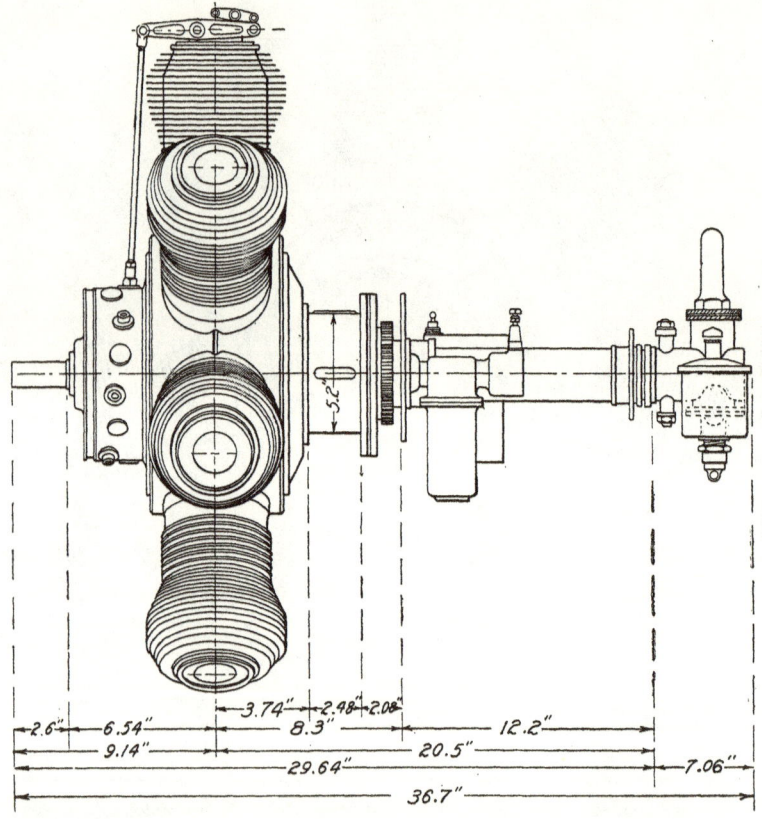

Fig. 50. End View of Seven-Cylinder Gnome Motor, Giving Dimensions

attached directly to the two-throw crank shaft in the usual manner, while the upper pistons transmit their power to the same cranks through long connecting rods passing outside of the lower pistons, but encased in a housing, so that the exhaust-valve-operating mechanism is the only moving part in view. The action of this is illustrated by Fig. 47. Above the exhaust valves of each group is placed a double rocker arm, which, at each turn of the shaft, opens one or the other of the two valves. To obtain the movement, each of the rocker arms e is fastened to a shaft a which is given a reciprocating movement by the lever t, attached to its other end. On the end of t is a shoe or follower, running in one or the other of the two grooves

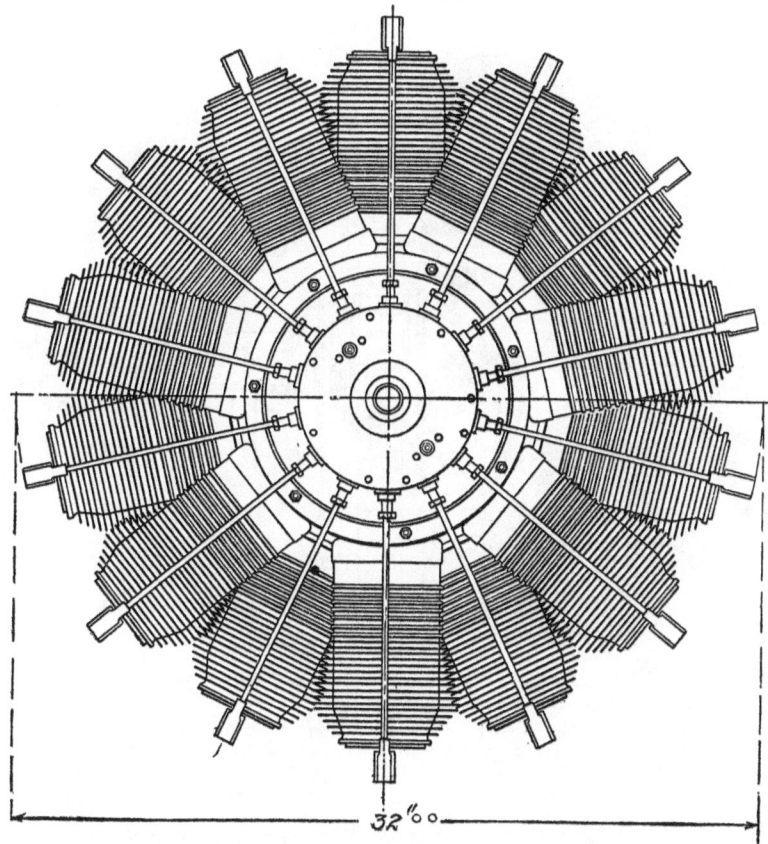

Fig. 51. Side View of Fourteen-Cylinder Gnome Motor

in the double cam c, keyed in the crank shaft. The two grooves cross at a certain point, thus switching the shoe from one to the other alternately. The inlet valves are all automatic, and are fed from a single carbureter, the inlet piping being so arranged that the course taken by the gas from the carbureter to every one of the cylinders is the same. Ignition is provided by two magnetos driv-

64 AERONAUTICAL MOTOR

ing through worm gearing and a shaft at right angles to the crank shaft, the magnetos revolving in opposite directions. A gear pump forces oil to all moving parts inside the crank case, while a centrifugal pump circulates the water, of which but four gallons are necessary. It generates 75 horse-power on a total weight of 330 pounds, or 1 horse-power for every 4.4 pounds, making it one of the lightest

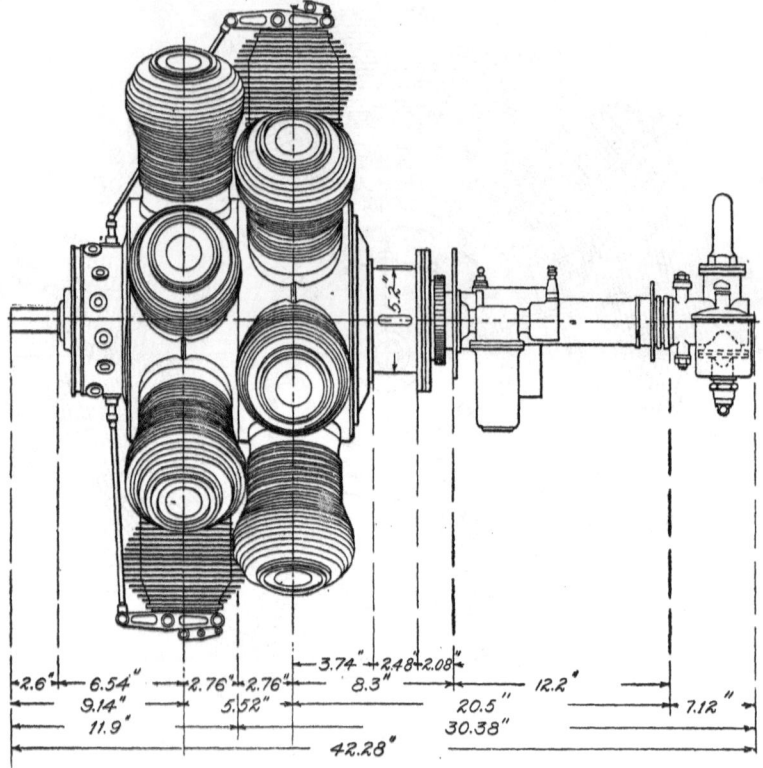

Fig. 52. End View of Fourteen-Cylinder Gnome Motor, Giving Dimensions

water-cooled motors. Automobiles of the same make have been equipped with motors operating on this principle, for several years.

Gnome Revolving=Cylinder Type. While the revolving-cylinder motor has been known for a number of years—the Adams-Farwell (American) being one of the first successful motors of this type did not come into great prominence until 1910, and this mainly through the performance of the Gnome motor on the numerous

AERONAUTICAL MOTOR 65

French machines competing at the International Meet (October, 1910). The Gnome motor is built in 50- and 100-horse-power models, the former of seven, shown in Figs. 48, 49, and 50, and the latter of fourteen cylinders—really two seven-cylinder motors, Figs. 51 and 52. The weight of the 100-horse-power model complete is 220 pounds, or 2.2 pounds per horse-power, which appears to be the minimum reached in a practical unit. The material and machine work throughout are of the very finest, the motor revolving in practically perfect balance. It is estimated, however, that the seven-cylinder motor expends at least 7 horse-power in overcoming the resistance of the air due to its revolution, the cylinders having air-cooling flanges which taper broadly near the heads, thus presenting considerable surface. The cylinders are mounted symmetrically about a drum-shaped crank case, as in the Clement, and have large exhaust valves placed in the heads and operated by rocker arms. The inlet valves are placed in the heads of the pistons and are automatic so that centrifugal force is taken advantage of to draw in the fuel as well as to expel the burnt gases through the exhaust valves. Both valves are counter-weighted to neutralize this force. The bore is about 4.4 inches and the stroke 4.8 inches, all seven connecting rods being attached to a common crank pin, or to a two-throw crank pin in the fourteen-cylinder type, *i. e.*, one rod acts on the pin and the others are articulated to it. Fuel is admitted to the crank case through the hollow crank shaft to one end of which the carbureter is directly attached, while lubricating oil is injected in the same manner by means of a two-cylinder reciprocating pump, with two distributors.

An improved model of the seven-cylinder Gnome was brought out during 1911. This is rated at 70 horse-power and the first of this type completed was brought to the United States by Earle Ovington on his new Bleriot monoplane with the "inverse curve" form of tail. It requires a skilled mechanic, thoroughly familiar with the Gnome construction, to dismount the 50-horse-power model, but in the new 70-horse-power model it is only necessary to remove a few nuts to take off the front half of the crank case, leaving the cylinders readily detachable, while the method of clamping them has also been made much more secure. The receptacles into which the spark plugs are screwed are internally threaded steel tubes welded into the side of the cylinder by a secret process, while the automatic inlet valves, balanced by counterweights to offset the action of centrifugal force, are made so that they can be withdrawn through the cylinder heads, making it unnecessary to take down the engine for this purpose. It was with one of the new 70-horse-power Gnome motors that Weyman won the 1911 Gordon-Bennett in a Nieuport monoplane.

As the motor revolves at 1,300 r. p. m. normally, the centrifugal force is terrific and the oil is practically pumped right through the motor—or, in other words, pumped in and thrown out. Castor oil is employed for the purpose and the consumption is very great— at least half a gallon of lubricant being necessary for every gallon of gasoline used. The consumption of fuel is also very high—300 grammes per horse-power hour—about 10.6 ounces of gasoline, or about 44.1 pounds per hour for the 50-horse-power motor and close to 90 pounds per hour for the 100-horse-power motor, which, with lubricant, would make 100 pounds of gasoline and oil to run the larger motor one hour. This extravagant consumption of fuel and oil, particularly such high-priced lubricant as castor oil, is the chief drawback of the revolving-cylinder motor, and the latter will undoubtedly have to be improved in this respect if it is to maintain its lead.

More than 500 Gnome revolving motors have been built and it has to its credit almost every world's record for 1910 except that of altitude (Wright), and including such events as the Gordon-Bennett Cup, London to Manchester, Paris-London, Crossing the Alps, Statue of Liberty, *Circuit de L'Est*, and other important speed, as well as altitude, and endurance flights, more than $500,000 in prize money having been won during 1910 alone in machines equipped with Gnome motors.

BUILDING AND FLYING AN AEROPLANE

PART I

One of the commonest phases of interest in aviation is the desire to build a flying machine. In fact, this is very frequently the first thing the experimenter undertakes after having gone into the theory of flight to some extent. Only too often, no effort whatever is made to get beyond theory and the machine is an experiment in every sense of the word. An experience of this nature is costly —far more so than is agreeable for the student, and is likely to result in disgusting him with aviation generally. There are hundreds of schemes and principles in the art that have been tried again and again with the same dismal failure in the end. Refer to the story of the Wright Brothers and note how many things they mention having tried and rejected as worse than useless. About once in so often someone "rediscovers" some of these things and, having no facilities for properly investigating what patent attorneys term the "prior art" (everything that has gone before, from the beginning of invention, or at least patented invention) becomes possessed of the idea that he has hit upon something entirely novel and wholly original. There is no desire in the present work to discourage the seeker after new principles—undoubtedly there are many yet to be discovered. The art of flight is in its infancy and there is still a great deal to be learned about it, but there is no more discouraged inventor than he who discovers a principle and, after having experimented with it at great expense, finds that it is only one of many things that numerous others have spent considerable money in proving fallacious, a great many years ago.

If it be your ambition to build a flying machine and you believe that you have discovered something new of value, it will be to your interest to retain a responsible patent attorney to advise you as to the prior art, before expending any money on its construction. You will find it very much more economical in the end. There are prob-

Copyright, 1912, by American School of Correspondence.

ably not more than half a dozen men alive in this country today who "know all the schemes that won't work." The average seeker after knowledge is assuredly not likely to be one of these few, so that until he knows he is working along new and untried lines that give promise of success, it will pay him to stick to those that have proved successful in actual practice. In other words, to confine his efforts in the building line to a machine that experience has demonstrated will fly if properly constructed and, what is of equal importance, skilfully handled. Build a machine, by all means, if you have the opportunity. It represents the best possible experience. But as is pointed out under the "Art of Flying," take a few lessons from some one who knows how to fly, before risking your neck in what is to you a totally untried element. Even properly designed and constructed machines are not always ready to fly. An aeroplane needs careful inspection of every part and adjustment before it is safe to take to the air in it, and to be of any value this looking-over must be carried out by an experienced eye.

BUILDING AEROPLANE MODELS

The student may enter upon the business of building to any extent that his inclination or his financial resources or his desire to experiment may lead him. The simplest stage, of course, is that of model building and there is a great deal to be learned from the construction and flying of experimental models. This has become quite a popular pastime in the public schools and some very creditable examples of work have been turned out. The apparent limitations of these rubber-band driven models need not discourage the student, as some of the school-boy builders have succeeded in constructing models capable of flying a quarter mile in still air and their action in the air is wonderfully like the full-sized machines.

Models with Rubber=Band Motor. The limitations of the available power at command must be borne in mind, as the rubber-band motor is at best but a poor power plant. It is accordingly not good practice to have the spread of the main planes exceed 24 inches, though larger successful models have been built. In attempting to reproduce any of the well-known models, difficulty is often experienced in accommodating the rubber-band motor to them, as even where the necessary space is available, its weight throws the balance

BUILDING AND FLYING AN AEROPLANE

out entirely, and the result is a model that will not fly. This has led to the production of many original creations, but these, while excellent flyers, would not serve as models for larger machines, as of necessity they have been designed around their power plants. The rubber bands for this purpose may be purchased of any aeronautic supply house. The most practical method of mounting the motor is to attach it to the rear end of the fuselage, usually a single stick, which is accordingly made extra long for that purpose. At the other end it is attached to a bent wire fastened to the propeller in order to revolve the latter. An easy way to wind up the motor is to employ an ordinary egg beater, modified as described below, or a hand

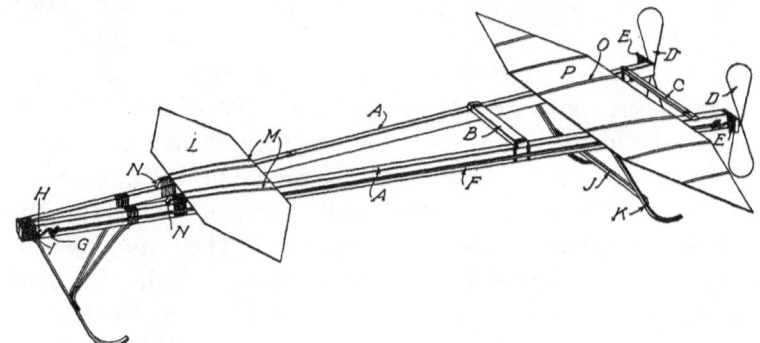

Fig. 1. Details of Main Frame of Rubber-Band Driven Aeroplane Model

drill, inserting a small wire yoke in the jaws in place of the usual drill, or bit. This yoke is placed so as to engage the propeller blades, and the latter is then turned in the opposite direction, storing energy in the rubber band by twisting its strands tightly.

For those students who do not care to undertake an original design at the outset, or who would prefer to have the experience gained by building from a plan that has already been tried, before attempting to originate, the following description of a successful model is given. This model can not only be made for less than the models sold at three to five dollars, but is a much more efficient flyer, having frequently flown 700 feet.

Main Frame. The main frame of the model monoplane consists of two strips A of spruce, each 28 inches long, and measuring in cross section $\frac{1}{4}$ by $\frac{3}{8}$ of an inch. As shown in Fig. 1, the two strips are tied together at the front with strong thread and are then glued, the glue being spread over and between the windings of the thread, Figs. 1 and 2. The rear ends of these strips are spread apart $4\frac{1}{4}$ inches to form a stout triangular frame, and are tied together by cross bars of bamboo B and C which are secured to the main strips A by strong thread and glue.

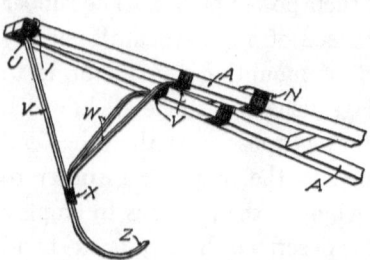

Fig. 2. Details of Forward Skids of Aeroplane Model

Propellers. The propellers D are two in number and are carried by the two long strips A. Each propeller is 5 inches in diameter, and is whittled out of a single block of white pine. The propellers have a pitch of about 10 inches. After the whittling is done they are sandpapered and coated with varnish. The thickness of the wood at the hub E_2, Fig. 3, of the propeller should be about $\frac{5}{8}$ inch. At the rear ends of the strips A, bearing blocks E_1 are secured. These bearing blocks are simply small pieces of wood projecting about $\frac{5}{8}$ inch laterally from the strips A. They are drilled to receive a small metal tube T_2 (steel, brass, or copper), through which tube the propeller shaft T_1 passes.

The propeller shaft itself consists of a piece of steel wire passing through the propeller hub and bent over the wood, so that it can not turn independently of the propeller. Any other expedient for causing the propeller to turn with the shaft may obviously be employed. Small metal washers T_3, at least three in number, are slipped over the propeller shaft so as to lie between the propeller and the bearing block.

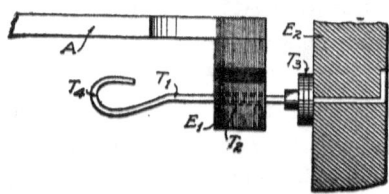

Fig. 3. Details of Propeller and Rudder of Aeroplane Model

That portion of the propeller shaft which projects forwardly through the bearing block E_1 is bent to form a hook T_4. To the hook T_1 rubber strips T, by which the propellers are driven, are secured. The rubber strips are nearly as long as the main strips A. At their forward ends they are secured to a fastening consisting of a double hook GH, the hook G lying in a horizontal plane, the hook H in a vertical plane. The hook G holds

BUILDING AND FLYING AN AEROPLANE

the rubber strips, as shown in Figs. 1 and 4, while the hook H engages a hook T. This hook is easily made by passing a strip of steel wire through the meeting ends of the main strips A, the portions projecting from each side of the strips being bent into the hooks I.

Skids. Three skids are provided, on which the model slides, one at the forward end, and two near the rear end. All are made of bamboo. As shown in Fig. 2 the front skid may be of any length that seems desirable. A 6-inch piece of bamboo will probably answer most requirements. This piece N is bent in opposite directions at the ends to form arms Z and U. The arm Z is secured to the forward ends of the two strips A, constituting the main frame, by means of thread and glue. The strips and skid are not held together by the same thread, but the skid is attached to the two strips after they have

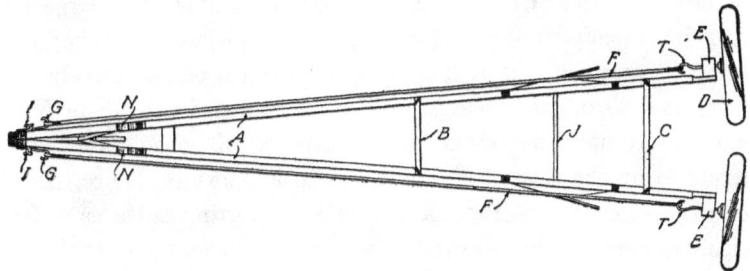

Fig. 4. Details of Rear Skids on Aeroplane Model

been wound. Hence, there are two sets of windings of thread, one for the two strips A themselves, and another for the skid and the strips. Strong thread and glue should be used, as before. In order to stiffen the skid, two bamboo struts W will be found necessary. These are bent over at the ends to form arms V_1, Fig. 2. Each of the arms is secured to the under side of a strip A by strong thread and glue. The arms X are superimposed and tied to the bamboo skid V with strong thread and glue.

The two rear skids, of which one is shown in Fig. 5, consist each of two 5-inch strips of bamboo S, likewise bent at either end in opposite directions to form arms S_2 and S_3. The arms S_2 are fastened to the strips A by strong thread and glue. To stiffen the skids a strut C_1 is provided for each skid. Each strut consists of a 3-inch strip of bamboo bent over so as to form arms C_2. Strong thread and glue are employed to fasten each strut in position on the strip and the skid. In the crotch of the triangular space B_1, a tie bar J, Figs. 4 and 5, is secured by means of thread and glue. This tie bar connects the two skids, as shown in Figs. 1 and 4, and serves to stiffen them. The triangular space B_1 is covered with paper, preferably bamboo paper. If bamboo paper is not available, parchment or stiff light paper of some kind may be used. It does not need to be waterproof. Thus triangular fins are formed which act as stabilizing surfaces.

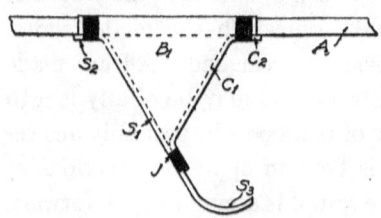

Fig. 5. Enlarged Details of One Rear Skid, Aeroplane Model

Main Planes. The main planes are two in number, but are different in size. Contrary to the practice followed in large man-carrying monoplanes, the front supporting surface is comparatively small in area and the rear supporting surface comparatively large. These supporting surfaces L and P are shown in detail in Figs. 6 and 7. It has been found that a surface of considerable area is required at the rear of the machine to support it, hence, the discrepancy in size. Although the two supporting surfaces differ in size, they are made in exactly the same manner, each consisting of a thin longitudinal piece of spruce R, to which cross pieces of bamboo Q are attached. In the smaller plane, Fig. 7, all the cross pieces are of the same size. In the larger plane, Fig. 6, the outer strips S are somewhat shorter than the others. Their length is $2\frac{1}{2}$ inches, whereas the length of the strips Q is $3\frac{1}{2}$ inches. In order to allow for the more gradual tapering of the plane, around the outer ends of the longitudinal strips R and the ribs Q a strip of bamboo O is tied. The

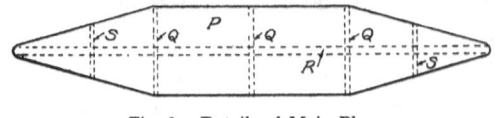

Fig. 6. Details of Main Plane of Aeroplane Model

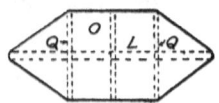

Fig. 7. Details of Smaller Plane of Aeroplane Model

frame, composed of the longitudinal strip and cross strips, is then covered with bamboo paper, parchment paper, or any other stiff light paper, which is glued in place.

BUILDING AND FLYING AN AEROPLANE

The forward or smaller plane has a spread of $8\frac{1}{2}$ inches and a depth of $3\frac{1}{4}$ inches. The main plane has a spread of 20 inches and a depth of $3\frac{1}{2}$ inches at the widest portion. The author has made experiments which lead him to believe that the tapering form given to the outer edge of the plane improves both the stability and endurance of the machine.

The planes are slightly arched, although it will be found that flat planes will also give good results. The rear edge of the main plane should be placed $4\frac{1}{4}$ inches distant from the forward edge of the propeller block E_1.

The front plane must have a slight angle of incidence, just how much depends upon the weight of the machine, the manner in which it is made, and various other factors. This angle of incidence is obtained by resting the front portion of the plane on two small blocks N, Figs. 1 and 2, which are fastened to the top of the main strip A by strong thread and glue.

The height of the blocks N should be about $\frac{1}{4}$ inch, although this will necessarily vary with the machine. The blocks should be placed approximately 4 inches from the forward end of the machine. The front end of the forward plane should be elevated about $\frac{1}{4}$ inch above the rear end, which rests directly on the main strips.

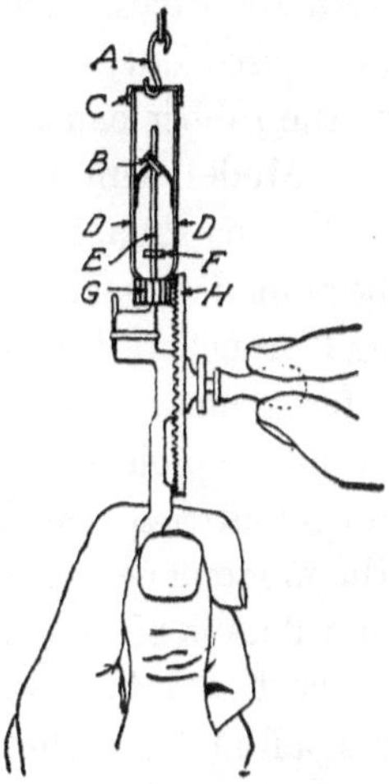

Both the front and rear planes L and P are removably lashed to the frame by means of ordinary rubber bands, which may be obtained at any stationery store. These rubber bands are lettered M in Fig. 1.

Fig. 8. Device for Winding up Rubber-Band Motors

Winding the Rubber Strips. The rubber strips can be most conveniently wound up by means of an egg beater, slightly changed for the purpose, Fig. 8. The beater and the frame in which it is carried are entirely removed, leaving only the main rod E, which is cut off at the lower end so that the total length is not more than 2 or 3 inches. The two brass strips D on either side of the rod, which are attached to the pinion Q meshing with the large driving wheel H, are likewise retained. A washer F is soldered to the rod near its upper end, so as to limit the motion of the small pinion G and the brass strips D attached to the pinion. Next a wire B is bent in the form of a loop, through which loop the central rod passes. The ends of the wire are soldered to the side strips D. Lastly, a piece of wire C is bent and soldered to the lower ends of the side strips. In order to wind up a rubber strip, the strip is detached from the forward end of the model, and the hook A slipped over the wire C. The opposite end of the rubber band is held in any convenient manner. Naturally the two strips must be wound in opposite directions, so that the two propellers will turn in opposite directions. By stretching the rubber while it is being wound, more revolutions can be obtained. It is not safe to have the propeller revolve more than 700 times. The ratio of the gears of the egg-beater winder can be figured out so that the requisite number of twists can be given to the rubber bands for that particular number of revolutions.

Model with Gasoline Motor. The next and somewhat more ambitious stage is the building of a power-driven model, which has been made possible by the manufacture of miniature gasoline motors and propellers for this purpose. Motors of this kind, weighing but a few pounds and capable of developing $\frac{1}{4}$ horse-power or more, may be had complete with an 18-inch aluminum propeller and accessories for about $45. As is the case with the rubber-band driven model, the monoplane is the simplest type to construct, and the dimensions and details of an aeroplane of this type are given here. It will be found that a liberal-sized machine is required to support even such a small motor. The planes, Fig. 9, have a spread of 7 feet 8 inches from tip to tip, each wing measuring $3\frac{1}{2}$ feet by a chord of 15 inches. They are supported on a front and rear wing spar of spruce, $\frac{1}{2}$ by $\frac{3}{8}$ inch in section, while the ribs in both the main plane and the rear stabilizing plane measure $\frac{1}{8}$ by $\frac{1}{2}$ inch in cross section. There are eight of these spruce ribs in the main plane, and they are separately heated and curved over a Bunsen burner, or over a gas stove, which is the same thing. They are then nailed to the wing spars 6 inches apart. The main spars of the fuselage are 7 feet long and they are made of $\frac{1}{2}$- by $\frac{3}{8}$-inch spruce, the struts being placed $1\frac{1}{2}$ feet apart, measuring from the rear, with several intermediate struts to brace the engine bed. Instead of using strut sockets for the fuselage, which would increase the cost of construction unnecessarily, a simple com-

BUILDING AND FLYING AN AEROPLANE 9

bination of a three-way wire fastener and a wire nail may be resorted to. The shape of these fasteners is shown at A in Fig. 9. They may be cut out of old cracker boxes or tin cans (sheet iron) with a pair of shears, the holes in the ends being made either with a small drill or by driving a wire nail through the metal placed on a board, and

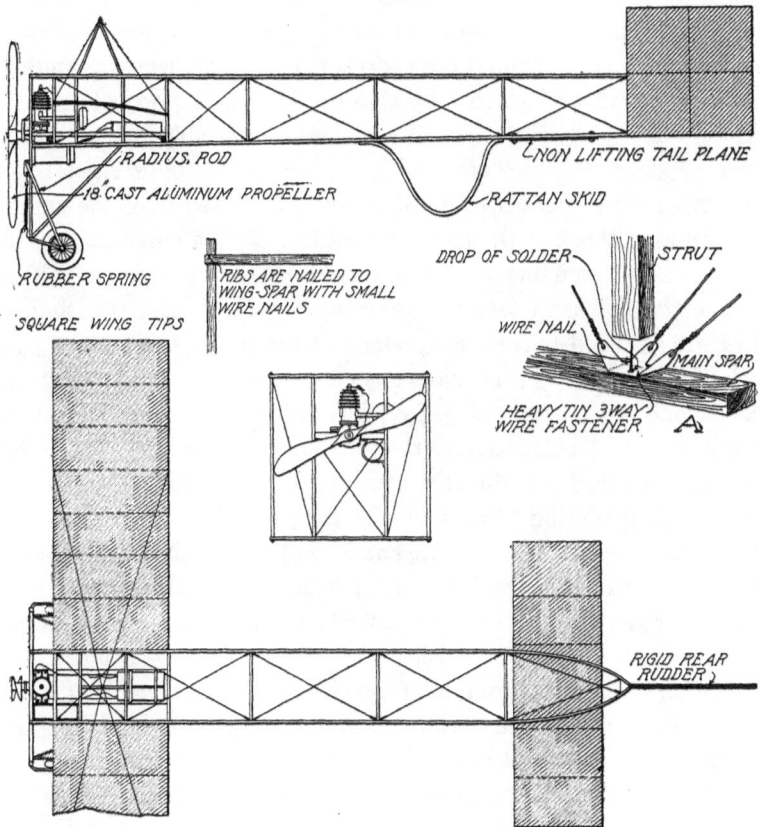

Fig. 9. Details of Power-Driven Aeroplane Model

filing the burrs off smooth. A central hole must also be made for the 1½-inch wire nail which is driven through the main spar and the fastener then slipped over it. As indicated, this nail also serves to hold the strut. A drop of solder will serve to attach the fastener to the nail. The front of the fuselage is 9 inches square, tapering down to 6 inches at the rear. The height of the camber of the main planes is 1½ inches and the angle of incidence is 7 degrees, measured with relation to the fuselage. The non-lifting tail plane at the rear which is to give the machine longitudinal stability, measures 4 feet in span by 14 inches in depth.

The running gear or front landing frame is made of ½-inch square spruce, all joints being made with $\frac{1}{16}$- by 1-inch bolts. Aluminum sleeves, procurable at an aeronautic supply house, are employed for the attachment of the rubber springs and the radius rods running down to the wheels, which may also be purchased ready to install. Old bicycle wheels will serve the purpose admirably. Light steel tubes ¼ inch in diameter are used to run these aluminum sleeves on. Two other steel tubes are joined to the lower corner of the frame by flattening them at the ends and drilling with a small hole for a nail. These are run diagonally up to the fuselage and serve as buffers to take the shocks of landing. For bracing the wings, two similar tubes are fastened to form a pyramid on top of the main plane just back of the engine. From these, guys are run to the wings as shown. The engine bed is made of ½- by ¾-inch white pine, and to make it solid it is carried as far back as the rear edge of the main plane. The batteries and coil are directly attached to this plane, care being taken in their placing to preserve the balance of the machine. The rudder measures 14 inches square and is made of ⅜-inch square spruce, reinforced with tin at the joints, as it is necessary to make the frame perfectly rigid. Both sides are covered with fabric. In this case a 1-horse-power motor furnishes the necessary energy and it is fitted with an 18-inch aluminum propeller which it is capable of turning at 2,400 r. p. m. The carbureter and gas tank are made integral, and the gasoline and oil are both placed in this tank in the proportion of about four parts to one, in order to save the weight of an extra tank for oil.

Flights of half a mile are possible with this model in calm weather, but a great deal of measuring and testing of the fuel is necessary in order to regulate the flight, and "grass-cutting" should be practiced by the builder in order to properly regulate the machine. Trials have shown that the flat non-lifting tail on the fuselage gives excellent longitudinal stability, the machine rising nicely and making its descent very easy angle, so that it is seldom damaged by violent collisions in landing.

Intentionally blank as was the original edition.

VIEW AT ONE OF THE FRENCH AVIATION GROUNDS SHOWING THE HANGARS RANGED ALONG THE EDGES OF THE FIELD
This Photograph Protected by International Copyright

BUILDING AND FLYING AN AEROPLANE

BUILDING A GLIDER

The building of hand- or power-driven models does not suffice to give that personal experience that most students are desirous of obtaining. The best method of securing this is to build a glider and practice with it. Any flying machine without a motor is a glider and the latter is the basis of the successful aeroplane. In the building of an aeroplane the first thing constructed is the glider, $i. e.$, the frame, main planes, stabilizing planes, elevators, rudders, etc. It is only by the installation of motive power that it becomes a flying machine. The biplane will be found the most satisfactory type of glider as it is more compact and therefore more easily handled, which is of great importance for practicing in a wind. The generally accepted rule is that 152 square feet of surface will sustain the weight of the average man, about 170 pounds, and it will be apparent that the length of the glider will have to be greater if this surface is to be in the form of a single plane than if the same amount is obtained by incorporating it in two planes—the biplane. A glider with a span of 20 feet and a chord of 4 feet will have a surface of 152 square feet. So far as learning to balance and guide the machine are concerned, this may be mastered more readily in a small glider than in a large one, so that there is no advantage in exceeding these dimensions—in fact, rather the reverse, as the larger construction would be correspondingly more difficult to handle. The materials necessary consist of a supply of spruce, linen shoe thread, metal sockets, piano wire, turnbuckles, glue, and closely-woven, light cotton fabric for the covering of the planes.

Main Frame. The main frame or box cell is made of four horizontal beams of spruce 20 feet long and $1\frac{1}{2}$ by $\frac{3}{4}$ inch in section. They must be straight-grained and perfectly free from knots or other defects. If it be impossible to obtain single pieces of this length, they may be either spliced or the glider may be built in three sections, consisting of a central section 8 feet long, and two end sections each 6 feet in length, this form of construction also making the glider much easier to dismantle and stow in a small space. In this case, the ends of the beams of each end section are made to project beyond the fabric for 10 inches and are slipped into tubes bolted to corresponding projections of the central section. These tubes are drilled with three holes each and bolts are passed through these holes and corresponding holes in the projecting ends after they have been fitted into the tubes, and drawn up tightly with two nuts on each bolt to prevent shaking loose. Ordinary $\frac{3}{16}$-inch stove bolts will serve very nicely for this purpose. The upper and lower planes forming the box cell, are held apart by 12 struts, 4 feet long by $\frac{7}{8}$ inch diameter, preferably of rounded or oval form with the small edge forward to minimize the head resistance. It is only necessary to space these equally, starting from both ends; this will bring the splices of the demountable sections in the center of the square on either side of the central section. The main ribs are 3 feet long by $1\frac{1}{4}$- by $\frac{1}{2}$-inch section and their placing should coincide with the position of the struts. Between these main ribs are placed 41 small ribs, equally spaced and consisting of pieces 4 feet long by $\frac{1}{2}$ inch square. These, as well as all the other pieces, should have the sharp edges of the square rounded off with sand paper. The ribs should have a camber of 2 inches in their length and the simplest method of giving them this is to take a piece of plank, draw the desired curve on it, and then nail blocks on both sides of this curve, forming a simple mould. The rib pieces should then be steamed, bent into this mould, and allowed to dry, when they will be found to have permanently assumed the desired curvature. Meanwhile, all the other pieces may be shellaced and allowed to dry.

Assembling the Planes. To assemble the glider, the beams are laid out on a floor, spaced the exact distance apart, *i. e.*, 3 feet, and exactly parallel—in the demountable plan, each section is assembled independently. The main ribs are then glued in place and allowed to set, after which they are strongly bound in place with the linen thread, and the various layers of thread given a coating of hot glue as they are put on. This method is not arbitrary, but it is simple and gives the lightest form of construction. If desired, tie-plates, clamps, or any other light method of fastening may be employed. This also applies to the ribs. They are assembled by placing them flush with the front beam and allowing them to extend back a foot beyond the rear beam, arched side up in every case. They may be glued and bound with thread, held by clamps, or nailed or screwed into place, care being taken to first start a hole in the beam with an awl and to dip the nails in soft soap to prevent splitting the

BUILDING AND FLYING AN AEROPLANE 13

wood. Twenty-one ribs, spaced one foot apart, are used in the upper plane, and 20 in the lower, owing to the space left for the operator in the latter. For fastening the two planes together, whether as a whole or in sectional units, 24 aluminum sockets will be required. These may be purchased either ready to fit, or an effective substitute made by sawing short lengths of steel tubing, slitting them with the hack saw an inch from the bottom, and then flattening out and drilling the right-angle flanges thus formed to take screws for attaching the sockets to the beams. In case these sockets are bought, they will be provided with eye bolts for the guy wires; if homemade, they may have extra holes drilled in the edges of the flanges for this purpose or some simple wire fastener such as that described in connection with the power-driven model may be used, heavier metal, however, being employed to make them. The sockets should all be screwed to the beams at the proper points and then the struts should be forced into them. The next move is to "tie" the frame together with guy wires, No. 12 piano wire being employed for this purpose. Each rectangle is trussed by running diagonal guy wires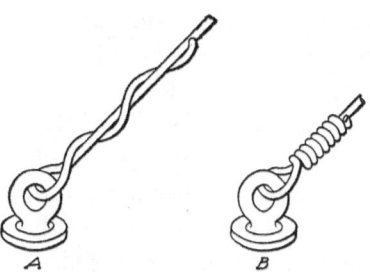

Fig. 10. Wrong and Right Way of Making a Wire Joint

from each corner to its opposite. To pull these wires taut, a turnbuckle should be inserted in each and after the wire has been pulled as tightly as possible by hand, it should be wound upon itself to make a good strong joint, as shown at B, Fig. 6. A fastening as shown at A will pull out under comparatively little strain and is not safe. As is the case with most of the other fittings, these turnbuckles may be bought or made at home, the simple bicycle type of turnbuckle mentioned in connection with "Building a Curtiss," being admirably adapted to this purpose. In fact, the construction of the latter will be found to cover the requirements of the glider, except that the ribs are simpler and lighter, as already described, and no provision for the engine or similar details is necessary. All the guy wires must be tightened until they are rigid, and the proper degree of tension for them may be simply determined in the following manner:

After the entire frame is wired, place each end of it on a saw horse so as to lift it two or three feet clear of the floor. Stand in the opening of the central section, as if about to take a glide, and by grasping the forward central struts, raise yourself from the floor so as to bring your entire weight upon them. If properly put together the frame will be rigid and unyielding, but should it sag even slightly, the guy wires must be uniformly tightened until even the faintest perceptible tendency to give under the weight is overcome.

Stretching the Fabric. The method of attaching the fabric will be determined by whether the glider is to be one piece or sectional, and the expense for this important item of material may be as little or as much as the builder wishes to make it. Some employ rubberized silk, others special aeronautic fabrics, but for the purposes of the amateur, ordinary muslin of good quality, treated with a coat of light varnish after it is in place, will be found to serve all purposes. The cloth should be cut into 4-foot strips, glued to the front horizontal beams, stretched back tightly, and tacked to both the rear horizontal beams and to the ribs. Tacks should also supplement the glue on the forward beams and the upholstery style should be used to prevent tearing through the cloth. In case the glider is built in sections, the abutting edges of the cloth will have to be reinforced by turning it over and stitching down a strip one inch wide, and it will make this edge stronger if an extra strip of loose fabric be inserted under the turn before sewing it down. Eyelets must then be made along these edges and the different sections tightly laced together when assembling the glider. It is also desirable to place a strip of cloth or light felt along the beams under the tacks to prevent the cloth from tearing out under the pressure.

To form a more comfortable support for the operator, two arm pieces of spruce, 3 feet by 1 inch by $1\frac{3}{4}$ inches, should be bolted to the front and rear beams about 14 inches apart over the central opening left in the lower plane. These will be more convenient than holding on to the struts for support, as it will not be necessary to spread the arms so much and there will be more freedom for manipulating the weight to control the glider in flight. In using the struts, it is customary to grasp them with the hands, while with the arm pieces, as the name implies, the operator places his arms over them, one of the strips coming under each armpit. After the fabric has

BUILDING AND FLYING AN AEROPLANE 15

been given a coat of varnish on the upper side and allowed to dry, the glider is ready for use. The cost of the material should be about $30 to $40, depending upon the extent to which the builder has relied upon his own ingenuity in fashioning the necessary fittings—in any case, it will be less than the amount required for the purchase of the engine alone for a power-driven model.

Glider with Rudder and Elevator. It will be noted that this is the simplest possible form of glider in that it is not even provided with a rudder, but for the beginning of his gliding education the novice will not require this, as first attempts should be confined to glides over level ground in moderate, steady wind currents and at a modest elevation. Some of the best gliding flights made by Herring, Chanute's co-worker, were in a rudderless glider. After having mastered the rudiments of the art, the student may go as far as the dictates of his ambition impel him in the direction of improvements in his glider, by adding a rudder, elevator, and warping control. In fact, it is not necessary to confine himself to the simple design of glider here outlined at all. He may take either the Wright or Curtiss machines as a model and build a complete glider, following the dimensions and general methods of construction here given, though these may also be improved upon by the man handy with tools, bearing in mind that the object to be achieved is the minimum weight consistent with the maximum strength.

Learning to Glide. The first trials should be made on level ground and the would-be aviator should be assisted by two companions to help him in getting under way. The operator takes a position in the center rectangle, back far enough to tilt up slightly the forward edges of the planes. A start and run forward is made at a moderate pace, the keepers carrying the weight of the glider and overcoming its head resistance by running forward at the same speed. As the glider cuts into the air, the wind caused by running will catch under the uplifted edges of the curved planes and will buoy it up, causing it to rise in the air taking the operator with it. This rise will be probably only sufficient to lift him clear of the ground a foot or two. Now he projects his legs slightly forward so as to shift the center of gravity a trifle and bring the edges of the glider on an exact level, parallel with the ground. This, with the momentum acquired at the start, will keep the glider moving forward for some distance. When the weight of the operator is slightly back of the center of gravity, the leading edges of the planes are tilted up somewhat, increasing the angle of incidence and in consequence the pressure under the planes, causing the glider to rise, and if the glide is being made into a wind, as should always be the case, quite a height may be reached as the result of this energy. Once it ceases, the tendency to a forward and upward movement is lost, and it is to prolong this as much as possible that the operator shifts the center of gravity to bring the machine on an even keel, or where at a little height, slightly below this, giving it a negative angle of incidence, which permits him to coast down the air until sufficient speed is acquired to reverse the angle of incidence and again rise so as to provide a "hill" for another coast, thus prolonging the flight considerably. To put it in the simplest language, when the operator moves backward, shifting the center of gravity to the rear, the planes are tilted so that they catch or "scoop up" the advancing air and rise upon it, whereas when he moves forward and the planes tilt downward, this air is "spilled" out behind and no longer acts as a support, and the glider coasts, either until the ground is reached or enough momentum is gained to again mount upon the wind. A comparatively few flights will suffice to make the student proficient in the control of his apparatus by his body movements, not only as concerns the elevating and depressing of the planes to ascend or descend, corresponding to the use of the elevator on a power machine, but also actual steering, which is accomplished by lateral movement to the left or right.

Stable equilibrium is one of the chief essentials to successful flight and this can not be maintained in an uncertain, gusty wind, especially by the novice. The beginner should certainly not attempt a glide unless the conditions are right. These are a clear, level space without obstructions such as trees, and a steady wind not exceeding 12 miles per hour. When a reasonable amount of proficiency has been attained in the handling of the glider over level ground, the field of practice may be changed to some gentle slope. In starting from this, it will be found easier to keep the glider afloat, but the experience at first will prove startling to the amateur, for as the glider sails away from the top of the slope, the distance between him and the ground increases so rapidly that he will imagine himself at

BUILDING AND FLYING AN AEROPLANE   17

a tremendous height, but by preserving the balance and otherwise manipulating his weight in the manner taught by the practice over the level, a nice flight of much greater distance will be made and the machine will gradually settle down to the ground much farther away from the starting place than was possible in the earlier trials, this being one of the great advantages of starting from an elevation. There is nothing that will fit the beginner so well for the actual handling of a power machine as a thorough course of gliding flights, and it is recommended that those who build gliders become proficient in their use before attempting to pilot an aeroplane, whether of their own make or not.

A further step in advance is the actual building of a full-fledged power machine, and for those who desire a simple and comparatively inexpensive type, requiring very little work that can not be performed in the home workshop, a description of the construction of a Curtiss biplane is given, while for those who are more ambitious and also have greater financial resources, the details of the building of a Bleriot monoplane are given.

BUILDING A CURTISS BIPLANE

Cost. First of all, the prospective builder will want to know the cost. The best answer to this is that the machine will cost all its builder can afford to spend upon it and probably a little more, as the man to whom the expense is not of vital consideration will doubtless not undertake its construction. Speaking generally, and there can be nothing very definite about it, in view of the great difference in the conditions, an expenditure of three to four hundred dollars will cover the complete outlay for everything but the motor. If the builder has the time and facilities for doing all the work himself, this amount may be reduced very materially. On the other hand, if he finds it necessary to purchase most of the material in form ready to assemble, it may exceed this. But it will be a great aid to many to know that there is practically nothing about the modern aeroplane which can not be found in stock at one of the aeronautic supply houses. This makes it possible for many to undertake the construction of a machine to whom it would not be feasible, or at least not an attractive project in view of the time involved, were it necessary to make every part at home. So far

18 BUILDING AND FLYING AN AEROPLANE

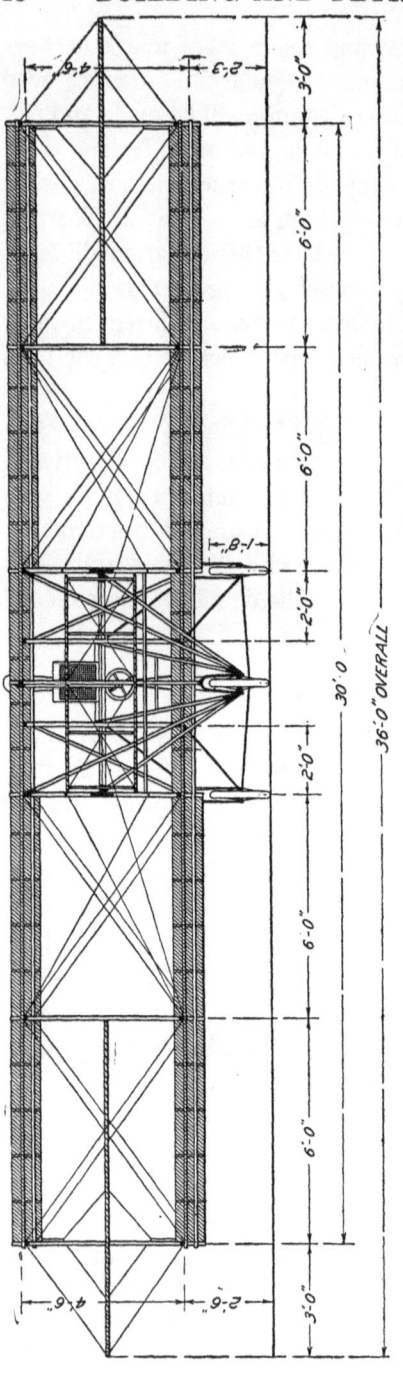

Fig. 11. Detailed Front View of Curtiss Biplane

as becoming involved in any legal difficulties is concerned owing to existing patents, the student need not worry himself about this in attempting the construction of a Curtiss biplane, so long as he restricts the use of his machine to experimental purposes and does not try to compete with the patentees in their own field—that of exhibiting and selling machines.

General Specifications. Just how long it will take to complete such a machine will depend very largely upon the skill of the builder and the extent of his resources for, as already mentioned, the expense may be cut down by making all the necessary parts at home, but it will naturally be at the sacrifice of a great deal of time. For instance, the oval struts and beams may be bought already shaped from the local planing mill, or they may be shaved down from the rough by hand. Turnbuckles can be made from bicycle spokes and nipples and strips of sheet steel, or they can be bought at 12 to 15 cents each. As a hundred or more of them are needed, their cost is quite a substantial item.

BUILDING AND FLYING AN AEROPLANE 19

Aeroplane construction doubtless impresses the average observer as being something shrouded in considerable mystery—something about which there is no little secrecy. Quite the contrary is the case in reality. Any man who is fairly proficient as a carpenter and knows how to use the more common machinist's tools, such as taps

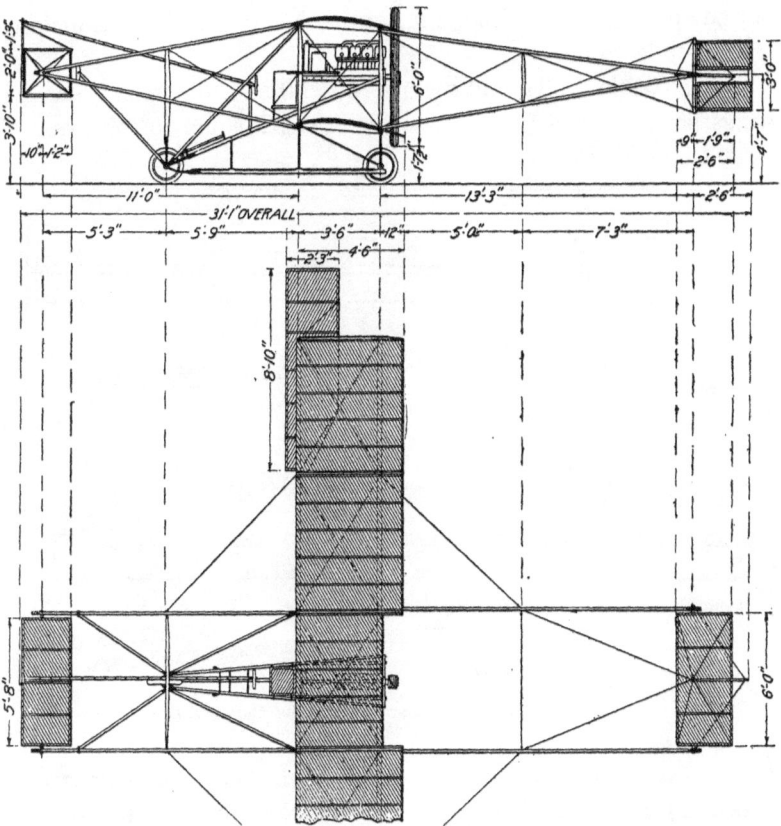

Fig. 12. Plan and Side Elevation of Curtiss Biplane

and dies, drills, hacksaw, and the like, will find no difficulty in constructing the machine of which the details are given here. Having completed its building, he will have to draw upon his capital to supply the motor. One capable of developing 25 to 30 horse-power at 1,000 to 1,200 r. p. m. will give the machine considerable speed, as it will be recalled that Curtiss made a number of his first flights

20   BUILDING AND FLYING AN AEROPLANE

with a 25-horse-power motor. As to the weight, the lighter the better, but 400 pounds for the complete power plant will not be excessive. The machine can sustain itself in the air with less power than that mentioned, but with a heavy, low-power motor it will be sluggish in action. This is an advantage for the amateur, rather than otherwise, as it will provide him with an aeroplane that will not be apt to get away from him during his first trials, thus making it safer to learn on.

The Curtiss biplane has a spread of 30 feet, the main planes or wings being divided into sections of a length equal to the distance

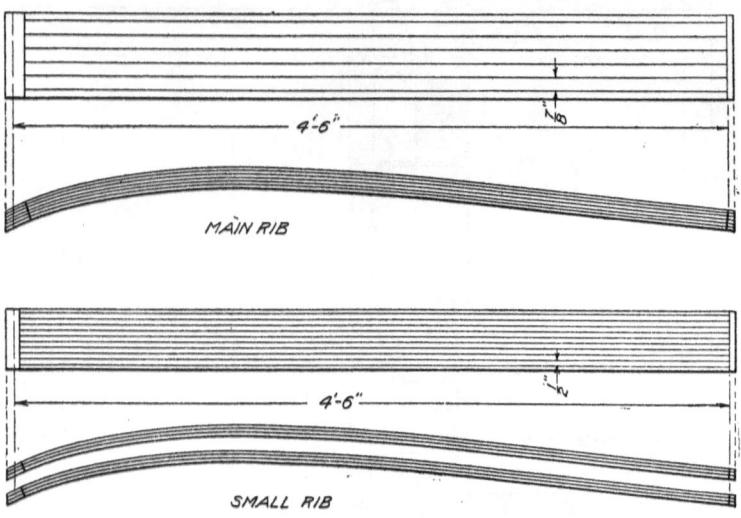

Fig. 13. Details of Main and Small Ribs, Curtiss Biplane

between struts, Figs. 11 and 12. There are five of these sections, each measuring six feet. The struts can be taken out and the sections laid flat on each other for storage. The framework for the front and rear rudders can also be jointed, if desired, making it possible to store the machine in small compass. The longest parts of the machine, when taken apart, are the two diagonal beams running from the front wheel back to the engine bed, and the skid. The horizontal front rudder is packed intact. The vertical rear rudder is unhung and laid flat on the tail. Two men can take the machine apart in a few hours, and can reassemble it in a day. Whether these particular

BUILDING AND FLYING AN AEROPLANE

TABLE I

Relative Strength of Clear Spruce and Elm as Demonstrated by Tests

Material	Size of Pieces (Inches)	Breaking Strain (Pounds)	Weight of Piece (Ounces)
Elm	$1\frac{1}{2} \times 1\frac{1}{8} \times 12$	900	$5\frac{1}{4}$
Spruce	$1\frac{1}{2} \times 1\frac{1}{8} \times 12$	900	$4\frac{1}{4}$
Elm	$1\frac{1}{16} \times 1\frac{1}{16} \times 12$	880	$4\frac{3}{4}$
Spruce	$1\frac{1}{16} \times 1\frac{1}{16} \times 12$	760	$3\frac{7}{8}$
Elm	$1 \times 1 \times 12$	450	4
Spruce	$1 \times 1 \times 12$	600	$3\frac{1}{2}$
Elm	$\frac{13}{16} \times 1\frac{1}{8} \times 12$	390	$3\frac{1}{2}$
Spruce	$\frac{13}{16} \times 1\frac{1}{8} \times 12$	475	3
Elm	$\frac{3}{4} \times \frac{3}{4} \times 12$	275	$2\frac{1}{2}$
Spruce	$\frac{3}{4} \times \frac{3}{4} \times 12$	280	$2\frac{1}{4}$
Elm	$\frac{9}{16} \times \frac{13}{16} \times 12$	175	$2\frac{1}{8}$
Spruce	$\frac{9}{16} \times \frac{13}{16} \times 12$	175	2

features of construction are covered by patents can not be said, as Curtiss has declined to commit himself regarding any rights he may have to them.

Ribs. Two distinct types of ribs are used, main ribs and small ribs, both of the same curvature, Fig. 13. The main ribs are used between pairs of struts, to hold apart the front and rear beams; they are heavy enough to be quite rigid. Three to four small ribs are laid across each section of the planes, between the pairs of main ribs, to give the cloth the proper curvature, and to maintain it in the form desired. The main ribs are built up of six $\frac{1}{4}$-inch laminations of wood $\frac{7}{8}$ inch wide and securely glued together. The small ribs are made of three layers $\frac{1}{2}$ inch wide.

The first part of the actual construction will be the making of these laminated ribs, but before describing this detail, the question of suitable material should be well considered. Both weight and strength must be figured on and this limits the choice to a few kinds of wood. Of these *spruce* and *elm* are the best available, with the occasional use of *ash* to give greater rigidity. Spruce is, of course, the first choice. This wood was once considered as having no great strength, but a series of careful tests shows this belief to be unfounded. With the exception of the bed, or support for the

22 BUILDING AND FLYING AN AEROPLANE

motor and a few other parts, the Wright machines are constructed wholly of spruce.

Table I gives results of tests made with spruce from Washington and Oregon, and with elm from Michigan and Indiana. Testing scales were employed, the pieces being supported at their ends with the load in the center.

These tests were made with clear wood in each case, as knots naturally decrease the strength of a piece greatly, this depending on their size and location.

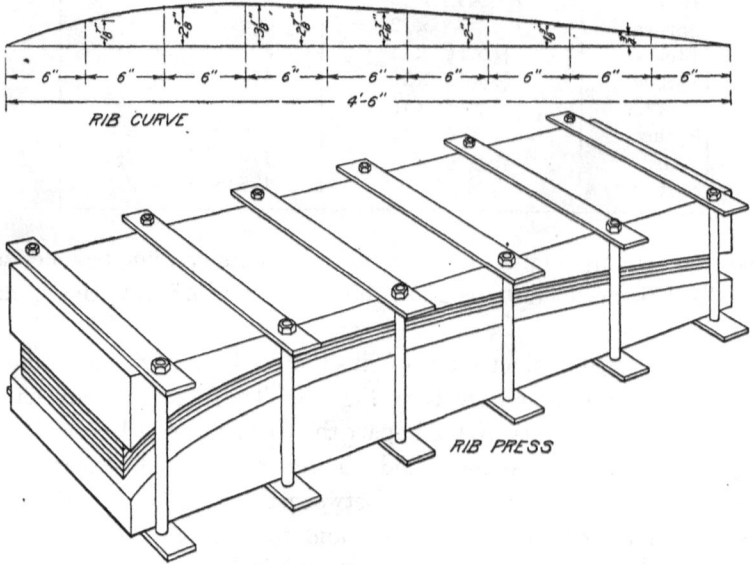

Fig. 14. Details of Rib Press, Curtiss Biplane

Before proceeding with the ribs themselves, the press for giving them the proper curvature must be made. Take a good piece of oak, ash, or other solid wood, 8 inches wide by 5 feet long, and dressed all over. On the side of the piece lay out the curve, the dimensions of which are illustrated in Fig. 14. First, rule the horizontal, or chord line, on it, marking off 4 feet 6 inches on this line, equidistant from each end. Then divide the chord into 6-inch sections and, at the point of each 6-inch section, erect perpendiculars beginning at the rear, $\frac{3}{4}$ inch, $1\frac{3}{8}$ inches, 2 inches, and so on, as indicated on the drawing. The upper ends of these perpendiculars will

BUILDING AND FLYING AN AEROPLANE

form locating points for the curve. Through them draw a smooth curve as shown, continuing it down through the chord at each end. Take the piece with the curve thus marked on it to the local planing, sash and blind, or sawmill—any plant equipped with a band saw—and have it cut apart along the curve. This will cost little or nothing—acquaintance will obtain it as a favor, and acquaintance with any wood-working concern in the aeroplane builder's home town will be of great aid. Failing this aid, the operation may be carried out with a hand saw (rip), but the job will not be as neat and will have to be cleaned up with a draw knife and sand paper, taking care to preserve the outline of the curve as drawn. As the rib press is really a mould or pattern from which all the ribs are to be bent to a uniform curvature, care must be taken in its construction.

To clamp the two halves of the press together, a dozen machine bolts will be required; they should measure $\frac{3}{4} \times 15$ inches. If obtainable, eye bolts will be found more convenient as they may be turned up with but one wrench and a bar. The steel straps are $\frac{3}{8}$ by $1\frac{1}{2}$ by 10 inches long with $\frac{3}{4}$-inch holes drilled 9 inches apart to centers, to enclose the 8-inch pieces.

Obtain a sufficient supply of boards of reasonably clear spruce, $\frac{1}{4}$ inch thick, 6 to 7 inches wide, and at least 4 feet 9 inches long (dressed both sides), to make all the ribs necessary both small and large. This material should be purchased from the mill as it is out of the question to attempt to cut the ribs from larger sizes by hand. Buy several pounds of good cabinet makers' glue and a water-jacketed gluepot. This glue comes in sheets and in numerous grades—a good quality should be used, costing from 40 to 50 cents a pound if bought in a large city. Laminating the ribs in this manner and gluing them together is not only the quickest and easiest method of giving them the proper curve, being much superior to steam bending, but is also stronger when well done, as the quality of the material can be watched more closely.

Start with the making of the small ribs; apply the glue thin and piping hot in a generous layer to three boards with a good-sized flat paint or varnish brush. Omit on the upper surface of third board and apply between three others, Fig. 13. This will give two series of three each in the press. Tighten up the end bolts first, as the upper part of the press near the top of the curve is likely to be weak unless liberally proportioned. Then turn down the nuts on the other bolts. Do not attempt to turn any one of them as far as it will go the first time, but tighten each one a little at a time, thus gradually making the compression over the whole surface as nearly uniform as possible. This should be continued until the glue will no longer ooze out from between the boards, indicating that they are in close contact. Twenty-four hours should be allowed for drying, and when taken out the cracks between the boards should be almost invisible in the finished ribs.

Have the laminated boards cut by a power rip saw at the planing mill, to the dimensions shown in the drawing, making an allowance of $\frac{1}{4}$ inch for the width of the saw blade at each cut in calculating the number of ribs which can be cut from each board. In addition, a margin should be allowed at each side, as it is impractical to get all the thin boards squarely in line. For the main ribs, apply the glue between all six boards, clamp and dry in the same manner. Thirty small ribs will be required, if three are used in each section, and forty if four are specified, while twelve main ribs will be needed for standard construction, and sixteen if the quick-demountable plan referred to is followed. It is advisable to make several extra ribs of each kind in addition. If the builder has not sufficient faith in spruce alone, despite the figures given in Table I, one of the laminations, preferably the center, or if two be employed, the outer ones, may be of ash, though this will add considerably to the weight.

To prevent the ribs from splitting open at the ends, they are protected by light steel ferrules, shown in Fig. 15. When received in the rough-sawed condition from the mill, the ribs must be tapered at the ends with a plane or spoke shave to fit these ferrules, and the sharp edges should be rounded off. In doing this, it must be remembered that the upper surface of the small ribs gives the curvature to the cloth surface, so that any tapering must be done on the lower side. The main ribs may be tapered from both sides, as it is the center line, or crack between the third and fourth laminations, that determines the curve. Every inch along this line $\frac{3}{16}$-inch holes are to be drilled for the lacing, Fig. 15.

The ferrules for the front ends of the small ribs are light $\frac{1}{2}$-inch seamless steel tubing; they may be flattened to the proper shape in a vise without heating and are drilled with a $\frac{1}{8}$-inch hole. They

BUILDING AND FLYING AN AEROPLANE

are driven tight on to the tapered ends of the ribs and fastened in place with a small screw. The rear-end ferrules are $\frac{1}{2}$-inch lengths of $\frac{3}{8}$-inch tubing, driven on and drilled with a $\frac{3}{32}$-inch hole for the rear-edge wire. The rear ferrules of the main ribs may be the same $\frac{1}{2}$-inch tubing used for the front of the small ribs; they should be cut off so that their ends will come in the same line as the holes in the ends of the small ribs. If the quick-demountable plan be followed, the second main rib from each end may be left long and

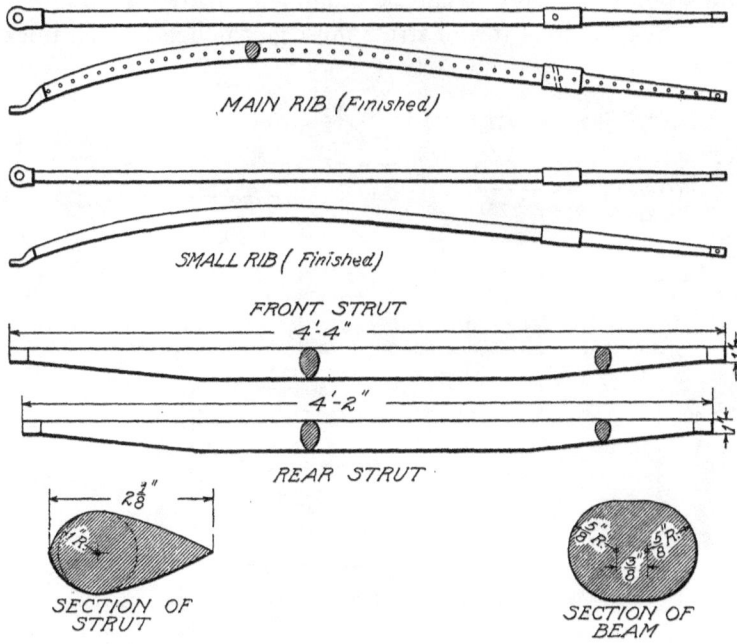

Fig. 15. Details of Ribs and Struts, Curtiss Biplane

drilled with a hole like the small ribs. The front ferrules of the main ribs should be $\frac{3}{4}$-inch tubing of heavier gauge, drilled with a $\frac{1}{4}$-inch hole. The finished ribs are sandpapered smooth and shellaced or coated with spar varnish. The latter is much more expensive and slower in drying but has the great advantage of being weather-proof and will protect the glue cracks from moisture. The ferrules may be painted with black enamel.

Struts. Before going into the detail of the construction of the remainder of the *main cell* and its attached framing, a brief descrip-

26   BUILDING AND FLYING AN AEROPLANE

tion of its parts and their relation to one another will make matters clearer. The upright struts, Fig. 15, which hold the two planes apart, fit at each end into sockets, which are simply metal cups with bolts projecting through their ends, Fig. 16. Those at the bottom of the front row of struts pass through the eyes of the turnbuckles and connections for the wire trussing, then through the flattened ferrules of the main ribs, and finally through the beam, all being clamped together with a nut. Those at the top go through the turnbuckles first, then through the beam, and finally the rib ferrule. The bolts at the back row of struts must go through the full thick-

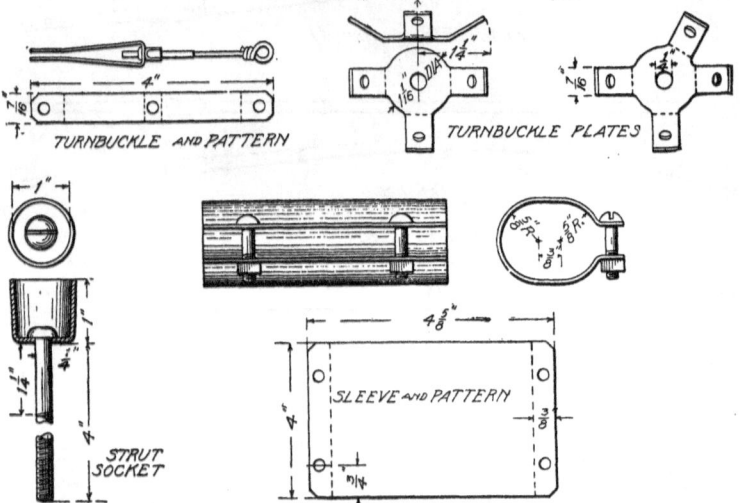

Fig. 16. Details of Metal Parts of Curtiss Biplane

ness of the main ribs, and so must be longer. The drawings, Figs. 15 and 16, show the method of attachment of both the main and the small ribs and illustrate a neat method of attaching the turnbuckles—instead of being strung on the socket bolt one after another, they are riveted to the corners of a steel plate which alone is clamped under the socket.

Beams. The beams are jointed at each strut connection, the ends being cut square and united by a sheet-steel sleeve, a pattern of which is shown in Fig. 16, clamped on by two small bolts. The hole for the socket bolt is drilled half in each of the two abutting beams. As it is very difficult to obtain long pieces of wood suf-

ONE OF THE FRENCH MILITARY DIRIGIBLES WITH THE BALLOON SHED SHOWN BELOW

Intentionally blank as was the original edition.

BUILDING AND FLYING AN AEROPLANE 27

ficiently straight grained and free from knots for the purpose, this jointed system considerably cheapens the construction. Both beams and struts are of spruce, but to give additional strength, the beams of the middle section may be ash. Special aero cloth, rubberized fabrics, or light, closely-woven duck (racing yacht sail cloth of fine quality, this being employed at first by the Wright Brothers in their machines) forms the surfaces of the wings. The front edge of each section of the surface is tacked to the beam and the rear edge is laced over the rear wire already referred to, this wire being stretched taut through the holes in the rear tips of the ribs, both main and small. After the cloth is stretched tight, it is tacked to the small ribs, a strip of tape being laid under the tack heads to prevent the cloth from pulling away from under them. If the aeroplane is intended to be taken apart very often, the standard design as shown by the large drawings, Figs. 11 and 12, may be modified so as to make it unnecessary to unlace the cloth each time. This is arranged by regarding the two outer sections at each end of the plane as one, and never separating them. Additional main ribs are then provided at the inner ends of these sections, and are attached directly to the beams, instead of being clamped under the strut sockets. In taking the machine apart, the struts are pulled from the sockets, leaving the latter in place. It will then be an advantage to shorten the main planes somewhat, say 3 inches on each section, so that the outer double sections will come under the "12-foot rule" of the Express Companies.

Running Gear. Three wheels are provided—one in front under the outrigger and two under the main cell for starting and landing. Two beams extend from the front wheel to the engine bed and serve to carry the pilot's seat, as will be seen from the elevator, Fig. 12. A third beam runs back horizontally from the front wheel and on rough ground acts as a skid. The rest of the running gear is made of steel tubing, the pieces being joined simply by flattening the ends, drilling and clamping with bolts; no sockets or special connections of any kind are necessary here. If desired, the wheels may be carried in bicycle forks and may be fitted with shock absorbers, some idea of the various expedients adopted by different builders for this purpose being obtainable from the sketches, Fig. 40 in "Types of Aeroplanes." Two separate tubes, one on each side of the wheel make a simple construction and will probably serve just as well. The details of the running gear will be given later.

Outrigging and Rudders. For the outriggers and the frames carrying the front horizontal or elevating rudder and the rear vertical rudder and tail, or horizontal keel, either spruce or bamboo may be employed. Bamboo will be found on machines turned out by the Curtiss factory, and while it is the lighter of the two, it is not generally favored, as spruce is easier to obtain in good quality and is far easier to work. At their ends, these outriggers are fitted with ferrules of steel tubing, flattened and drilled through. The outriggers are attached to the main framework of the machine by slipping the ferrules over the socket bolts of the middle section struts, above and below the beams. It is preferable, however, to attach the rear outriggers to extra bolts running through the beams, so that when the machine is to be housed the tail and rudder can be unshipped and the triangular frames swung around against the main frame, considerably reducing the space required.

The tail, horizontal and vertical rudders, and the ailerons are light frames of wood, covered on both sides with the same kind of cloth as the main planes or wings. These frames are braced with piano wire in such a manner that no twisting strains can be put on them. The front horizontal rudder, which is of biplane construction like the main cell, is built up with struts in the same way. Instead of being fitted with sockets, however, the struts are held by long screws run through the planes and into their ends, passing through the eyes of the turnbuckles.

DETAILS OF CONSTRUCTION

Main Planes and Struts. It is preferable to begin with the construction of the main planes and their struts and truss wires, the ribs already described being the first step.

The main beams offer no special difficulties. They are ovals $1\frac{1}{4}$ by $1\frac{5}{8}$ inches, all 6 feet long except the eight end ones, which are 6 feet 2 inches. The beams of the central section should be of ash, or should be thicker than the others. In the latter case, they must be tapered at the ends so that the clamping sleeves will fit and the additional wood must be all on the lower side, so that the rib will not be thrown out of alignment. The spruce used for the other beams

BUILDING AND FLYING AN AEROPLANE 29

should be reasonably clear and straight grained, but a small knot or two does not matter, provided it does not come near the ends of the beam. The beams may be cut to the oval shape by the sawmill or planed down by hand.

"Fish-shaped" or "stream-line" section, as it is more commonly termed, is used for the struts, Fig. 15. It is questionable whether this makes any material difference in the wind resistance, but it is common practice to follow it in order to minimize this factor. It is more important that the struts be larger at their centers than at the ends, as this strengthens them considerably. At their ends the struts have ferrules of the 1-inch brass or steel tubing, and fit into the sockets which clamp the ribs and beams together. The material is spruce but the four central struts which carry the engine bed should either be ash or of larger size, say $1\frac{1}{4}$ by 3 inches.

Care Necessary to Get Planes Parallel. The front struts must be longer than the rear ones by the thickness of a main rib at the point where the rear strut bolt passes through it, less the thickness of the rib ferrule through which the bolt of the front strut must pass. However, the first distance is not really the actual thickness of the rib, but the distance between the top of the rear beam and the bottom of the strut socket. In the drawings the difference in length between the front and rear struts is given as 2 inches, but it is preferable for the builder to leave the rear struts rather long and then measure the actual distance when assembling, cutting the struts to fit. The ends of the struts should also be countersunk enough to clear the head of the socket bolt.

One of the items which the builder can not well escape buying in finished form is the strut sockets. These are cup-shaped affairs of pressed steel which sell at 20 cents each. Sixteen of them will be required for the main frame, and a dozen more can advantageously be used in the front and rear controls, though for this purpose they are not absolutely necessary. They can also be obtained in a larger oval size suitable for the four central struts that carry the engine bed, as well as in the standard 1-inch size. The bolts which project through the bottom of the sockets are ordinary $\frac{1}{4}$-inch stove bolts, with their heads brazed to the sockets.

For the rear struts, where the bolt must pass through the slanting main rib, it is advisable to make angle washers to put under the socket and also between the beam and rib. These washers are made by sawing up a piece of heavy brass tubing, or a bar with a ¼-inch hole drilled in its center, the saw cuts being taken alternately at right angles and at 60 degrees to the axis of the tube.

The sleeves which clamp together the ends of the beams are made of sheet steel of about 20 gauge. The steel is cut out on the pattern given in the drawing, Fig. 16, and the $\frac{3}{16}$-inch bolt holes drilled in the flanges. The flanges are bent over by clamping the sheet in a vise along the bending line and then beating down with a hammer. Then the sleeves can be bent into shape around a stray end of the beam wood. The holes for the strut socket bolts should not be drilled until ready to assemble. Ordinarily, $\frac{3}{16}$-inch stove bolts will do to clamp the flanges together.

Having reached this stage, the amateur builder must now supply himself with turnbuckles. As already mentioned, these may either be purchased or made by hand. It is permissible to use either one or two turnbuckles on each wire. One is really sufficient, but two— one at each end—add but little weight and give greater leeway in making adjustments. As there are about 115 wires in the machine which need turnbuckles, the number required will be either 115 or 230, depending upon the plan which is followed. Those of the turnbuckles to be used on the front and rear controls and the ailerons, about one-fifth of the total number, may be of lighter stock than those employed on wires which carry part of the weight of the machine.

Making Turnbuckles for the Truss Wires. On the supposition that the builder will make his own turnbuckles, a simple form is described here. As will be seen from Fig. 16, the turnbuckles are simply bicycle spokes, with the nipple caught in a loop of sheet steel and the end of the spoke itself twisted into an eye to which the truss wire can be attached. The sheet steel used should be 18 or 16 gauge, and may be cut to pattern with a heavy pair of tin snips. The spokes should be $\frac{3}{32}$ inch over the threaded portion. The eye should be twisted up tight and brazed so that it can not come apart. The hole in the middle of each strip is, of course, drilled the same size as the spoke nipple. The holes in the ends are $\frac{3}{16}$ inch.

In the original Curtiss machines, the turnbuckles were strung on the socket bolts one after another, sometimes making a pack of them half an inch thick. A much neater construction is shown in the drawings, in which the bolt pierces a single plate with lugs to which to make the turnbuckles fast by riveting. The plates are of different shapes, with two, three, or four lugs, according to the places where they are to be used. They are cut from steel stock $\frac{3}{32}$ inch thick, with $\frac{1}{4}$-inch holes for the socket bolts and $\frac{3}{16}$ inch, or other convenient size, for the rivets that fasten on the turnbuckles.

The relative merits of cable and piano wire for trussing have not been thoroughly threshed out. Each has its advantages and disadvantages. Most of the well-known builders use cable; yet if the difference between 1,000 feet of cable at $2\frac{1}{4}$ cents per foot (the price for 500-foot spools), and 8 pounds of piano wire at 70 cents a pound, looks considerable to the amateur builder, let him by all means use the wire. The cable, if used, should be the $\frac{3}{32}$-inch size, which will stand a load of 800 pounds; piano wire should be 24 gauge, tested to 745 pounds. It should be noted that there is a special series of gauges for piano wire, known as the music wire gauge, in which the size of the wire increases with the gauge numbers, instead of the contrary, as is usual with machinery wire gauges.

One by no means unimportant advantage of the piano wire is that it is much easier to fasten into the turnbuckles. A small sleeve or ferrule, a $\frac{1}{4}$-inch length of $\frac{1}{8}$-inch tubing, is first strung on the wire. The end of the wire is then passed through the turnbuckle eye, bent up, thrust through the sleeve, and again bent down. When the machine is taken apart, the wire is not disconnected from the eye, but instead the turnbuckle spoke is unscrewed from the nipple. The shape of the sheet-steel loop should be such as to hold the latter in place. Cable, on the other hand, must be cut with about 2 inches to spare. After being threaded through the turnbuckle eye, the end is wound back tightly on itself and then soldered, to make certain that it can not loosen.

With a supply of turnbuckles and cable or piano wire at hand, the builder may go ahead with the main box-like structure or cell, which should be completed except for the cloth covering, and in proper alignment, before taking up the construction of the running gear and controls.

Running Gear. The running gear of the machine is built of seamless steel tubing, those parts which carry the weight of the machine direct being of $\frac{3}{4}$-inch outside diameter, 16-gauge tubing,

32 BUILDING AND FLYING AN AEROPLANE

while the others are ⅝-inch outside diameter, either 18 or 20 gauge. About 25 feet of the heavy and 45 feet of the light tubing will be required, in lengths as follows: Heavy, four 3-foot, three 4-foot; light, one 6-foot, two 4-foot 6-inch, and seven 4-foot pieces. Referring to Fig. 17, two diagonal braces from the rear beam to the engine bed, the V-shaped piece under the front engine bed struts and all of the rear frame except the horizontal piece from wheel to wheel, are of heavy tubing. The horizontal in the rear frame, diagonals from the rear wheels and the rear end of the skid to the front beam, the two horizontals between the front and rear beam, and the forward V are of light tubing.

Three ash beams are used in the running gear. Two of these run diagonally from the rear end of the engine bed to the front wheel.

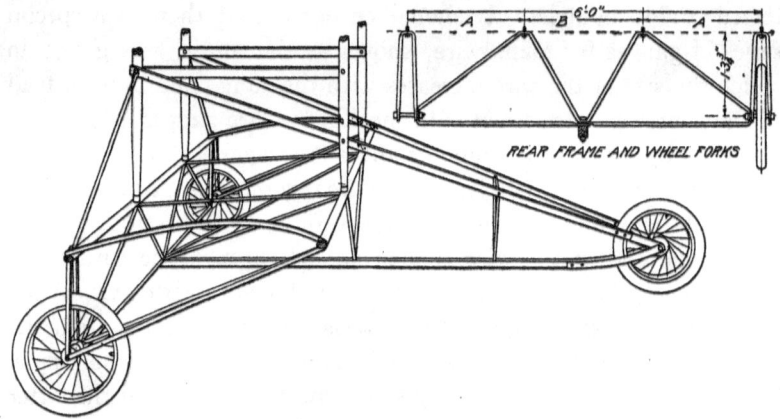

Fig. 17. Details of Curtiss Running Gear

These are about 10 feet long and 1 by 1¾ inches section. The third, which on rough ground acts as a skid, is 8½ feet long and about 2 inches square. Between the points where the tubing frames are attached to it, the upper corners may be beveled off with a spoke shave an inch or more down each side. The beams are attached to the front wheel with strips of steel stock 1½ inches wide and ¼ inch thick. The engine bed beams are also ash about 1 by 1¾ inches section. Their rear ends are bolted to the middle of the rear engine bed struts and the front ends may be ½ inch higher.

The wheels are usually 20 by 2 inches, and of the bicycle type,

BUILDING AND FLYING AN AEROPLANE 33

but heavier and wider in the hub; the tires are single tube. These wheels, complete with tires, cost about $10 each. This size is used on the standard Curtiss machines, but novice operators, whose landings are not quite as gentle as they might be, find them easily broken. Therefore, it may be more economical in the end to pay a little more and get heavier tires—at least to start with.

For working the tubing into shape, a plumber's blow torch is almost indispensable—most automobilists will already possess one of these. The oval, flat variety, holding about one pint, is very handy and packs away easily, but on steady work requires filling somewhat too frequently. With a dozen bricks a shield can be built in front of the torch to protect the flame and concentrate the heat. Whenever it is to be flattened and bent, the tubing should be brought to a bright red or yellow heat. Screwing the vise down on it will then flatten it quickly without hammer marks. Where the bend is to be made in the middle of the piece, however, it may be necessary to resort to the hammer and anvil.

It is convenient to start with the framework under the rear beam. This may be drawn accurately to full size on the workshop floor, and the tubes bent to fit the drawing. With this framework once in place, a definite starting point for the remainder of the running gear is established. Here and in all other places, when boring through wood, the holes should be drilled out full, and larger washers should be placed under the bolt head and nut. All nuts should be provided with some sort of locking device The perspective drawing, Fig. 17, should show the general arrangement clearly enough to enable the builder to finish the running gear.

Outriggers. Both the front and rear control members, or "outriggers" as they are termed, Fig. 12, may be conveniently built up on the central section of the main frame, which, it is assumed, has now been fitted with the running gear.

The horizontal rudder, or "elevator," is a biplane structure like the main cell of the machine, but with fewer struts; it is carried in front of the main planes on two A-shaped frames. The vertical rudder, at the rear, is split along the middle and straddles a fixed horizontal plane, or *tail*. This also is carried on two A-shaped frames. Lateral stability is controlled by two auxiliary planes or ailerons, one at each side of the machine and carried on the two outer

34   BUILDING AND FLYING AN AEROPLANE

front struts. These three control units—*elevator, tail* and *rudder,* and *ailerons*—will now be taken up separately and their construction, location on the machine, and operation will be described.

Horizonal Rudder or Elevator. The two planes of the elevator are 2 feet wide by 5 feet 8 inches long and are spaced 2 feet apart,

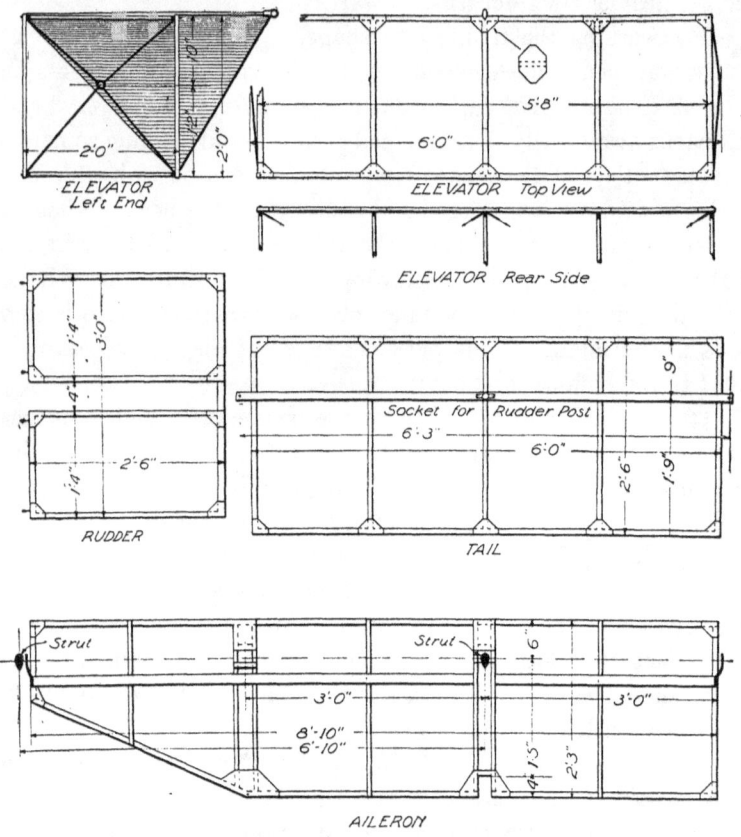

Fig. 18. Details of Rudders and Ailerons, Curtiss Biplane

being held in this position by ten struts. The frames of the planes are built of spruce sticks $\frac{1}{2}$ by 1 inch, each plane having two sticks the full length and five evenly spaced crosspieces or ribs. These are joined together with squares of X-sheet tin, as shown in the detailed drawing, Fig. 18. With a little experimenting, paper patterns can be made from which the tin pieces can be cut out. The sticks are then nailed through the tin with $\frac{3}{4}$-inch brads.

It is convenient to draw the frames out accurately on a smooth wood floor and then work over this drawing. The first few brads will hold the sticks in place. When all the brads have been driven, a little drop of solder should be run in around the head of each one. This is a tedious job. One must be careful to use no more solder than necessary as it increases the weight very rapidly. Two pounds of wire solder should be sufficient for all the control members which are built in this way. When the top side is soldered, pry the frame loose from the floor with a screwdriver and turn it over. Then the projecting points of the brads must be clinched and the soldering repeated.

At this stage, the two frames should be covered on both sides with the prepared cloth used for covering the main planes. The method of preparing this cloth is detailed a little farther along.

The struts, so-called, to continue the analogy with the main planes, are turned sticks of spruce $\frac{3}{8}$ inch in diameter. They are fitted at each end with ferrules of thin $\frac{3}{8}$-inch brass, or steel tubing, driven on tight. Instead of using sockets, the struts are held at each end, simply by a long wood screw driven through the tin and wood of the plane frame and into the strut. These screws also hold the turnbuckles for the truss wires. For trussing purposes, the elevator is regarded as consisting of two sections only, the intermediate struts being disregarded.

The turnbuckles and wire used here and in the other control members may well be of lighter stock than those used in the main planes. Piano wire, No. 18, or $\frac{1}{16}$-inch cable is amply strong. The sheet steel may be about 22 gauge, instead of 16, and the bicycle spokes smaller in proportion. No turnbuckle plates are necessary. The screws running into the struts may be passed directly through the eyes of the turnbuckles, where they would have been attached to the turnbuckle plate. In order to secure a square and neat structure, those struts which have turnbuckles at their ends should be made a trifle shorter than the others.

At each end, the elevator has an **X**-shaped frame of $\frac{1}{4}$-inch steel tubing; at the intersection of the **X**'s are pivots on which the elevator is supported. Each **X** is made of two tubes, bent into a **V** and flattened and brazed together at the points. The ends of the **X**'s are flattened and bent over so that the screws which hold the struts in place may pass through them.

36 BUILDING AND FLYING AN AEROPLANE

Fig. 19. Curtiss Biplane Ready for Flight

To the front middle strut is attached an extension which acts as a lever for operating the elevator. This is a stick of spruce ¾ inch in diameter and 3 feet 3 inches long. At its upper end it has a ferrule of steel tubing, flattened at the end. The lower part of the stick may be fastened to the strut by wrapping the tube with friction tape, or by improvising a couple of sheet steel clamps. The upper end of the stick is braced by a ¼-inch steel tube, extending to the top of the rear middle strut, and held by the same screw as the strut. This extension lever is connected to the steering column by a bamboo rod, 1 inch in diameter and about 10 feet long, provided with flattened ferrules of steel tubing at each end. Each ferrule should be held on by a ⅛-inch stove bolt passing through it.

Front and Rear Outrigger Frames. Both the front elevator and the tail and rudder at the rear, are carried, as mentioned above, each on a pair of **A**-shaped frames, similar to one an-

BUILDING AND FLYING AN AEROPLANE 37

other, except that those in the rear are longer than those in the front. Both are made of spruce of about the same section as used for the struts of the main frame. These pieces may either be full length, or they may be jointed at the intersection of the crosspieces, the ends being clamped in a sheet-steel sleeve, just like that used on the beams of the main frame. In this case, it is advisable to run a $\frac{1}{8}$-inch stove bolt through each of the ends.

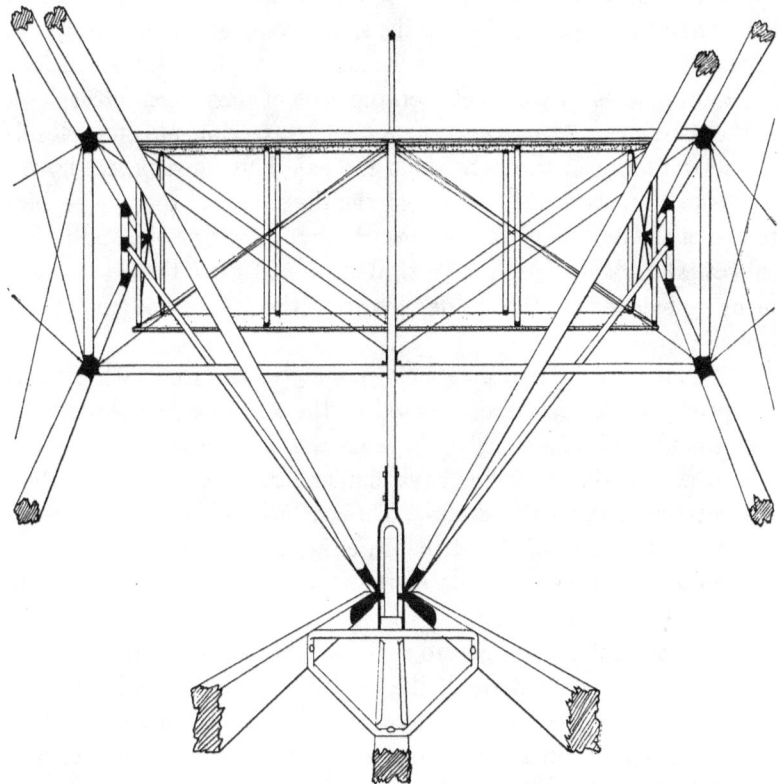

Fig. 20. Details of Outriggers and Front Elevating Planes as Seen from Driver's Seat

The crosspieces of the **A**-frames are spruce of the same section, or a little smaller. At their ends may be used strut sockets like those of the main frame; or, if it is desired to save this expense, they may be fastened by strips of $\frac{1}{16}$-inch steel stock with through bolts.

The front outrigger has, besides the two **A**-frames, a rather complicated arrangement of struts designed to brace the front wheel against the shocks of landing. This arrangement does not appear very plain in a plan or elevation, and may best be understood by reference to the photograph, Fig. 19, and the perspective drawing, Fig. 20. Fig. 20 is a view from the driver's seat. The elevator is seen in front, the **A**-frames at each side, and at the bottom the two diagonal beams to the engine bed and the skid.

Reference to this drawing will show the two diagonals run from the front wheel up and back to the top of the main frame, and two more from the wheel forward to the short crosspieces near the apexes of the **A**-frame: there is also a vertical strut which intersects two horizontal pieces running between the ends of the longer crosspieces of the **A**-frames. Altogether, there are five attachments on each side of the front wheel, through which the axle bolt must pass, viz, the connections to the skid, to one of the diagonals to the engine bed, to one of the rear diagonals, to one of the front diagonals, and to one side of the fork carrying the vertical strut. Of these the skid attachments should be on the inside closest to the wheel, and the engine bed diagonals next.

The four additional diagonals running to the front wheel may be spruce of the same section used in the **A**-frames, or turned one inch round. At each end they have flattened ferrules of steel tubing. The beams of the **A**-frames have similar ferrules at the ends where they attach to the main frames. These attachments should be made on the socket bolts of the struts on either side of the middle 6-foot section and on the outer side of the main beams—not between the beam and the socket itself.

It is possible, of course, to make all the **A**-frames and diagonal braces of bamboo, if desired, the qualities of this material already having been referred to. Bamboo rods for this purpose should be between 1 and $1\frac{1}{4}$ inches in diameter. Where ferrules are fitted on the ends, the hole of the bamboo should be plugged with wood glued in place.

Generally, in the construction of the outrigger frames, the builder can use his own discretion to a considerable extent. There are innumerable details which can be varied—far too many to consider even a part of the possibilities in this connection. If the builder runs across any detail which he does not see mentioned here, he may safely assume that any workmanlike job will suffice. Often, the method may be adapted to the materials on hand. The diagonal wires from the crosspieces of the **A**-frames to the struts should be crossed.

Rudder and Tail Construction. The frame for the rudder and tail are constructed in much the same way as those for the elevator, Fig. 18. Spruce sticks 1 by $\frac{1}{2}$ inch are used throughout, except for the piece at the back edge of the rudder and the long middle piece across the tail; these should be $1\frac{1}{2}$ by $\frac{1}{2}$ inch. This long middle piece of the tail is laid across on top of the rest of the framework. When the cloth is put on, this makes the upper surface slightly convex while the lower surface remains flat. The ends of this piece should be reinforced with sheet steel, fairly heavy and drilled for $\frac{1}{4}$-inch bolts, attaching the tail to the **A**-frames.

The rudder is hung from two posts extending above and below the tail. These posts may be set in cast aluminum sockets, such as may be obtained from any supply house for 20 cents apiece. The posts need not be more than $\frac{3}{4}$ inch in diameter. At their outer ends, they should have ferrules of steel tubing, and the turnbuckles or other attachments for the truss wires should be attached by a wood screw running into the end of each. From these posts the rudder may be hung on any light hinges the builder may find convenient, or on hinges improvised from screw eyes or eye bolts, with a bolt passing through the eyes of each.

In steering, the rudder is controlled by a steering wheel carried on a hinged post in front of the pilot. This post should be ash about 1 by $1\frac{1}{4}$ inches. It hinges at the bottom on a steel tube of $\frac{1}{2}$-inch diameter which passes through it and is supported at the ends on diagonal beams to the engine bed. Two diagonals of lighter tubing may be put in to hold the posts centered between the two beams.

The post is, of course, upright, and the hub of the wheel is horizontal. The wheel may be conveniently mounted on a piece of tubing of the same size as the hub hole, run through the post and held by a comparatively small bolt, which passes through it and has a big washer on either end. The wheel is preferably of the motor-boat variety with a groove around the rim for the steering cable.

The rear edge of the tail should be about 1 inch lower than the front. To make the rudder post stand approximately vertical, wedge-shaped pieces of wood may be set under the sockets.

40   BUILDING AND FLYING AN AEROPLANE

The steering connections should be of flexible cables of steel such as are made for this purpose. There should be a double pulley on the post just under the wheel, and the cables should be led off the post just at the hinge at the bottom, so that swinging the post will not affect them. The cable is then carried under the lower main plane and out the lower beams of the A-frames. It is attached to the rudder at the back edge; snap hooks should be used for easy disconnection in packing. Perhaps the best way of guiding the cable, instead of using pulleys, is to run it through short pieces of tubing lashed to the beams with friction tape. The tubing can be bent without flattening by first filling it with melted lead, which, after the bending, can be melted out again.

Ailerons for Lateral Stability. The framework of the ailerons is made in the same way as that for the elevator, tail, and rudder, Fig. 18. The pieces around the edges should be $1\frac{1}{2}$ by $\frac{1}{2}$ inch, as also the long strip laid over the top of the ribs. The ribs should be $\frac{1}{2}$ by $\frac{3}{4}$ inch. Each aileron has two holes, one for the strut to pass through, and the other for the diagonal truss wires at their intersection. The back edge also has a notch in it to clear the fore and aft wires. Each aileron is hung on four strips of soft steel about $\frac{1}{2}$ by $\frac{1}{16}$ inch, twisted so that one end is at right angles to the other. These are arranged one on each side of the strut which passes through the aileron, and one at each end. Bolts through the struts carry three of them and the outer one is trussed by wires to each end of the outer strut.

A frame of $\frac{1}{4}$-inch steel tubing fits around the aviator's shoulders and is hinged to the seat, so that he can move it by leaning from one side to the other. This is connected by flexible cable to the rear edges of the ailerons, so that when the aviator leans to the left, he will raise the left and lower the right aileron. The upper edges of the ailerons are directly connected to each other by a cable running along the upper front beam, so that they must always move together.

Covering of the Planes. Mention has already been made of the fact, in the general description of the machine, that light sail cloth, as employed on the Wright machines, may be used for the planes or wings. As a matter of fact, many different materials may be successfully employed, the selection depending upon the builder himself and his financial resources. About 55 square yards of material

BUILDING AND FLYING AN AEROPLANE   41

will be required, and in comparing prices always compare the width as this may vary from 28 to 55 inches. Rubberized silk which is used on the standard Curtiss machines is the most expensive covering, its cost running up to something like two hundred dollars. There are also several good aero fabrics on the market which sell at 60 cents a square yard, as well as a number of brands of varnish for the cloth—most of them, however, quite expensive. The most economical method is to employ a strong linen cloth coated with shellac, which will be found very satisfactory.

The covering of the frames with the cloth may well be postponed until after the engine has been installed and tested, thus avoiding the splashing of oil and dirt which the fabric is apt to receive during this operation. The wire to which the cloth is laced, must be strung along the rear ends of the ribs of each plane. The wires pass through holes in the ends of the small ribs and are attached to the main ribs with turnbuckles. At the ends of the planes the main ribs must be braced against the pull of the wire by a piece of $\frac{1}{4}$-inch tubing running from the end of the rib diagonally up to the rear beam. Both turnbuckles and tube are fastened with one wood screw running into the end of the rib.

The cloth should be cut to fit the panels between the main ribs and hemmed up, allowing at least an inch in each direction for stretch. Small eyelets should be put along the sides and rear edges an inch apart for the lacing. At the front edge, the cloth is tacked directly to the beam, the edge being taken well under and around to the back. Strong fish line is good material for the lacing.

After the cloth is laced on, it must be tacked down to the small ribs. For this purpose, use upholstery tacks as they have big cup-shaped heads which grip the cloth and do not tear out. As an extra precaution a strip of heavy tape must be run over each rib under the tack heads. All the control members are covered on both sides, the edges being folded under and held by tacks.

Making the Propeller. If the completed biplane is to fly properly and also have sufficient speed to make it safe, considerable care must be devoted to the design and making of the propeller. Every aeroplane has a safe speed, usually referred to in technical parlance as its *critical speed*. In the case of the Curtiss biplane under consideration, this speed is about 40 miles an hour.

42   BUILDING AND FLYING AN AEROPLANE

By speeding up the motor considerably, it may be able to make 42 to 43 miles an hour in a calm, such a condition representing the only true measure of an aeroplane's ability in this direction, while on the other hand, it would not be safe to let its speed with relation to the wind (not to the ground) fall much below 35 miles an hour. At any slower rate of travel, its dynamic stability would be precarious and the machine would be likely to dive to the ground unexpectedly. The reasons for this have been explained more in detail under the heading of "The Internal Work of the Wind."

The necessity of making the propeller need not discourage the ambitious builder—if he can spare the time to do it right, it will be excellent experience. If not, propellers designed for driving a machine of this size can be purchased ready to mount from any one of quite a number of manufacturers. But as the outlay required will be at least $50, doubtless most experimenters will prefer to undertake this part of the work as well as that of building the framework and main cell, particularly as more than 90 per cent of the sum mentioned is represented by labor. The cost of the material required is insignificant by comparison.

True-Screw Design. First it will be necessary to design the propeller to meet the requirements of the biplane itself. As this is a matter that has already been gone into in considerable detail under the appropriate heading, no further explanation of propeller characteristics or of the technical terms employed, should be needed here. We will assume that the biplane is to have a speed of 40 miles per hour in still air with the motor running at 1,200 r. p. m. With this data, it will not be difficult to calculate the correct pitch of the propeller to give that result. Thus

$$\frac{40 \times 5280 \times 100}{60 \times 1200 \times 85} = 3.45$$

or in round numbers a pitch of $3\frac{1}{2}$ feet. 40 (the speed in miles per hour) times 5,280 (feet per mile) divided by 60 (minutes in an hour) gives the speed of the aeroplane in feet per minute. Dividing this by 1,200 (revolutions per minute) gives the number of feet the aeroplane is to advance per revolution of the propeller. The "$\frac{100}{85}$" part of the equation represents the efficiency of the propeller which can safely be figured on, *i. e.*, 85 per cent, or an allowance for slip of 15

Intentionally blank as was the original edition.

AN OLD DUTCH WINDMILL AND A MODERN FRENCH AEROPLANE
This Photograph Protected by International Copyright

BUILDING AND FLYING AN AEROPLANE 43

per cent. Forty miles an hour is the maximum speed to be expected, while the r. p. m. rate of the engine should be that at which it operates to the best advantage.

The merits of the *true-screw* and *variable-pitch* propellers have already been dwelt upon. The former is not only more simple to build, but experience has shown that, as generally employed, it gives better efficiency. Hence, the propeller under consideration will be of the true-screw type. Its pitch has already been calculated as $3\frac{1}{2}$ feet. For a machine of this size and power, it should be 6 feet in diameter. Having worked out the pitch and decided upon the diameter, the next and most important thing is to calculate the pitch angle. It will be evident that no two points on the blade will travel through the air at the same speed. Obviously, a point near the tip of the propeller moves faster than one near the hub, just as in rounding a curve, the outer wheel of an automobile has to travel faster than the inner, because it has to travel farther to cover the same ground. For instance, taking the dimensions of the propeller in question it will be seen that its tips will be traveling through the air at close to 4.3 miles per minute, that is,

$$\frac{6 \times \pi \times 1200}{5280} = 4.28$$

in which 6, the diameter of the propeller in feet, times π gives the circumference of the circle which is traveled by the blade tips 1,200 times per minute; this divided by the number of feet per mile gives the miles per minute covered. On the other hand, a point on the blade but 6 inches from the hub will turn at only approximately 3,500 feet per minute. Therefore, if every part of the blade is to advance through the air equally, the inner part must be set at a greater angle than the outer part. Each part of the blade must be set at such an angle that at each revolution it will move forward through the air a distance equal to the pitch. This is known as the pitch angle. The pitch divided by the circumference of the circle described by any part of the blade, will give a quantity known as the *tangent* of an angle for that particular part. The angle corresponding to that tangent may most easily be found by referring to a book of trigonometric tables.

For example, take that part of the blade of a $3\frac{1}{2}$-foot pitch pro-

TABLE II
Propeller Blade Data

Radius in Inches	Tangent	Pitch Angle	Add	Final Angle
6	1.1141	48° 5'	....	48°
9	.7427	36° 36'	....	37°
12	.5571	29° 7'	3° 13'	32° 20'
15	.4457	24° 1'	3° 9'	27° 10'
18	.3719	20° 24'	3° 6'	23° 30'
21	.3183	17° 40'	3°	20° 40'
24	.2785	15° 40'	2° 50'	18° 30'
27	.2476	13° 54'	2° 46'	16° 40'
30	.2228	12° 40'	2° 45'	15° 25'
33	.2025	11° 27'	2° 43'	14° 10'

peller which is 6 inches from the center of the hub. Then

$$\frac{3.5 \times 12}{6 \times 2\pi} = 1.1141 \text{ tangent of 48 degrees 5 minutes}$$

in which 3.5×12 reduces the pitch to inches, while 6×2π is the circumference of the circle described by the point 6 inches from the hub. However, in order to give the propeller blade a proper hold on the air, it must be set at a greater angle than these figures would indicate. That is, it must be given an angle of incidence similar to that given to every one of the supporting planes of the machine. This additional angle ranges from 2 degrees 30 minutes, to 4 degrees, depending upon the speed at which the particular part of the blade travels; the greater the speed, the less the angle. This does not apply to that part of the blade near the hub as the latter is depended upon solely for strength and is not expected to add to the effective thrust of the propeller.

Table II shows the complete set of figures for a blade of 3½-foot pitch, the angles being worked out for sections of the blade 3 inches apart.

These angles are employed in Fig. 21, which shows one blade of the propeller and its cross sections.

It should be understood that these calculations apply only to the type of propeller known as the *true screw*, as distinguished from the *variable pitch*. The design of the latter is a matter of personal skill and experience in its making which is hardly capable of

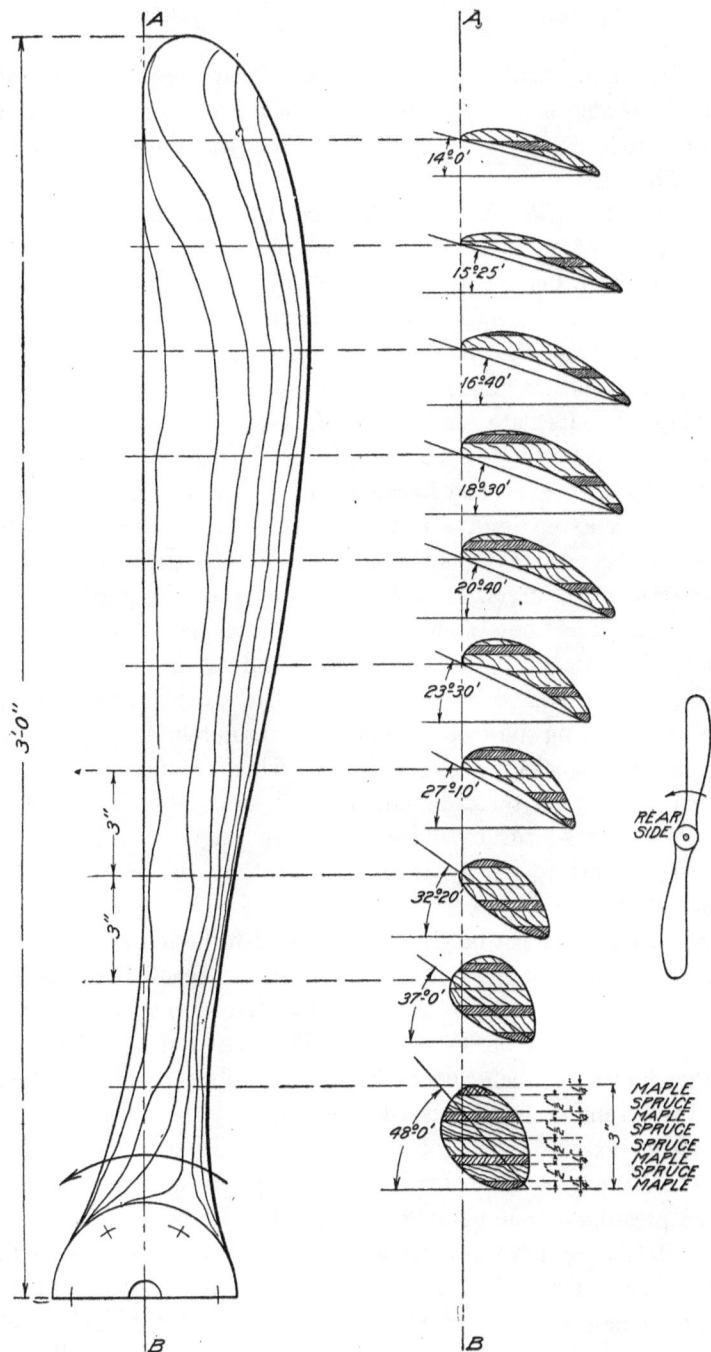

Fig. 21. Details of Propeller Construction, Curtiss Biplane

expression in any mathematical formula. There are said to be only about three men in this country who know how to make a proper variable-pitch propeller, and it naturally is without advantage when made otherwise.

Shaping the Blades. Like the ribs, the propeller is made up of a number of laminations of boards finished true and securely glued, afterward being cut to the proper shape, though this process, of course, involves far more skill than in the former case. Spruce is the strongest wood for its weight, but it is soft and cracks easily. Maple, on the other hand, is tough and hard, so that it will be an advantage to alternate the layers of these woods with an extra maple board, in order to make both outside strips of the harder wood, so as to form a good backing for the steel flanges at the hub, the rear layer extending the full length of the thin rear edges of the blades. Other woods may be employed and frequently are used by propeller manufacturers, such as mahogany (not the grained wood used for furniture, but a cheaper grade which is much stronger), walnut, alternate spruce and whitewood, and others.

The boards should be selected with the greatest care so as to insure their being perfectly *clear*, *i.e.*, absolutely free of knots, cross-grained streaks, or similar flaws, which would impair their strength and render them difficult to work smoothly. They should measure 6 inches wide by 6 feet 1 inch in length. Their surfaces must be finished perfectly true, so that they will come together uniformly all over the area on which they bear on one another, and the various pieces must be glued together with the most painstaking care. Have the glue hot, so that it will spread evenly, and see that it is of a uniform consistency, in order that it may be smoothly applied to every bit of the surface. They must then be clamped together under as much pressure as it is possible to apply to them with the means at hand, the rib press already described in detail forming an excellent tool for this purpose. Tighten up the nuts evenly a little at a time, avoiding the application of excessive or uneven pressure at one point, continuing the gradual tightening up process until it can not be carried any farther. This is to prevent the boards from assuming a curve in drying fast. Allow at least twenty-four hours for drying, during which period the laminated block should be kept in a cool, dry place at as even a temperature as possible.

BUILDING AND FLYING AN AEROPLANE 47

Before undertaking the remainder of the work, all of which must be carried out by hand, with the exception of cutting the block to the outline of the propeller, which may be done with a band saw, a set of templates or gauges should be made from the drawings. These will be necessary as guides for finishing the propeller acurately. Draw the sections out full size on sheets of cardboard or tin and cut out along the curves, finally dividing each sheet into two parts, one for the upper side and one for the lower. Care must be taken to get the sides of the template square, and when they are used, the propeller should be laid on a perfectly true and flat block. Each template should be marked as it is finished, to indicate what part of the blade it is a gauge for. The work of cutting the laminated block down to the lines represented by the templates is carried out with the aid of the plane, spoke shave, and gouge. After the first *roughing out* to approximate the curvature of the finished propeller is completed, the cuts taken should be very fine, as it will be an easy matter to go too deep, thus spoiling the block and necessitating a new start with fresh material. For finishing, pieces of broken glass are employed to scrape the wood to a smooth surface, followed by coarse and finally by fine sandpaper.

Mounting. The hub should be of the same diameter as the flange on the engine crank shaft to which the flywheel was bolted, and should have its bolt holes drilled to correspond. To strengthen the hub, light steel plates of the same diameter are screwed to it, front and back, and the bolt holes drilled right through the metal and wood. This method of fastening is recommended where it is possible to substitute the propeller for the flywheel formerly on the engine, it being common practice to omit the use of the flywheel altogether. The writer does not recommend this, however, as the advantages of smoother running and more reliable operation gained by the use of a flywheel in addition to the propeller far more than offset any disadvantage represented by its weight. It will be noted that the Wright motors have always been equipped with a flywheel of ample size and weight and this is undoubtedly responsible, in some measure at least, for the fact that the Wright biplanes fly with considerably less power than is ordinarily employed for machines of the same size. If the motor selected be equipped with an unusually heavy flywheel, and particularly where the wheel is of comparatively small diameter, making it less effective as a balancer, it may be replaced with one of lighter weight and larger diameter. It may be possible to attach it by keying to the forward end of the crank shaft, thus leaving the flange from which the flywheel was taken free for mounting the propeller. An ordinary belt pulley will serve excellently as the new flywheel, as most of its weight is centered in its rim, but as the common cast-iron belt pulley of commerce is seldom intended to run at any such speed as that of an automobile motor, it should be examined carefully for flaws. Otherwise, there will be danger of its bursting with disastrous results under the influence of centrifugal force. Its diameter should not exceed 16 inches in order to keep its peripheral speed within reasonable limits. Where the mounting of the motor permits of its use, a wood pulley 18 to 20 inches in diameter with a steel band about $\frac{1}{8}$- to $\frac{1}{4}$-inch thick, shrunk on its periphery, may be employed. Most builders will ridicule the idea of a flywheel other than the propeller itself. "You do not need it; so why carry the extra weight?" will be their query. It is not absolutely necessary, but it is an advantage.

In case the flywheel of the engine selected is keyed to the crank shaft, or in case it is not possible to mount both the flywheel and the propeller on different ends of the crank shaft, some other expedient rather than that of bolting to the flange must be adopted. In such a case, the original flywheel, where practical to retain it, may be drilled and tapped and the propeller attached directly to it. Where the flywheel can not be kept, it will usually be found practical to cut off its rim and bolt the propeller either to the web or spokes, or to the flywheel hub, if it be cut down to the latter.

The drawing, Fig. 21, shows the rear or concave side of the propeller. From the viewpoint of a man standing in its wind and facing forward, it turns to the left, or anti-clockwise. On many of the propellers now on the market, the curved edge is designed to go first. This type may have greater advantages over that described, but the straight front edge propeller is easier for the amateur to make.

Mounting the Engine. Having completed the propeller, the next step is the mounting of the engine. Reference to the types available to the amateur aeroplane builder has already been made. There are a number of motors now on the market that have been

BUILDING AND FLYING AN AEROPLANE 49

designed specially for this purpose and not a few of them are of considerable merit. Their cost ranges from about $250 up to $2,500, but it may be possible to pick up a comparatively light-weight automobile motor second hand which will serve all purposes and which will cost far less than the cheapest aeronautic motor on the market. It must be capable of developing 30 actual horse-power at 1,000 to 1,200 r. p. m. and must not exceed 400 pounds complete with all accessories, such as the radiator and piping, magneto, water, oil, etc. Considerable weight may be saved on an automobile motor by removing the exhaust manifold and substituting a lighter flywheel for the one originally on the engine—or omitting it altogether, as just mentioned. A light-weight aeronautic radiator should be used in preference to the usual automobile radiator.

When placing the engine in position on the ash beams forming its bed or support, it must be borne in mind that the complete machine, with the operator in the aviator's seat, is designed to balance on a point about $1\frac{1}{2}$ feet back of the front edge of the main planes. As the operator and the motor represent much the larger part of the total weight, the balance may easily be regulated by moving them slightly forward or backward, as may be required. It will be necessary, of course, to place the engine far enough back in any case to permit the propeller blades to clear the planes. The actual installation of the engine itself will be an easy matter for anyone who has had any experience in either automobile or marine gasoline motor work. It is designed to be bolted to the two engine beams in the same manner as on the side members of the frame of an automobile, or the engine bed in a boat. Just in front of the engine is the best place for the gasoline tank, which should be cylindrical with tapering ends, to cut down its wind resistance. If the designer is not anxious to carry out points as fine as this, a light copper cylindrical tank may be purchased from stock. It should hold at least ten gallons of gasoline. In front of the tank is the radiator.

Controls. The controls may be located to conform to the builder's own ideas of accessibility and convenience. Usually the switch is placed on the steering column, and it may be of the ordinary *knife* variety, or one of the special switches made for this purpose, as taste may dictate. The throttle control and spark advance may

50 BUILDING AND FLYING AN AEROPLANE

either be in the form of pedals, working against springs, or of small levers working on a notched sector, at the side of the seat. The complete control, levers, and sector may be purchased ready to mount whenever desired, as they are made in this form for both automobile and marine work. This likewise applies to the wheel, which it would not pay the amateur to attempt to make.

Another pedal should work a brake on the front wheel, the brake shoe consisting of a strip of sheet steel, fastened at one end to the fore part of the skid and pressed against the wheel by a bamboo rod directly connected with the brake pedal. An emergency brake can also be made by loosely bolting a stout bar of steel on the skid

Fig. 22. Method of Starting the Engine of an Aeroplane

near its rear end; one end of this bar is connected to a lever near the seat, so that when this lever is pulled back the other end of the bar tends to dig into the ground. As making a landing is one of the most difficult feats for the amateur aviator to master and sufficient space for a long run after alighting is not always available, these brakes will be found a very important feature of the machine.

The engine is started by swinging the propeller, and this is an operation requiring far more caution than cranking an automobile motor. Both hands should be placed on the same blade, Fig. 22, and the latter should always be pulled downward—never upward.

BUILDING AND FLYING AN AEROPLANE   51

With the switch off, first turn the propeller over several times to fill the cylinders with gas, leaving it just ahead of dead center of one of the cylinders, and with one blade extending upward and to the left at a 45-degree angle. After closing the switch, take the left blade with both hands and swing it downward sharply, getting out of the way of the following blade as quickly as possible.

Tests. The first thing to be done after the propeller is finished and mounted on the engine is to test the combination, or power plant of the biplane, for speed and thrust, or pulling power. From these two quantities it will be easy to figure the power that the engine is delivering. The only instruments necessary are a spring balance reading to 300 pounds or over; a revolution counter, such as may be procured at any machinist's supply house for a dollar or two; and a watch. One end of the spring balance is fastened to the front end of the skid and the other to a heavy stake firmly driven in the ground a few feet back. The wheels of the biplane should be set on smooth boards so that they will not offer any resistance to the forward thrust. When the engine is started the spring balance will give a direct reading of the pull of the propeller.

With one observer noting the thrust, another should check the number of revolutions the engine is turning per minute. To do this, a small hole should previously have been countersunk in the hub of the propeller to receive the conical rubber tip of the revolution counter. The observer stands behind the propeller, watch in one hand and revolution counter in the other. At the beginning of the minute period, the counter is pressed firmly against the hub, and quickly withdrawn at the end of the minute. A stop watch is naturally an advantage for the purpose. The horse-power is figured as follows, assuming, for example, a thrust of 250 pounds at 1,200 r. p. m.

$$\frac{250 \times 1200 \times 3.5 \times 100}{33.000 \times 85} = 37 \text{ h. p.}$$

As before, the "$\frac{100}{85}$" allows for the slip and represents the efficiency of the propeller; 33,000 is the number of foot pounds per minute or the equivalent of one horse-power, and 3.5 is the pitch of the propeller.

Assembling the Biplane. Assembling the machine complete requires more space than is available in the average workshop.

However, it is possible to assemble the sections of the planes in a comparatively small room, carrying the work far enough to make sure that everything will go together properly when the time comes for complete assembly at the testing ground. In this case, it is preferable to assemble the end sections first, standing them away when complete to make room for the central section, on which the running gear and outriggers are to be built up.

The builder will have decided by this time whether he will make his machine on the regular plan, with one main rib between each section, or on the quick-detachable plan, which has two main ribs on either side of the central section, as previously explained.

It is desirable to be able to assemble two sections at once and this should be possible anywhere as it requires a space only about 6 by 13 feet. Two wood 2×4's, about 12 feet long, should be nailed down on the blocks on the floor; make these level and parallel to each other at a distance of 3 feet 6 inches on centers, one being 3 inches higher than the other. Strips of wood should be nailed on them, so as to hold the main beams of the frame in place while assembling.

The two front and two rear beam sections are laid in place and joined with the sheet-steel sleeves, the flanges of the sleeves on the inner side of the beams. Then through the sleeves in the front beams, which are, of course, those on the higher bed, drill the holes for the strut socket bolts ($\frac{1}{4}$ inch). The holes for the outer ones go through the projecting ends of the beams; those for the inner ones are half in each of the two abutting beams. At the end where the central section joins on, a short length of wood of the same section may be inserted in the sleeve while drilling the hole. An assistant should hold the beams firmly together while the holes are being drilled.

Now lay in place the three main ribs belonging to the two sections under construction and fasten them at the front ends by putting in place the strut sockets for which the holes have been drilled, with a turnbuckle plate under each socket, Fig. 16. The strut socket bolt passes through the main rib and the beam. The bed on which the assembling is being done, should be cut when sufficiently under the joints to leave room for the projecting bolt ends. Set the ribs square with the front beams, then arrange the rear beams so that

BUILDING AND FLYING AN AEROPLANE 53

their joints come exactly under the ribs; clamp the ribs down and drill a true, vertical hole through the rib beam, holding the two sections of the beam together as before. Then put the rear strut sockets in place, using the angle washers previously described, above and below the rib.

When the quick-detachable plan is followed, the ribs at the inner ends of the double section, where they join the central section, should be bolted on an inch from the ends of the beam, using $\frac{1}{4}$-inch stove bolts instead of the socket bolts. The sleeves should be slotted, so that they can slide off without removing these bolts, as the sleeves and ribs which occupy the position over the joints of the beams, belong to the central section.

The sections should now be strung up with the diagonal truss wires which will make them rigid enough to stand handling. The wires are attached at each end to the flange bolts of the sleeves. Either one or two turnbuckles may be used on each wire, as already explained; if but one turnbuckle be used, the other end of the wire may be conveniently attached to a strip of sheet steel bent double and drilled for the bolt, like the sheet-steel slip of a turnbuckle. The attachment, of whatever nature, should be put between the end and the flange of the sleeve, not between the two flanges.

Three or four ribs can be used on each section; four are preferable on sections of full 6-foot length. They are, of course, evenly spaced on centers. At the front ends, they are attached to the beam by wood screws through their flattened ferrules. The attachment to the rear beam is made with a slip of sheet steel measuring $\frac{1}{2}$ by 3 inches, bent over the rib and fastened to the beam at each side with a wood screw. A long wire nail is driven through the rib itself on the beam.

Four double sections should be built up in this manner, the right and left upper and the right and left lower sections. Uppers and lowers are alike except for the inversion of the sockets in the upper sections. Rights and lefts differ in that the outer beams are long enough to fill up the sleeves, not leaving room for another beam to join on.

Inserting the struts in their sockets between the upper and lower sections of the same side will now form either of the two sides of the machine complete. Care should be taken to get the rear struts the proper length with respect to the front ones to bring the upper and lower planes parallel. The distance from the top of the lower front beam to the top of the upper front beam should be the same as the distance between the rows of bracing holes in the upper and lower main ribs just above and below the rear struts—about 4 feet 6 inches. It should hardly be necessary to mention that the thick edges of the struts come to the front—they are fish-shaped and a fish is thicker at the head than at the tail.

The truss wires may now be strung on in each square of the struts, beams, and main ribs, using turnbuckles as previously described. The wires should be taut enough to sing a low note when plucked between the thumb and forefinger. If the construction is carried out properly, the framework will stand square and true with an even tension on all the wires. It is permissible for the struts to slant backward a little as seen from the side, but all should be perfectly in line.

For adjusting the turnbuckles, the builder should make for himself a handy little tool usually termed a nipple wrench. It is simply a strip of steel $1\frac{1}{2}$ by $\frac{1}{2}$ by $\frac{3}{32}$ inches, with a notch cut in the middle of the long sides to fit the flattened ends of the turnbuckle nipples. This is much handier than the pliers and does not burr up the nipples.

It has been assumed in this description of the assembling that the builder is working in a limited space; if, on the contrary, he has room enough to set up the whole frame at once, the work will be much simpler. In this case, the construction bed should be 30 feet long. First build up the upper plane complete, standing it against the wall when finished; then build the lower plane, put the struts in their sockets, and lay on the upper plane complete.

Returning to the plan of assembly by sections, after the side sections or wings of the machine have been completed, the struts may be taken out and the sections laid aside. The middle section, to which the running gear and outriggers will be attached, is now to be built up in the same way. If the builder is following the plan in which there is one main rib between each section, it will be necessary to take off the four inner main ribs from the sections already completed, to be used at the ends of the central section. The plan drawing of the complete machine shows that the ribs of the central

BUILDING AND FLYING AN AEROPLANE 55

section are cut off just back of the rear beam to make room for the propeller. This is necessary in order to set the motor far enough forward to balance the machine properly. The small ribs in this section have the same curve but are cut off 10 inches shorter at their rear ends, and the stumps are smoothed down for ferrules like those for the other small ribs. In the plan which has one main rib between each section, the main rib on each side of the central section must be left full length. In the quick-detachable plan with two main ribs on each side of the central section, the inner ones, which really belong to this section, are cut off short like the small ribs.

In the drawing of the complete machine, the distance between the struts which carry the engine bed is shown as 2 feet. This is only approximate, as the distance must be varied to suit the motor employed. By this time, the builder will have decided what engine he is going to use—or can get—and should drill the holes for the sockets of these struts with due respect to the width of the engine's supporting feet or lugs, remembering that the engine bed beams go on the inside of the struts. In the drawing of the running gear, Fig. 17, the distance between the engine-bed struts has been designated A. The distances, B, on each side are, of course, approximately $(6'-2A)$, whatever A may be.

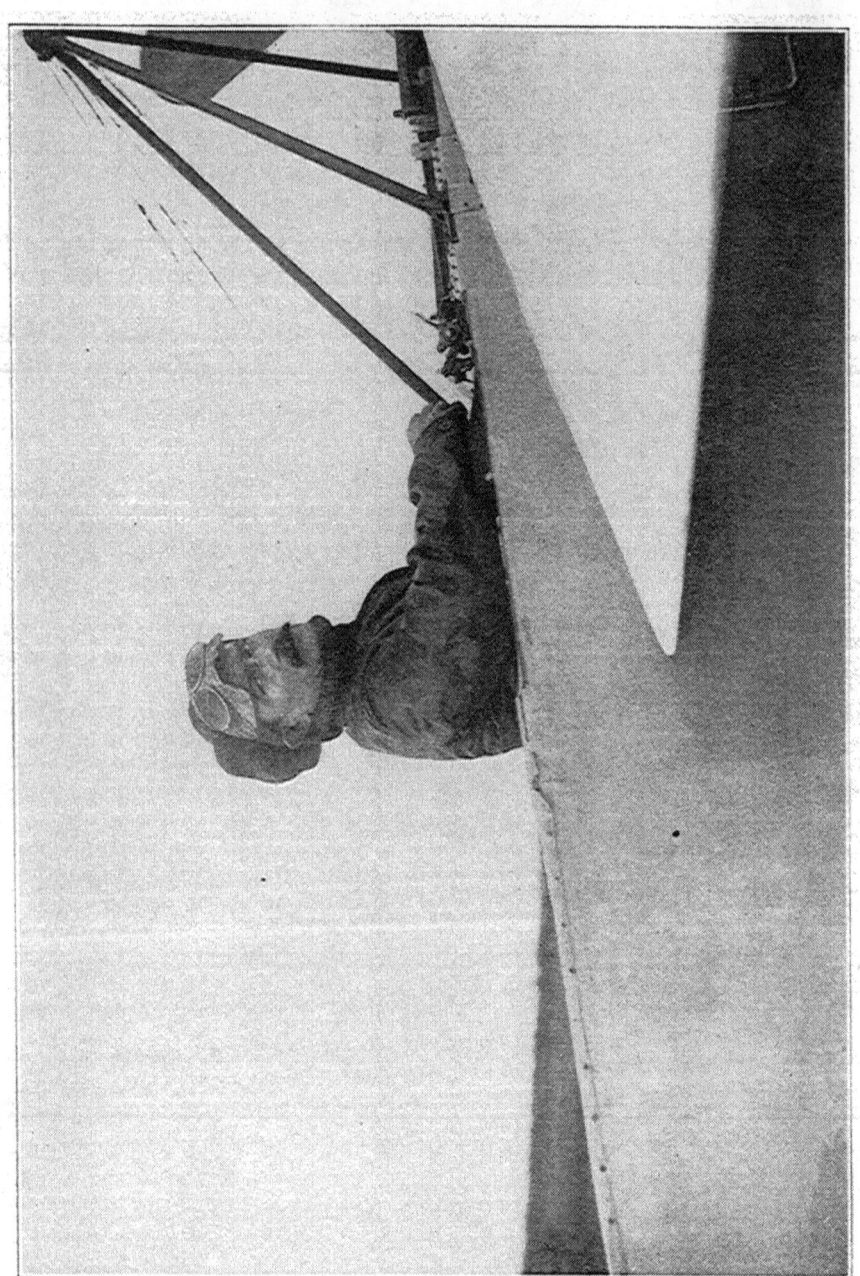

VEDRINES, ONE OF THE MOST FAMOUS AND SUCCESSFUL OF EUROPEAN AEROPLANE PILOTS, SEATED IN A DEPERDUSSIN MONOPLANE

BUILDING AND FLYING AN AEROPLANE

PART II

BUILDING A BLERIOT MONOPLANE

As mentioned in connection with the description of its construction, the Curtiss biplane was selected as a standard of this type of aeroplane after which the student could safely pattern for a number of reasons. It is not only remarkably simple in construction, easily built by anyone with moderate facilities and at a slight outlay, but it is likewise the easiest machine to learn to drive. The monoplane is far more *difficult* and *expensive* to build.

The Bleriot may be regarded as the most typical example in this field, in view of its great success and the very large numbers which have been turned out. In fact, the Bleriot monoplane is the product of a factory which would compare favorably with some of the large automobile plants. Its construction requires skillful workmanship both in wood and metal, and a great many special castings, forgings, and stampings are necessary. Although some concerns in this country advertise that they carry these fittings as *stock parts*, they are not always correct in design and, in any case, are expensive. Wherever it is possible to avoid the use of such parts by any expedient, both forms of construction are described, so that the builder may take his choice.

Bleriot monoplanes are made in a number of different models, the principal ones being the 30-horse-power "runabout," Figs. 23 and 24, the 50- and 70-horse-power passenger-carrying machines, and the 50-, 70-, and 100-horse-power racing machines. Of these the first has been chosen as best adapted to the purpose. Its construction is typical of the higher-power monoplanes of the same make, and it is more suitable for the beginner to fly as well as to build. It is employed exclusively by the Bleriot schools.

Motor. The motor regularly employed is the 30-horse-power, three-cylinder Anzani, a two-cylinder type of which is shown in

Copyright, 1912, by American School of Correspondence.

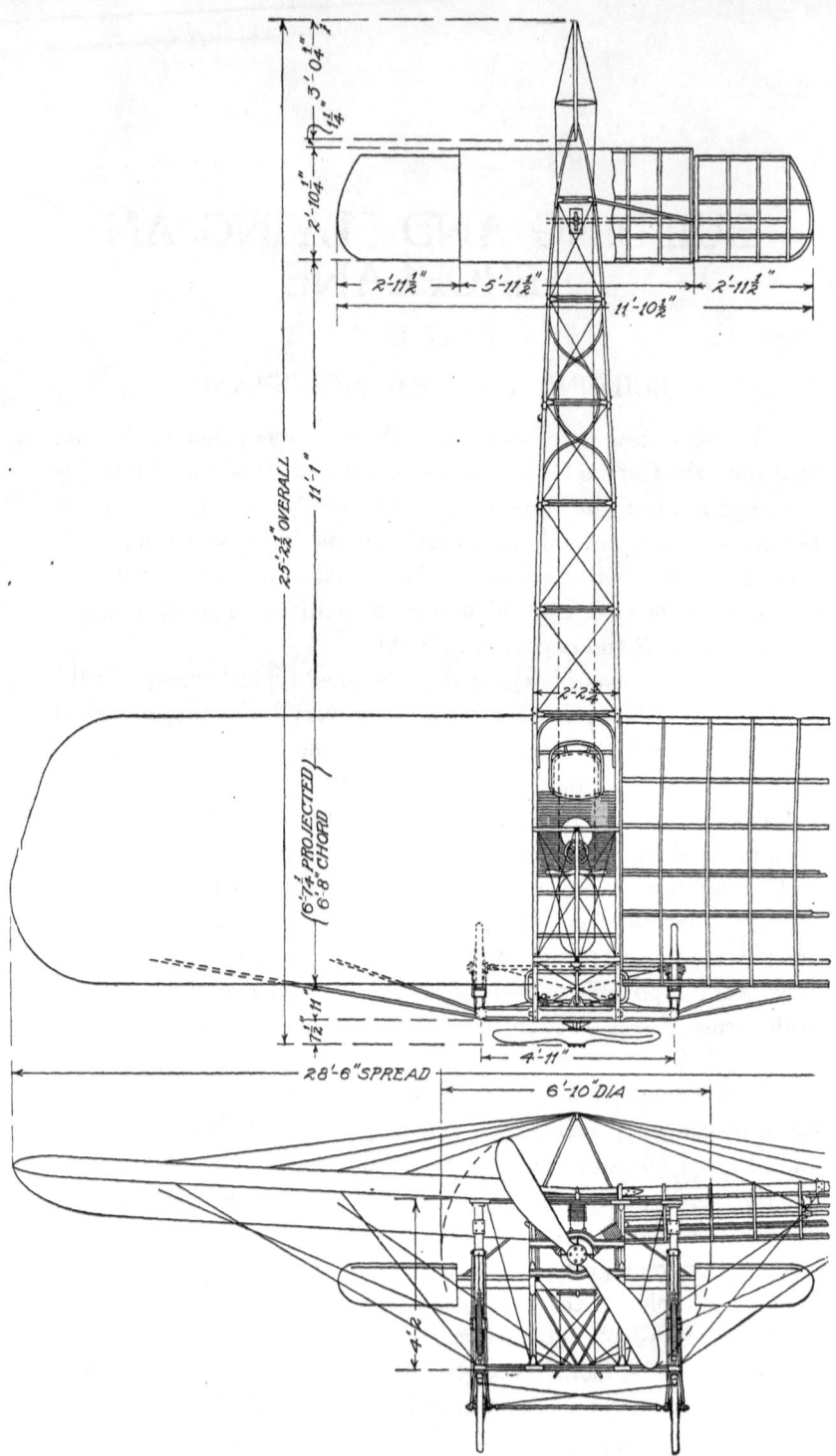

Fig. 23. Details of Bleriot Monoplane

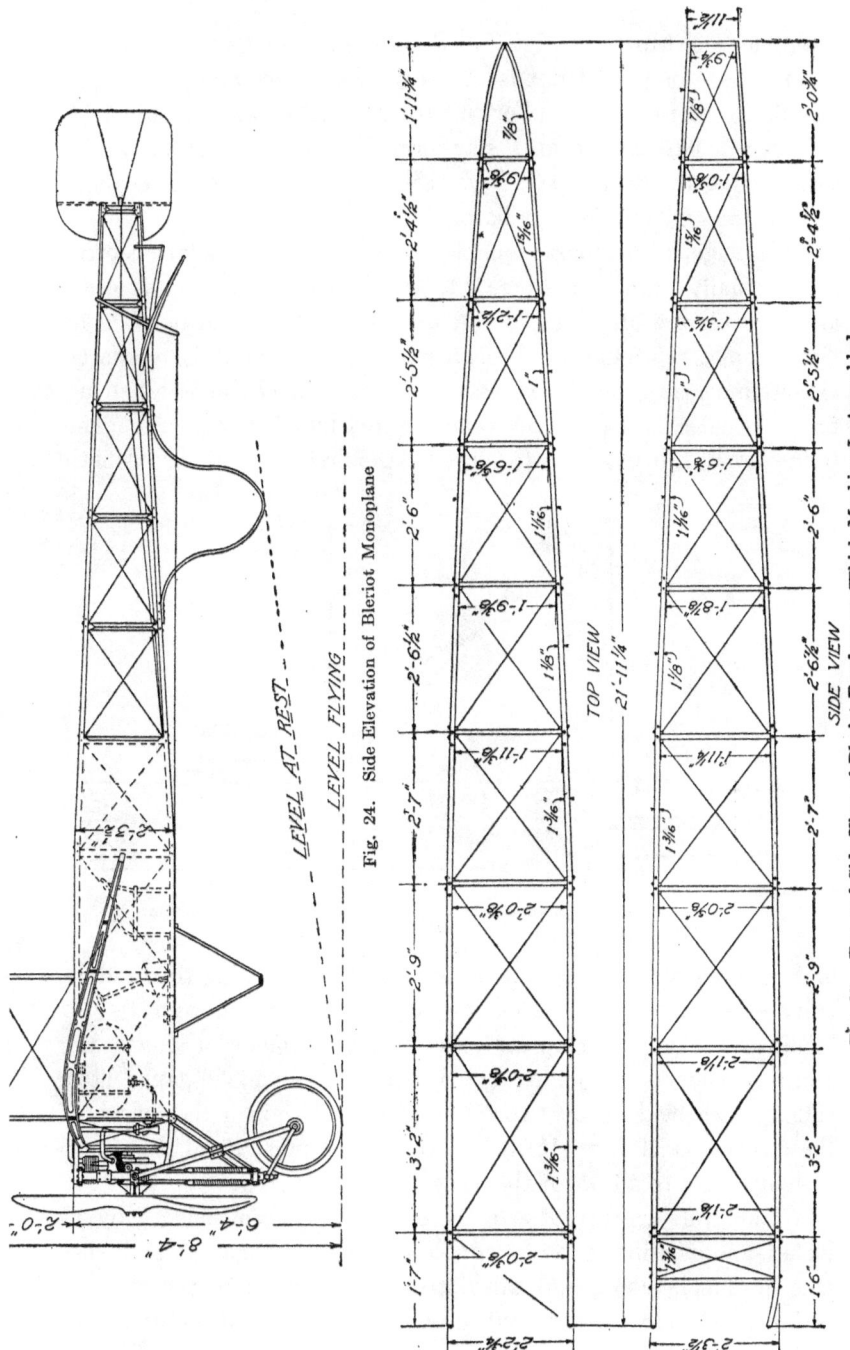

Fig. 24. Side Elevation of Bleriot Monoplane

Fig. 25. Top and Side View of Bleriot Fuselage on Which Machine Is Assembled

60 BUILDING AND FLYING AN AEROPLANE

"Aeronautical Motors," Fig. 40. From the amateur's standpoint, a disadvantage of the Bleriot is the very short space allowed for the installation of the motor. For this reason, the power plant must be fan shaped, like the Anzani; star form, like the Gnome; or of the two-cylinder opposed type. It must likewise be air-cooled, as there is no space available for a radiator.

Fuselage. Like most monoplanes, the Bleriot has a long central body, usually termed "fuselage," to which the wings, running gear, and controls are all attached. A drawing of the fuselage with all dimensions is reproduced in Fig. 25, and as the machine is, to a large extent, built up around this essential, its construction is taken up first. It consists of four long beams united by 35 crosspieces. The beams are of ash, $1\frac{3}{16}$ inches square for the first third of their length

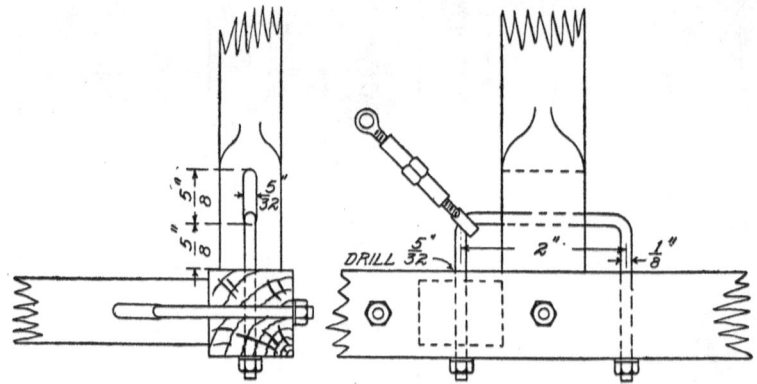

Fig. 26. Details of U-bolt Which Is a Feature of Bleriot Construction

and tapering to $\frac{7}{8}$ inch square at the rear ends. Owing to the difficulty of securing good pieces of wood the full length, and also to facilitate packing for shipment, the beams are made in halves, the abutting ends being joined by sleeves of $1\frac{1}{8}$-inch, 20-gauge steel tubing, each held on by two $\frac{1}{8}$-inch bolts. Although the length of the fuselage is 21 feet $11\frac{1}{4}$ inches, the beams must be made of two 11-foot halves to allow for the curve at the rear ends.

The struts are also of ash, the majority of them being $\frac{7}{8}$ by $1\frac{1}{4}$ inches, and oval in section except for an inch and a half at each end. But the first, second, and third struts (counting from the forward end) on each side, the first and second on the top, and the first strut

BUILDING AND FLYING AN AEROPLANE

on the bottom are $1\frac{3}{16}$ inches square, of the same stock as the main beams. Practically all of the struts are joined to the main beams by U-bolts, as shown by the detail drawing, Fig. 26, this being one of Louis Bleriot's inventions. The small struts are held by $\frac{1}{8}$-inch bolts and the larger ones by $\frac{3}{16}$-inch bolts. The ends of the struts must be slotted for these bolts, this being done by drilling three holes in a row with a $\frac{5}{32}$- or $\frac{7}{32}$-inch drill, according to whether the slot is for the smaller or larger size bolt. The wood between the holes is cut out with a sharp knife and the slot finished with a coarse, flat file.

All of the U-bolts measure 2 inches between the ends. The vertical struts are set 1 inch forward of the corresponding horizontal struts, so that the four holes through the beam at each joint are spaced 1 inch apart, alternately horizontal and vertical. To the projecting angles of the U-bolts are attached the diagonal truss wires, which cross all the rectangles of the fuselage, except that in which the driver sits. This trussing should be of 20-gauge piano wire (music-wire gauge) or $\frac{1}{16}$-inch cable, except in the rectangles bounded by the large struts, where it should be 25-gauge piano wire or $\frac{3}{32}$-inch cable. Each wire, of course, should have a turnbuckle. About 100 of these will be required, either of the spoke type or the regular type, with two screw eyes—the latter preferred.

Transverse squares, formed by the two horizontal and two vertical struts at each point, are also trussed with diagonal wires. Although turnbuckles are sometimes omitted on these wires, it takes considerable skill to get accurate adjustments without them. The extreme rear strut to which the rudder is attached, is not fastened in the usual way. It should be cut with tongues at top and bottom, fitting into notches in the ends of the beams, and the whole bound with straps of 20-gauge sheet steel, bolted through the beams with $\frac{1}{8}$-inch bolts.

Continuing forward, the struts have no peculiarity until the upper horizontal one is reached, just behind the driver's seat. As it is impossible to truss the quadrangle forward of this strut, owing to the position of the driver's body, the strut is braced with a U-shaped half-round strip of $\frac{1}{2}$ by 1 inch of ash or hickory bolted to the beams at the sides and to the strut at the rear, with two $\frac{1}{8}$-inch bolts at each point. The front side of the strut should be left square where this brace is in contact with it. The brace should be steam bent with the curves on a 9-inch radius, and the half-round side on the inside of the curve.

The vertical struts just forward of the driver's seat carry the inner ends of the rear wing beams. Each beam is attached with a single bolt, giving the necessary freedom to rock up and down in warping the wings. The upper 6 inches of each of these struts fits into a socket designed to reinforce it. In the genuine Bleriot, this socket is an aluminum casting. However, a socket which many would regard as even better can be made from a 7-inch length of 20-gauge $1\frac{1}{8}$-inch square tubing. One end of the tube is sawed one inch through the corners; two opposite sides are then bent down at right angles to form flanges, and the other two sides sawed off. A 1- by 3-inch strip of 20-gauge sheet steel, brazed across the top and flanges completes the socket. With a little care, a very creditable socket can be made in this way. Finally, with the strut in place, a $\frac{3}{8}$-inch hole is drilled through 4 inches from the top of the socket for the bolt securing the wing beam.

The upper horizontal strut at this point should be arched about six inches to give plenty of elbow room over the steering wheel. The bending should be done in a steam press. The strut should be $1\frac{3}{16}$ inches square, cut sufficiently long to allow for the curve, and fitted at the ends with sockets as described above, but set at an angle by sawing the square tube down further on one side than on the other.

On the two lower beams, is laid a floor of half-inch boards, extending one foot forward and one foot back of the center line of the horizontal strut. This floor may be of spruce, if it is desired to save a little weight, or of ordinary tongue-and-grooved floor boards, fastened to the beams with wood screws or bolts. The horizontal strut under this floor may be omitted, but its presence adds but little weight and completes the trussing. Across the top of the fuselage above the first upper horizontal strut, lies a steel tube which forms the sockets for the inner end of the front wing beams. This tube is $1\frac{3}{4}$ inches diameter, 18 gauge, and $26\frac{3}{4}$ inches long. It is held fast by two steel straps, 16 gauge and 1 inch wide, clamped down by the nuts of the vertical strut U-bolts. The center of the tube is, therefore, in line with the center of the vertical struts, not the horizontal ones. The U-bolts which make this attachment are, of course, the $\frac{3}{16}$-inch size, and one inch longer on each end than usual. To make a neat job, the tube may be seated in wood blocks, suitably shaped, but these must not raise it more than a small fraction of an inch above the top of the fuselage, as this would increase the angle of incidence of the wings.

The first vertical struts on each side are extras, without corresponding horizontal ones; they serve only to support the engine. When the Gnome motor is used, its central shaft is carried at the centers of two x-shaped, pressed-steel frames, one on the front side, flush with the end of the fuselage and one on the rear.

Truss Frame Built on Fuselage. In connection with the fuselage may be considered the overhead truss frame and the warping frame. The former consists of two inverted v's of 20-gauge, 1- by $\frac{3}{8}$-inch oval tubing, joined at their apexes by a 20-gauge, $\frac{3}{4}$-inch tube. Each v is formed of a single piece of the oval tubing about 5 feet long. The flattened ends of the horizontal tube are fastened by a bolt in the angles of the v's. The center of the horizontal tube should be 2 feet above the top of the fuselage. The flattened lower ends of the rear v should be riveted and brazed to strips of 18-gauge steel, which will fit over the bolts attaching the vertical fuselage struts at this point. The legs of the front v should be slightly shorter, as they rest on top of the wing socket tube. Each should be held down by a single $\frac{3}{16}$-inch bolt, passing through the upper wall of the tube and its retaining strap; these bolts also serve the purpose of preventing the tube from sliding out from under the strap. Each side of the frame is now braced by diagonal wires (No. 20 piano wire, or $\frac{1}{16}$-inch cable) with turnbuckles.

At the upper corners of this frame are attached the wires which truss the upper sides of the wings. The front wires are simply fastened under the head and nut of the bolt which holds the frame together at this corner. The attachment of the rear wires, however, is more complex, as these wires must run over pulleys to allow for the rocking of the rear wing beams when the wings are warped. To provide a suitable place for the pulleys, the angle of the rear v is enclosed by two plates of 20-gauge sheet steel, one on the front and one on the rear, forming a triangular box 1 inch thick fore and aft, and about 2 inches on each side, only the bottom side being open. These plates are clamped together by a $\frac{3}{16}$-inch steel bolt, on which are mounted the pulleys. There should be sufficient clearance for pulleys 1 inch in diameter. The wires running over these pulleys must then pass through holes drilled in the tube. The holes should not be drilled until the wings are on, when the proper angle for them can be seen. The cutting and bending of the steel plates is a matter of some difficulty, and should not be done until the frame is otherwise assembled, so that paper patterns can be cut for them. They should have flanges bent around the tube, secured by the bolts which hold the frame together, to keep them from slipping off.

The oval tubing is used in the vertical parts of this frame, principally to reduce the wind resistance, being placed with the narrow side to the front. However, if this tubing be difficult to obtain, or if price is a consideration, no harm will be done by using $\frac{3}{4}$-inch round tubing. Beneath the floor of the driver's cockpit in the fuselage is the warping frame, the support for the wires which truss the rear wing beams and also control the warping.

This frame is built up of four $\frac{3}{4}$-inch, 20-gauge steel tubes, each about 3 feet long, forming an inverted, 4-sided pyramid. The front and back pairs of tubes are fastened to the lower fuselage beams with $\frac{3}{16}$-inch bolts at points 15 inches front and back of the horizontal strut. At their lower ends the tubes are joined by a fixture which carries the pulleys for the warping wires and the lever by which the pulleys are turned. In the genuine Bleriot, this fixture is a special casting. However, a very neat connection can be made with a piece of $\frac{3}{16}$-inch steel stock, $1\frac{1}{4}$ by 6 inches, bent into a U-shape with the legs 1 inch apart inside. The flattened ends of the tubes are riveted and brazed to the outside upper corners of the U, and a bolt to carry the pulleys passes through the lower part, high enough to give clearance for 2-inch pulleys. This frame needs no diagonal wires.

Running Gear. Passing now to the running gear, the builder will encounter the most difficult part of the entire machine, and it is impossible to avoid the use of a few special castings. The general plan of the running gear is shown in the drawing of the complete machine, Figs. 23 and 24, while some of the details are illustrated in Fig. 27, and the remainder are given in the detail sheet, Fig. 28. It will be seen that each of the two wheels is carried in a double fork, the lower fork acting simply as a radius rod, while the upper fork is attached to a slide which is free to move up and down on a 2-inch steel tube. This slide is held down by two tension springs, consisting

BUILDING AND FLYING AN AEROPLANE

of either rubber tubes or steel coil springs, which absorb the shocks of landing. The whole construction is such that the wheels are free to pivot sideways around the tubes, so that when landing in a quartering wind the wheels automatically adjust themselves to the direction of the machine.

Framework. The main framework of the running gear consists of two horizontal beams, two vertical struts, and two vertical tubes. The beams are of ash, $4\frac{3}{4}$ inches wide in the middle half, tapering to $3\frac{3}{4}$ inches at the ends, and 5 feet $2\frac{3}{4}$ inches long overall. The upper beam is $\frac{13}{16}$ inch thick and the lower 1 inch. The edges of the beams are rounded off except at the points where they are drilled for bolt holes for the attachment of other parts. The two upper beams of the fuselage rest on these beams and are secured to them by two $\frac{3}{16}$-inch bolts each.

The vertical struts are also of ash, $1\frac{3}{16}$ inch by 3 inches and 4 feet 2 inches long overall. They have tenons at each end which fit into corresponding square holes in the horizontal beams. The two lower fuselage beams are fastened to these struts by two $\frac{3}{16}$-inch through bolts and steel angle plates formed from $\frac{1}{16}$-inch sheet steel. The channel section member across the front sides of these struts is for the attachment of the motor, and will be taken up later. The general arrangement at this point depends largely on what motor is to be used, and the struts should not be rounded or drilled for bolt holes until this has been decided.

From the lower ends of these struts CC, Fig. 27, diagonal struts DD run back to the fuselage. These are of ash, $1\frac{3}{16}$ by $2\frac{1}{2}$ inches and 2 feet 6 inches long. The rear ends of the struts DD are fastened to the fuselage beams by the projecting ends of the U-bolts of the horizontal fuselage struts, and also by angle plates of sheet steel. At the lower front ends the struts DD are fastened to the struts CC and the beam E by steel angle plates, and the beam is reinforced by other plates on its under side.

Trussing. In the genuine Bleriot, the framework is trussed by a single length of steel tape, $1\frac{1}{8}$ by $\frac{1}{16}$ inch and about 11 feet long, fastened to U-bolts in the beam A, Fig. 27. This tape runs down one side, under the beam E, and up the other side, passing through the beam in two places, where suitable slots must be cut. The tape is not made in this country, but must be imported at considerable

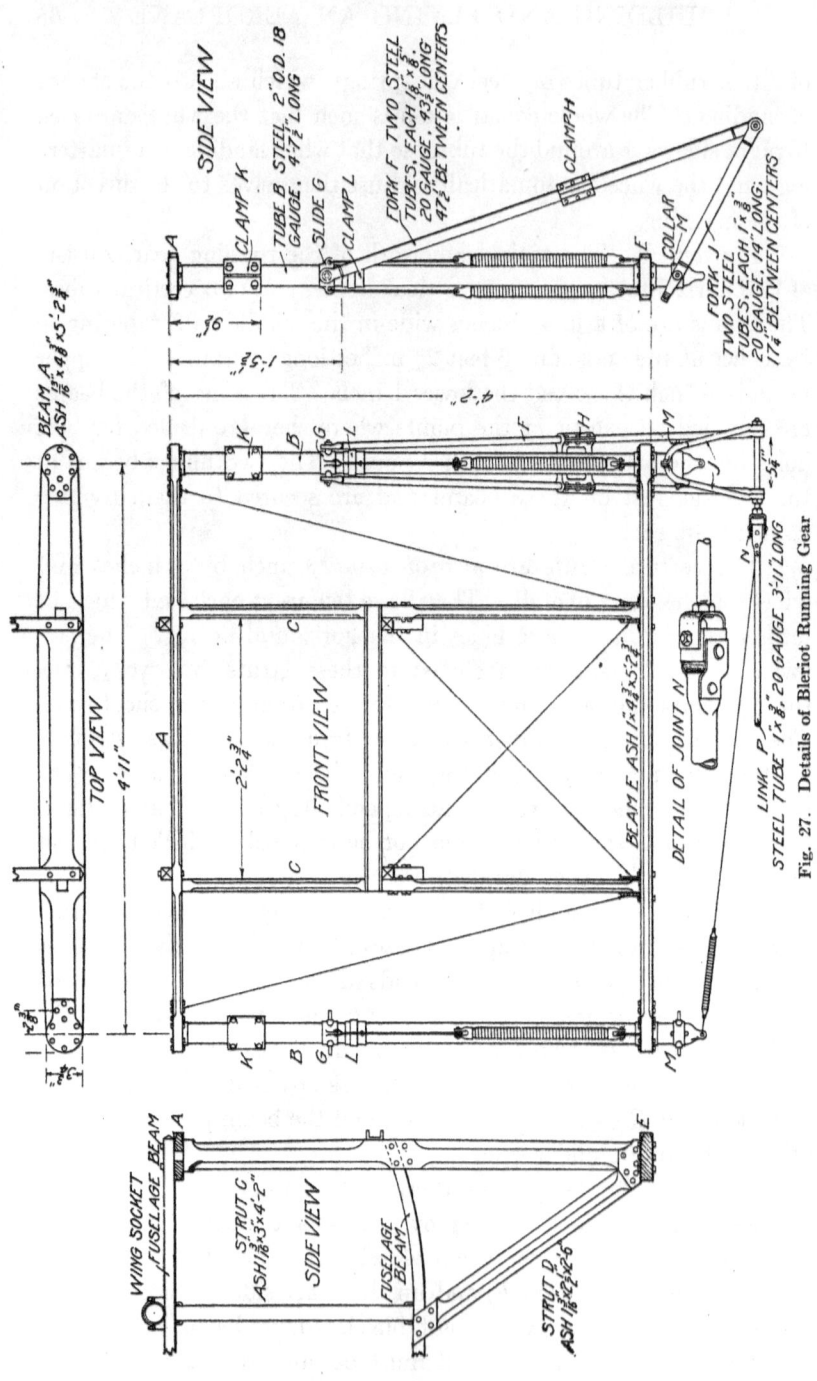

Fig. 27. Details of Bleriot Running Gear

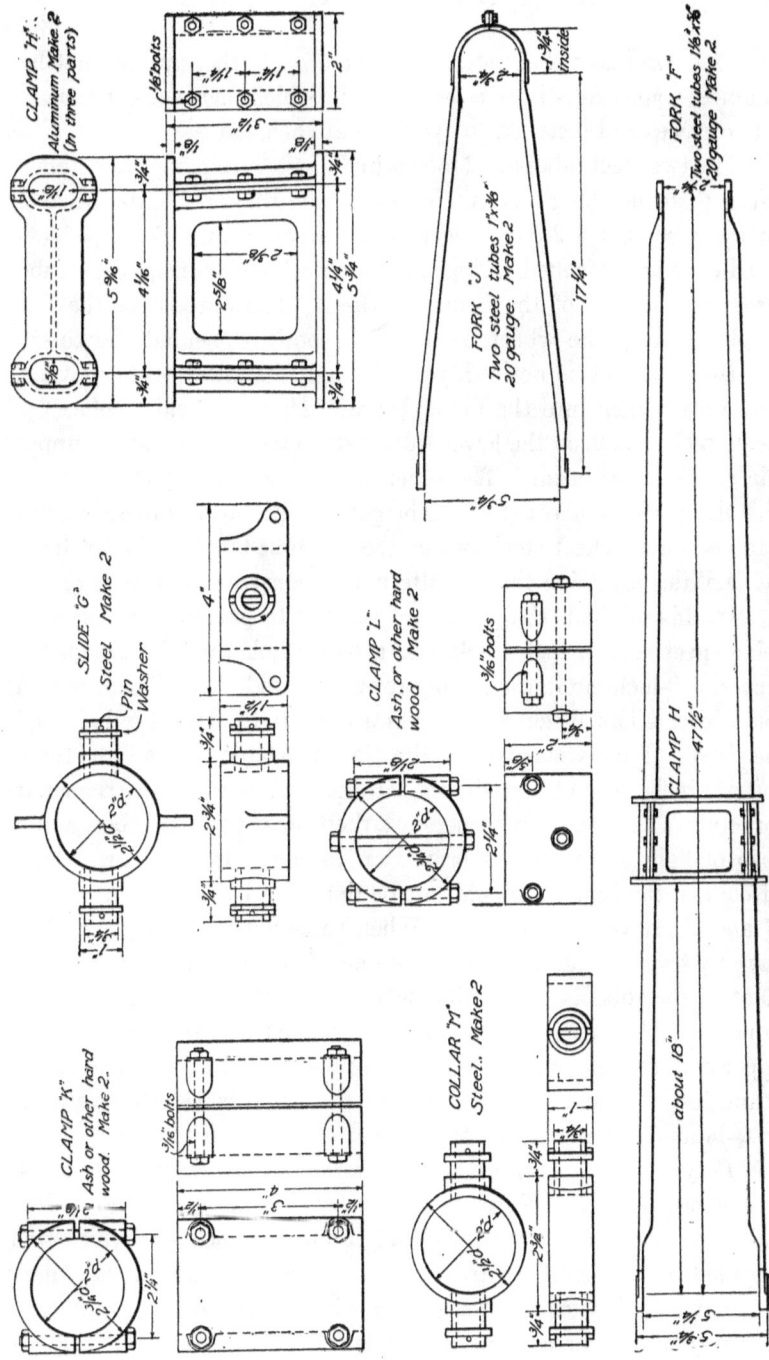

Fig. 28. Details of Various Fittings for Bleriot Monoplane

expense. Ordinary sheet steel will not do. If the tape can not be obtained, a good substitute is $\frac{1}{8}$-inch cable, which then would be made in two pieces and fastened to eye bolts at each end.

The two steel tubes are 2 inches in diameter, 18-gauge, and about 4 feet 10 inches long. At their lower ends they are flattened, but cut away so that a 2-inch ring will pass over them. To these flattened ends are attached springs and wires which run from each tube across to the hub of the opposite wheel. The purpose of these is simply to keep the wheels normally in position behind the tubes. The tubes, it will be noticed, pass through the lower beam, but are sunk only $\frac{1}{8}$ inch into the upper beam. They are held in place by sheet-steel sockets on the lower side of the upper beam and the upper side of the lower beam. The other sides of the beams are provided with flat plates of sheet steel. The genuine Bleriot has these sockets stamped out of sheet steel, but as the amateur builder will not have the facilities for doing this, an alternative construction is given here.

In this method, the plates are cut out to pattern, the material being sheet steel $\frac{1}{16}$ inch thick, and a $\frac{1}{2}$-inch hole drilled through the center, a 2-inch circle then being drawn around this. Then, with a cold chisel a half dozen radial cuts are made between the hole and the circle. Finally this part of the plate is heated with a blow-torch and a 2-inch piece of pipe driven through, bending up the triangular corners. These bent up corners are then brazed to the tubes, and a strip of light sheet steel is brazed on to cover up the sharp edges. Of course, the brazing should not be done until the slides *GG*, Figs. 27 and 28, have been put on. When these are once in place, they have to stay on and a breakage of one of them, means the replacement of the tube as well. This is a fault of the Bleriot design that can not well be avoided. It should be noticed that the socket at the upper end, as well as its corresponding plate on the other side of the beam, has extensions which reinforce the beam where the eye bolts or U-bolts for the attachment of the steel tape pass through.

Forks. Next in order are the forks which carry the wheels. The short forks *JJ*, Figs. 27 and 28, which act simply as radius rods, are made of 1- by $\frac{3}{8}$-inch oval tubing, a stock size which was specified for the overhead truss frame. It will be noticed that these are in two parts, fastened together with a bolt at the front end. The regular Bleriot construction calls for forged steel eyes to go in

BUILDING AND FLYING AN AEROPLANE 69

the ends of tubes, but these will be hard to obtain. The construction shown in the drawings is much simpler. The ends of the tubes are heated and flattened until the walls are about $\frac{1}{16}$ inch apart inside. Then a strip of $\frac{1}{16}$-inch sheet steel is cut the right width to fit in the flattened end of the tube, and brazed in place. The bolt holes then pass through the combined thickness of the tube and the steel strip, giving a better bearing surface, which may be further increased by brazing on a washer.

The long forks FF, which transmit the landing shocks to the springs, are naturally made of heavier material. The proper size tubing for them is $1\frac{1}{8}$ by $\frac{5}{8}$ inches, this being the nearest equivalent to the 14 by 28 mm French tubing. However, this is not a stock size in this country and can only be procured by order, or it can be made by rolling out $\frac{13}{16}$-inch round tubing. If the oval tubing can not be secured, the round can be employed instead, other parts being modified to correspond. The ends are reinforced in the same way as described for the small forks.

These forks are strengthened by aluminum clamps H, Figs. 27 and 28, which keep the tubes from spreading apart. Here, of course, is another call for special castings, but a handy workman may be able to improvise a satisfactory substitute from sheet steel. On each tube there are four fittings: At the bottom, the collar M to which the fork J is attached, and above, the slide G and the clamps K and L, which limit its movement. The collar and slide should be forged, but as this may be impossible, the drawings have been proportioned for castings. The work is simple and may be done by the amateur with little experience. The projecting studs are pieces of $\frac{3}{4}$-inch, 14-gauge steel tubing screwed in tight and pinned, though if these parts be forged, the studs should be integral.

The clamps which limit the movement of the slides are to be whittled out of ash or some other hard wood. The upper clamp is held in place by four bolts, which are screwed up tight; but when the machine makes a hard landing the clamp will yield a little and slip up the tube, thus deadening the shock. After such a landing, the clamps should be inspected and again moved down a bit, if necessary. The lower clamps, which, of course, only keep the wheels from hanging down too far, have bolts passing clear through the tubes.

To the projecting lugs on the slides GG are attached the rubber tube springs, the lower ends connecting with eye bolts through the beam *E*. These rubber tubes, of which four will be needed, are being made by several companies in this country and are sold by supply houses. They should be about 14 inches long, unstretched, and $1\frac{1}{4}$ inches in diameter, with steel tips at the ends for attachment.

Hub Attachments. The hubs of the two wheels are connected with the link *P*, with universal joints *N N* at each end. In case the machine lands while drifting sidewise, the wheel which touches the ground first will swing around to head in the direction in which the machine is actually moving, and the link will cause the other wheel to assume a parallel position; thus the machine can run diagonally on the ground without any tendency to upset.

This link is made of the same 1- by $\frac{3}{8}$-inch oval tubing used elsewhere in the machine. In the original Bleriot, the joints are carefully made up with steel forgings. But joints which will serve the purpose can be improvised from a 1-inch cube of hard wood and three steel straps, as shown in the sketch, Fig. 27. From each of these joints a wire runs diagonally to the bottom of the tube on the other side, with a spring which holds the wheel in its normal position. This spring should be either a rubber tube, like those described above, but smaller, or a steel coil spring. In the latter case, it should be of twenty $\frac{3}{4}$-inch coils of No. 25 piano wire.

Wheels. The wheels are regularly 28 by 2 inches, corresponding to the 700 by 50 mm French size, with 36 spokes of 12-gauge wire. The hub should be $5\frac{1}{4}$ inches wide, with a $\frac{3}{8}$-inch bolt. Of course, these sizes need not be followed exactly, but any variations will involve corresponding changes in the dimensions of the forks. The long fork goes on the hub inside of the short fork, so that the inside measurement of the end of the big fork should correspond to the width of the hub, and the inside measurement of the small fork should equal the outside measurement of the large fork.

Rear Skid. Several methods are employed for supporting the rear end of the fuselage when the machine is on the ground. The first Bleriot carried a small wheel in a fork provided with rubber springs, the same as the front wheels. The later models, however, have a double u-shaped skid, as shown in Figs. 23 and 24. This skid is made of two 8-foot strips of ash or hickory $\frac{1}{2}$ by $\frac{3}{4}$ inches, steamed and bent to the u-shape as shown in the drawing of the complete machine.

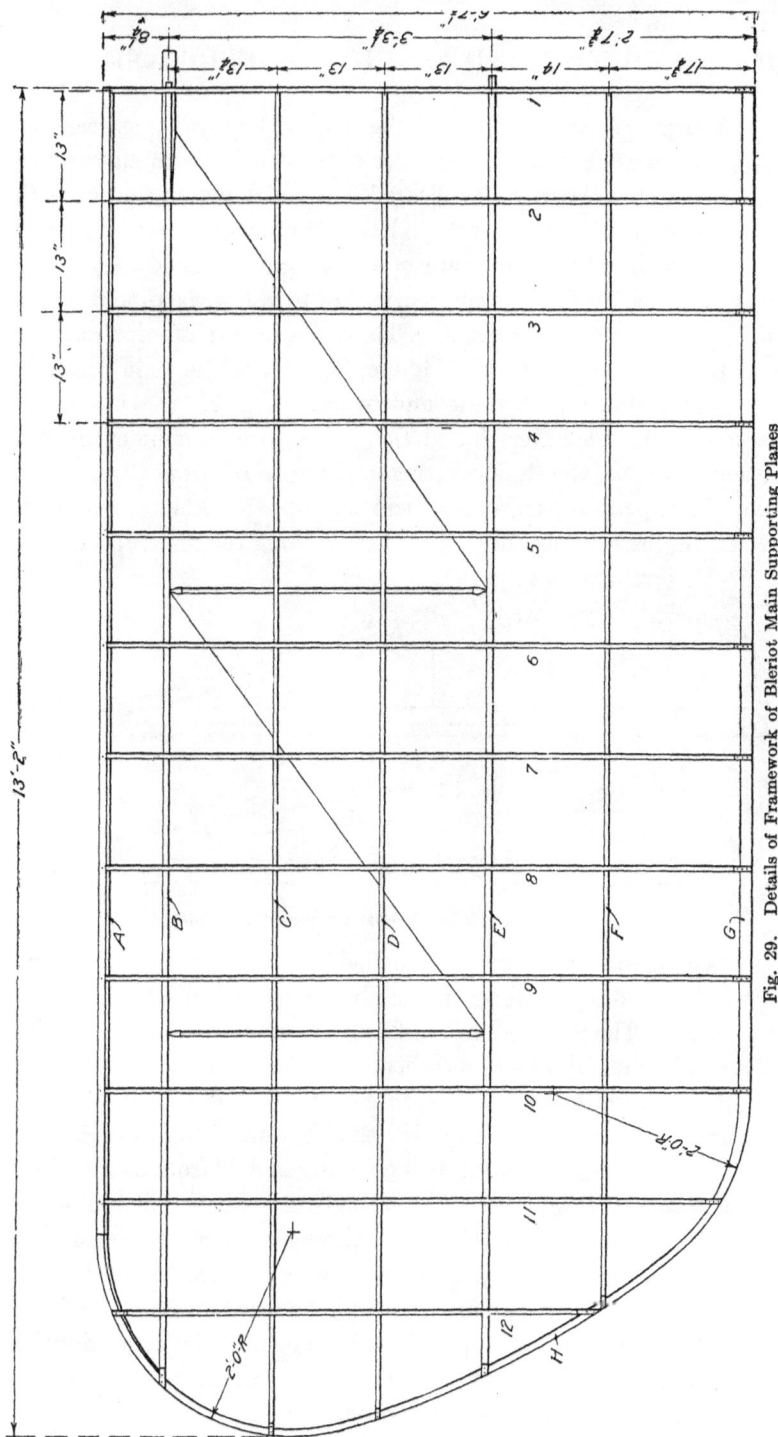

Fig. 29. Details of Framework of Bleriot Main Supporting Planes

295

72   BUILDING AND FLYING AN AEROPLANE

Wings. Having completed the fuselage and running gear, the wings are next in order. These are constructed in a manner which may seem unnecessarily complicated, but which gives great strength for comparatively little weight. Each wing contains two stout ash beams which carry their share of the weight of the machine, and 12 ribs which give the proper curvature to the surfaces and at the same time reinforce the beams. These ribs in turn are tied together and reinforced by light strips running parallel to the main beams.

In the drawing of the complete wing, Fig. 29, the beams are designated by the letters B and E. A is a sheet aluminum member intended to hold the cloth covering in shape on the front edge. C, D, and F are pairs of strips (one strip on top, the other underneath) which tie the ribs together. G is a strip along the rear edge, and H

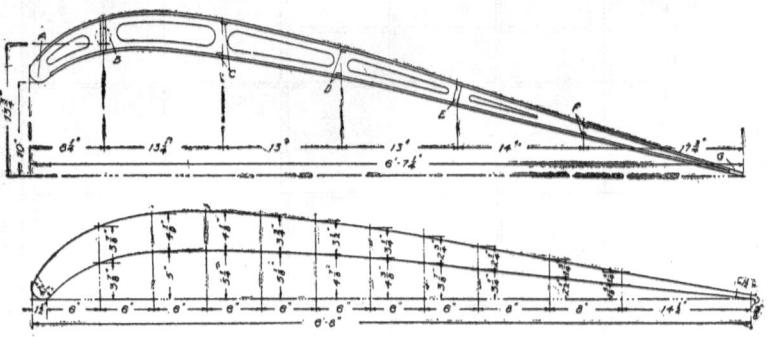

Fig. 30. Complete Rib of Bleriot Wing and Pattern from Which Web Is Cut

is a bent strip which gives the rounded shape to the end of the wing. The ribs are designated by the numbers 1 to 12 inclusive.

Ribs. The first and most difficult operation is to make the ribs. These are built up of a spruce board $\frac{3}{16}$ inch thick, cut to shape on a jig saw, with $\frac{3}{16}$- by $\frac{5}{8}$-inch spruce strip stacked and glued to the upper and lower edges. Each rib thus has an I-beam section, such as is used in structural steel work and automobile front axles. Each of the boards, or webs as they are usually called, is divided into three parts by the main beams which pass through it. Builders sometimes make the mistake of cutting out each web in three pieces, but this makes it very difficult to put the rib together accurately. Each web should be cut out of a single piece, as shown in the detail drawing, Fig. 30, and the holes for the beams should be cut in after the top and bottom strips have been glued on.

BUILDING AND FLYING AN AEROPLANE 73

The detail drawing, Fig. 30, gives the dimensions of a typical rib. This should be drawn out full size on a strip of tough paper, and then a margin of $\frac{3}{16}$ inch should be taken off all round except at the front end where the sheet aluminum member A goes on. This allows for the thickness of the top and bottom strips. In preparing the pattern for the jig saw, the notches for strips C, D, and F should be disregarded; neither should it be expected that the jig-saw operator will cut out the oval holes along the center of the web, which are simply to lighten it. The notches for the front ends of the top and bottom strips should also be smoothed over in the pattern.

When the pattern is ready, a saw or planing mill provided with a saw suitable for the work, should cut out the 40 ribs (allowing a sufficient number for defective pieces and breakage) for about $2. The builder then cuts the notches and makes the oval openings with an auger and keyhole saw. Of course, these holes need not be absolutely accurate, but at least $\frac{3}{4}$ inch of wood should be left all around them.

Nine of the twelve ribs in each wing are exactly alike. No. 1, which forms the inner end of the wing, does not have any holes cut in the web, and instead of the slot for the main beam B, has a $1\frac{3}{4}$-inch round hole, as the stub end of the beam is rounded to fit the socket tube. (See Fig. 23.) Rib No. 11 is 5 feet $10\frac{1}{2}$ inches long, and No. 12 is 3 feet long. These can be whittled out by hand, and the shape for them will be obvious as soon as the main part of the wing is put together.

The next step is to glue on the top and bottom strips. The front ends should be put on first and held, during the drying, in a screw clamp, the ends setting close up into the notches provided for them. Thin $\frac{1}{2}$-inch brads should be driven in along the top and bottom at 1- to 2-inch intervals. The rear ends of the strips should be cut off to the proper length and whittled off a little on the inside, so that there will be room between them for the strip G, $\frac{1}{4}$ inch thick. Finally, cut the slots for the main beams, using a bit and brace and the keyhole saw, and the ribs will be ready to assemble.

Beams and Strips. The main beams are of ash, the front beam in each wing being $3\frac{1}{4}$ by $\frac{3}{4}$ inches and the rear beam $2\frac{1}{2}$ by $\frac{5}{8}$ inches. They are not exactly rectangular but must be planed down slightly on the top and bottom edges, so that they will fit into the irregularly-

74 BUILDING AND FLYING AN AEROPLANE

shaped slots left for them in the ribs. The front beams, as mentioned above, have round stubs which fit into the socket tube on the fuselage. These stubs may be made by bolting short pieces of ash board on each side of the end of the beam and rounding down the whole.

To give the wings their slight inclination, or dihedral angle, which will be apparent in the front view of the machine, the stubs must lie at an angle of $2\frac{1}{2}$ degrees with the beam itself. This angle should be laid out very carefully, as a slight inaccuracy at this point will result in a much larger error at the tips. The rear beams project about 2 inches from the inner ribs. The ends should be reinforced with bands of sheet steel to prevent splitting, and each drilled with a $\frac{3}{8}$-inch hole for the bolt which attaches to the fuselage strut. A strip of heavy sheet steel should be bent to make an angle washer to fill up the triangular space between the beam and the strut; the bolt hole should be drilled perpendicularly to the beam, and not to the strut. The outer ends of the beams, beyond rib No. 10, taper down to 1 inch deep at the ends.

The aluminum member A, Fig. 29, which holds the front edge of the wing in shape, is made of a 4-inch strip of fairly heavy sheet aluminum, rolled into shape round a piece of half-round wood, $2\frac{1}{4}$ inches in diameter. As sheet aluminum usually comes in 6-foot lengths, each of these members will have to be made in two sections, joined either by soldering (if the builder has mastered this difficult process) or by a number of small copper rivets.

No especial difficulties are presented by the strips, C, D, and F, which are of spruce $\frac{3}{16}$ by $\frac{5}{8}$ inch, or by the rear edge strip G, of spruce $\frac{1}{4}$ by $1\frac{1}{2}$ inches. Each piece H should be 1 by $\frac{1}{2}$ inch half-round spruce, bent into shape, fitted into the aluminum piece at the front, and at the rear flattened down to $\frac{1}{4}$ inch and reinforced by a small strip glued to the back, finally running into the strip G. The exact curve of this piece does not matter, provided it is the same on both wings.

Assembling the Wings. Assembling the wings is an operation which demands considerable care. The main beams should first be laid across two horses, set level so that there will be no strain on the framework as it is put together. Then the 12 ribs should be slipped over the beams and evenly spaced 13 inches apart to centers, care being taken to see that each rib stands square with the beams, Fig. 31.

THE ANCIENT AND THE MODERN
The Wright Flyer at Le Mans, France.

Intentionally blank as was the original edition.

BUILDING AND FLYING AN AEROPLANE

The ribs are not glued to the beams, as this would make repairs difficult, but are fastened with small nails.

Strips C, D, and F, Fig. 29, are next put in place, simply being strung through the rows of holes provided for them in the ribs, and fastened with brads. Then spacers of $\frac{3}{16}$-inch spruce, 2 or 3 inches long, are placed between each pair of strips halfway between each rib, and fastened with glue and brads. This can be seen in the broken-off view of the wing in the front view drawing, Fig. 23. The rear edge strip fits between the ends of the top and bottom

Fig. 31. Assembling the Main Planes of a Bleriot Monoplane

strips of the ribs, as mentioned above, fastened with brads or with strips of sheet-aluminum tacked on.

Each wing is trussed by eight wires, half above and half below; half attached to the front and half to the rear beam. In the genuine Bleriot steel tape is used for the lower trussing of the main beams, similar to the tape employed in the running gear, but American builders prefer to use $\frac{1}{8}$-inch cable. The lower rear trussing should be $\frac{3}{32}$- or $\frac{7}{64}$-inch cable, and the upper trussing $\frac{3}{32}$-inch.

The beams are provided with sheet-steel fixtures for the attachment of the cables, as shown in the broken-off wing view, Fig. 23. These are cut from fairly-heavy metal, and go in pairs, one on each side of the and beam, fasten with three $\frac{3}{16}$-inch bolts. They have lugs top and bottom. They are placed between the fifth and sixth and ninth and tenth ribs on each side.

To resist the backward pressure of the air, the wings are trussed with struts of 1-inch spruce and $\frac{3}{16}$-inch cable, as shown in Fig. 23. The struts are placed between the cable attachments, being provided with ferrules of flattened steel tubing arranged to allow the rear beam freedom to swing up and down. The diagonal cables are provided with turnbuckles and run through the open spaces in the ribs.

Control System. The steering gear and tail construction of the Bleriot are as distinctive as the swiveling wheels and the U-bolts, and the word "cloche" applied to the bell-like attachment for the control wires, has been adopted into the international vocabulary of aeroplaning. The driver has between his knees a small steering wheel mounted on a short vertical post. This wheel does not turn, but instead the post has a universal joint at the bottom which allows it to be swung backward and forward or to either side. The post is really a lever, and the wheel a handle. Encircling the lower part of the post is a hemispherical bell—the cloche—with its bottom edge on the same level as the universal joint.

Four wires are attached to the edge of the cloche. Those at the front and back are connected with the elevator, and those at the sides with the wing-warping lever. The connections are so arranged that pulling the wheel back starts the machine upward, while pushing it forward causes it to descend, and pulling to either side lowers that side and raises the other. The machine can be kept on a level keel by the use of the wheel and cloche alone; the aviator uses them just as if they were rigidly attached to the machine, and by them he could move the machine bodily into the desired position.

In practice, however, it has been found that lateral stability can be maintained more easily by the use of the vertical rudder than by warping. This is because the machine naturally tips inward on a turn, and, consequently, a tip can be corrected by a partial turn in the other direction. If, for example, the machine tips to the right, the aviator steers slightly to the left, and the machine comes back to a level keel without any noticeable change in direction. Under ordinary circumstances this plan is used altogether, and the warping is used only on turns and in bad weather.

BUILDING AND FLYING AN AEROPLANE 77

It will be noticed that the Bleriot control system is almost identical with that of the Henri Farman biplane, the only difference being that in the Farman the cloche and wheel are replaced by a long lever. The movements, however, remain the same, and as there are probably more Bleriot and Farman machines in use than all other makes together, this control may be regarded almost as a standard. It is not as universal as the steering wheel, gear shift, and brake levers of the automobile, but still it is a step in the right direction.

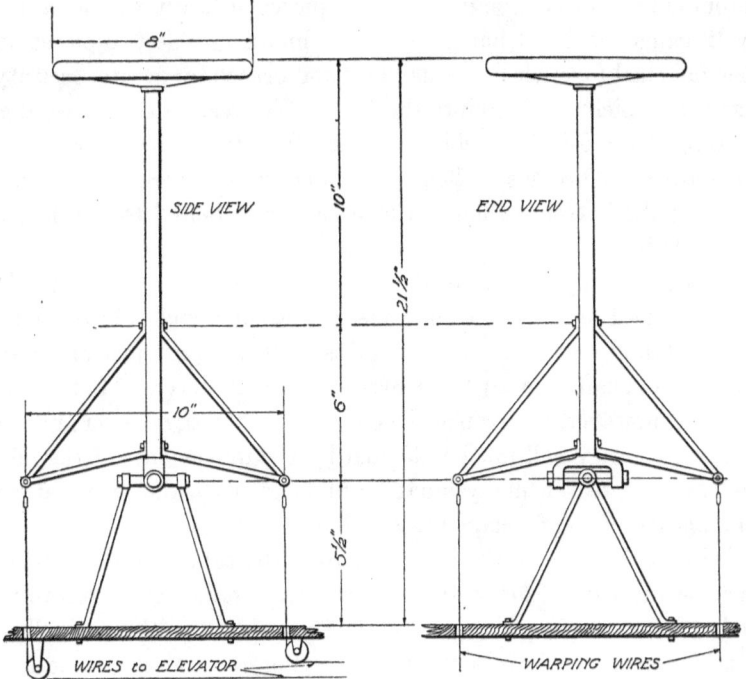

Fig. 32. Control Device of Steel Tubing instead of Bleriot "Cloche"

In the genuine Bleriot, the cloche is built up of two bells, one inside the other, both of sheet aluminum about $\frac{1}{16}$ inch thick. The outer bell is 11 inches in diameter and $3\frac{1}{2}$ inches deep, and the inner one 10 inches in diameter and 2 inches deep. A ring of hard wood is clamped between their edges and the steering column, an aluminum casting passing through their centers. This construction is so complicated and requires so many special castings and parts that it is almost impossible for the amateur.

Steering Gear. While not so neat, the optional construction shown in the accompanying drawing, Fig. 32, is equally effective. In this plan, the cloche is replaced by four V-shaped pieces of $\frac{1}{2}$-inch, 20-gauge steel tubing, attached to a steering post of 1-inch, 20-gauge tubing. At the lower end, the post has a fork, made of pieces of smaller tubing bent and brazed into place, and this fork forms part of the universal joint on which the post is mounted. The cross of the universal joint, which is somewhat similar to those employed on automobiles, can best be made of two pieces of heavy tubing, $\frac{1}{2}$ inch by 12 gauge, each cut half away at the middle. The two pieces are then fastened together by a small bolt and brazed for greater security. The ends which are to go into the fork of the steering post must then be tapped for $\frac{3}{8}$-inch machine screws. The two other ends of the cross are carried on V's of $\frac{1}{2}$-inch, 20-gauge tubing, spread far enough apart at the bottom to make a firm base, and bolted to the floor of the cockpit.

The steering wheel itself is comparatively unimportant. On the genuine Bleriot it is a solid piece of wood 8 inches in diameter, with two holes cut in it for hand grips. On the post just under the wheel are usually placed the spark and throttle levers. It is rather difficult, however, to arrange the connections for these levers in such a way that they will not be affected by the movements of the post, and for this reason many amateur builders place the levers at one side on one of the fuselage beams.

From the sides of the cloche, or from the tubing triangles which may be substituted for it, two heavy wires run straight down to the ends of the warping lever. This lever, together with two pulleys, is mounted at the lower point of the warping frame already described. The lever is 12 inches long, 11 inches between the holes at its ends, and 2 inches wide in the middle; it should be cut from a piece of sheet steel about $\frac{1}{16}$ inch thick. The pulleys should be $2\frac{1}{2}$ inches in diameter, one of them bolted to the lever, the other one running free. The wires from the outer ends of the rear wing beams are joined by a piece of flexible control cable, which is given a single turn over the free pulley. The inner wires, however, each have a piece of flexible cable attached to their ends, and these pieces of cable, after being given a turn round the other pulley, are made fast to the opposite ends of the warping lever. These cables should be

BUILDING AND FLYING AN AEROPLANE 79

run over the pulleys, not under, so that when the cloche is pulled to the right, the left wing will be warped downward.

It is a common mistake to assume that both pulleys are fastened to the warping lever; but when this is done the outer wire slackens off and does not move in accord with the inner wire, on account of the different angles at which they work.

Foot Levers. The foot lever for steering is cut from a piece of wood 22 inches long, hollowed out at the ends to form convenient rests for the feet. The wires connecting the lever to the rudder may either be attached to this lever direct, or, if a neater construction is desired, they may be attached to another lever under the floor of the cockpit. In the latter case, a short piece of 1-inch steel tubing serves as a vertical shaft to connect the two levers, which are fastened to the shaft by means of aluminum sockets such as may be obtained from any supply house. The lower lever is 12 inches long and 2 inches wide, cut from $\frac{1}{16}$-inch steel similar to the warping lever.

Amateur builders often cross the rudder wires so that pressing the lever to the right will cause the machine to steer to the left. This may seem more natural at first glance, but it is not the Bleriot way. In the latter, the wires are not crossed, the idea being to facilitate the use of the vertical rudder for maintaining lateral equilibrium. With this arrangement, pressing the lever with the foot on the high side of the machine tends to bring it back to an even keel.

Tail and Elevator. The tail and elevator planes are built up with ribs and tie strips in much the same manner as the wings. However, it will hardly pay to have these ribs cut out on a jig saw unless the builder can have this work done very cheaply. It serves the purpose just as well to clamp together a number of strips of $\frac{3}{16}$-inch spruce and plane them down by hand. The ribs when finished should be $24\frac{1}{4}$ inches long. The greatest depth of the curve is $1\frac{1}{4}$ inches, at a point one-third of the way back from the front edge, and the greatest depth of the ribs themselves $2\frac{1}{4}$ inches, at the same point. Sixteen ribs are required.

A steel tube 1 inch by 20 gauge, *C*, Fig. 33, runs through both tail and elevators, and is the means of moving the latter. Each rib at the point where the tube passes through, is provided with an aluminum socket. Those on the tail ribs act merely as bearings for the tube, but those on the elevator ribs are bolted fast, so that

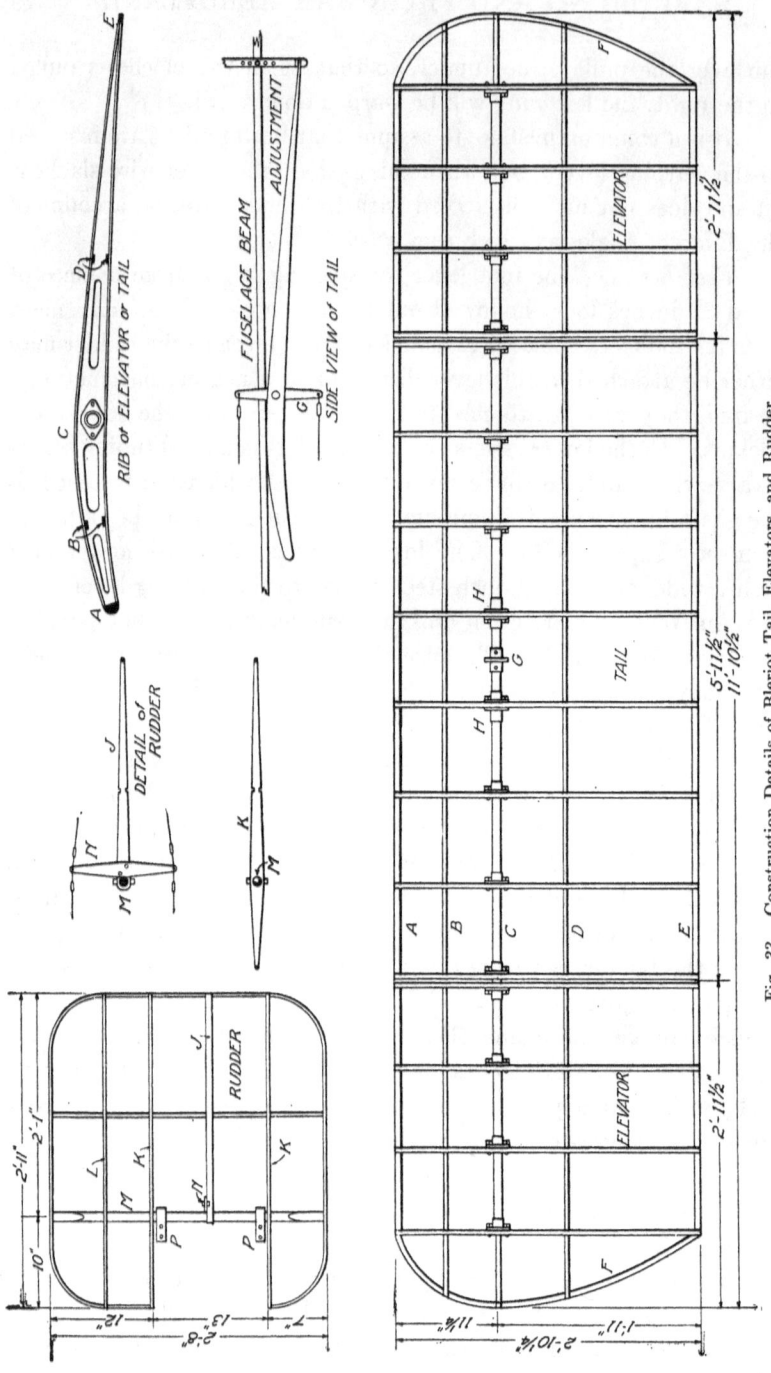

Fig. 33. Construction Details of Bleriot Tail, Elevators, and Rudder

304

BUILDING AND FLYING AN AEROPLANE 81

the elevators must turn with the tube. At its center the tube carries a lever G, of $\frac{1}{16}$-inch steel 12 by 2 inches, fastened on by two aluminum sockets, one on each side. From the top of the lever a wire runs to the front side of the cloche, and from the bottom a second wire runs to the rear side of the cloche.

The tube is carried in two bearings HH, attached to the lower beams of the fuselage. These are simply blocks of hard wood, fastened by steel strips and bolts. The angle of incidence of the tail is adjustable, the tail itself being held in place by two vertical strips of steel rising from the rear edge and bolted to the fuselage, as shown in the drawing, Fig. 33. To prevent the tail from folding up under the air pressure to which it is subjected, it is reinforced by two $\frac{3}{4}$-inch, 20-gauge steel tubes running down from the upper sides of the fuselage, as shown in the drawing of the complete machine, Fig. 23.

The tail and elevators have two pairs of tie strips, B and D, Fig. 33, made of $\frac{3}{16}$- by $\frac{5}{8}$-inch spruce. The front edge A is half round, 1- by $\frac{1}{2}$-inch spruce, and the rear edge E is a spruce strip $\frac{1}{4}$- by $1\frac{1}{2}$-inches. The end pieces are curved.

Rudder. The rudder is built up on a piece of 1-inch round spruce M, corresponding in a way to the steel tube used for the elevators. On this are mounted two long ribs KK, and a short rib J, made of spruce $\frac{3}{8}$ inch thick and $1\frac{3}{8}$ inches wide at the point where M passes through them. They are fastened to M with $\frac{1}{8}$-inch through bolts. The rudder lever N, of $\frac{1}{16}$-inch steel, 12 by 2 inches, is laid flat on J and bolted in place; it is then trussed by wires running from each end to the rear ends of KK. From the lever other wires also run forward to the foot lever which controls the rudder.

The wires to the elevator and rudder should be of the flexible cable specially made for this purpose, and should be supported by fairleaders attached to the fuselage struts. Fairleaders of different designs may be procured from supply houses, or may be improvised. Ordinary screw eyes are often used, or pieces of copper tubing, bound to the struts with friction tape.

Covering the Planes. Covering the main planes, tail, elevators, and rudder may well be left until the machine is otherwise ready for its trial trip, as the cloth will not then be soiled by the dust and grime of the shop. The cloth may be any of the standard brands which are on the market, preferably in a rather light weight made specially for double-surfaced machines of this type; or light-weight sail cloth may be used, costing only 25 or 30 cents a yard. About 80 yards will be required, assuming a width of 36 inches.

Except on the rudder, the cloth is applied on the bias, the idea being that with this arrangement the threads act like diagonal truss wires, thus strengthening and bracing the framework. When the cloth is to be put on in this way it must first be sewed together in sheets large enough to cover the entire plane. Each wing will require

Fig. 34. Method of Mounting Fabric on Main Supporting Frame

a sheet about 14 feet square, and two sheets each 6 feet square will be required for the elevators and tail. The strips of cloth run diagonally across the sheets, the longest strips in the wing sheets being 20 feet long.

Application of the cloth to the wings, Fig. 34, is best begun by fastening one edge of a sheet to the rear edge of the wing, stretching the cloth as tight as can be done conveniently with one hand. The cloth is then spread forward over the upper surface of the wing and is made fast along the inner end rib. Small copper tacks are used, spaced 2 inches apart on the upper side and 1 inch on the

BUILDING AND FLYING AN AEROPLANE

lower side. After the cloth has been tacked to the upper sides of all the ribs, the wing is turned over and the cloth stretched over the lower side. Finally the raw edges are trimmed off and covered with light tape glued down, tape also being glued over all the rows of tacks along the ribs, making a neat finish and at the same time preventing the cloth from tearing off over the tack heads.

Installation of Motor. As stated previously, the ideal motor for a Bleriot-type machine is short along the crank shaft, as the available space in the fuselage is limited, and air-cooled for the same reason. Genuine Bleriots are always fitted with one of the special types of radial or rotary aeronautic motors, which are always air-cooled. Next in popularity to these is the two-cylinder, horizontal-opposed motor, either air- or water-cooled. However, successful machines have been built with standard automobile-type, four-cylinder, water-cooled motors, and with four-cylinder, two-cycle, aeronautic motors.

When the motor is water-cooled, there will inevitably be some difficulty in finding room for a radiator of sufficient size. One scheme is to use twin radiators, one on each side of the fuselage, inside of the main frame of the running gear. Another plan is to place the radiator underneath the fuselage, using a supplementary water tank above the cylinders to facilitate circulation. These two seem to be about the only practicable arrangements, as behind the motor the radiator would not get enough air, and above it would obstruct the view of the operator.

It is impossible to generalize to much effect about the method of supporting the motor in the fuselage, as this must differ with the motor. Automobile-type motors will be carried on two heavy ash beams, braced by lengths of steel tubing of about 1 inch diameter and 16 gauge. When the seven-cylinder rotary Gnome motor is used, the crank shaft alone is supported; it is carried at the center of two x-shaped frames of pressed steel, one in front of and the other behind the motor. The three-cylinder Anzani motors are carried on four lengths of channel steel bent to fit around the upper and lower portions of the crank case, which is of the motorcycle type.

Considerable care should be taken to prevent the exhaust from blowing back into the operator's face as this sometimes carries with it drops of burning oil, besides disagreeable smoke and fumes. The

84 BUILDING AND FLYING AN AEROPLANE

usual plan is to arrange a sloping dashboard of sheet aluminum so as to deflect the gases down under the fuselage.

The three sections of the fuselage back of the engine section are usually covered on the sides and bottom with cloth like that used on the wings. Sometimes sheet aluminum is used to cover the section between the wing beams. However, those who are just learning to operate machines and are a little doubtful about their landings often leave off the covering in order to be able to see the ground immediately beneath their front wheels.

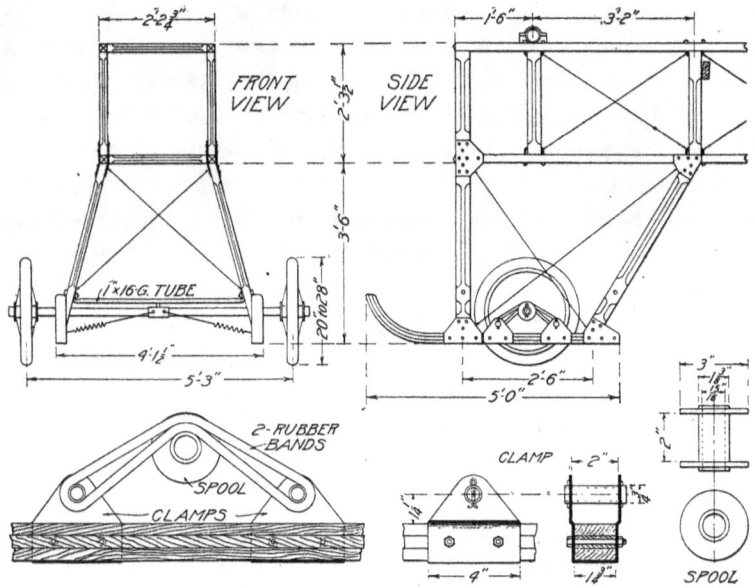

Fig. 35. Running Gear of Morane Type of Bleriot Monoplane

New Features. *Morane Landing Gear.* Although the regular Bleriot landing gear already described, has many advantages and has been in use with only detail changes for several years, some aviators prefer the landing gear of the new Morane monoplane, which in other respects closely resembles the Bleriot. This gear, Fig. 35, is an adaptation of that long in use on the Henri Farman and Sommer biplanes, combining skids and wheels with rubber-band springs. In case a wheel or spring breaks, whether due to a defect or to a rough landing, the skids often save an upset. Besides, the

BUILDING AND FLYING AN AEROPLANE 85

tension of the springs is usually such that on a rough landing the wheels jump up and allow the skids to take the shock; this also prevents the excessive rebound of the Bleriot springs under similar conditions.

Another advantage which may have some weight with the amateur builder, is that the Morane running gear is much cheaper and easier to construct. Instead of the two heavy tubes, the four forks of oval tubing, and the many slides, collars, and blocks—most of them special forgings or castings—the Morane gear simply requires two short laminated skids, four ash struts, and some sheet steel.

The laminated skids are built up of three boards each of $\frac{5}{8}$- by 2-inch ash, $3\frac{1}{2}$ feet long. These must be glued under heavy pressure in forms giving the proper curve at the front end. When they are taken from the press, three or four $\frac{1}{2}$-inch holes should be bored at equal distances along the center line and wood pins driven in; these help in retaining the curve. The finished size of the skids should be $1\frac{3}{4}$ by $1\frac{3}{4}$ inches.

Four ash struts $1\frac{1}{4}$ by $2\frac{1}{2}$ inches support the fuselage. They are rounded off to an oval shape except at the ends, where they are attached to the skids and the fuselage beams with clamps of $\frac{1}{16}$-inch sheet steel. The ends of the struts must be beveled off carefully to make a good fit; they spread out 15 degrees from the vertical, and the rear pair have a backward slant of 30 degrees from vertical.

Additional fuselage struts must be provided at the front end of the fuselage to take the place of the struts and beams of the Bleriot running gear. The two vertical struts at the extreme front end may be of the same $1\frac{1}{4}$- by $2\frac{1}{2}$-inch ash used in the running gear, planed down to $1\frac{3}{16}$ inches thick to match the thickness of the fuselage beams. The horizontal struts should be $1\frac{3}{16}$ by $1\frac{3}{4}$ inches.

The wheels run on the ends of an axle tube, and usually have plain bearings. The standard size bore of the hub is $\frac{15}{16}$ inch, and the axle tube should be $\frac{15}{16}$ inch diameter by 11 gauge. The tube also has loosely mounted on it two spools to carry the rubber band springs. These are made of $2\frac{1}{4}$-inch lengths of $1\frac{3}{8}$-inch tubing, with walls of sufficient thickness to make an easy sliding fit on the axle tube. To the ends of each length of tube are brazed $2\frac{1}{2}$-inch washers of $\frac{3}{16}$-inch steel, completing the spool.

The ends of the rubber bands are carried on rollers of ¾-inch, 16-gauge tubing, fastened to the skids by fittings bent up from $\frac{3}{16}$-inch sheet steel. Each fitting is bolted to the skid with two ⅜-inch bolts.

Some arrangement must now be made to keep the axle centered under the machine, as the rubber bands will not take any sidewise strain. A clamp of heavy sheet steel should be made to fit over the axle at its center, and from this heavy wires or cables run to the bottom ends of the forward struts. These wires may be provided with stiff coil springs, if it is desired to allow a little sidewise movement.

New Bleriot Inverse Curve Tail. Some of the latest Bleriot

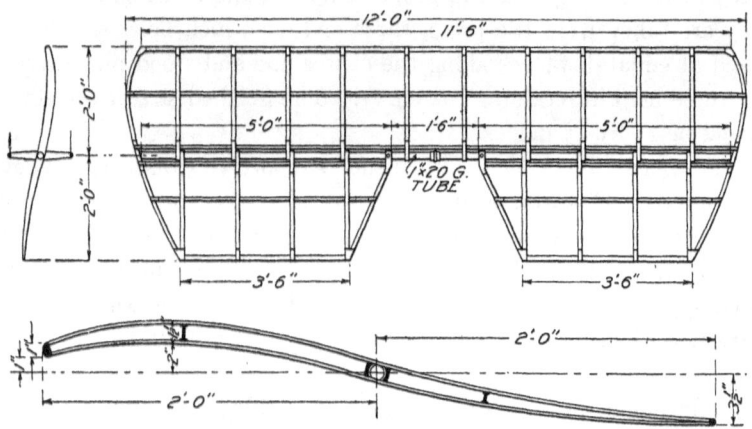

Fig. 36. Details of Bleriot Inverse Curve Tail

machines have a new tail which seems to add considerable to their speed. It consists of a fixed tail, Fig. 36, nearly as large as the old-style tail and elevators combined, with two elevator flaps hinged to its rear edge. The peculiarity of these elevators, from which the tail gets its name, is that the curve is concave above and convex below—at first glance seeming to have been attached upside down.

In this construction, the 1-inch, 20-gauge tube, which formerly passed through the center of the tail, now runs along the rear edge, being held on by strips of ½- by $\frac{1}{16}$-inch steel bent into U-shape and fastened with screws or bolts to the ribs. Similar strips attach the elevators to the tube, but these strips are bolted to the tube.

BUILDING AND FLYING AN AEROPLANE 87

The construction is otherwise like that previously described. It is said that fitting this tail to a Bleriot in place of the old-style tail adds 5 miles an hour to the speed, without any other changes being made.

Another slight change which distinguishes the newer Bleriots is in the overhead frame, which now consists of a single inverted V instead of two V's connected by a horizontal tube. The single V is set slightly back of the main wing beam, and is higher and, of course, of heavier tubing than in the previous construction. Its top should stand 2 feet 6 inches above the fuselage, and the tubing should be 1 inch 18 gauge. It also requires four truss wires, two running to the front end of the fuselage and two to the struts to which the rear wing beams are attached. All of the wires on the upper side of the wings converge to one point at the top of this V, the wires from the wing beams, of course, passing over pulleys.

These variations from the form already described may be of interest to those who wish to have their machines up-to-date in every detail, but they are by no means essential. Hundreds of the old-style Bleriots are flying every day and giving perfect satisfaction.

ART OF FLYING

Knowledge of the science of aeronautics and ability to fly are two totally different things. Long-continued study of the problem from its scientific side enabled the Wright Brothers to learn how to build a machine that would fly, but it did not teach them how to fly with it. That came as the result of persistent attempts at flying itself. A study of the theoretic laws of balancing does not form a good foundation for learning how to ride a bicycle—practice with the actual machine is the only road to success. The best evidence of this is to be found in the fact that several of the most successful aviators today have but a slight knowledge of the science of aeronautics. They are not particularly well versed in what makes flight possible, but they know how to fly because they have learned it in actual practice.

Reference to the early work of the Wright Brothers shows that during a period of several years they spent a large part of their time in actual experiments in the air, and it was not until these had proved

88 BUILDING AND FLYING AN AEROPLANE

entirely satisfactory that they attempted to build a power-driven machine.

Methods Used in Aviation Schools. Aviation schools are springing up all over this country and there are a number of well-established

Fig. 37. Monoplane Dummy Used for Practice in Aviation Schools

institutions of this kind abroad. In the course of instruction, the student must first learn the use of the various controls on a dummy machine. In the case of an English school, this dummy, Fig. 37, is a motorless aeroplane mounted on a universally-jointed support so

Fig. 38. Aerocycle with Treadle Power for Practice Work

as to swing about a pivot as desired. This is employed for the purpose of familiarizing the beginner with the means of maintaining equilibrium in the air.

BUILDING AND FLYING AN AEROPLANE 89

A French school, on the other hand, employs a wingless machine, which is otherwise complete, as it consists of a regulation chassis with motor and propeller, all steering and elevating controls. On this, the student may practice what has come to be familiarly known as "grass-cutting," to his heart's content, without any danger of the machine taking to the air unexpectedly, as has frequently been the case where first attempts have been made on a full-fledged machine. Usually, most of such attempts result disastrously, often destroying in a moment the result of months of work in building the machine.

Fig. 39. Voisin Biplane with Double Control for Teaching Beginners

A French aerocycle, Fig. 38, a comparatively inexpensive machine, is also useful for practice in balancing and in short, low flights. The French apparatus in question may accordingly be considered an advance, not only over the English machine, even of the type shown in Fig. 39, which has a double control, and is especially designed for the teaching of beginners, but very much over the practice of attempting to actually fly for the first time in a strange machine, as it provides the necessary practice in the handling of the motor and the lateral steering. The machine can make high speed over the ground, but is perfectly safe for the beginner, as it is incapable of rising. Having gone through the stages represented by either of these contrivances, the best course for the learner to follow is to try gliding, taking short glides to attain the ability to quickly meet varying conditions of the atmosphere.

The fact that these glides are of extremely short duration at first need not be discouraging when it is recalled that, after several years of work, the Wright Brothers considered that great progress had been made when, in 1902, they were able to make glides of 26 seconds. During six days of the practice season of that year, they made 375 gliding flights of various distances, most of them comparatively short, but each one of value in familiarizing the glider with the conditions to be met. It is not material whether gliding or manipulation of the control levers is taken up first, as both should be mastered as far as possible before attempting to fly a regular machine.

Use of the Elevating Plane. So many things are necessary to the control of an aeroplane that thinking becomes entirely too slow a process—the aviator must be endowed with something approaching the instinct of the bird; he must be so familiar with his machine and its peculiarities that a large part of the work of controlling it is the result of subconscious movement. The control levers of many machines are so arranged that this subconscious movement on the part of the aviator directly operates the balancing mechanism. There is no time to think. When a machine rises from the ground, facing the wind as it should, its path of flight should be a gradual upward inclination, this being something difficult to accomplish at first, owing to the sensitiveness of the elevating rudder, the tendency almost invariably being to give the latter too great an angle of incidence. At this stage, the maximum velocity of flight has not yet been attained and care must be taken to keep the angle of ascent small. Otherwise, the power of the engine, which may not have reached its maximum, would not be sufficient to cause the machine to ascend an inclined path at the starting speed. If the speed of flight be reduced by the increased resistance at this point, the whole machine will slide back in the air, and if a sudden gust of wind happens to coincide with the attempt to rise at too great an angle, there is danger of it being blown over backward.

Where the machine is just leaving the ground and the elevator has been set at an excessive angle, the rear end of the skids or the tail may slap the ground hard and break off, or they will impose so much resistance upon its movement by scraping over the turf that the machine can not attain its soaring speed. It must be borne in mind, of course, that remarks such as the present can be only of the most general nature, every type of machine having its own peculiarities—in some instances, the extreme opposite of those characterizing similar machines. For example, in the Voisin 1910 type, the very large and powerful light tail tends to lift before the main planes, and if this be not counteracted, the whole machine may turn up on its end. In order to offset this tendency, the elevator must be raised so as to keep sufficient pressure beneath it; the moment of this pressure about the center of gravity must be at least equal to the pressure under the tail planes about the center of gravity of the machine, or the tail will rise unduly in the air. At least that is the theory of it—naturally, only practice with that particular machine would suffice to enable an aviator to familiarize himself with that particular peculiarity. Again, some machines are "tail heavy." But there is great difficulty in even approximating the degree of relative motion, for which reason it has been suggested, under "Accidents and Their Lessons," that a gradometer, or small spirit level, in plain sight of the aviator, should form part of the equipment of every machine. The Wrights long ago adopted the expedient of attaching a strip of ribbon to the elevator to provide an indication of motion relative to the wind.

Aeroplane in Flight. The sensation of motion after the machine leaves the ground is almost imperceptible, and it is likewise extremely difficult to tell at just what moment the aeroplane ceases running on the solid ground and takes to the air. There is a feeling of exhilaration but very little of motion. Whereas 40 miles an hour over the ground, particularly in an automobile, brings with it a lively appreciation of the speed of travel, the same speed in an aeroplane is a very gentle motion when high above the ground. If there be no objects close at hand, with which to compare the speed, the sense of motion is almost entirely lost.

Center of Gravity. The static balance of a machine should be carefully tried before commencing to fly, and particularly that of a biplane of the Wright type, in which the aviator sits beside the engine.

When provision is made for carrying a passenger, his seat is placed in the center line of the machine, so that his presence or absence does not materially affect the question of lateral balance. As men are not all of the same weight, in cases in which the aviator only partly balances the engine about the center line, his weight being insufficient for the purpose, extra weights should be placed on the wing tip at the lightest end until the true balance is secured, otherwise a permanent warping, or *gauchissement* as the French term it, is required at this side in order to keep the machine on an even keel. In other words, the machine will carry what sailors term a port helm where the left side of the machine is lighter than the right, and *vice versa*, and it will be necessary to keep the rudder over to that side slightly during the entire flight to counteract this tendency.

In aeroplanes fitted with tails, the center of gravity is usually in the vicinity of the trailing edge of the main planes and, of course, should be on the center line of the machine. The center of gravity of the aviator on a monoplane should approximately coincide with that of the machine. If this be not the case, the stabilizers or the elevator must be permanently set to produce longitudinal balance. Much downward set, or the increase of the angle of incidence of the tail, will create undue resistance to flight and should be avoided when possible by bringing the weight farther forward. The center of pressure should coincide with the center of gravity, and balance will result.

Before even ground work is attempted, the position of the center of gravity should be determined in the manner shown in Fig. 40, the approximate location for four types of machines being shown. At what point the machine must be suspended, so that it can tip only frontward and backward and be evenly balanced, is a question that must be answered in order to ascertain the probability of the machine's pitching forward whenever mud, grass, or rough ground is encountered in alighting. If the center of gravity should lie in front of the axles of the ground wheels in a machine of the Farman type, trouble is sure to follow. Always consider the relation of the center of gravity to the wheels, in order that you may gain some idea of the distribution of the weight on the running gear when the machine is tipped forward 10 degrees. If the wheels are not forward far enough there will be trouble in running on the ground. The elevators must correct whatever variance there may be from the correct center of gravity and position of the wheels, and the manipulation of the elevators for that purpose requires skill. If the tail be very heavy, the elevator may not be able to counteract that defect.

The position of the center of gravity of a machine in regard to lateral stability in flight is a matter of far greater importance than untried aviators realize. Having it too low is quite as bad as too high, as in either case there is a tendency to upset. Although the dihedral angle is considered wasteful of power, it seems to do more to secure inherent stability than any other device. Devices for maintaining stability automatically are to be frowned upon in the present state

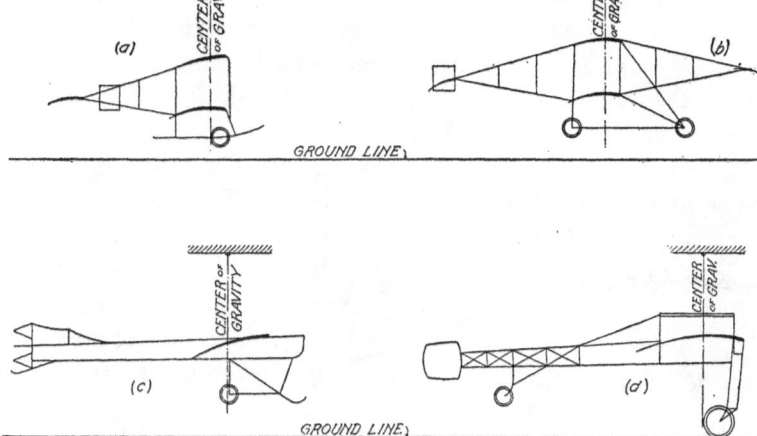

Fig. 40. Method of Determining Center of Gravity of Different Types of Machines

of the art. The sensitive perception and quick response which come with intimate knowledge of a machine's peculiarities, are at present worth more than gyroscopes and pendulums. To acquire this intimate knowledge, the aviator must familiarize himself thoroughly with the machine; he must become so accustomed to controls that he and the machine are literally one. A practiced bicycle rider does not have to think about balance, neither does the practiced aviator, yet he must always be prepared to meet motor stoppages, unusual air disturbances, and breakages. A leap from the ground directly into the air, without preliminary practice, means certain accident, to put it mildly.

94   BUILDING AND FLYING AN AEROPLANE

Center of Pressure. But although the center of gravity remains approximately constant, the center of pressure is continually varying and is never constant for many seconds. The center of pressure on an aerocurve constructed to Phillips' design, Fig. 41, is about one-third of the chord from the leading edge of the plane under normal conditions, *i. e.*, when the angle of incidence is about 8 degrees between the direction of motion of the plane and that of the air. At the moment this angle is increased the center of pressure moves toward the rear, and *vice versa*. The center of gravity must be moved to coincide with this new position, or the center of pressure must be artificially restored by the use of supplementary planes or elevators, moving in a contrary direction. A forward movement of the center of pressure tends to lower the tail of the machine, when the intensity of the pressure is unchanged, and to counterbalance this the rear elevator must have its angle of incidence increased in order to increase the lift at the rear of the machine, or it will slide down backward. The alternative to be adopted in case of temporary lack of engine power is to decrease the angle of the elevator and allow the aeroplane to sweep downward, thus gaining momentum. The increase of speed will then be sufficient probably to enable the machine to continue in a horizontal flight, when the center of pressure is again restored to its normal position.

Fig. 41. Aerocurve of Phillip's Design

Ground Practice. First of all, the aviator should familiarize himself with his seat for it is from that place that he must judge wind effects, vibration, motor trouble, and the thousand and one little creaks and hums that will ultimately mean so much to him. Not until he has thoroughly accustomed himself to his seat, should he try to run along the ground. This done, hours should be spent running up and down and around the field to learn the use of the rudder, particularly on rough ground. The runs should be straight so that when the time comes to leap into the air, the aviator may be sure that he is on an even keel, and flying straightaway. In order to prevent the possibility of leaving the ground unexpectedly in practice, trials should be made only in calm weather and with the motor well throttled down so that the machine will be reduced to a

BUILDING AND FLYING AN AEROPLANE 95

speed of not more than 15 miles per hour. After a time this may be increased to 20, but the latter is the maximum for ground practice, as the machine will rise at speeds slightly exceeding this. In these practice runs on the ground, the student should learn to gauge the rush of air against his face, as when aloft his best gauge will be the wind pressure on his cheeks, as that will tell him whether he is moving with sufficient speed to keep up or not. It will also tell him ultimately whether he is moving along the ground fast enough to leap up.

In this stage of experimenting on the ground, the elevator is kept neutral as far as possible. With increasing skill its use may be ventured, but only sparingly, for it takes very little to lift the machine from the ground with a speed in excess of 20 miles per hour. It will soon be discovered that the elevator can be used as a brake to prevent pitching forward. The tail elevators on the Farman or Bleriot running gear are very effective owing to the blast of the propeller, even when the main planes are not moving forward at lifting speed. With the Curtiss type of running gear and a front elevator only, it is often possible at 18 to 20 miles per hour to raise the front wheel off the ground for a second or two—facts which indicate that at 25 to 28 miles per hour, the elevator is far more effective.

First Flight. The first actual flight should be confined to a short trip parallel to the ground and not more than one or two feet above it. At first, the student should see how close he can fly to the ground without actually touching it, which he can do by gradually increasing his forward speed. This must be done in an absolute calm as an appreciable amount of wind will bring in too many other factors for the student to master at so early a stage. This practice should be continued in calm air until short, straight flights can be made a foot or two from the ground with the motor wide open. If it be found that the machine barely flies straightaway with the full power of the motor, the latter is either badly out of adjustment, or a more powerful engine is required. In an under-powered machine turning would be suicidal. Moreover, the resistance encountered in the air is greater than on the ground and may be such that the speed is not sufficient for sustentation. Fig. 42, (a) and (b), show why it is possible to run along the ground faster than it is possible to travel in the air, under certain conditions, and why the ground can be left at low speed. If it were possible to drive a machine with such enormous

96 BUILDING AND FLYING AN AEROPLANE

projected areas as *BB*, shown in Fig. 42 (b), a man could fly slowly for an indefinite period. But the projected area is greater than the air displaced by the propeller, and it is impossible to fly except with a moderate angle of incidence, giving projected areas *AA*, Fig. 42 (a).

The student, as he increases in skill, may venture to a height of 10 feet, which should be maintained as accurately as before, and after making a run of 100 yards, the machine should be pointed down, but ever so slightly. The wind pressure on the face immediately becomes greater. Within a foot or two of the ground the motor should be cut off or throttled. This should be tried ten or fifteen times, and the height increased to 30 or 40 feet, in order that the student may familiarize himself with the sensation of coasting. At the end of each glide the machine will seem to become more responsive, as indeed it does, for gliding down greatly increases the efficiency of the elevator and other controls, because of the increased speed. Gliding down steep angles is often the aviator's salvation in a tight

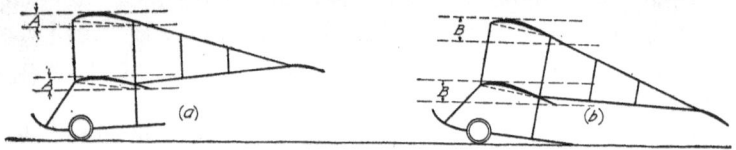

Fig. 42. Diagrams Showing Greater Projected Area of Main Plane when Running along Ground

place, particularly when the motor fails, a side gust threatens, or an air pocket is encountered.

Warping the Wings. When sufficient confidence has been attained at a height of 30 to 40 feet, the ailerons or warping devices may be tried judiciously. Here the intention should be to correct any tendency to side tipping, and not purposely to incline the machine as far as possible without actually causing a wreck. The use of the lateral control may cause the machine to swerve a little, but that may be ignored. Before landing, a straight course should be taken so that the machine will always come down on an even keel. With increasing practice, the student may fly higher, but always with the understanding that there is a limit to the angle of incidence. An automobile is retarded when it strikes a short, steep hill; so is an aeroplane. No aeroplane has yet been built that can take a steep angle and climb right up that grade continuously. Altitude is reached by a series of small steps and at comparatively low angles, as unless the course is straightened out at regular intervals, a machine will lose its speed and tend to plunge tail first, just as is the case when an attempt is made to rise from the ground at too sharp an angle.

In warping the wings an increase of lift imparted to one wing of the machine is produced by increasing the angle of incidence of the whole or part of the wing, or by an increase of pressure under that wing, and will tend to cause that side of the machine to rise and the other side to lower, the result being that the machine will be liable to slide through the air diagonally. In the majority of aeroplanes there are no fins or keels to counteract this movement, and lateral stability must be restored by artificially increasing the lift of the depressed wing. This can be done by warping, or lowering the trailing edge of the depressed wing and increasing its lift, and simultaneously raising the trailing edge of the other wing, thus decreasing the angle of incidence of the latter and reducing its lifting effect. This applies to flight on a straight course, whatever the cause may be that tends to upset lateral stability. It will be seen, therefore, that the center of gravity remains constant and the center of pressure must be manipulated to restore stability. This manipulation is much more rapid and positive than the alteration of the center of gravity by the movement of the aviator's body resorted to in the early gliding flights of pioneer experimenters.

Making a Turn. The first turn should be made over a large field and the diameter of the turn should be at least half a mile. The height should be not less than 50 feet. After that level has been maintained, the rudder should be moved very gingerly. The machine will lean in almost immediately, because the outer end travels at a higher speed than the inner and therefore has a greater lift. Warping or working the ailerons should be resorted to as a means of counteracting this tendency, and the rudder swung to the opposite direction, if necessary. It is obvious that if the rudder will cause the machine to bank when swung in one direction, it will right the machine again when swung in the opposite direction. It is even possible to turn the machine on an even keel by anticipating the banking, simply by correctly using the rudder, which was necessary in the old Voisin machine flown by Farman in 1908, because it had no mechanical lateral control. The student should learn the correct angle of banking, i. e., the angle at which the machine will neither skid nor slide down and which is most economical of power because it requires less use of the lateral controls. The necessity of "feeling the air" is greater in turning than in any other phase of flying. By "feeling the air" is meant the ability to meet any contingency intuitively and not until this is acquired can the student become an expert aviator. When it has been acquired, safe flying is assured and is dependent only upon the integrity of the planes, motor, and controls. By using the rudder discreetly and by banking simply far enough to partially offset the centrifugal force of turning, the use of the lateral control will not be necessary in still air. Even too short a turn can be corrected by a quick use of the rudder.

The peculiarities existing between different types of monoplanes become even more marked than between the biplane and the monoplane. For example, in piloting a Bleriot monoplane, Fig. 43, it is necessary to take into account the effect of the engine torque. As the engine rotates in a right-hand direction, from the point of view of the pilot, the left wing tends to rise in the air, owing to the depression of the right side of the machine. The machine also tends to turn to the right, and this must be counteracted by putting the rudder over to the left. An aeroplane answers its controls with comparative slowness, with the exception, perhaps, of the Wright machine, which is noted for its sensitive and quick response to every movement of the levers. All control movements must, therefore, be very gentle, as the behavior of an aeroplane is more like that of a boat than that of an automobile. The action of the elevator has already been described, and it is, perhaps, the most difficult of all the controls to manipulate, in that it requires the exercise of a new sense. The direction rudder is naturally a more familiar type of control, and in action is similar to the rudder of a boat.

The torque of the motor renders it advisable for a novice to turn his machine to the right, if a right-hand propeller be used, and *vice versa*. If two propellers, turning in opposite directions, are employed, as in the Wright biplane, there is no inequality from the torque of the motor. Since torque is not noticeable in straight flying, straightening out again will always serve the student when he finds himself in trouble on a turn. When the use of the rudders and ailerons has reduced the speed, a downward glide will increase

BUILDING AND FLYING AN AEROPLANE 99

Fig. 43. Making a Start with Bleriot Monoplane

it again, and if the motor should stop on a turn, such a downward glide is immediately imperative. When the machine is thus gliding, a change in the fore-and-aft balance becomes at once apparent, because the blast of the propeller no longer acts on the tail, and the elevator must then be used with greater amplitude to obtain the same effect.

Only by constant practice in calm air can the student familiarize himself with exactly the amount of warping and rudder control to employ to properly offset the lowering of the inner wing in rounding a turn. If this be not corrected, the whole machine tends to bank excessively and will be apt to slide downward in a diagonal direction, Fig. 44. This is a perilous position for the aviator and must be guarded against by the manipulation of the warping control so as to increase the lift of the inner wing of a biplane, at the same time, employing the rudder to counteract this tendency. The use of the rudder is of even greater importance on the monoplane, as, in this case, warping the inner wing tends to direct the whole machine downward instead of raising the inner wing itself. Several bad accidents have resulted from monoplanes refusing to respond to the warping of the inner wing when making a turn. In such machines, the rudder must be practically always employed in connection with the warping of the wings in order to keep the machine on an even keel, although the controls may not actually be interconnected, this being one of the grounds on which foreign manufacturers are trying to make use of the Wright principle, without infringing the Wright patents, as while they employ warping in connection with the simultaneous use of the rudder, the controls are not attached to the same lever as in the Wright machine.

Lateral resistance must also be taken into consideration in turning, otherwise the machine, if kept on an even keel, will tend to skid through the air and turn about its center of gravity as a pivot. In the case of an automobile, the resistance to lateral displacement is great, though on a greasy surface it may be small, as when the machine skids sideways, a suitable banking of the road being necessary to prevent this on turns. Many hold that the banking of the aeroplane on turns is only the direct effect of the turning itself, but the fallacy of this will be apparent upon a consideration of the law of centrifugal force. It is obvious that to make a turn, some force

BUILDING AND FLYING AN AEROPLANE 101

Fig. 44. An Aeroplane "Banking" as it Rounds a Pylon

must be imparted to the machine to counteract the effect of the centrifugal force upon the machine as a whole. And as the sidewise projection of the machine is small, a compensating force must be introduced. This can be done only by previously banking up the machine on the outer wing, so that the pressure of the air under the main plane can counteract the tendency to lateral displacement. The force then acting under the planes is in a diagonal direction, and the angle at which it is inclined vertically depends upon the banking of the planes, it being normal to their greater dimension. This force can be resolved into two forces, one perpendicular and one horizontal, the magnitude of each being dependent upon the degree of banking. When the speed of the machine is higher, the amount of banking must be greater in order to increase the value of the horizontal component in proportion to the increase of the value of the centrifugal force at the higher speed, in spite of the fact that the forces acting under the planes are also greater due to the higher speed.

As the curve commences, the rudder being put over, the difference of the pressures on the two wings, owing to their different flying speeds comes into account, as already explained, and care must be taken that the banking does not increase abnormally. When the turn is completed, the rudder is straightened and the machine is again brought to an even keel with the aid of the wing-warping control, or the ailerons. The effect of a reverse warping to prevent excessive banking, lowering the inside wing tip incidentally, puts a slight drag on that wing and assists in the action of turning, as does also the provision of small vertical planes between the elevator planes of the original Wright machine. Since the adoption of the headless type, these surfaces are placed between the forward ends of the skids and the braces leading down to them.

In making a turn, say, to the left, the outside or right-hand wing is first raised by lowering the wing tip on that side and the rudder is then put over to the left. When the correct amount of banking is acquired, the wing tip is restored to its normal position, and probably the left wing tip may have to be lowered slightly to increase the lift on that side owing to its reduced speed. When the turn is completed, the rudder is straightened out and the left wing tip lowered to restore the machine to an even keel. Both Glenn

BUILDING AND FLYING AN AEROPLANE   103

Curtiss in this country and R. E. Pelterie in France have shown that it is possible to maneuver without using the rudder at all, the ailerons or wing tips alone being relied upon for this purpose.

Before flights in other than calm air are attempted, much practice is required. The machine must be inspected over and over again, and the wind variations studied with a watchful eye. Not until this familiarity with machine and atmosphere be acquired should flying in a wind be attempted. To the man on the ground, wind is simply air moving horizontally, but to the man in the air it is quite different. Not only must he consider horizontal movement, but vertical draughts and vortices as well. A rising current of air lifts a machine, a downward current depresses it, and he must learn to take advantage of the former as the birds do. Horizontal currents affect forward speed over the ground; swirls and vortices create inequalities in wind pressure on the planes and disturb lateral balance. Familiarity with all these atmospheric conditions can be acquired only after long practice. Against every tree, house, hill, fence, and hedge beats an invisible surf of air; upward currents on one side and downward on the other. The upward draught is not usually dangerous, for it simply lifts the machine; but the down draught will cause it to drop. A swift downward glide under the full power of the motor must then be made, to increase the forward speed and consequently the lift. This explains why it is dangerous to fly near the ground in a wind; likewise why the beginner should never attempt flying at first in anything but a dead calm.

Turning in a Wind. When turning in a wind, two velocities must be borne in mind, that of the machine relative to the air and that relative to the earth. The former is limited at its lower value to that of the flying speed of the machine, and the latter must be considered on account of the momentum of the machine as a whole. Change of momentum is a matter of horse-power and weight and is the governing factor in flying in a wind on a circular course. Suppose the flying speed of a machine is a minimum of 30 miles an hour relative to the air, and a wind of 20 miles an hour is blowing. The actual speed of the machine relative to the earth in flying against the wind will be 10 miles an hour. If it be desired to turn down the wind, the speed of the machine relative to the earth must be increased from 10 miles to 50 miles an hour during the turn and a corresponding change of momentum must be overcome. There are two ways of accomplishing this, either by speeding up the motor to give the maximum power, or by rising just previous to making the turn and then sweeping down as the turn is made, thus utilizing the acceleration due to gravity to assist the motor. The wind's velocity will assist the machine also and during the turn it will make considerable leeway, a small amount of which is deducted to counteract the centrifugal force of the machine.

Turning in a contrary direction, *i. e.*, up into the wind when running with it, requires considerable skill, as when flying 50 miles an hour, the tendency on rounding a corner into a 20-mile-an-hour wind would be for the machine to rise rapidly in the air. The centrifugal force at such a speed is also considerable, causing the machine to make much leeway with the wind during the turn. Turning under such circumstances should be commenced early, particularly if there are any obstructions in the vicinity, and considerable skill should be acquired before an attempt is made to fly in such a wind.

Starting and Landing. A machine should always be started and landed in the teeth of the wind, and no one but the most experienced aviators can afford to disregard this advice, certainly not the novice. The precaution is necessary because in landing the machine should always travel straight ahead without the possibility of lurching and consequently breaking a wing, as frequently happens. Contact with the ground is necessarily made at a time when the machine is traveling over it at a speed of 30 to 40 miles per hour and skidding sideways at 10 to 15 miles per hour, all circumstances which tend to wreck an aeroplane.

Planning a Flight. It is easy to lose one's way in the air. For that reason it is best to follow the Wright idea of starting out with a definite plan, and of landing in some predetermined spot, as aimless wandering about may prove disastrous to the inexperienced aviator. He may forget which way the wind was blowing, or how much fuel he had, or the character of the ground beneath him. Should the motor stop, he may make an all too hasty decision in landing. It is an easy matter to lose one's bearings in the air, not only because the vehicle is completely immersed in the medium in which it is traveling, but also because the earth assumes a new aspect from the seat of an aeroplane. Cecil Grace was one of those who lost his bearings and, as a consequence, his life. Ordinary winds blowing over a level country can be negotiated with comparative safety. Not so the puffy wind. To cope with that, constant vigilance is required, particularly in turning. In a circular flight in a steady wind, the only apparent effect is that the earth is swept over faster in one direction than in the other. Before a cross-country flight is attempted, the starting field should be circled over at a great height, as not until then may the long distance flight be started in safety. Cross-country flying is, of course, fascinating, and it is a sore temptation, at an altitude of a few hundred feet, to throw off all caution and fly off over that strange country below, which is, indeed, a new land as viewed from aloft. To quote a professional aviator: "Here the greatest self-restraint must be exercised. Not until the necessary practice has been acquired, not until the right kind of confidence has been gained, may one of these trips be attempted, and then only after it has been properly planned."

Training the Professional Aviator. Look back over the achievements in the air during the comparatively short time that man has actually been flying, and it will be noted that the beginners, burning up with the enthusiasm of the novice, have performed the most spectacular feats and flown with the greatest fearlessness. Curtiss was comparatively new at aviation when he won the Gordon-Bennett at Rheims in 1909. John B. Moisant, the sixth time he ever went up in an aeroplane, flew from Paris to London with a 187-pound passenger and 302 pounds of fuel, oil, and spare parts. Hamilton made his successful flight from New York to Philadelphia and return when he was hardly more than a novice, while Atwood's great flights from St. Louis to New York and Boston to Washington were made before his name had become known, and Beachey had been flying only a few months when he broke the world's altitude record at Chicago, while more recent achievements, notably Dixon's flight across the Rockies, have emphasized the work of the beginner. All of this substantiates the belief held at every aviation headquarters in the country—namely, that the older men already in aviation may improve the art by executive ability and scientific experiments, but most of them will degenerate as flyers. Beyond a certain point, frequency of flight does not necessarily create a feeling of confidence and safety; rather it brings a fuller appreciation of the dangers, and the men who best know how to fly are most content to stay upon the ground.

Professional aviators are drawn from every walk of life, but trick bicycle performers, acrobats, parachute jumpers, and racing automobile drivers make the most promising applicants. By a kind of sixth sense, both the Wrights and Curtiss weed out the promising ones after a brief examination. They select men who have an almost intuitive sense of balance. Most of these, provided they have nerve, have in them the stuff of which aviators are made, even though they may have had no experience in any line akin to aviation. Neither Curtiss nor the Wrights will accept women under any condition. The Moisant school does not share this discrimination and trained three women for pilot's licenses during 1911.

Curtiss and the Wrights are keen in their realization that recklessness is pulling a wing feather from aviation every time a man is killed, and they are doing their utmost to promote conservatism. Curtiss said in an interview:

> I do not encourage and never have encouraged fancy flying. I regard the spectacular gyrations of several aviators I know as foolhardy and unnecessary. I do not believe that fancy or trick flying demonstrates anything except an unlimited amount of a certain kind of nerve and perhaps the possibilities of what is valueless—aerial acrobatics. Some aviators develop the sense of balance very rapidly, while others acquire it only after long practice. It may be developed to a large extent by going up as a passenger with an experienced man. Therefore, in teaching a beginner, I make it a point to have him make as many trips as possible with someone else operating the machine. In this way the pupil gains confidence, becomes accustomed to the sensation of flying, and is soon ready for a flight on his own hook. This is the method used in training army and navy officers to fly. I have never seen novices more cautious and yet more eager to fly than these young officers. They have always learned every detail of their machines before going aloft, and largely because of this they have developed into great flyers. Perhaps it is due to the military bent of their minds; at any rate, they have made good almost without exception.

ACCIDENTS AND THEIR LESSONS

Press Reports. Whenever an industry, profession, or what not, is prominently before the public, every event connected with it is regarded as "good copy" by the daily press. Happenings of so insignificant a nature that in any commonplace calling would not be considered worthy of mention at all, are "played up." This is particularly the case with fatalities, and the eagerness to cater to the morbid streak in human nature has been responsible for the unusual amount of attention devoted to any or all accidents to flying machines, and more especially where they have a fatal ending. In fact, this has led to the chronicling of many deaths in the field of aviation that have not happened—some of them where there was not even an accident of any kind. For instance, in many of the casualty lists published abroad from time to time, such flyers as Hamilton, Brookins, and others have figured among those who have been killed, ever since the date of mishaps that they had months ago.

It will be recalled that five years ago, when the automobile began to assume a very prominent position, every fatality for which it was responsible was heralded broadcast where deaths caused by other vehicles would not be accorded more than local notice. To a large extent, this is still true and will probably continue to be the case until the automobile assumes a rôle in our daily existence as commonplace as the horse-drawn wagon and trolley car. There is undoubtedly ample justification for this and particularly for the editorial comment always accompanying it, where the number of lives sacrificed to what can be regarded only as criminal recklessness is concerned. Still, the fact that in a city like New York the truck and the trolley car are responsible for an annual death roll more than twice as large as that caused by the automobile, does not call for any particular mention. Horses and wagons, we have always had with us, and the trolley car long since became too commonplace an institution around which to build a sensation.

As the most novel and recent of man's accomplishments, the conquest of the air and everything pertaining to it is a subject on which the public is exceedingly keen for news and nothing appears to be of too trivial import to merit space. Where an aviator of any prominence is injured, or succumbs to an accident, the event is accorded an amount of attention little short of that given the death of some one prominent in official life. During the four years that aviation has been to the fore, about 104 men and one woman have been killed, not including the deaths of three or four spectators resulting from accidents to aeroplanes, during this period—*i. e.*, from the beginning of 1908 to the end of 1911. In view of the lack of corroboration in some cases, the figures are made thus indefinite.

Naturally most of these deaths have occurred in 1910 and 1911—in fact, 50 per cent took place from 1908 to the end of 1910, and the remainder during 1911, since these years were responsible for a far greater development, and particularly for a greater increase in the number engaged, than ever before. More was accomplished in these two years than in the entire period intervening between that day in December, 1903, when the Wright Brothers first succeeded in leaving the ground in a power-driven machine, and the beginning of 1910.

Fatal Accidents. Conceding that the maximum number mentioned, 105, were killed during the four years in question, throughout the world, it will doubtless come as a surprise to many to learn that this is probably not quite twice the number who have succumbed to football accidents during the same time in the United States alone. Authentic statistics place the number thus killed at 13 during 1908, 23 in 1909, 14 during 1910, and 17 in 1911, or a total of 67. But we have been playing football for a couple of centuries or more and this is regarded as a matter of course. The death of a football player occurring in some small, out-of-the-way place would not receive more than local attention, unless there were other reasons for giving it prominence, so that, in all probability, the statistics in question fall far short of the truth, rather than otherwise.

The object of mentioning this phase of the matter is to place the question of accidents in its true light. That the development of any new art is bound to be attended by numerous mishaps, many of them fatal, goes without saying and it is something that can not be ignored. Nothing could be worse than attempting to gloss over or belittle the loss of life for which aviation has been responsible and doubtless will continue to be. Progress invariably takes its toll and it is more often founded upon failure than unvarying success, for every accident is a failure, in a sense, and every accident carries with it its own lesson.

Where the cause is apparent, it gives an indication of the remedy which will bring about the prevention of its recurrence. In other words, it serves to point out weaknesses and shows what is necessary to overcome them. For that reason alone is the question of accidents taken up here, as a study of those that have occurred points the way to improvement. Table III gives a resumé of the more impor-

Fatal Aeroplane Accidents

Date	Aviator	Nationality	Locality	Type	Machine Make	Probable Cause
Sept. 17-08	Lt. Selfridge	American	Ft. Myer, Va.	Biplane	Wright	B
Sept. 7-09	E. Lefebvre	French	near Paris	Biplane	French Wright	A or B
Sept. 22-09	Capt. Ferber	French	Boulogne	Biplane	Voisin	C
Dec. 6-09	A. Fernandez	Spanish	near Nice	Biplane	Fernandez	B
Jan. 4-10	L. Delagrange	French	Bordeaux	Monoplane	Bleriot	B
Apr. 2-10	H. Le Blon	French	San Sebastian	Monoplane	Bleriot	B
May 13-10	Hauvette-Michelin	French	Lyons	Monoplane	Antoinette	C
June 18-10	T. Robl	German	Stettin	Biplane	Aviatik	A
July 3-10	C. Wachter	French	Rheims	Monoplane	Antoinette	B
July 15-10	D. Kinet	Belgian	Ghent	Biplane	H. Farman	C
July 12-10	C. S. Rolls	English	Bournemouth	Biplane	French Wright	B
Aug. 3-10	N. N. Kinet	Belgian	Brussels	Biplane	H. Farman	A
Aug. 20-10	Lt. Vivaldi	Italian	Monte Mario	Biplane	M. Farman	A
Aug. 27-10	C. Van Maasdyk	Dutch	Arnhem	Biplane	Sommer	A
Sept. 25-10	E. Poillot	French	Chartres	Biplane	Savary	A
Sept. 27-10	G. Chavez	Peruvian	Domodossola	Monoplane	Bleriot	B
Sept. 29-10	E. Plochman	German	Mulhausen	Biplane	Aviatik	A
Oct. 1-10	H. Haas	German	Wellen	Biplane	German Wright	B
Oct. 7-10	Capt. Mazievitch	Russian	St. Petersburg	Biplane	H. Farman	B
Oct. 23-10	Capt. L. Madiot	French	Douai	Biplane	Breguet	A
Oct. 25-10	Lt. W. Mente	German	Magdeburg	Biplane	German Wright	B
Oct. 26-10	F. Blanchard	French	Paris	Monoplane	Bleriot	B
Oct. 27-10	Lt. Saglietti	Italian	Rome	Biplane	Asteria	A
Nov. 17-10	R. Johnstone	American	Denver	Biplane	Wright	B
Dec. 3-10	Cecil Grace	American	England	Biplane	English Wright	D
Dec. 3-10	Engr Camarota and a private	Italian	Rome	Biplane	H. Farman	A
Dec. 31-10	J. B. Moisant	American	New Orleans	Monoplane	Bleriot	B
Dec. 31-10	Arch. Hoxsey	American	Los Angeles	Biplane	Wight	B

A—represents loss of control or the result of some miscalculation on the part of the aviator through inexperience, lack of judgment, or similar cause.
B—covers causes that may be summed up as a failure of the machine in some essential. Either a vital part broke through weakness due to excessive air pressure, failed from vibration or similar cause, or loosened and came in contact with the propeller or other moving part.
C—colliding with obstruction either on the ground or in flight. This is practically a subdivision of A, so far as the actual cause of the accident is concerned, but as there were only two fatalities from this particular cause, they are given a separate classification.
D—lost 'at sea.

tant fatalities that have resulted from the use of a heavier-than-air machine during the *past four years:*

Fatalities greatly increased in number during 1911, but not out of proportion to the greatly augmented number of aviators. With comparatively few exceptions, however, the accidents were more or less similar in their nature to those already tabulated, so that it would be of no particular value to extend the comparison in this manner to cover them. Many of the fatalities during that year were not of the aviators themselves, but of the spectators, a fact which calls attention to a danger that has not been fully appreciated before. At the start of the Paris-Madrid race, the French minister of war and another official were killed by a monoplane plunging into the crowd, and on the same day, May 21, 1911, five people were killed at Odessa, Russia, in the same manner. An unusual type of mishap, not mentioned in the tabulation and in which three or four aviators lost their lives during 1911, was the burning of the aeroplane in midair, or the explosion of the gasoline, setting fire to the wings and either burning the aviator at his post or killing him by the fall. One such accident occurred in France in September, another in Spain two days later, and a third in Germany, in which two men were killed. Accidents of an even more unusual nature were the collision of two biplanes in midair at St. Petersburg, the collision of a motorcycle with a biplane as it swooped down on a race track, and the partial wrecking of Fowler's biplane by a bull upon landing near Fort Worth, Texas, but these, of course, had no bearing on the design of the machines.

Apart from those specially referred to, the great majority of accidents during 1911 may be ascribed to two or three of the causes detailed in connection with the comparative table. Of these, lack of experience and foolhardiness stand out prominently, the latter undoubtedly causing the double fatality at Chicago when two aeroplanes plunged into Lake Michigan, drowning one of the aviators, while a third machine collapsed in mid-air, hurling the aviator to his death on the field. Careful reading of the reports of a large number of these accidents usually brings to light the statement "in attempting to make a quick turn," or similar phrase, showing that the moving cause of the accident was due to subjecting the parts of the machine to excessive stresses, as outlined in the following pages.

Causes. *Lack of Experience.* It will be at once noticeable by Table III that out of a total of 28, no less than 16, or considerably more than half of the accidents, were due in one way or another to lack of experience. In other words, the aviators had not fully complied with the cardinal principle for success in flying upon which the Wright Brothers have always laid so much stress, *i. e.*, you must first learn to fly before you can attempt to go aloft safely. Nothing short of a thorough mastery of the machine can suffice to give the aviator the ability to do the right thing at the right moment, in the great majority of cases. There will always be occasions when even the most skilled aviator will make errors of judgment and frequently they cost him his life. But this is equally true of every dangerous calling, whether it be running an automobile, driving a locomotive, or doing any of the thousand and one things where the responsibility for his own and other lives is placed in one man's hands and depends to a large extent on his discretion and judgment in cases of emergency, so that there will be fatalities from this cause as long as man continues to fly. This involves the personal equation that must always be reckoned with. Just how many of the accidents that have resulted in the fatalities set forth, have been due to the fallibility of the operator and for how much the design of the current types of machines is responsible, would be hard to say. Fig. 45, for example, which shows H. V. Roe in the act of striking the ground in his triplane, illustrates an accident due to bad design. Methods of control will be improved and simplified and made as nearly "fool-proof" as human ingenuity can accomplish, but experience in other fields has demonstrated unmistakably that they can never be developed to a point where it is impossible to do the wrong thing. With skill at such a premium in callings of responsibility which involve only conditions that have been familiar for years, how much more so must it be in the air about which so little is known? Consequently, the real danger is to be found in the personal equation, just as it is in every other mode of conveyance, despite the fact that it has been perfected to a point which apparently admits of little further development where safeguarding it is concerned.

Obstructions. Obstructions are bound to play a prominent part in accidents to any method of conveyance, but less so in aviation than in any other, as it is only in rising and alighting that this danger

112   BUILDING AND FLYING AN AEROPLANE

Fig. 45. Roe's Multiplane as it Struck the Ground. An Accident Due to Poor Design

BUILDING AND FLYING AN AEROPLANE 113

Fig. 46. DeLesseps' Machine after Striking an Obstruction

337

114 BUILDING AND FLYING AN AEROPLANE

is present. Of the two fatal accidents ascribed to this cause, one resulted from colliding with an obstruction while running along the ground preparatory to rising, and the other from striking an obstruction in flight, Fig. 46. In view of the numerous cross-country flights that have been made, trips across cities and the like, it is to be marveled at that up to the present writing no fatalities have been caused by what the aviator most dreads when leaving the safety of the open field, that is, being compelled to make a landing through stoppage of the motor, whether from a defection or lack of fuel. While no fatalities have as yet to be put down to this ever-present danger in extended flights, an accident that might have had a fatal termination, occurred to Le Blanc during the competition for the Gordon-

Fig. 47. Overturned Monoplane Due to a Start in a Gale

Bennett trophy, which was the chief event of the International Meet in October, 1910, at Belmont Park, near New York. Le Blanc and his fellow compatriots who were eligible were all experienced cross-country flyers, the former having won the *Circuit de L'Est*, a race around France, and by far the most ambitious of its kind which had been attempted up to that time. They accordingly protested most vigorously against flying over the American course to compete for the cup which Curtiss had captured at Rheims the year before, owing to the fact that it presented numerous dangerous obstructions in the form of trees and telegraph poles. But as it was impossible to provide any other convenient five-kilometer circuit (3.11 miles) as called for by the conditions, the protest was of no avail. After

BUILDING AND FLYING AN AEROPLANE 115

having covered 19 of the 20 laps necessary to complete the distance of 100 kilometers in time that had never been approached before, Le Blanc was compelled to descend through lack of fuel, and as he had not risen more than 80 to 100 feet at any time during the race, this meant coming down the moment the motor stopped. The result was a collision with a telegraph pole, breaking it off and wrecking the monoplane, the aviator fortunately escaping any serious injury. During the same meet Moisant demolished his Bleriot monoplane by trying to start in the face of a high wind, Figs. 47 and 48.

Stopping of Motor. The mere fact that the motor stops does not necessarily mean a disastrous ending to a flight, as is very com-

Fig. 48. View of Moisant Monoplane after a Bad Spill

monly believed, this having been strikingly illustrated by Brookins' glide to earth from an altitude of 5,000 feet with the motor dead, and Moisant's glide from an even greater height in France. But it does mean a wreck unless a suitable landing place can be reached with the limited ability to control the machine that the aviator has when he can no longer command its power. Motors will undoubtedly become more and more reliable as development progresses, but the human equation—the partly-filled fuel tank, the loose adjustment that is overlooked before starting, and a hundred and one things of a similar nature—will always play their rôle, so that compulsory landing in unsuitable places will always constitute a source of danger as flights become more and more extended.

Breakage of Parts of Aeroplanes. In studying the foregoing table, it can only be a source of satisfaction to the intelligent student and believer in aerial navigation, to note how large a proportion of the accidents is due to the breakage of parts of the machine. This implies a fault in construction, but not in *principle*. It reveals the fact that, in the attempt to secure lightness, strength has sometimes been sacrificed, chiefly through lack of appreciation of the stresses to which the machine is subjected in operation. At a time when weight is regarded almost as the paramount factor by so many builders, it is inevitable that some should err by shaving things too fine. Lightness is an absolute necessity and failure to achieve it in every instance without eliminating the factor of safety has been due more to the crude methods of construction and lack of suitable materials, than any other cause—conditions that are bound to obtain in the early days of any art. Construction is improving rapidly, but progress is bound to be attended with accidents of this nature. The fact that their proportion is greatly diminishing despite the rapidly increasing number of aviators is the best evidence of what is being accomplished. When machines are built with such a high factor of safety in every part that breakage is an almost unheard-of thing, failures from this cause will have been reduced to an unsurpassable minimum.

Failure of the Control Mechanism. Under the general classification B, are included not alone those accidents directly due to breakage of some vital part, but also those instances in which some element of the control, such as the elevator, has become inoperative through jamming. When an accident happens in the air, it takes place so quickly and the machine is so totally wrecked by falling to the ground, that it is usually difficult to determine the exact nature of the cause through a subsequent examination of the parts, so that it can seldom be stated with certainty just what the initial defection consisted of, though it may be regarded as a foregone conclusion that, in the case of experienced aviators who have previously demonstrated their ability to cope with all ordinary emergencies, nothing short of the failure of some vital part could have caused their fall.

This was the case with Johnstone's accident at Denver—an occurrence illustrating another phase of the personal equation that must be taken into consideration when noting the lessons to be

BUILDING AND FLYING AN AEROPLANE 117

learned from a study of accidents and their causes. It is simply the old, old story of familiarity breeding contempt — the miner thawing out sticks of dynamite before an open fire. Due to the rarefied air of Denver, which is at an elevation of more than 5,000 feet, Johnstone had underestimated the braking powers of the air on the machine in landing the day previous and had crashed into a fence, breaking one of the right outermost struts between the supporting planes.

Proper regard for safety should naturally have called for its replacement by an entirely new strut, but conditions at flying meets as at present conducted make quick repairs to damaged machines imperative. The damaged upright was accordingly glued and braced by placing iron rings around it, the rings themselves being held in place by ordinary nails passing through holes in the iron large enough to let the nail head slip through. The vibration of the motor and the straining of the strut in warping the wings caused the nails to work out of the holes, permitting the rings to slide out of place as well. Johnstone was an accomplished aviator, much given to the execution of aerial maneuvers only possible to the skilled flyer of quick and ready judgment. But such performances impose excessive stresses on the supporting planes and their braces, and one of Johnstone's quick turns caused the repaired struts to collapse through the strain of sharply warping the wing tips on that side. He immediately attempted to restore the balance of the machine by bringing the left wing down with the control, then tried to force the twisting on the right side, succeeding momentarily, and a few seconds later losing all control and crashing to the ground. It appeared to demonstrate that even when disabled an aeroplane is not entirely without support, but has more or less buoyancy—something which is really more of an optical illusion than anything else due to underestimating the speed at which a body falls from any great height. Johnstone's accident was the first of its kind, in that he fell from a height of about 800 feet, during the first 500 of which he struggled to regain control of the machine, finally dropping the remaining 300 feet apparently as so much dead weight. It showed in a most striking manner the vital importance of the struts connecting the supporting surfaces of the biplane, any damage to them resulting in the crippling of the balancing devices and the end of all aerial support.

Biplane vs. Monoplane. It requires only a glance at Table III to show that the greater number of accidents have happened to the biplane, yet the latter is generally regarded as the safer of the two. Prior to Delagrange's fatal fall in January, 1910, there had been only four fatalities with modern flying machines: Selfridge and Lefebre were killed in Wright machines, the latter of French manufacture, Ferber lost control of his Voisin biplane, and Fernandez was killed flying a biplane of his own design. In one case at least, that of Lieutenant Selfridge, the accident appears to have been due to the failure of a vital part—the propeller. It has since become customary to cover the tips of propellers for at least a foot or so with fabric tightly fitted and varnished so as to become practically an integral part of the wood. This prevents splintering as well as avoiding the danger of the laminations succumbing to centrifugal force and flying apart. At the extremely high speeds, particularly at which direct-driven propellers are run, the stress imposed on the outer portion of the blades by this force is tremendous. In making any attempt to compare the number of accidents to the biplane and the monoplane, it must also be borne in mind that the former has been in the majority.

Delagrange's accident offers two special features of technical interest. It was the first fatality to happen with the monoplane and was likewise the first fatal accident which appeared to be distinctly due to a failure of the main structure of the machine. For obvious reasons, it is usually difficult to definitely fix the cause of an accident, but in this case there seemed good reason to suppose that the main framing of one of the wings gave way altogether. Curiously enough, Santos-Dumont had an accident the day following from an exactly similar cause, the machine plunging to the ground. But with the good fortune that has attended this experimenter throughout his long aerial career, he was uninjured. It was definitely established that the cause was the fracture of one of the wires taking the upward thrust of the wing. In the case of the biplane, the top and bottom members are both of wood, with wooden struts, the whole being braced with numerous ties of wire. In the monoplane, however, the main spars are trussed to a strut below by a comparatively small number of wires. The structure of each wing is, in fact, very much like the rigging of a sailboat, the main spars taking the place of the mast while the wire stays take that of the shrouds, with this very important difference, that the mast of the boat is provided with a forestay to take the longitudinal pressure when going head to the wind, while the wing of an aeroplane often has no such provision, the longitudinal pressure due to air resistance being taken entirely by the spar.

It is quite possible that this had something to do with Delagrange's accident, as, in the effort to make a new record, his Bleriot had just been fitted with a very much more powerful motor. In fact, double that for which the machine was originally designed, and this was given by the maker as the probable cause of the mishap. As the new motor was of a very light type, the extra weight, if any, was quite a negligible proportion of the total weight of the machine. The vertical stresses on the wings and their supporting wires would, therefore, not be materially increased. But as the more powerful engine drove the wings through the air a great deal faster, the stresses brought upon them by the increased resistance would be substantially augmented and, unless provision were made for this, the factor of safety would be much reduced. Whether the failure of the wing was actually from longitudinal stress or the breaking of a supporting wire, as in Santos-Dumont's case, will never be known, but it is quite clear that the question of ample strength to resist longitudinal stresses should be carefully considered, especially when increasing the power of an existing machine.

The question of the most suitable materials and fastenings for the supporting wires is, moreover, a matter which requires very careful consideration. In the case of the biplane, the wires are so numerous that the failure of one, or even more, may not endanger the whole structure, but those of the monoplane are so few that the breaking of but one may mean the loss of the wing. In this respect, as in others, the conditions are parallel to the mast of the sailboat. It is only reasonable to expect, therefore, that similar materials would be best adapted to the purpose. At present, however, the stays of aeroplane wings are almost invariably solid steel wire, or ribbon, while marine shrouds are always of stranded wire rope, solid wire not having been found satisfactory. Weight for weight, the solid wire will stand a greater strain when tried in a testing machine than will the stranded rope, but practice has always demonstrated that it is not so reliable. The stranded rope never breaks without warning, and sometimes several of its wires may go before the whole gives way. As the breakage of the strands can be easily seen, it is possible to replace a damaged stay before it becomes unsafe. In the case of a single wire, there is nothing to show whether it has deteriorated or not. It seems a doubtful policy to use in an aeroplane what experience has shown not to be good enough for a boat, and stranded wire cables particularly designed for aeronautic use are now being placed on the market in this country.

Record Breaking. Striving after records has undoubtedly proved one of the most prolific causes of accident. What is wanted to make the aeroplane of the greatest practical use is that it should be safe and reliable. The tendency of record-breaking machines is the exact opposite of this, as the weights of all the most essential parts must be cut down to the finest limits possible in order to provide sufficient power and fuel-carrying capacity for the record flight. It is, in fact, generally the case in engineering that the design and materials which will give the best results for a short time are essentially different from those which are the most reliable, and striving after speed records consists simply in disregarding safety and reliability to the greatest extent to which the pilots are willing to risk their necks, and there is no difficulty in getting men to take practically any risk for the substantial rewards offered.

The performance of specially sensational feats in the air is likewise a fertile source of accidents. One noted aviator who has the reputation of being a most conservative and expert operator, while endeavoring to land within a set space, made too sudden a turn, which resulted in the tail of the machine giving way, precipitating him to the ground. In fact, the number of failures resulting from abrupt turns shows conclusively that there is too small a factor of safety in the construction, not because the added weight could not be carried, but because the extreme lightness alone made possible the stunts for which there is always applause or financial reward. It may seem strange to the man whose only interest in aeronautics is that of an observer, that so many should be willing to take such unheard-of chances; that an aeronaut will rise to great heights, knowing in advance that a vital part of his machine has been deranged, or is only temporarily repaired; and that many others will attempt ambi-

BUILDING AND FLYING AN AEROPLANE 121

tious flights with engines or other parts that have never been tested previously in operation in the air. Many young and inexperienced aviators are not content to thoroughly test out each new part on the ground, or close to it, but must go aloft at once to do their experimenting, with the usual result of such foolhardiness. If in other sports safe conditions were absolutely disregarded in this manner —take football as an instance—the resulting fatalities would not be charged against the sport itself. But aviation is so extremely novel and likewise so mysterious to the uninitiated that this is never taken into consideration.

Excessive Lightness of Machines. If, even at the present early stage of aviation, machines are being made excessively light for purposes of competition, it is time that the contest committees of organizations in charge of meetings formulate rules as to the size of engines, weight of machines, and similar factors, so that accidents will not only be reduced to a minimum, but competition along proper lines will develop types of machines which are useful and not merely racing freaks, as has already been done in the automobile field. Hair-raising performances also should be prohibited, at least until such time as improvements in the construction of machines make it reasonably certain that they are able to withstand the terrific strains imposed upon them in this manner. Suddenly attempting to bring the machine to a horizontal plane after a long dip at an appalling angle is an extremely dangerous maneuver, whether it be taken in the upper air or is one of the now familiar long glides to earth, which require pulling up short when within a few feet of the ground and after the dropping machine has acquired considerable inertia. The aviator is simply staking his life against the ability of the struts and stays to withstand the terrific stresses imposed upon them every time this is done.*

As at present constructed, many of the machines are not sufficiently strong to withstand the utmost in the way of speed and sudden turns which the skilled operator is likely to put on them. They should be made heavier, or of materials providing greatly increased strength with the same weight. That they can be made heavier without seriously damaging their flying ability has been

---

*This is exactly what occurred at the Chicago Meet, August 15, 1911, when Badger's Baldwin biplane collapsed at the end of a long dive, causing the death of the aviator.

122   BUILDING AND FLYING AN AEROPLANE

clearly demonstrated by the numerous flights with one and two passengers, and on one occasion in which three passengers besides the driver were taken up on an ordinary machine. This was likewise tempting fate by overloading, but it served to show the possibilities.

Landings. Then there is a class of accidents for which neither the aviator nor the machine is responsible, as where spectators have crowded on the field, causing the flyers to make altogether too sudden

Fig. 49. Monoplane is Liable to Stand on its Head if Landing is Not Properly Made

or impromptu landings at angles which would otherwise not be considered for a moment. This, of course, refers solely to exhibition meets, and the comparative immunity of cross-country flights from fatal accidents as compared with the latter, speaks for itself in this respect. In the open, even the novice seems to be able to pick a safe landing, especially if high enough to glide some distance before reaching the ground. This brings out the fact that, as a rule, the machines are

BUILDING AND FLYING AN AEROPLANE 123

safer in the air—a large part of the danger lies in making a landing. Starting places are usually smooth, but landing places may be the reverse. When alighting directly against the wind, which is the only safe practice, most of the machines will remain on an even keel until they come to a stop, but the slightest bump or depression, in connection with a side gust of wind, may swerve it around and capsize it, as demonstrated by the illustration of a bad landing by De Lesseps, Fig. 49. This was emphasized by some of the minor accidents at the International Meet near New York. There is no precision or accuracy in the movements of a flying machine when rolling slowly over the ground after the engine has been shut off, and the aviator is, to a certain extent, helpless. The wheels on most machines are placed too near the center and too close together. When an attempt is made to land with the wind on the quarter or side, although the machine may strike the ground safely, owing to the accuracy with which it may be controlled in the air while at speed, it is apt to turn after rolling a short distance and the wind will then easily capsize it, breaking a wing, smashing a propeller, and sometimes injuring the motor or the aviator. Accidents from this cause have been common.

These accidents and collisions with obstructions make plain the fact that brakes are quite as necessary on an aeroplane as on any other vehicle intended to run on the ground. Practically all aeroplanes are fitted with pneumatic tires and ball-bearing wheels and, as there is very little head resistance, they will run a considerable distance after alighting at a speed of 20 to 30 miles an hour. The employment of a brake on the wheels would have averted one of the fatal accidents abroad, as noted in Table III. They would have enabled Johnstone to stop his machine before colliding with the fence surrounding the aviation grounds at Denver, and they would have prevented several minor accidents at various meets, which, though not endangering the aviator in every instance, have often seriously damaged his machine. Every exhibition field is obstructed by fences, posts, buildings, and the like, and to avoid coming in contact with these, as well as with the irrepressible spectator, the aviator should certainly have an effective means of bringing the machine to a standstill when it is running along the ground. How much more so is this necessary for cross-country flying when the choice of a landing place is a difficult matter at best. Ability to come to a stop quickly would make it possible to land in restricted places where only a very limited run along the ground could be had.

Lack of Sufficient Motor Control. Another class of accidents that take place on the ground suggests the necessity for improving the motor control. In alighting, the motor is usually stopped by cutting off the ignition—ordinarily by grounding or short-circuiting. Throttling to stop appears to be seldom resorted to, but as several instances have occurred in which the aviator found it impossible to cut off the ignition, resulting in a collision with another machine or a building, it is evident that the control should be arranged so that both methods could be employed. With the increasing use of air-cooled motors that may continue to run through self-ignition after the spark has been cut off, this is more necessary than ever.

While it has been demonstrated that the stoppage of the motor does not necessarily involve a fall, most aviators will naturally prefer to command the assistance of the motor at all times, and in the case of motors using a carbureter this should be jacketed either from the cooling water or the exhaust, and means provided for increasing the air supply to prevent the motor stopping at a great height owing to the cold and the rarefied air. The reasons for this have been gone into more at length under the heading of "Altitude." With these and similar improvements that will be suggested by experience and further accidents, there appears to be no reason why aviation can not be made as safe as the personal equation will permit it to be. There will always be reckless flyers. Ignorance and incompetence can not be altogether eliminated any more than they can in sailing, hunting, or any other sport. The annual hunting fatalities from these causes in this country alone make a total beside which the aggregate of four years in aviation the world over, is but an insignificant fraction.

Parachute Garment as a Safeguard. To save as many as possible of these reckless ones from themselves, so to speak, a parachute garment has been devised to ease the shock of the fall. It will be recalled that Voisin would not fly in his biplane until he had provided himself with a heavily-padded helmet, somewhat on the order of the football headpiece. But neither a padded headpiece nor padded clothing would avail much against a fall of any kind from an aeroplane; hence, the parachute garment. Its object is not to take the shock of a fall, as are the pads, nor is it to prevent a fall, but to reduce the rate of drop by interposing sufficient air resistance to make the fall safe. This new parachute is in the form of a loose flowing garment, securely fastened to the body and fitted over a framework carried on the aviator's back. The lower ends of the garment are secured to the ankles. The arrangement is such that when the aviator throws out his arms, the garment is extended somewhat in umbrella or parachute form, thus creating sufficient resistance to prevent too rapid a descent. Experiments have been made with this parachute dress in which the wearer has jumped from buildings, cliffs, and other heights, and the garment has assumed its rôle of parachute at once, permitting a safe and easy descent.

Study of Stresses in Fancy Flying. To sum up, it will be seen that the most prolific cause of fatalities is the personal equation. Of all the many dangers encountered in aeroplaning, one of the most clearly defined, as well as one of the most seductive, results from fancy flying: from wheeling round sharp, horizontal curves; from conic spiraling; from cascading, swooping, and undulating in vertical plane curves, popularly dubbed "stunts." These are forms of flying in which aviators constantly vie with one another. They frequently result in imposing stresses upon the machine which are far beyond its capacity to withstand. The danger is particularly alluring to reckless young aviators engaged in public exhibitions. The death of St. Croix Johnstone, at the Chicago Meet in the summer of 1911, affords a typical illustration of what may be expected as the result of such performances. Nevertheless, partly because they do not adequately appreciate the risk, and largely, no doubt, because of the liberal applause accorded by an admiring throng which also fails to realize the hazardous nature of the fascinating maneuvers, there will doubtless always be aviators to undertake such feats.

Singularly enough, the exact magnitude of such hazards, or more accurately, the extent of the increased stress in the machine, though beyond even the approximate guess of the aviator, is capable of nice computation in terms of the speed and curvature of flight. During an exhibition meet in Washington, D. C., during the summer of 1911, Glenn H. Curtiss found difficulty in restraining one of his young pupils from executing various hair-raising maneuvers. He would plunge from a great elevation to acquire the utmost speed, then suddenly rebound and shoot far aloft. He would undulate about the field, and on turns would bank the machine until the wings appeared to stand vertical. Curtiss solemnly warned the young aviator and earnestly restrained him, pointing out the dangers of sweeping sharp curves at high speed, of swooping at such dangerous angles, and the like. Curtiss then turned to A. F. Zahm and expressed the wish that someone would determine exactly the amount of the added stress in curvilinear flight. The following, published by Zahm, in the *Scientific American*, gives the method of calculating this:

When a body pursues a curvilinear path in space, the centripetal force urging it at any instant may be expressed by the equation

$$Fn = m\frac{V^2}{R} \text{ (absolute units)}$$

$$= \frac{m}{g} \cdot \frac{V^2}{R} \text{ (gravitational units)}$$

in which Fn is the centripetal force, m the mass of the body, V its velocity, and R the instantaneous radius of curvature of the path followed by its center of mass. Since the mass may be regarded as constant for any short period, the equation may be expressed by the following simple law:

The centripetal force varies directly as the square of the velocity of flight and inversely as the instantaneous radius of the curvature of its path.

In applying the above equation to compute the stress in an aeroplane of given mass m, we may assume a series of values for V and R, compute the corresponding values for Fn, and tabulate the results for reference. Table IV has been obtained in this manner. It may be noted that on substituting in the equation, V is taken as representing miles per hour, R as feet, and g as 22 miles an hour, in order to simplify the figuring, this being 32.1 feet per second. The table shows at a glance the centripetal force acting on an aeroplane to be a fractional part of the gravitational force, or weight of the machine and its load. For example, if the aviator is rounding a curve of 300 feet radius at 60 miles per hour, the centripetal force is 0.55 of the total weight. At the excessively high speed of 100 miles per hour and the extremely short radius of 100 feet, the centripetal force would be 4.55 times the weight of the moving mass. The pilot would then feel heavier on his seat than he would sitting still with a man of his own weight on either shoulder. For speeds below 60 miles per hour and radii of curvature above 500 feet, the centripetal force is less than one third of the weight. The table gives values for speeds of 30 to 100 miles per hour, by increments of 10 miles, and for

BUILDING AND FLYING AN AEROPLANE 127

TABLE IV
Centripetal Force Acting on Aeroplane at Various Speeds and Curvatures of Flight

(V) Velocity or Speed of Aeroplane	(R) Radius of Curvature in Feet				
	100	200	300	400	500
Miles per hour	Weight	Weight	Weight	Weight	Weight
30	0.41	0.20	0.14	0.10	0.08
40	0.73	0.36	0.24	0.18	0.15
50	1.14	0.57	0.38	0.28	0.23
60	1.64	0.82	0.55	0.41	0.33
70	2.23	1.11	0.74	0.56	0.45
80	2.91	1.45	0.97	0.73	0.58
90	3.68	1.84	1.23	0.92	0.74
100	4.55	2.27	1.52	1.14	0.91

radii of curvature of 100 to 500 feet, by increments of 100 feet, so that intermediate speeds and radii may readily be calculated.

The entire stress on the aeroplane in horizontal flight, being substantially the resultant of the total weight and the centripetal force, can readily be figured by compounding them. Thus in horizontal wheeling, the resultant force as shown in the diagram, Fig. 50, is approximately

$$F = \sqrt{Fn^2 + W^2}$$

In swooping, or undulating in a vertical plane, the resultant force at the bottom of the curve has its maximum value

$$F = (Fn + W)$$

and at any other part of the vertical path, it has a more complex though smaller value, which need not be given in detail.

It is obvious that the greatest stress on the machine occurs at the bottom of a swoop, if the machine be made to rebound on a sharp curve. The total force ($Fn + W$) sustained at this point may be found from the table, if V and R be known, simply by adding 1 to the figures given, then multiplying by the weight of the machine. For example, if the speed be 90 miles per hour and the radius of

Fig. 50. Force Diagram in Horizontal Wheeling

curvature 200 feet, the total force on the sustaining surface would be 2.84 times the total weight of the machine. In this case, the stress on all parts of the framing would be 2.84 times its value in level flight, when only the weight has to be sustained. The pilot would feel nearly three times his usual weight.

From the foregoing, it is apparent that in ordinary banking at moderate speeds on moderate curves, the additional stress due to centripetal force is usually well below that due to the weight of the machine, and that in violent flying, the added stress may considerably exceed that due to the weight of the machine and may accordingly be dangerous, unless the aeroplane be constructed with a specially high factor of safety. But there is nothing in the results here obtained that seems to make sharp curving and swooping prohibitive. If the framing of the machine be given an extra factor of safety, at the expense perhaps of endurance and speed, it may be made practically unbreakable by such maneuvers, and still afford to the pilot and spectators alike all the pleasures of fantastic flying.

Methods of Making Tests. In order to obtain actual data for the fluctuations of stress in an aeroplane in varied flying, it is suggested that the stress or strain of some tension or compression member of the machine be recorded when in action; or simpler still, perhaps, that a record of the aeroplane's acceleration be taken and particularly its transverse acceleration. A very simple device to reveal the transverse acceleration of an aeroplane in flight would be a massive index elastically supported. A lath or flat bar stretching lengthwise of the machine, one end fixed, the other free to vibrate, and carrying a pencil along a vertical chronograph drum, would serve the purpose. This could be protected from the wind by a housing as shown in the sketch, Fig. 51.

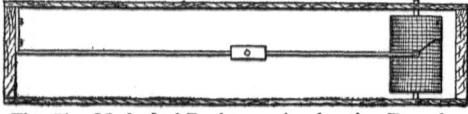

Fig. 51. Method of Boxing an Acceleration Recorder

An adjustable sliding weight could be set to increase or diminish the amplitude of the tracing, and an aerial or liquid damper could be added to smooth the tracing. The zero line would be midway between the tracings made on the drum by the stationary instrument when resting alternately in its normal position and upside down; the distance between this zero line to the actual tracing of the stationary instru-

BUILDING AND FLYING AN AEROPLANE 129

ment would be proportional to the aeroplane stresses in level, rectilinear flight; while in level flight on a curve, either horizontal or vertical, the deviation of the mean tracing from the zero line would indicate the actual stress during such accelerated flight. Of course, the drum could be omitted and a simple scale put in its place, so that the pilot could observe the mean excursion of the pencil or pointer from instant to instant; also, the damper of such excursion could be adjusted to any amount in the proposed instrument if the vibrating lath fitted its encasing box closely with an adjustable passage for the air as it moved to and fro; or if light damping wings were added to the lath, or flat pencil bar.

Another method would be to obtain by instantaneous photography the position of the centroid of the aeroplane at a number of successive instants, from which could be determined its speed and path, or V and R of the first equation, by which data, therefore, the stress could be read from Table IV.

Perhaps the simplest plan would be to add an acceleration penholder, with its spring and damper, to any recording drum the aeroplane may carry for recording air pressure, temperature, speed, and so forth. Indeed, all such records could be taken on a single drum.

A score of devices, more or less simple, but suitable for revealing the varying stress in an aeroplane, will occur to any engineer who may give the subject attention. And it is desirable in the interests both of aeroplane design and of prudent manipulation that someone obtain roughly accurate data for the stresses developed in actual flight.

Increment of Speed in Driving. It is commonly supposed by aviators that the *increment* of speed due to driving is very prodigious. An easy formula will determine the major limit of such speed increment. If the initial and natural speed of the aeroplane be v, and the change of level in diving be h, while the speed at the end of the dive be V, the minimum change of level necessary to acquire any increment of speed, $V-v$, may be found from the equation

$$h = \frac{(V-v)}{2g}$$

If, as before, g be taken as 22 miles per hour, the equation reduces

TABLE V

Minimum Change of Level Necessary to Produce Various Speed Increments

Natural Speed v of the Aeroplane	Increments of Speed $V-v$		
	Miles per hour, 10	Miles per hour, 20	Miles per hour, 30
Miles per hour	Feet	Feet	Feet
30	23.3	53.3	90.0
40	30.0	66.7	110.0
50	36.7	80.0	130.0
60	43.3	93.3	150.0
70	50.0	106.7	170.0

to the convenient formula

$$h = \frac{(V-v)}{30}$$

in which V and v are taken in miles per hour. Assuming various values for V and v, Table V has been found for the corresponding values of h in feet: For example, if the natural speed of the aeroplane in level flight be 50 miles per hour, and the aviator wishes to increase the speed by 20 miles per hour, he must dive at least 80 feet, assuming that the aeroplane falls freely, like a body *in vacuo*, or that its propeller overcomes the air resistance completely; otherwise the fall must be rather more than 80 feet.

It has been suggested that a contest be arranged to determine which aviator could dive most swiftly and rebound most suddenly, the prize going to the one who should stress his machine most as indicated by the accelerograph above proposed. But to avoid danger, the contest would have to be supervised by competent experimentalists, and would be best conducted over water. It is safe to say that more than one well-known aeroplane would be denied entry in such a contest because of lack of a sufficient factor of safety in its construction.

Dirigible Accidents. Because its wrecks are spectacular and the loss involved tremendous, the dirigible has probably earned an undeserved reputation, though it must be admitted that the big airships have come to grief with surprising regularity. The fact must be noted, however, that when an aeroplane is wrecked, the

BUILDING AND FLYING AN AEROPLANE 131

aviator seldom escapes with his life, while the spectators' lives are endangered to an even greater extent, whereas in the case of the dirigible, the loss is simply financial, both the crew and passengers usually escaping without a scratch. This is largely due to the fact that the majority of accidents to dirigibles have happened on the ground, and have been caused by lack of facilities for properly handling or "docking" the huge gas bag. Of course, lack of flotation or an accident to the motors, or both combined, have brought two of the numerous Zeppelins to earth in a very hazardous manner, though no one was killed, while four French army officers lost their lives in the Republique disaster, the exact cause of which was never definitely ascertained. This was likewise the case with Erbsloeh and his companion who were dropped from the sky, their airship having taken fire. It was thought that ignition was caused by atmospheric electricity, in this instance.

By far the great majority of later dirigible accidents have been due solely to the crude methods of handling the airships on the ground, and the frequency with which these have occurred should certainly have been responsible for the adoption of improvements in this respect at an earlier day.

For instance, the Morning Post, a big Lebaudy type bought for English use, had the envelope ripped open by an iron girder projecting from its shed. Repairs took several months, and at the end of the first trial thereafter, the ship was again wrecked in landing. A company of soldiers failed to hold the big craft and it drifted broadside into a clump of trees, hopelessly wrecking it. In attempting to dock the Deutschland I, 200 men were unable to hold it down, a heavy gust of wind catching the big airship and pounding it down on top of a wind break that had been specially erected at the entrance of the shed for protection. A similar accident happened to the big Parseval, a violent gust of wind casting it against the shed and tearing such a hole in the envelope that the gas rushed out and the car dropped 30 feet to the ground. The big British naval dirigible of the rigid type, the Mayfly, was broken in half in attempting to take it out of the shed the first time. A cross wind was blowing and the gas bag of one of the central sections was torn, deflating it and showing in a striking manner that the solidity of a rigid dirigible results chiefly from the aerostatic pressure of the gas in its various compartments. Without the gas lift, a rigid frame is so in reality only for certain limited distances, as was shown by the total collapse of the Mayfly's frame after having been subjected to the opposed leverage of the parts on either side of the original break. This, of course, was an error in design, as the frame of a rigid dirigible should certainly not be so weak in itself as to collapse upon the deflation of a single one of the central compartments. The incident on the trip of the Zeppelin III to Berlin, in 1909, when the flying blades of a broken propeller pierced the hull without causing an accident, shows how much resistance it may offer.

AMATEUR AVIATORS

It will probably come as a surprise to the average reader to learn that at the end of 1910, there were more than a thousand amateur aviators in this country, though all the flights which form the subject of newspaper reports have been the work of not more than a dozen flyers and doubtless half the population has not as yet seen an aeroplane in flight. The desire to fly, whether it be to satisfy one's desire to soar above the world in seeming defiance of natural laws, or merely to obtain the financial reward that is won by successful flight, attracts a great many from all stations and walks of life. This is particularly true among older boys who look on aviation as an advanced form of kite-flying. An example of rather serious work along this line may be cited of two high school boys of Chicago, Harold Turner and Fred Croll, who built a monoplane weighing 125 pounds, Fig. 52. This machine, although too small for a motor, was equipped with rudder and other operating planes and levers, the elevating plane and ailerons being automatically operated by an electrical device. On one of its flights the machine, carrying a 120-pound operator, was started and propelled by attaching it to an automobile; it rose to a height of 15 feet, and remained in the air 43 seconds.

Contrary to all precedent, the average amateur is bent upon achieving what the skilled professional considers as beyond even his talent and resources—that of building his own flying machine. With every other mechanical vehicle, the amateur learns to drive first and the majority are content with that achievement—for example, very few chauffeurs have any great ambition to build their own

BUILDING AND FLYING AN AEROPLANE 133

automobiles. With flying machines (one of the most difficult of mechanical contrivances), nearly all amateurs want to construct new types for themselves and all confidently expect to fly with no more knowledge than that gained in constructing them. We all have to be apprentices before becoming masters, so all aviators necessarily have to be learners and "grass cutters" before being professionals. Charles K. Hamilton was an exception, but he was already an expert pilot of dirigible balloons, and he did not try to build his own aeroplane. Willard, Mars, and Ely, all Curtiss pupils, flew after a very short training, but they did not attempt to construct aeroplanes for

Fig. 52. What an Amateur Aviator Can Do in Building an Aeroplane

themselves. This is also true of Clifford B. Harmon, the champion amateur.

Classes of Amateurs. *Inventors.* Generally speaking, amateurs are of two classes. Those of *the first class* believe they have conceived some entirely new system or invention, or an improvement on some machine that has previously proved a failure; they think they have discovered the secret which other inventors who preceded them failed to grasp. They expend their meager capital in trying to realize high hopes. A comparatively small number ever get as far as completing the machine and one trial on the field is usually sufficient to put a quietus on those who do, as it is disappointing, to say the least, to see the result of a number of months' work undone in a twinkling without the machine having shown the least disposition or ability to get off terra firma.

Would-Be Performers. The second class finds its chief incentive in the munificent reward to be gained with what appears to be comparatively little effort or expenditure, and the amateur who is seeking financial returns has no alternative except to build his own machine, or enter either the Wright or Curtiss school of flying and secure a berth with one of these companies.

Wright and Curtiss Patents. This is the result of conditions at present obtaining in the field of aviation. The only generally successful types of American aeroplanes are the Wright and Curtiss, and the acquirement of a biplane of either type means the expenditure of at least $5,000 for the machine alone, and they are sold only to individuals on the express condition that the machines are not to be used for exhibition or as a means of profit to the owner. The manufacturers have expert flyers of their own who attend meets and fairs throughout the country. It would make their monopoly impossible to allow outsiders to fly their aeroplanes publicly or to exhibit them. By this restriction the price of the machines is kept up and large returns are gained by exhibitions and flying.

To break this monopoly by importing European machines is not possible. All the successful aeroplanes made abroad such as the Farman, Cody, and Sommer biplanes; and the Bleriot, Antoinette, and Grade monoplanes are fitted with devices of control or stability, or both, covered by the Wright patents and can not be flown in this country without legal trouble. The numerous foreign aviators who brought over their machines in the fall of 1910 to compete at the International Meet, did so only on being granted a concession by the Wright Company to the effect that they would not be considered as infringers and sued. Similar arrangements were made at subsequent meets and this handicap will always be present where foreign machines are used.

Evasion by Invention of New Types. But when he thinks of the unprecedented sums paid professionals for simply exhibiting their machines and making short flights, the amateur is anxious to obtain a share of the profits. No thought is given the fact that were he and all his kind permitted to fly, the achievement would soon be commonplace and the aviator's golden age would be over. There

BUILDING AND FLYING AN AEROPLANE   135

are accordingly hundreds of would-be aviators in this country today who are striving to evade the Wright basic patents by either devising entirely new types of aeroplanes, or by inventing new methods of control and stability that will not infringe. Others, reasoning that the old aeroplanes built before the advent of the Wright machine cannot be held as infringements owing to priority, propose to develop Maxim, Langley, and Ader machines, though the dictum in the New York Court of Appeals decision referred to under the head of "Legal Status of Wright Patent," which states that a prior machine which *had never been known to fly* would not be considered an anticipation of a modern successful machine, may prove a stumbling block in their case as well. Thus, a round of the workshops of these enthusiasts reveals a host of heavier-than-air machines of every conceivable type and shape, every one of which, according to its builder, is *an aeroplane that will fly*. Mineola and Garden City, Long Island, harbor a score of these little shops the year round, but the same scenes are being enacted on a smaller scale in almost every state in the Union, and particularly in California, Ohio, Kansas, Massachusetts, and Arizona, in addition to which there are many who are carrying their experiments on in secret. Each believes deep in his heart that he will succeed where a master failed.

"Maxim failed with this type of machine," quotes one. "How did he expect to fly when his control was not proportionate to the machine's lift capacity?" Seemingly, nobody ever thought of that and our friend will make a fortune by going Maxim one better, but he does not. After months of labor and a great deal of expense he finds that some unforeseen difficulty develops which keeps his machine to earth as if it were part and parcel of it. Another has conceived a type of monoplane that is entirely new—different from any existing type—and as the latter are all foreign, he prides himself on having developed a monoplane that will be entirely American—the first and only American monoplane. Theoretically, it is a wonder; mechanically it is correct; and it speeds over the turf with surprising velocity; but when the elevating rudder is operated to make the machine rise, it balks and plunges head first into the ground. Again and again, the propeller and other broken parts are replaced at no small expense; again and again the inventor goes over every part of the machinery and computes the dimensions of the supporting surface to see if it all corresponds with the formula of his special theory. But time after time, the aeroplane acts like a jumping frog and lands head first. At last, its builder becomes convinced that there is something radically wrong and begins to depart from his original plans, involving changes that simply mean a waste of effort and money, since the inventor does not himself know what he is trying to correct and no one else knows better than he what the trouble is.

Evasion by Acquiring European Types. Others still, realizing from the foregoing experiences that it is almost impossible to construct an entirely new type of aeroplane off-hand, acquire European types and propose to fit them with new control and stability devices, such as are not covered by the Wright patents. So far, none has succeeded. Somehow, the Wrights seem to have covered all the conceivable working devices for control and stability, and the numerous attempts have accordingly resulted in failure. Undoubtedly, some of these aeroplanes built by amateurs may really be capable of flight; but how is the inventor to know it when he lacks the ability to operate it? To know how to fly an aeroplane is a condition precedent to success in the field of aviation that can not be met by building of a machine. The beginner is thus badly handicapped. Even though his machine may embody the elements essential to successful flight, he may never be able to establish the fact, since his first blundering attempt or two frequently ends by wrecking the machine, and many have neither the means nor the stamina to persevere further after a few bad wrecks, involving weeks and weeks of rebuilding each time. He can not engage an expert to fly his machine for him, as the expert's time per minute figures out a price that makes him gasp, and even at that the expert professional's time is pretty much all taken. Furthermore, very few would run the risk of attempting to fly an untried aeroplane—they have more to lose through accidental injury than the builder has through the failure of his theories.

And so it is with most inventors. They may have conceived something really good, but it is not complete, and an aeroplane is hardly worth its weight as junk unless it is. Hundreds of patents are taken out every year on devices to be used on heavier-than-air machines; inventors by scores make daily rounds trying to interest financiers in some seemingly wonderful mechanical scheme, and dozens of companies are organized each year to exploit some especially promising inventions. Numbers of aeroplanes are constructed and hailed as marvels, but, somehow, when a successful flight is made by an amateur it is always with some standard aeroplane, either of the Curtiss or Farman types, and mostly the former. In fact, the Curtiss has become a favorite with the amateur since the Federal court refused to sustain the granting of a preliminary injunction in favor of the Wright Company against Glenn H. Curtiss. It is accordingly being taken for granted in general that the outcome of the Wright vs. Curtiss litigation will be to declare the Curtiss machine non-infringing. Should it be the other way about, there will certainly be gloom and despair in the amateur camps throughout the country. However, neither the Wrights nor Curtiss impose any restriction upon the building of machines of their types for experimental purposes, so that the amateur who wishes to copy them may safely do so, provided no attempt be made to employ the machine for purposes of public exhibition or financial gain.